DATE DUE

SEP 8 '14			

DEMCO 38-296

The Awakening Nightmare

The Awakening Nightmare

A Breakthrough in Treating the Mentally Ill

by

Albert M. Honig

American Faculty Press   Rockaway, N.J.

*To my wife, Sylvia, and our children,
Karin, Kim, Eric, and Peter.*

Author's Preface

For over 15 years, almost every Friday, I've spent at home or at the Physicians and Surgeons Library in Philadelphia putting together this manuscript.

An author friend told me with encouragement "Anyone who has spent 15 years putting together his thoughts has a book with a story to tell."

As I wrote I've been just a step removed from my patients . . . enough to realize that although almost all the material is about other people I've encountered, within it all is a moving history of my own professional development.

This brief preface is my last opportunity before going to press to reread the manuscript and bring my thinking up to date.

Why the title "The Awakening Nightmare"? I have chosen this title for many reasons: Firstly, to plunge an arrow into the recurring myth that glorifies insanity as something mystical and beautiful and idealizes its sufferers as "Chosen people—special." Insanity, in fact, is living Hell! All of us have been at one time awakened by a nightmare, tormented as if it was real. Remember that feeling, and then try to feel what it would be like to live in this nightmare, day and night, unending, for years with no relief.

Recently a young girl who had pierced her chest wall with an 8 inch knife and lived only because she barely missed her aorta, said the following, "Last night I felt this panic and was drawn toward it. Why? Because at least it was better than feeling nothing at all. It was terrible; I felt as if I would kill myself or someone else. Was it what I deserved, some punishment? It always happens when I am close to falling asleep. The panic keeps me from being alone, as if my mother is with me. Only it's not pleasant and soothing. It's all distorted. It's very deep, as if there is a grip around my brain cells. What I want from her controls me completely."

No one should think it's easy to get on top of this nightmare and indeed those who recover are the most beautiful and sensitive of human beings. But this is, as they know, only because of the great amount of humanness that they have felt from others that has gotten them over their suffering.

Many patients have exploited the theme that their insanity gives them individuality and uniqueness—to lose it would make them dull and conforming. This is indeed one of the cruelest tricks of the mind. Oh, how many Jesus Christs and Joan of Arcs inhabit the back wards of our mental institutions! No one is born to suffer for all mankind and it is everyone's right, today, to be freed of this bondage.

I have noticed steps or phases that occur within an individual who is brought for treatment "extremely spaced out" with delusions and hallucinations and against his or her will. At first barely anyone understands why they are at the Foundation.

　　a. The first step is to admit that there is something wrong . . . it is not because I am bad that I am here—this is not a punishment.

　　b. Step two is a consideration of what is wrong with me. It is not a brain tumor that wracks my brain. I am really "nutty, crazy, insane or odd."

　　c. Step three—What must I do to get out of here.

It is within the exploration of step three that the patient gets relief and strength to arise out of the nighmare.

Heroin is Big Mother. Every junkie knows this. The drug problem is not given special treatment within these pages—underneath every addict there is a person hidden. Although heroin is the biggest seducer of all, methadone is not far behind. These drugs don't give, but take and eventually they will take away life itself. At present 45% of our patient population at Delaware Valley Mental Health Foundation have drug related problems.

Because they are human beings and not just addicts they are treated as members of a family included with people that initially presented other problems.

What represents true paradise? Is it crawling back into the maternal womb? Is it that heavenly maternal breast? It is a tablet of STP or Berkeley Blue Acid?

Perhaps it is not just one, but many beautiful feelings that when achieved repeatedly, make up a beautiful, happy, wholesome personality.

All human suffering emerges from frustrated human interaction.

The lover relationship between son and mother, mother and daughter, father and daughter and father and son are special "trips" within themselves that arise out of the family constellation and enhance the love relationship between adult male and female.

The hypocritical and corrupted upbringings of too many today have made a mockery of the family, the church, the school, the law and the state.

At Delaware Valley Mental Health Foundation we have learned a lot through communal living—interspersing comparatively healthy people with social and emotional rejects. Not only does it lend itself vastly to useful treatment of the mentally ill, but within our community are perhaps answers to successful husband and wife relationships, the raising of small children, family planning and some answers to problems of prejudice and problems of government.

It is extremely difficult to describe with words, the real spirit behind what makes the Delaware Valley Mental Health Foundation work. It's relaxed, seemingly unstructured (but really highly disciplined and differently structured) atmosphere gives off a subtle charge of emotion so powerful that it literally "freaks people out." I remember one medical student who came with his wife to serve as a vacation relief family over summer vacation. He was well qualified, ranking first in his class. After three days on the job, he begged to leave. If he continued here he would go insane, he said. I know his situation, having seen it before. He was really a "sick boy" who functioned well in certain intellectual spheres. However, pure "gut emotion" did him in. Fortunately, after being relieved of his duty he sought personal therapy.

There is no moderate reaction. One either loves the atmosphere passionately or hates it. Even first visitors have this impression. One 20 year old tough heroin addict put it this way: "I know I should split—go back to my gang . . . but I stay, Why, Why, Why?"

Recently a full length film entitled, "Other Voices" was made at the Foundation. Those interested in learning more about our work are invited to view it.

The paranoid position has always fascinated me. Analytic psychology rigidly teaches its origin to be repressed love feelings toward someone of one's own sex. This explained why men patients expressed hostile and hateful feelings toward me—but left me puzzled by the same feelings expressed by my women patients. Only recently have I realized that these women actually visualize me as a woman within the transference. In the chapter on Pathological Identifications I have presented similar points in much detail.

In Chapter II I have made community psychiatry seem like the answer. Indeed it did when it first arrived—so refreshing in its theory. Gradually, however, it has been molded into graven images. Large salaries for 9–5 psychiatrists and administrators and political patronage have diffused its original intent. I hear the cry once again "What about the patient and his needs?"

Will society ever change? Indeed it is changing. Not only the mentally ill but all oppressed peoples are in revolt—blacks, women, homosexuals, alcoholics, drug addicted, the poor and the earth's wretched.

Eventually, all the world will belong to all the people. I passionately believe that out of all the chaos, after the emergence of the individual, the family unit will emerge as the stabilizing force of social order.

What is and where is the revolution in mental health today? The prisons are being turned over, prisoners reading Marx, Mao and Che Guevera, have found rebirth in the revolutionary spirit, but the large mental hospitals, similar in appearance to prisons are silent still. The acute psychotic reaction is probably a natural restitutive reaction. However, chronic schizophrenia is not. It is an oppressive clinical syndrome of civilization contributed to (probably unkowingly) by physicians, large centralized hospital systems and sometimes autocratic paternalistic families. The autocratic father, usually a self-determined, self-made, independent type, still wields God-like power in his ability to recommit his "mentally ill" siblings to confinement type hospitalization. Too often mental hospitals are run by kindly grey-haired father image physicians whose main tools of therapy include insulin and electric shock. The hospital is usually programmed by an R.N. of the "Nurse Rachett" variety illustrated well by Ken Kesey in his book, "One Flew Over the Cuckoo's Nest."

I write openly on the subject only because I see what happens to "chronic schizophrenics" when they are free to feel their own feelings in a therapeutic family environment. They become like adult-children, with open-eyed regression—losing their animal like defensive, protective hospitalitis. But they can assume the old role of hospital patient quickly under the incisive questioning of an interrogator well versed in the language of the Manual of the American Psychiatric Association.

Perhaps the true revolution is in the current generation. Drugs have created a new comradeship—a buffer against decadent mental health thinking of the past. Here it has been successful. The old "chronic schizophrenia" seems to be changing in its outward manifestation. The essential human "weakness or illness" remains and must be helped, but it is group drug culture tinged instead of the single lonely isolation of the schizophrenic.

ALBERT M. HONIG

Table of Contents

The Awakening Nightmare

CHAPTER I

... simply human ...

"We are all more simply human than otherwise."
HARRY STACK SULLIVAN

It was snowing heavily, with people bundled up against the thrusting wind. I finished with my last patient at the clinic—adjusted her dosage of digitalis and walked her to the door and up the steps to the corner. I could hear the sound of the approaching trolley. It was late afternoon and already dark. In thirty minutes I was to be at Philadelphia General Auditorium. It was time for surgical presentation for the junior class at the medical school. Routinely, I skipped class to hear Dr. William Strecker. I was fascinated by his presentation of human dynamics, which he always illustrated with case presentations, both in neurology and psychiatry.

If I didn't hurry I would be late, but today was different. I stopped at Diamond's Stationery store and purchased a little leather-bound loose-leaf book, pocket size. I still carry that often re-filled notebook in my pocket, twenty-two years later. I never took notes in a patient session. However, frequently after a session I would record in outline form any observation I thought unusual and important, especially if it had universal meaning.

Without that little notebook, this book wouldn't have been possible.

Perhaps this book has two purposes. The first might be a personal one. It is my attempt to achieve immortality in the only way I know how, through my work. But this wouldn't be possible unless I had something of value to write about that would be of interest to others. This then is the second reason for the book—something to be taught and something to learn.

Many books have been written explaining the dynamics of schizophrenia

1

and some of the therapy of psychosis. Few, if any, describe mental illness from *intensive contact*, by living with it, day after day.

This book is directed to anyone interested in understanding the human mind and its soul in the depths of despair. It also will be of interest to those fascinated with the delicate balance between insanity and sanity, and the changes from one to the other.

It is different. Some readers may be revolted, others angered, still others made anxious. Even professionals may feel as unfamiliar as laymen with its presentation. Actors with an audience or a salesman with a customer may understand more of some aspects than does the psychiatrist. Perhaps other sections may appeal to the theologian or philosopher. But all those interested in people are invited to read its contents.

Deliberately not presented, but not ignored, is the medical or bio-chemical approach to mental illness. Research in these areas should continue. Whatever is found will only augment and substantiate, but never displace the dynamics of the mind.

What is presented is a great diversity of human experiences. The book portrays actual happenings and collected data. It does not pretend to be a neatly wrapped package of statistical proof.

There are taped word for word recordings of patients. There are day by day anecdotes. The patients are for the most part cases which were given up as hopeless. They were labelled schizophrenic, epileptic, or in the cases of children, autistic or retarded.

Statistical tabulation, very popular in the behavioral sciences today, is at best pseudoscientific. Attempts at dehumanization, that is, seeing people as symptoms or disease entities, can also be dangerous when magnified out of proportion.

All through the book there is one emphasis . . . DEDICATION.

Unfortunately the world is trending toward the opposite. "More Money for Less Work" is too often the motto. This is the theme of human effort displaced by mechanical and chemical devices. Starting with the industrial revolution and the harsh realities of exploitation and ending now in a surplus of material advantage, dedication has been swept aside, scorned and laughed at. Human efforts to help other humans, with the pleasure of success its own reward, are rare today. However, the pendulum must swing back, for no material gain can ever supplant man's natural gift to give comfort to his fellow man. But people are *afraid to get involved*. Even professionals hide behind a degree—for it is hard to face oneself and learn that ONE DOESN'T NEED A DEGREE *or a doctorate* to be able to understand and help another. No doctorate is a magic wand of competence in the art of therapy.

I have opened the door to my own personal background for you readers. Some of my frailties are exposed. This, too, is for a reason.

I believe good therapists are made, not born. If the interest is there, and one is willing to expose himself to his patient's psychopathology and therefore indirectly (and on the couch—directly) to his own pathology, he will become a better therapist. Patients pick out one's weak points—especially psychotic patients. They are "tuned in to phoniness." They also understand devotion and dedication and when it is there they will respond to it.

My father was a lawyer, but the healing arts were always more of an attraction to me. While serving in the Navy during World War II, I heard of the schizophrenic break of my physician-uncle's thirteen-year-old son and the seeds of psychiatry began to take root.

It was this very uncle, tall, strong and independent who practiced the osteopathic approach to medicine. As my family physician he had saved me from dying of blood poisoning as well as saving my sister when she contracted pneumonia.

My uncle believed in and taught me A. T. Still's [1] philosophy that the body contains within itself all things necessary for its own regeneration. I studied this philosophy, used it in my early days of general practice and finally took it with me when I entered work in mental illness.

I had gone into general practice on the New Jersey side of the George Washington Bridge. On my Wednesdays off, I attended ward rounds in neurology at one of the larger teaching institutions in New York City. I also attended case presentations in psychiatry. There, after one such seminar, I agreed to a Rorschach test proposed by a psychologist. After the results of the test were known, this psychologist sexually propositioned me. The fear that I might have shown dormant homosexual inclinations forced me to seek out Dr. Theodor Reik. And so began my personal psychoanalysis.

I had over 100 hours on Dr. Reik's couch. His venerable age, his personal warmth and the richness of his associations with the origins of psychoanalysis bound me securely to the profession.

To Dr. Reik, the practice of psychotherapy and psychoanalysis was more than just a business transaction between two people. He abhorred professional prejudice and petty jealousies. His devotion to Freud was extensive. "He was a wonderful man," Dr. Reik would say, and his consultation room was filled with pictures of the master teacher and other pioneers in the science. I have amused recollections of my time on Reik's couch, for it was also his bed and his pajamas were kept under the pillow.

After one year with Dr. Reik I was offered the first opportunity for an osteopathic physician to study psychiatry in a state unit. I would study at Norristown State Hospital with Dr. Arthur P. Noyes. A chance to learn more psychiatry, an opportunity to get to know my wife and children, and the prospect of a welcome relief from the trappings of general practice urged me on. I consulted with Dr. Reik. "Go!" he said, and within one month I had arranged for a young surgical resident to cover my practice for one year and I moved into further study.

Dr. Noyes felt osteopathic physicians should have equal opportunity to study psychiatry; the law gave then license to practice it as a specialty of medicine. However, personal prejudices against osteopaths in organized psychiatric circles persisted. Noyes' attempt to give me a salary and staff position was blocked. Although I was resident in work duties, to appease the AMA, I was not officially so designated. Though this meant an extra financial burden to me, it also meant unique opportunities. I was able to work with whomever I wanted; I was not bogged down with administrative duties and paper work.

Mary E. was the first patient I worked with closely. A fifteen year old student, she called out on hearing footsteps in the hall, "Help, I can't see. I'm blind." I walked to her. She was shackled to an iron bed. "Eyes are like daggers." I said, and removed her shackles. She quieted down. "If you are blind," I continued, "You cannot kill. I will love you, protect you and feed you."

The next day this patient expressed murderous hostility toward her foster mother and her real mother. On the third day she saw clearly and began to improve. In a month she was presented to staff for discharge. Admission notes on this girl had included "acute mania, disorientation, confabulation, assertiveness, bizarre behavior, blindness, 3-day hallucinatory coma." In the staff's final diagnosis, which read "adolescent reaction-temper tantrum," these were disregarded. It was not thought at that time that psychotherapeutic intervention could be helpful in such cases.

I spent considerable time with Billy M., a thirteen year old boy who, his mother said, had had personality problems all his life. When Billy was five years old, his lack of aggression tempted his brother to take away all Billy's friends. He showed manneristic slapping of his buttocks, had varied hallucinations about outer space, God, Christ, bizarre religion, nature and the universe.

I saw the boy every day for eleven months. At first I fed him and he reacted with drooling. Later he masturbated anally using a doorstop. Lastly, he discovered his penis and masturbated with ejaculation. Psycho-sexually, he went through all the important stages as described by Freud, but the psychosis was left intact. Hallucinations controlled his life. It was obvious that more involvement of myself was needed to effect a cure. Later I learned that just one hour a day did not satisfy the needs of a psychotic patient. Much more time and energy was needed to overcome the hallucinations masking underlying anxiety.

Then there was Larry, an autistic thirteen year old boy who had been ill since he was two and a half. He spent considerable time rocking and talking about himself in the third person. Communication was difficult and I found that the only way I could reach him was to hold him on my lap and feed him with a bottle. His face would flush, his lips would become warm and he would often urinate over me. Gradually he became toilet trained and his eyes became brighter. He became less aggressive and more alert. Other subtle changes made me think that childhood autism was not hopeless. Some of the things I learned in this case were incorporated into the chapter on Subnormal Mental Functioning many years later.

I remember J.M., a manneristic, laughing hebephrenic who had been in the State Hospital for over forty years. According to his yellowed and ancient file, he had been an active school leader, had received good grades and had been a member of the football team. At thirteen years of age his behavior changed. He saw visions of God and couldn't sleep at night. His parents brought him to the State Hospital for treatment.

Though his parents were long dead, J.M. refused to budge from his psychosis. "What for?" he would ask. "There's no one out there." Only once did he show any signs of letting down his barrier. Getting angry once, I grabbed his arm and turned him around. He reacted with his own anger and took a punch at me shouting, "Leave me alone or I'll tell my father." In reverse, he was asking for more involvement. Today I would take up such a challenge; having my own hospital, I can treat the way I think is best.

I remember Jane N., a pretty red-haired eighteen year old who walked naked, her hands folded in prayer, in a bare, locked sideroom in a cold basement. She had been like this approximately two weeks and had slept on a mattress in a corner.

The floor resident, a close friend of mine, knew of my interest in psychosis and called me in. "Aren't you cold?" I asked her. "Henry, I love you," she said. Who was Henry? I didn't know. "Here, eat," I said and gave her coffee. Finally she sighed, "You've come. Oh, Henry, I love you."

When she was dressed, she expressed a desire to go outside. Once there she saw a car; we entered and talked again. She noticed the sun, felt the cool air and said she was waking from a dream. She was out of the psychosis and in reality. But I was in trouble! I had taken a suicidal patient off the ward without permission and, worse luck, we had picked the chief nurse's car to sit in! The clinical director said, "Honig, this is the last straw. You are finished," and he phoned Dr. Noyes who was, luckily, for me, at the State Capitol on business and couldn't be reached. Given the chance, I explained the situation and was given a reprieve.

However, I saw a young pediatrician suffering from a first breakdown make an encouraging response to psychotherapy and then be subjected to electric shock by his own classmate, my superior on the ward, and I vowed to complete my year at the state institution and leave. I came across this same pediatrician five years later on another ward where an honest effort was being made to rehabilitate him. In the intervening years, he had lost his spirit. He seemed to have regressed and degenerated after five years of electric shock treatment. Given up as hopeless, he was finally returned to the Veterans' Hospital.

I became disgusted with routine bureaucracy, its cold lack of considera-tion, and its basic disregard for human dignity. I am now convinced that a state institution is a many-tentacled monster, powerful and dangerous. For instance, the state doesn't always respect the private psychiatrist's opinions concerning driving privileges for patients, neither will it employ former patients. Readmission is all too easy. Fortunately the Federal Government is now in agreement with much of what I am thinking and a de-emphasis away from large hospitals to community clinics is taking place.

I began to look around, knowing that I couldn't stay at the state hos-pital much longer. I had written to Dr. John N. Rosen, and he invited me to see his workshop in Bucks County, Pennsylvania. I was immediately impressed with Dr. Rosen's candor, strength and methods of reaching the unconscious. I readily accepted the fellowship he offered and remained with him two years, accompanying him on daily rounds.

Rosen worked by renting homes throughout the countryside. In these homes he would have a male and female mother and father surrogate. They were usually college students or former patients. Most often they were young and single. The homes were spread out throughout the rolling hills at random, wherever a house could be found. Often it would take us over half an hour to get from one to another. We travelled from one to another discussing cases on the way. Rosen's intuitive skill in understand-ing the unconscious was more than just training. His ability to stimulate mental processes was uncanny. Under his discipline I developed a tough-ness toward the unconscious that enabled me to feel a greater tenderness and compassion for my fellow human beings. His "Direct Analysis—Selected Papers" has always been a stimulus to my thinking; I feel this work will rank as a classic in the literature of psychiatry.

I also owe a debt of gratitude to others; the sensitive writing of H. S. Sullivan, the American Mid-western approach of Karl Menninger and the teachings of the Master, Freud, have had a subtle effect upon my profes-sional thinking.

When I completed my training with Dr. Rosen, my thoughts about prac-tice were in conflict. The glamour and prestige of Park Avenue in New York City or Rittenhouse Square in Philadelphia intrigued me. The idea of my name exhibited on a shiny brass plaque for all to see and the stimulation of the bustling metropolis bade me make two train trips to New York looking for an office. The rents were exorbitant, and the pace impersonal and all too quick. There was a feeling of being crowded in.

I realized that I was running away. Bucks County had beautiful scenery, natural recreation and none of the pressures of the big city. Here, I could do my work easily and enjoyably, and not have to weigh each day's work in coin. As I look back, I wonder if office psychiatry so practiced is really therapeutic. To change behavior, much more devotion is necessary. Can this be given in the one or two often rather impersonal office visits per week?

My first referrals came from Dr. Rosen, and I rented homes in the countryside much as he did. I realized the inconvenience and isolation of widely spaced individual houses and dreamed of a centralized community where knowledge and experience could be shared and where the cost of treatment could be reduced and the quality increased.

In 1963, with Harold J. Fine, Ph.D., the Honig-Fine Clinic was founded from the remnants of two early American farms. At first proprietary (we bought the land with our own funds), it is now the nonprofit Delaware Valley Mental Health Foundation. The Foundation is devoted to community service, research and training. It is a comprehensive mental health center and the uniqueness of its work with psychotics was the subject of a feature article in the April, 1966, issue of *Look Magazine*.

Since then, I have been bombarded with over 10,000 letters from patients, families, clergymen, mental health organizations, governmental organizations, professionals, semi-professionals and others both interested and curious.

The requests for information and on-site visits are never-ending. The Foundation was chosen by a Scandinavian journal as having made the major advance in mental health in 1965–66. It was written up, along with other major advances in medicine and surgery throughout the world.

All this has prodded me to write this book. It represents my complete professional thinking at this date. Although one sees things differently day by day I find that ideas that I wrote about ten years ago are still just as practical today. It is the understanding and finer interpretation of the basic ideas that deepen.

Anyone and everyone who reads this book or its individual sections might find a different use for it.

Perhaps some will be inspired to work with deep psychoses. Others may merely learn to be better human beings.

References

[1] Still, A. T. FOUNDER OF OSTEOPATHY. Waukegan, Hunting, 1925.

CHAPTER II

The Delaware Valley
Mental Health Foundation

". . . madmen are too often man-made, *and he who is potentially a madman may keep a saving grip on his own reason if he be fortunate enough to receive that kindly and intelligent treatment to which one on the brink of chaos is of right entitled."* [1]

"You can no longer hide in the discomfort of your private office, appropriately fitted out with an overstuffed couch and a picture of Freud visiting Worcester, Massachusetts in 1909. As the Angel Gabriel observed in Marc Connelly's 'Green Pastures': 'Everything nailed down is coming loose.' A U.S. Court of Appeals judge, a devoted friend of psychiatry, complained publicly that it was almost impossible to implement the landmark Durham decision of 1954 because psychiatrists testifying in court used 'technical, stereotyped language which is not only unintelligible to the jury, but a substitute for hard thinking about the defendant's personality and his life history.' The judge accused psychiatrists of being either unwilling or unable to convey to the layman an understanding of why the accused acted as he did." [2]

It has been a sad state of affairs. The impetus for more humanization in psychiatry has always been sparked by interested laymen rather than by the organized profession itself.

Dean W. S. Curran, director of the Law-Medicine Institute, Boston University School of Medicine, said the revolution is a "revolt of the patients." He pointed out a parallel struggle for human rights within the law.

None of us as professionals can any longer act in what we believe is the best interest of our clients or patients without consulting them fully on the proposed course of action or treatment of choice. More and more they may disagree with us and, in their concerted members, they may have their way. They may not be wise everytime they do this—any more than we have been.[3]

Plato in 350 B.C. said: "If a man is insane he shall not be at large in the city, but his relations shall keep him at home in any way which he can." [4]

Man has pondered the most humanistic methods for mental health care. Where there has been courage of conviction and pioneering zeal there has been organized progress. Except for isolated incidents such as the efforts of the Greek, Asclepiades in 100 B.C.; Caelius Aurelianus in the 5th century; Pinel in the 1780's at the Bicetre; [5] Tuke, the English Quaker in the 1830's; the early America colonists at York Retreat; and Conolly [6] at Hanwell in the 1840's, most efforts succumbed to what seemed to be more important issues of the times. An exception has been the Rijks colony at Gheel, Belgium.[7] Some efforts at humanitarianism have even backfired, for instance, the efforts of Dorothea Dix in the 1850's. It was she and men like Kirkbride who conceived of the idea of small hospitals, with a capacity of not more than 250. In this attempt they were almost completely unsuccessful, and mental hospitals grew almost more monstrous through the years.

The personal experiences of Clifford Beers in the early 1900's were incorporated in his autobiography.[8] The abuses he suffered caused a mild stir at the time and aroused the encouragement of men like William James. Beers showed the deleterious effects of both mechanical and chemical restraint and advocated a policy of nonrestraint. Even today however, one can walk into a state hospital and find the same things going on. It was better to forget than to correct.

Harry Solomon in the 1958 Presidential address to the American Psychiatric Association stated;

The large mental hospital is antiquated, outmoded, and rapidly becoming obsolete. We can still build large hospitals but we cannot staff them; and therefore we cannot make true hospitals of them. After 114 years of effort, state hospitals still do not have an adequate staff as measured against the minimum standards as set by our association; and these standards represent a compromise between what was thought to be adequate and what it was thought had some possibility of being realized. Only 15 states have more than 50% of the total number of physicians needed to staff the public mental hospitals according to these standards. On the national average registered nurses are calculated to be only 19.4% adequate, social workers 36.4%, psychologists 65%. Even the least highly trained, the attendants, are only 80% adequate. I do not see, how any reasonably objective view of our mental hospitals today can fail to conclude that they are bankrupt beyond remedy. I believe, therefore, that our large mental hospitals should be liquidated as rapidly as can be done in an orderly and progressive fashion.

Solomon concluded by saying: "I tentatively suggest that facilities be established devoted to the care and custody of a group of chronically ill individuals for whom, at the present time, we have no clear cut definite medical or psychiatric treatment. I suggest that such facilities be planned as a colony or home rather than as a hospital." [9]

The World Health Organization committee in 1953 recommended that the effort to provide more beds in mental hospitals was over-emphasized to the neglect of the development of services which, if adequately supplied, would reduce the need for admission. Instead of adding beds to already oversized hospitals, they recommended that additional staff be recruited and that one third of the time of a staff person be spent in community activities.[10]

By 1955 the dissatisfaction with treatment programs for the mentally ill in the U.S. was so widespread that Congress appropriated money to establish the Joint Commission on Mental Illness and Health. This committee finished its study and reported to Congress in March, 1961.[11]

Let us take some excerpts from the Message of the President of the United States relative to mental illness and mental retardation, February 5, 1963:

There are now about 600,000 patients for mental illness and 200,000 mentally retarded patients in our nation's institutions. Every year, nearly 1,500,000 people receive treatment in institutions for the mentally ill and mentally retarded. Most of them are confined and compressed within an antiquated, vastly overcrowded, chain of custodial state institutions. The average amount expended on their care is only $4.00 a day. Too little to do much good for the individual, but too much if measured in terms of efficient use of our mental health dollars. In some states, the average is less than $2.00 per day.

The total cost to the taxpayers is over $2.4 billion a year in direct public outlays for services—about $1.8 billion for mental illness and $600 million for mental retardation. Indirect public outlays, in welfare costs and in the waste of human resources are even higher. But the anguish suffered by both those afflicted and by their families transcends financial statistics, particularly in view of the fact that both mental illness and mental retardation strike so often in childhood, leading in most cases to a lifetime of disablement for the patient and a lifetime of hardship for his family.

The time has come for a bold, new approach. New medical, scientific, and social tools and insight are now available . . . For too long the shabby treatment of the many millions of the mentally disabled in custodial institutions and many millions more now in communities needing help, has been justified on grounds of inadequate funds, further studies and future promises.

We can procrastinate no more . . . We need a new type of health facility, one which will return mental health care to the main stream of American medicine, and at the same time upgrade mental health services.[12]

The Congress enacted Public Law 88-164, Title II, Community Mental Health Centers Act of 1963. To be considered a community mental health center certain essential services must be provided:

a. inpatient services.
b. outpatient services.
c. partial hospitalization services, which must include at least a day care service.
d. emergency service which must be available 24 hours a day within at least one of the first three services listed above.
e. construction and education services available to community agencies and professional personnel.

Additional services are:

1. diagnostic services.
2. rehabilitative services, including vocational and educational programs.
3. pre-care and after-care services in the community, including foster-home placement, house visiting and half-way houses.
4. training.
5. research and evaluation.

The Present Application of the Community Mental Health Center Act

In March, 1908, Clifford Beers wrote, "an effective beginning might be made if the government would establish a federal commission for the adequate statistical investigation of insanity." On February 5, 1963, President Kennedy delivered his famous address. Public Law 183 was passed by the 84th Congress soon after. The passage of the Act in October provided $329,000,000 to help states build community mental health centers and develop programs related to mental retardation. Federal monies began being allocated to the states more in dribbles than in extremely beneficial amounts. For instance, in 1964 Pennsylvania received only two million dollars and this money went to the big established centers—not really where it was needed most.

But the ax had struck a mighty blow—at least at the planning level. The idea of community psychiatry had been reborn. Perhaps it is here to stay. This yet remains to be seen. Unfortunately, the adaptation of the original five points of the law has been both inadequate and probably opportunistic.

In their efforts to participate, the nearly 300 state hospitals much resemble an old lady trying on a young girl's dress. With these 300 hospitals, go thousands of buildings, tens of thousands of acres of developed property, and half a million resident patients—about 80% of the total number of mental patients who are hospitalized at any given time. And their staffs are wedded to this total system of antiquation. All this constitutes a great mass of inertia limited in speed of change or of dissolution.

State hospitals are adopting the latest therapeutic methods as far as their budget will allow.[13] This has created a paradox. Between 1956 and 1962 annual admissions increased 46% (from 186,000 to 271,000) while released increased 73% (from 133,000 to 231,000). This seems to indicate an earlier release but a greater amount of readmission. If this is truly the situation, patients are being released, not well, but pasted together, mainly with drugs, and then, unable to survive in the real world, are readmitted to the hospital again. Very few are getting real psychotherapeutic intervention into their illness. The state hospitals during this time were busy. But, however they may try, there will be little progress. Hunt says, "many state hospitals are still ancient, gloomy, fortress-like redoubts, locked and barred".[14] Some states spend less than $3.00 per day on their mental patients; others spend $8.00 or $9.00. Some have one doctor for every two hundred patients. The best has one for every 40. On a recent visit to a New Jersey State Hospital, I was told that the doctor-patient ratio for time was figured to be 5 minutes of doctor time per patient per week. Dr. Nina Ridenour in her recent book writes, "In many mental hospitals there is a little core of heroic, dedicated doctors who are doing the very best they can to treat a tenth of their hospital population while the other 9/10 vegetate, waiting to die." [15]

No matter how the state hospitals attempt to cleanse themselves, I doubt if they can scrub out the subhuman smell which has permeated them for over one hundred years. They should be abolished and replaced with community facilities.

A somewhat different picture exists in the well-established private hospital. The National Association of Private Psychiatric Hospitals says there are about 200 to 220 private hospitals having 13,000 beds. They handle 25% of all mental patients admitted each year. It is said that ten hospitals are added yearly. They have always handled the economically elite, but because of increased medical insurance and the individual desire for better care, they now have opened their doors to all but the very poor. Hunt states two things have fostered their growth:

a. The individualism of Americans—a desire to pay their own way.
b. The smallness, the intimacy, the personal and even idiosyncratic flavor of private hospitals, which tend to have widely different looks, moods, styles of therapy. Many express the personality of the psychiatrist who heads them. A freedom to choose among them appeals to many physicians and their patients.[16]

The range of cost varies from $180.00 a month for custodial care to $2,000.00 a month. The higher fee might cover a stay in what could be in the category of a plush resort hotel, rest home or country inn. Those on the lower scale offer the patient less all around than does the state hospital, except for the services of the patient's own physician. I would venture to say that more shock treatment, both insulin and electric, is used in these places than in our more progressive state hospitals.

Most private hospitals are geared for short-term therapy and will not take the more severely ill patient, such as the schizophrenic, for a long enough time to do him any good. Then again, they may do harm by nonselective use of electric shock treatment. If a patient has been subjected to this treatment during his first break with reality, he develops a bitter attitude toward psychiatry.

Most private hospitals have been proprietarily run, that is, for profit. The more money that is spent on patient care, the less will be the proprietary profit. This in itself is no longer a feasible or even an understandable concept in our present day thought.

The facilities of both the state hospital and the private profit-making hospital have been condemned by public law. For the future they are dead. It is best to extract the good from each as quickly as possible so that it may be incorporated in the concept of the community mental health center.

From the private hospital, with its goal for profit, we can learn efficiency of operation. Its private enterprise has allowed personal initiative and creativity. It has taught the efficacy of "moral" treatment, that is: nonrestraint, psychotherapy and the preservation of individual dignity. It has enlisted patient responsibility by giving equal or 1–1 ratio between patient and therapist.

The state hospital has revealed the patients' need for re-birth in a severe mental illness. It has shown that time is essential for recovery. It has shown that one can return, in due *time*, from the depths of human despair. It has shown that to live in a subhuman or regressed state for a period of time does not mean that one must *always* remain there. All this has been possible in the state hospital because these hospitals have been places of last resort and by law were forced to take all people regardless of ability to pay.

Some Concepts of Community Mental Health Clinics:

At present, the Community Mental Health Center takes one of two directions:

   I. psychiatric beds in general hospitals
  II. a therapeutic community

I. Psychiatric Beds in General Hospitals

Public law 186 suggested that a Community Mental Health Center have affiliation with a general hospital. Many authorities in psychiatry have followed this suggestion by establishing their mental health centers around a general hospital. For years many of the large medical centers have had psychiatric wards. In these wards they cater to medicopsychiatric problems, e.g., the psychosomatic ward at Temple University Medical Center, Philadelphia, Pennsylvania. Green, Bush, Odoroff and Brooks point out the increase from 32 hospital units in general hospitals in 1920 to 548 in 1956.[17, 18, 19] Even so, in 1956 only 11% of the general hospitals in the United States had psychiatric facilities.

Cameron has suggested that in addition to the inpatient and ambulant service already provided by hospital psychiatric units, they should go a step further and establish actual diagnostic and treatment centers for populations requiring intensive care.[20] The bed capacity of the centers would then be regarded as simply a central core from which would radiate a variety of community psychiatric facilities.

Schulberg questions the "fashionable" trend, stating that almost all treatment changes in the field of mental health have not had their origin in careful research, but instead stem from loose observations, followed by current theory or fad, and an absolute certainty on the part of their proponent as to their validity.[21] He points out the difficulties that might ensue if a medical frame of reference is applied to a psychiatric illness. What might be right for heart disease or cancer may not be best for emotional illness.

It is my own feeling that only a psychiatric emergency suite should exist in a general hospital. This should be completely suicide- or violent-proof and should serve as an immediate, temporary service until further disposition of the patient can be made. Here, diagnostic tests can be performed. It would serve as a "cooling" area and would allow the patient to remain close to his home and his medical physicians until proper transfer to a therapeutic community. If chemical restraint (the use of medication) is necessary, it need only be for a short period of time. This would fit in with the philosophy of a general medical community hospital—that of short term care.

II. The Therapeutic Community

The "therapeutic community" reveals in its name both a special place and a definite attitude toward the mental patient. It includes certain goals and treatment procedures that enhance the self-esteem of an individual. It embraces the principles of non-restraint, non-custodial or "watch-dog" approaches and emphasizes that all therapies used are to rehabilitate the patient both socially and internally. Movement instead of lethargy or stasis is implied by its very nature. Here psychiatry can be comfortable with its original meaning Psych (soul)-iatreia (healing) Greek.

The idea of the Therapeutic Community is not a new one. The town of Gheel, in Flemish, Belgium, has been famous for its therapeutic community for over 1,000 years. Based on a tradition of sainthood and martyrdom of Dymphna, the patron saint of the mentally ill, this whole city of 16,000 is involved in the care of mental illness. The city is divided into pie shaped quadrants, radiating out from a central hospital. There are currently 1,400 patients living in homes in the community, and this was so with their mothers and fathers back far into history. If one visits Gheel, as I have, one will see patients living and working on farms, in the rear family rooms of butcher shops, bakeries, carpenter shops, with contractors, and in many other skills and trades.

Gheel learned what we have also learned at the Delaware Valley Mental Health Foundation: isolation and restraint, whether chemical or physical, lead only to human despair, despondency and then inertia. One psychiatrist in Gheel, who himself had been raised in a family with mental patients, told me that this was probably the best approach to understanding the mental patient. However, the therapeutic community at Gheel is a Government hospital. The families are given only $1.00–$5.00 per day per patient depending on the patient's ability to work. Since the standard of living in Begium is increasing, it no longer pays families to continue housing and employing these patients. Like all state and government hospitals, Gheel is understaffed. Three physicians, and a few psychologists see patients perhaps once a month. Larger numbers of male and female nurses, who travel from house to house on bicycles do most of the work in the homes. All in all, Gheel is in danger of extinction.

Another example is Japan. In national surveys in 1963, Japan estimated it had approximately 1,240,000 cases of mental illness, including 570,000 psychotics 280,000 were in need of inpatient care. One city, Choshi City, greatly alarmed by its 12.6% of mental illness, declared itself, "Mental Health City," and began a total program of rehabilitation.[22]

In Nigeria and Haiti, where the native witch and voodoo doctors have cared for the mentally ill for centuries, innovations are being made. The mental hospitals in these countries were nothing more than jails where patients were beaten with clubs. Recently patients have been taken out, and are now living in huts in surrounding villages, with families. The psychiatrists have joined forces with the native healers in devising new techniques to help patients. For instance, faced with any type of stressful life situation, the uneducated, usually illiterate, low-class Haitian is apt to attribute his misfortunes to malicious supernatural external forces. Even educated persons faced with repeated failures may fall back on previously discarded voodoo beliefs. Gradually modern psychiatry is being introduced, blending with ancient beliefs where possible.[23]

Robert H. Felix, a director of the National Institute of Mental Health, states that statistics from mental health clinics and day hospitals that treat patients in a community setting show that 40% of these patients are employed, as opposed to 10% in state hospitals. He says there is a large body of new scientific evidence to substantiate the conviction that isolation is harmful and that more *understanding of human relationship* is therapeutic.[24]

The application of PL 88-164 has been ingenious in places like the State of Illinois where every area of 50,000 population has been divided into eight zones, each with comparative mental health services.[25] Each zone has approximately 280 beds, 30 for mentally retarded children, 20 for emotionally disturbed children and 230 for adults. There are also day care, outpatient and full diagnostic facilities. The diagnostic facilities are run by interdisciplinary teams including psychiatrists, psychologists and social workers. Except for emergencies, all medical problems are referred to a general hospital. Consultation and liaison with various agencies in the community to make full use of the community's total resources are paramount in treating as many patients as possible.

Another program worthy of mention is the Home Treatment Service at Boston State Hospital.[26] Here, the entire Dorchester section of Boston (a community of more than 180,000 persons), is served by a staff of two psychiatrists, two social workers, four registered nurses, and one occupational therapist, plus residents in psychiatry and students of nursing, social work and occupational therapy. The patient remains in his own home and avoids the stigma of hospitalization with its concomitant loss of dignity and civil rights.

"Community psychiatry makes so much sense it seems incredible it was not discovered a hundred years ago." [27]

Its basic principles are:

1. People need people.
2. Transitions must be provided from widely differing social context, much as we rear children in social stages.
3. Reward and reinforcement of behavior come through "doing" in a setting that provides social ambiance with its accompanying feedback. The old bromides "virtue is its own reward" and "nothing succeeds like success" have their counterparts in social psychiatry.
4. The earlier a disease, disorder, or deviation is recognized, the easier it is to correct.

Jackson says, "It is apparent that psychiatrists and psychiatrically-oriented reporters oversold psychiatry to the American public and public reaction boomeranged on the professionals. Psychiatrists and psychoanalysts are yanked from the shelter of couch and shockbox to the awful realities of P.T.A. meetings, divorced parents clubs, teachers' conferences and the law."[28]

This is the function of the community mental health worker. The kind of person who makes the best community mental health worker is one who accepts the quirks of human nature philosophically, and is not personally threatened by the unusual behavior which he will see when he works with a broad range of people.

The Delaware Valley Mental Health Foundation—How It Operates

"If you wish to learn from the theoretical physicist anything about the methods which he uses, I would give you the following piece of advice: don't listen to his words, examine his achievements. For to the discoverer in that field, the construction of his imagination appear so necessary and so natural that he is apt to treat them not as creations of his thoughts but as given realities . . ."

Albert Einstein

MEDICAL DIRECTOR   Essential to the founding of, and the growth and development of a Community Clinic, is the medical director. One can learn much from post-mortem examinations and the reader is referred to "The Life and Death of a Mental Hospital," by Stotland and Kobler.[29] Within its covers can be learned many things that might well mean the difference between failure and success. The authors state "it is important that the independence and autonomy of a hospital be respected, which in large measure is a consequence of the respect awarded to the independence and autonomy of the medical director."

The medical director must believe completely in the institution and must be able to impart the depth and strength of his conviction to the hospital staff and to the professional community.

A way of communicating basic belief in a hospital is to develop this belief in plant, staff and refinement of treatment methods. The hospital cannot stand smugly pat, but must face continual growth. It must not expand for expansion's sake alone, but must develop out of created need, always along the guidelines of its basic philosophy. The director must be a leader facing out into the community, drawing from it new support, new ideas, new people. In that way he does not have to "face in" to the staff in any way that threatens their integrity. Then again he must receive a high degree of professional respect from his colleagues and his staff.

When the Delaware Valley Mental Health Foundation was founded by Dr. Fine and myself in 1961 (as the Honig-Fine Clinic) its purpose was three-fold: (1) service (2) training (3) research. In essence, its story is just beginning, although it has been operating for ten years. Many things have changed, but the *theoretical construction* has withstood pressure and remained the same.

STRUCTURE:

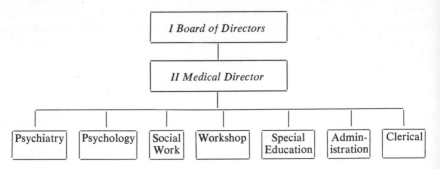

Each department is autonomous; all are responsible to the medical director, who in turn is responsible to the Board of Directors.

SERVICES: Our Foundation offers the following services:

1. Inpatient
   a. Teenage and adult
   b. Children—Psychotic and Autistic
2. Outpatient
3. Community
   a. Prison Work
   b. School Consultations
   c. Private Legal Consultations

INPATIENT: All professional personnel who are housed at the Foundation are responsible for the care of inpatients, for whom they have 24-hour responsibility. We call them family therapists. For their patients they provide custodial care, emotional support, a warm family atmosphere and psychotherapy within the limits of their psychotherapeutic training and experience.

The inpatient department is perhaps, the most unique part of the Foundation's services. It provides a 24-hour live-in family therapy (day and night care) with trained personnel. This is both unusual and extremely effective. For instance, one family therapist, (a Ph.D. in Clinical Psychology) and her husband, have five patients living with them. She also sees several outpatients in psychotherapy. Another family therapist has had little clinical training except his former position as an attendant in a state hospital. He has two of his own children, the last born at the Foundation. He has two patients living with him. This family provides a warm, energetic young home. His wife has no background in psychology but has a degree in art. Her 'ability as a mother with her own children is conveyed to the patients living in their home. The husband is attending the local college, studying psychology, and is representative of our training program of non-professionals for family therapy.

Besides the live-in family, a psychiatrist is on call on a 24-hour consultation basis, at the Foundation. When a patient is accepted into a therapeutic family, he lives with that family and does his therapeutic work within the Foundation. When he is well enough to leave 24-hour therapy he may become just a night patient, returning at night. Some patients attend school during the day, returning at night. Recently it has been Foundation policy to have inpatients tutored by public school teachers who do their tutoring at the Foundation. This has involved the community and has allowed the patients to live at home. When a patient first enters the inpatient unit, it has been found advisable that he be removed from the stresses of everyday living, forget all of his social and work activities, and put all of his energies into his full time psychotherapy. He is given a room with or without a roommate, and immediately becomes an integral part of the therapeutic family. Usually, withdrawal from the world and regression have already taken place before the patient is admitted to a live-in unit. By living-in, within a family, the theoretical assumption is that the withdrawal from the outside world and regression that will ensue, are necessary and useful steps to the understanding of the patient's problems and to helping him with these problems. The first step in therapy is to anchor the patient to a secure base. It is the function of the family unit to make itself that home base. It becomes a place of refuge, of complete acceptance, ideally a "maternal breast from which to 'seep in' nourishment through all one's body openings." Superficial efforts at pasting a patient together are avoided. A complete personality rebirth is the goal. *I know of no other unit, be it general hospital bed, insulin ward, group therapy ward, etc., that can serve this function so well.* It is no longer an idea in my mind. I have accepted it as reality. Without it, I feel that a patient is being cheated of something that is essential to recovery. One can think of day care centers, halfway houses, ex-patient clubs and they may all be useful, but they are *no substitute* for the 24-hour live-in family unit.

This has proven itseslf to me, not by statistical evidence, but by patients returning to visit the family once they have been discharged. This is a regular occurence at our Foundation. It is hard to find a Sunday when a former patient does not arrive at one of the units, perhaps with his wife and family, to take a current patient out for a ride and to talk to his own former family therapists over a cup of coffee. The former patient has accepted the Foundation and its family unit as "home base."

The Family Milieu Remains Home Base

The patient is introduced to new experiences which at first may involve only other patients and other families. But his family milieu never loses its initial function, "Mother Base or Home Base."

The individual does not yet feel love; he accepts and is accepted by the "total therapeutic team or milieu."

I have found that these individuals *cannot put their trust in one individual.* One can only speculate that this inability is due to previous experiences

—real and imagined. Whatever the reason, the patient cannot now tolerate the intensity of a one-to-one relationship.

I accept this during treatment with the hope that the desired trust will grow with time. Discipline, seeming rebuffs and analysis of resistances emanating from the main therapist to encourage maturation, at the same time discourage "closeness." Frequently, and because the patient needs this closeness, one of the family therapists emerges as his or her friend and protector—the good person, the compassionate acceptor.

Frequently a patient will not completely confide in his physician therapist or his family theraphists. He splits his trust even further into good and bad people. This is especially true where the physician therapist and family therapists are united, unswervingly, on a point of discipline. He then goes to confide in another family therapist, a relief therapist or even one of the secretaries at the Foundation. In a small therapeutic community, such as ours, the importance of sharing secrets cannot be emphasized enough. A large part of a weekly staff meeting is devoted to discussion of patient problems and each day these things are discussed informally.

Community Participation

The individual family unit and the total therapeutic family at the Foundation act as the home base. Its education is directed toward the essentials of life. Its aim is to build the inner security and to replace the essential lack of life base with a firm human fibre. This is the essence of the patient's illness. I feel that one of the failures of large institutions is their autonomy and self-containment. Some of these places exist as communities within themselves. By doing so they lose their essential purpose, that of helping an individual to independence and self-sufficiency.

This self-sufficiency is the ultimate goal of our society; it is only through this accomplishment that a person can rear a family and perpetuate social structure. Where but within a family structure itself can this be best learned?

Only the essentials of work therapy, occupational therapy, shop therapy and understanding people are taught at the clinic. *For development of these essentials,* we resort to community resources such as schools, sheltered workshops, YMCA's, health clubs and social gathering places.

The daily living together allows a patient to see his family therapist's weak and strong points. This has more good than bad in it, for he sees humanism and can reflect his own humanism. It allows the patient to evaluate properly what people really are and aren't. It allows him to see his own parents in proper perspective—and to see them as human too.

This way overvalued myths and false perceptions are punctured. They have no function in a solid environment.

Daily problems in living become situational problems that are analyzable. Should a hallucinatory patient attend school? One patient, adjusted and resigned to "3 hots and a cot" for 10 years while in a hospital, be came interested in our autistic children. He voiced his desired to further his work in education, although he was then 35 and a trained engineer. He wanted to train to be a teacher. When the academic atmosphere reawakened earlier problems about girls, and studying, and he didn't want to withdraw, he was allowed to continue. But now the reason was for therapeutic, not academic gain (on our part) and he was closely supervised—he was driven to school and his homework was checked daily.

It is amazing how the eventual calm at day's end may turn to pure chaos the next morning. (Although rare, this has happened on occasion.) At this writing there is only one patient in one of the family units—an autistic youth so confused that he would be completely lost if he were to run away. Yesterday, there were four. The three others:

S.R., age 42, went home yesterday with her husband who is on an alcoholic binge. Whenever this had occurred before, she would fall apart in psychosis. Now she is home nursing him, she has thoroughly cleaned her house, her husband has begged her to "stay home" because he "needs" her. She was successful in getting him off to his job this morning, and from our conversation on the telephone I feel she will probably make full recovery now and continue in outpatient treatment.

Jerry W., age 18, was a wild hallucinatory boy who had been in three mental hospitals. It finally looked as if he might make the 10th grade, for the second time, but yesterday he cut three classes, took money from a guidance teacher's purse and threw the purse into the woods. Although Jerry denied taking the money, the principal had sufficient evidence to discount his story and intended to call the police. I immediately left the session I was conducting with a neurotic outpatient— claiming emergency—and went to the school. The boy came home with me, confessed the theft and said he gave the money to lower classmen. Although the principal promised no vindictiveness, he suspended the boy from class. I do not know whether the boy will complete the year.

After this incident, he ran away while supposedly mowing the lawn. We put out a four-state alarm but were able to cancel it when his mother called to say he had walked into the house after spending the night in a car.

On this same day, E.L., a senior at the local school, went home without permission on the pretense of seeing his niece, age 6, who had been operated on and was in the hospital. He called me at the General Hospital where I am Chief of Psychiatry and asked for permission to go on the Pediatric Ward, a privilege reserved for parents only. I granted my permission although I knew I'd be in trouble with the Chairman of the Pediatric Department. The boy promised to return to school the next day. Did he come? No. Instead, when his family therapist went to get him, and with graduation only a week away, he held a knife to his chest and threatened suicide. The family therapist called the State Police and Rescue Squad. At this point and in front of an extremely hysterical mother, the boy dropped his knife. Peacefully, he returned to the family milieu to face his first prom—something he obviously didn't want to do.

Again on this same day L.W., age 22, recently discharged from the Navy, who had been hospitalized at the State Hospital with feelings of having been hypnotized, took his car to the Navy Base, boarded a plane and tried to escape voices and insanity by flying away. He was stopped by four burly Shore Patrol men and his parents were called. He is being treated in his own home and comes to the office as an outpatient. He is extremely negativistic, and now feels that I am hypnotizing him. He begs me to please take away the hypnosis. He feels his parents are being hypnotized also and are under my influence. This is obviously a negative homosexual-type transference and I cannot bow out of the case. I will have to place him in a local hospital until there is room in one of our units.

All is done by trial and error. Frequently, with open doors to the outside world constantly beckoning, a patient attempts too much, too early. Most often he may learn something from his acting out.

Would it not have been easier to have these four patients safely locked on a ward? But would they get well? Calculated risks are necessary in treatment: without them little constructive insight is reached. Occasionally such episodes end in permanent disaster, such as suicide. On such occasions, human instinct tends toward tighter restrictions and closed doors. However, although changes in the management of a case with new refinements occur all the time, the basic philosophy continues to remain the same.

Reisman writes that a drive is instilled in a child to urge him to live up to his ideals and to test his ability to be "on his own" by continuous experiments in self-mastery instead of following tradition. As the growing child begins his duty of self-observation and character training, he prepares himself to meet novel situations. Indeed, if he rises in the occupational hierarchy, that becomes increasingly elaborated in the phase of transitional growth, or if he moves toward the various opening frontiers of life, he finds he can flexibly adapt his behavior without changing his character. He can separate the two because he is an individual with a new level of self-awareness.[30]

Because patients who have recovered from the psychosis must learn by doing, as do children, it is no wonder many of them refuse to give up their symptoms and change their behavior. Age, loss of energy, a feeling of "What is there for me anyway?" are sometimes not imaginations but feelings based upon a seemingly impossible situation. It is easy to motivate a young person because one's own narcissism or love of life-self —joie de vivre—is the moving force. But this is not always true with one forty and over, especially if he is without a mate who cares for him or wants him. The person who has no one out there who cares, lacks what is probably the most motivating factor.

I must stress one more important element in the struggle for mental health. I adjure parents and families not to do anything "halfway." If, in one year, a person becomes well enough to hold a laborer's job but has the mental capacity to become a college graduate, it would be foolish, if not stupid, to deny him a longer stay within his therapeutic environment so that he may develop as fully as his capacities permit.

All other departments derive their basic philosophy from the philosophy of the inpatient department. The inpatient department is the *"laboratory"* of the Delaware Valley Mental Health Foundation. The total philosophy of the Foundation has evolved from its tenets. The principle of the family milieu care has been modified and adapted to handling patients in other home and family situations.

The Self Help Commune

At present plans are underway for the establishment of a Self Help Commune. This will be a community house—off the grounds of the Foundation where people from the Foundation can live. It is being planned by former inpatients. The rules will be few and simple at first. To be eligible a person must be: a. a former inpatient at the Foundation, b. self-supporting and occupied in meaningful work (employment or school), c. able to live in a house with others with enough internal discipline to take active part in the running of the house.

The people who live here presently want a central kitchen but personal privateness in other ways. It eventually may be open to others, such as staff members (who are not living at the Foundation) or outsiders who can meet the admission rules. It is not just a halfway house because if a person so decides, he may be a permanent resident (with the full realization that many patients, especially those who are older, may never reach the ability to share marriage). It will be a buffer between the "Mother" Foundation and the competitive world.

The establishment of the Self Help Commune is to me a recognition by the Foundation that the outside world is in the throes of revolutionary change. Leon Trotsky remarks about the High Court of the Tsar being preoccupied with spirits, witches, the supernatural, and the occult in the hopes of ignoring the uprooting feeling in the streets of the capital.[31] Alas, Trotsky reminds us, it was the women, born to the revolution on Woman's Day, February 23, 1917 who won over the Cossacks and soldiers. Is there a lesson to be learned here? A recovered psychotic person is indeed a revolutionary—overcoming the worst tyranny of all. . . . *The oppression of the soul.*

It can be very confusing for a mind with a tenuous control of itself to have to deal with the "Madding crowd."

It is hoped that the Self Help Commune with its loose but loyal ties to the Foundation will provide a measure of stability.

Outpatient Department

Frequently dedication and proper understanding can be taught to other family members so that a patient can be treated while remaining in his own home and visiting the clinic as an outpatient. This can only work with a patient who can accept the role of patient, accept the fact of "sickness" and is willing to subordinate his or her "independence" for help and aid. Strict discipline and control are essential and flouting of recommendations means no therapeutic gain.

The Autistic Day Care Program

Around 1963, I began experimenting with the treatment of autism. My first patient was a boy 19, ill since he was 15 months old. His case has been written up in more detail in the chapter on *Thought Process and Subnormal Mental Functioning.** Several young children ages five to ten were brought to my care in the ensuing years. All were given up as hopeless by at least one authority. To my delight, these children responded to intrusive techniques, much as did the chronic schizophrenic patients. The method of intrusion varied—for instance a baby bottle filled with sugary milk produced the most violent reactions when placed in the mouth of these children. They would refuse to suck; they bit the nipple voraciously, and indeed showed a great deal of energy devoted toward non-involvement.

At first, I would see these children several times a week or as often as possible. With a mother who could follow my orders, much could be accomplished at home. As I saw more children, I noticed degrees of withdrawal. Those who were more withdrawn needed more care. Some were brought out of their homes and placed with families that formerly worked in our inpatient department as family therapists. The need for a "day care" or school program emerged. Here the children go through a variety of early learning experiences to enhance their perception and to keep them in reality. These include tactile stimulation through water, clay, etc., and visual and sound stimulation. Those patients who are more advanced are taught some lessons. All are taught sociability. Constant intrusion takes place. In teaching the fundamentals of interpersonal relationships, an intense one-to-one relationship is necessary. Plans for a residential unit are now at the planning and thinking stage. It has been given the name of Carousel House.

Community Involvement

Since the addition of a social worker in 1967, more community activities have been added. They include:

*Chapter XII. This chapter discusses the ramifications of autism (merely a symptom complex) in detail.

1. Cooperation with other agencies such as child welfare, other psychiatric clinics, The Bucks County Planning Commission, the county Mental Health and Mental Retardation Board.

2. Visiting Nurse Program. The visiting nursing program consists of a team of nurses who are available 24 hours per day. They may visit patients at the Delaware Valley Hospital, a general hospital where I am Chairman of the Department of Neurology and Psychiatry and where other members of our psychiatric staff have consultation privileges. Frequently they assist patients home from the hospital and they are in contact with our staff and the patient's own general practictioner.

Prison Work

The Foundation is involved in prison rehabilitation in the following ways:

1. Under the direction of the Chairman of the Psychology Department: Counseling of prisoners and of guards in handling prisoners.

2. Through the State Bureau of Rehabilitation: Prisoners have the opportunity for examination and outpatient psychotherapy.

Until this last year, the pressures of work and steady growth prevented statistical tabulation and structural shoring. With the hiring of an administrator, an annual report was released. (See Appendix.)

The story of the Delaware Valley Mental Health Foundation has been presented in this chapter with emphasis on its inception, development, and structure. One might compare this with the skeletal system of the human body.

The rest of this book will be devoted to its heartbeat, pulse, and emotion. As you read further, all its humanism will be exposed. Love, violence, devotion, sweat, tears, grief and pain, all are here.

References

[1] Beers, C. W. A MIND THAT FOUND ITSELF, N.Y., Longmans, Green, 1917.

[2] Gorman, M. "Psychiatry and public policy." THE AMERICAN JOURNAL OF PSYCHIATRY. *122*:55–60 (1965).

[3] Curran, W. J. "Legislative progress and planning for community mental health." In: FRONTIERS OF HOSPITAL PSYCHIATRY. Nutley, Roche, Jan. 1966.

[4] Plato. THE LAW BOOK XI. London, Dent, 1960.

[5] Reidy, J. P. ZONE MENTAL HEALTH CENTERS. Springfield, Thomas, 1964. p. VII–X.

[6] Page, C. MECHANICAL RESTRAINT AND SECLUSION OF INSANE PERSONS. N.Y., Longmans, 1964. App. I.

[7] Gheel. THE PRESENT POSITION OF FAMILY CARE AT GHEEL. Brussels, S.C.T., 1951.

[8] Beers, C. W. *op. cit.* p. 5–36.

[9] Solomon H. S. "The presidential address: The American Psychiatric Association in relation to American psychiatry. THE AMERICAN JOURNAL OF PSYCHIATRY. *115*:7–8 (1958).

[10] World Health Organization. Expert Committee on Mental Health. THIRD REPORT TECH. REP. v. 73 (1953).

[11] Joint Commission on Mental Health and Illness. ACTION FOR MENTAL HEALTH. Final report of the Commission. N.Y., Basic Books, 1961. p. 388.

[12] Kennedy, J. F. "Message from the President of the United States." THE AMERICAN JOURNAL OF PSYCHIATRY. *120*:729 (1964).

[13] Hunt, M. A REPORT ON THE STATE MENTAL HOSPITAL. West Point, Merck, Sharp and Dohme, 1965. *1(2)*:4 (1965).

[14] *idem.*

[15] *idem.*

[16] *idem.*

[17] Green, R. S. "A comparison of sanitoriums and psychiatric units in a general hospital." JOURNAL OF MICHIGAN MEDICAL SOCIETY. *58*:1474 (1959).

[18] Bush, C. K. "The growth of general hospital care of psychiatric patients." THE AMERICAN JOURNAL OF PSYCHIATRY. *113*:1059 (1957).

[19] Odoroff, M. E. and Brooks, B. W. "General hospitals heighten load of long-term care. MODERN HOSPITAL. *93(5)*:84–86.

[20] Cameron, D. E. and Ewen, M. D. "Treating the mentally ill in general hospitals." CONNECTICUT MEDICINE. *22*:290 (1958).

[21] Schulberg, H. "Psychiatric units in general hospitals." THE AMERICAN JOURNAL OF PSYCHIATRY. *120*:30 (1963).

[22] Kato, M. "Rehabilitation and community care of psychiatric patients in Japan." THE AMERICAN JOURNAL OF PSYCHIATRY. *121*:844 (1965).

[23] Wittkower, E. and Bijou, L. "Psychiatry in developing countries." THE AMERICAN JOURNAL OF PSYCHIATRY. *120*:218 (1965).

[24] Reidy, J. P. *op. cit.* 1964. p. 9.

[25] *idem.* p. 12–27.

[26] Schimel, J. "Physicians panorama." MENTAL HEALTH ACHIEVEMENT AWARDS. *2(5)*:17–19 (May 1965).

[27] Jackson, D. "Community psychiatry," TRENDS IN PSYCHIATRY. *2(3)*:5.

[28] *idem.* p. 6–7.

[29] Stotland, E. and Kobler, A. LIFE AND DEATH OF A MENTAL HOSPITAL. Seattle, Univ. of Washington, 1965. p. 214.

[30] Reisman, D. THE LONELY CROWD. Garden City, Doubleday, 1953. p. 59.

[31] Trotsky, L. THE RUSSIAN REVOLUTION. Garden City, Doubleday, 1959.

CHAPTER III

A New Method of Diagnosis

Is there such a thing as a mental illness? If there is, is it a disease process or must we settle for the ambiguous term "mental disorder?" Many social dangers and danger to human freedom lie in wait for all of us who would try to establish a concept of mental illness. But neither does an answer lie in the denial of its existence.

This denial is reminiscent of several years ago when I walked into one of my treatment units and found my distraught patient on hands and knees desperately praying to an overhead light bulb. As I tried to dissuade him from his preoccupation, the assistant therapist* turned on me shouting, "What right do you have interfering? If this man wants to believe this way, you have no right to stop him."

Perhaps this denial might also be compared to the time when a patient, two years in therapy, went so far as to call an attorney to ask if her husband could force her to continue. The first three months of her treatment were spent in combating a severe mania, the rest in intractible depression. At this point, she had reached a feeling of not wanting extreme dependency any longer.

This was good. But it was not good to deny that she had been ill, "crazy," or that her behavior was absurd. This denial would allow her no inner alarm system to warn her if symptoms were recurring.

How do we draw the conclusion that an individual is mentally sick? Before that question is answered, it should be stated that there are those who would even challenge that concept "mentally sick." There is, perhaps, relative justice in doing this.

---

* The term assistant therapist is used here for a single male student living with the patient. It has been replaced by the establishment in 1961 with the concept of family therapist.

Although dissatisfaction with the medical basis and conceptual framework of phsychiatry is not of recent origin, little has been done to make the problem explicit, and even less to remedy it. To declare a person sick or ill, who is basically troubled or mentally or emotionally disabled, "sick" sounds at first like a great boon, for it bestows on the patient the dignity of suffering from a "real illness." On the other hand, perhaps it has delayed recognition of the essential nature of the phenomena much as Guillotin's perfection of his guillotine delayed the essential question of capital punishment. It made execution less cruel, less painful and easier. However, it delayed the more basic problems of why? Similarly, to say a mental sufferer has a mental disease or illness or sickness relegates his care to healers, physicians and biochemists, pharmacologists and surgeons. One might say that this removes the patient from the care of hate mongers, sadists, witch believers and mystics, and at least physicians are regulated by the Hippocratic oath—a humane bill of rights.

However, much as pneumonia, cancer and tuberculosis are considered diseases—something that must be removed from a person as soon as possible—the emphasis is on the procedure of removal rather than the human person. In these illnesses or diseases, such treatment has proven effective—quickly, painlessly—and it has thus removed the human suffering caused by disease*—whether it be a bacteria, a proliferating immature cell or an anatomical part misshapen from overwork.

This has given rise to surgical procedures to remove defective anatomical parts and injections of chemical, such as serotonin and Vitamin B_3 to combat deficiencies in normal body chemistry. It has also fostered a use of chemicals and electricity to "shock" people out of their condition or to reinstate normal electrical potential. Recently, the known mood-changing effect of certain chemicals on the human organism has led to neurochemical interpretation of their action. With the experimentation with the hallucinogenic agents this has led further, to form a cultism in our society whose theme is: 1. Do your thing (tune in); 2. Drop out; 3. Turn on.[1]

Now in the 1970's, it is safe to say that the general trend in diagnosis is away from the concept of "mental disease." Many official forms still require precise diagnostic terms. The term "mental disorder" is being substituted for "mental disease" or "mental illness," but it is still another label, and few have ever taken time to think out what the difference would mean in the overall life of a person so diagnosed, hospitalized in the state system and treated in a state hospital. Even though the term "mental

---

* According to Koch's Postulate on the cause of diseases, the following four criteria must be present:
  a. The organism must be present in the tissues or fluids of the affected animal.
  b. It must be isolated and cultivated outside the body for several generations.
  c. The cultivated organism, on innoculation into a suitable animal, should reproduce the disease.
  d. It should be again isolated from the artificially infected animal.

disorder" replaces "mental disease," the whole system of diagnosis, the method and places of hospitalizations and the methods of treatment have not changed.

The recording systems now used are all inclusive in item description, and provide for a wealth of detail.

All this makes a very elaborate and inclusive patient record. When the patient is transferred from one institution to another, for whatever reason, be it financial—as from a private to state or veterans hospital (when the patient does not have adequate funds to continue treatment) or from one hospital to another because the patient is not getting well—or the family is not happy—or if the patient is sent home "on extended leave," usually heavily medicated—then another term is used: "in remission." If the "illness is fulminating," in other words, if the patient is markedly excited, anxious, hallucinating and in need of hospitalization, the illness is said to be in a state of exacerbation. Another example: Carcinoma of the rectum . . . in remission. This means the diseased cancer is *quiet*, the patient is feeling better—the fingers are crossed in the hopes that the disease will not erupt again. A mental disorder may also be so labeled.

Let us examine the case history of L.V. Here is a summary of his record sent North with the patient after he was taken from the ward of a leading Southern University, against advice, by an irate parent who felt his son wasn't being helped:

Our records reveal that L.V. was, at the time of his admission to our clinic March 29, 1966, twenty-three years of age and an unmarried biology teacher living with his parents. The reason for admission involved his ideas that people were following him, that he was going to be harmed by members of the Catholic Church, and these symptoms lasted about a week previous to his admission. I assume that you have already explored the background family and personal history of the patient.

The illness during his short hospitalization involved many fears and notions that he might be a second Apostle Paul, and many systematic delusions which eventuated in his asking his father to put him in jail for his protection.

His physical exam revealed him to be in good general physical health with a normal neurological exam, negative electroencephalogram, and laboratory studies within normal limits. On April 1, 1966 he developed a fever with reddened throat and a small area of pneumonitis for which he received antibiotics and responded readily. Patient was sufficiently ill in his early hospitalization to require constant nursing. He received sedation with Thorazine and then eventually a series of eleven electro-shock treatments.

Father signed him out against medical advice on April 17, 1966 and it was the staff's opinion that he was still psychotic at the time of removal from the hospital. It was our understanding that the father thought a trip to California would be beneficial although we were quite concerned with the father's lack of understanding of his illness.

Final diagnosis based on this short period of observation of treatment was Schizophrenic Reaction, Paranoid Type.

The father was urged to place him under the care of another psychiatrist."

L.V. was brought by this father, by plane, to our clinic, after he had read about the work at the Foundation in a copy of *LOOK* magazine while sitting in a dentist's office.[2] Initial examination showed a meek, "beaten" 23 year old male obsessed with a system of fanatical religiosity. Most of it centered around serving a feared yet protective "Lord over All" and then a well-thought-out system of checks and balances with the answers to most banal everyday human questions. There were structured prayers for eating, defecating and extreme punishments and suffering for sexual thoughts. L.V. had made extensive study of the "Scripture" (the New Testament). He amazed his churchmen by "babbling" in seven languages on an evangelistic tour through the South. He had fears that "Little green men living under the sea" would get him and generally he would be exterminated for his religious beliefs.

L.V., in our unit for 9 months, became less fearful mainly because, as he said, "I've been walking through the streets and no one has attacked me." He held a job and he was placed in a boarding care arrangement— that is, farmed out to a nice home that included a widow, an eighteen year old daughter who had been a patient briefly at the Foundation, and an unle in the throes of divorce. L.V. liked his "whole family" at his sessions. He worked outdoors at a local nursery and I saw him once a week in the evening.

He would continue in his self-entangling religiosity week after week.

One week, "his mother," the widow herself brought up as a Protestant "it's better to do without and wait for heaven" attitude, nagged him all week says "L.V., stop this nonsense. You level and tell Dr. H. what really is on your mind." L.V. on his next visit spoke freely and openly about his sexual experiences at age eleven with his six year old sister. He told of his fears that his sister would be pregnant. He told of sexual experiences with other girls; then he made a vow with God never to think of sex again. Eventually, under the strain of living with this attractive eighteen year old female, his "paranoid schizophrenic" structure suddenly burst. It was too much. Actually, one day he was caught naked in bed with the eighten year old daughter, by her mother. The daughter had been bedded with influenza. She claimed she was so sick and weak she couldn't fight off the boy's advances.

He soon tightened up and wrote down the following:

Some history, from approximately June, 1962, till December, 1965:

In this period of time I hope I can explain in as full detail as possible the highpoints, lowpoints, feelings, emotions, experiences, etc., of what I believe was a very crucially important period of my life.

It was back in and around and preceding June, 1962, that I was experiencing a very bothering spirit within me, so strange that it made me feel very bound and troubled. I was just absolutely, even with the help of a doctor and other assistants, wasn't able to release myself from this bondage feeling. To describe it, it was very inferior feeling and mainly I just couldn't carry a conversation with other people. I felt very nervous and self-centered yet, I knew that I was the outgoing type that always liked to be with other people, but I noticed myself to have been almost controlled by some sort of mental quirk, that was astoundingly frightening and bothersome. So as I said earlier than June of '62 I had visited with Dr. B., my family doctor to whom I grant did help me somewhat, yet as I say, I just couldn't seem to be able to rid myself of it. Seeming to be able to blame it upon a guilt complex and having been fairly religious in my life, my past minor, but seemingly major, mishaps in my life, sexually, brought me to this condition, I supposed strongly. As I've said or implied up to the present, it has been hard to describe though. I, even to this day, don't know exactly why or exactly how it happened, but I think it was the "breaking of my sexual vows with God" which to me was like the END OF THE WORLD. I tried many avenues of cure, but the only relief came when I began to read, seek, and pray towards God until gradually it removed to a great degree. Now going back to June of 1962, I began seeing a favorite friend and neighbor and past 3rd Grade Teacher with whom I had visited customarily almost once every year just for friendly religious curious reason. Now, I was visiting her mainly because it was urgent and I needed help and I didn't care who it was or what. It was very odd for a person my age and background to be visiting frequently with a very elderly lady, but now I am almost positive it was the Lord's way of directing me into a *very deep walk* with Him.

Miss W. and I shared some very comforting experiences and things together, yet there were many times of hardship and a continual feeling of discomfort that still continued onward with me, so I still wasn't what I felt cured, but I was gradually, slowly moving towards a feeling of tranquility much more so than I had ever had before, yet again, I repeat, there was a different agonizing feeling taking over to replace the lost guilt feelings. It was one of tribulation within and an outward experience of public dismissal, in the sense that I became very narrow-minded. But, as I continued on in this state of mind and with Miss W. I had some of the most spiritually electrified feelings that even to this day, often having been through extra various hardships, denials, etc., disappointments, still it remains overall a predominating glorious emotional state of mind, just flowing with happiness, yet intermingled with sadness.

So as I said, we had wonderfully real experiences together. She would teach me the Bible from the Bible and other books, as the Haley's Bible Handbook and other reading books, such as Sammy Morris' Life, a book I obtained either through the Baptist Book Store or the Pentecostal Book Store. Also I read many other books near this time as "The Man Called Peter," by Catherine Marshall, "World Aflame," by Billy Graham, "Out of His Life and Works," by Albert Schweitzer, "The Life of Jesus Christ," by James Stalkner, "The Life of Paul," by James Stalkner, "Pilgrims Progress," by Paul Bunyan, which by the way I found to be very informative, and many other forms of religious materials as pamphlets, magazines, cards, gifts, etc. Here my life was opening up into a *brand new* atmosphere, one of religious Godliness and spiritual tranquility so grand I *honestly* can't explain *fully* even to this day. Anyway, everytime I look back to those experiences, I find such joy, glory, happiness, peace of mind, purity, honor, etc., that *I Love It.*

Her brother, P.W., was a minister and Miss W. had been quite a Godly person throughout her life, having taught down lowly ways in country towns with children. She expressed the Lord throughout all her work in school and everywhere. A very devoted to God woman she was and still is to this day as I know. Her life was cut short in her teaching career because of a nervous condition which from what she tells me must have not only been inherited naturally, but developed through her hard times teaching God and school TOGETHER so strictly. Anyway she shared her life experiences with me and was what I call "nurturing me in the admonition of the Lord." It did me good for as I said, it helped remove that mysterious feeling of pain and I gained a new one in return. Ha! Anyway, so then, I went on doing much better and I was on my way back to Health. Boy, was it *great!*

Mainly I enjoyed her cooking and trying to founder me, but yet I felt God directing me to work with her spiritually! "For where two or three are gathering together in my name, there I am in the midst of you." I used to pick blackberries for her and myself. She used to make jellies and jams for me and pies and cobblers. This one fruit, blackberries, has been such an inspiringly different treat, even from the time our original family moved from the city to the country and I met Danny Blakeman and his family. Mrs. Blakeman used to make much blackberry jam, which stood out in my taste for fantastic delicacies. It was the greatest I felt. Here again I was a linking of joyful, childhood experiences with the present at that time and this was great. In great addition, I was gradually being shown what I call by God, the most beautiful outlook upon life I had ever had in my life. It simply magnificent.

We even took trips together for I took the summer off because I was going to summer school and this left me more time to do things with her. One trip that was very thrilling, inspiring, and significant to me was the one she and I made to Fort Wayne, Indiana. Our objective on the trip to this place was to visit Sammy Morris' burial place. He was the person that I read about in the book, "The Life of Samuel Morris," which was supposed to have been a very spiritually, heart-warming story of a young boy's desperate trip from Africa to America and his life with Jesus. The boy was supposed to have had a very close relationship with God for His life was beautiful according to my judgement. "Everything was simply Jesus in his life." This boy (Negro) life inspired me greatly an dhelped stimulate a new ideal in my life, such that I became very independent, even so strongly that I found myself approaching a nearness to God so astounding that God seemed so close and so real to me, like He had never been before. In the book, Sammy was very close to God and he evidently walked so close to God that when he did die, around 20 years of age, he heard angels flapping their wings while on his death bed. Also, I remember he loved snow very much and I had a most wonderful connection in relationship to snow and God that here again I began to float in what I describe as the Spirit of God. I was going so high, I even thought I saw Jesus looking at me one Sunday while in the Gospel Assembly Church in Nashville; God, just seemed to fall right smack into my life, so wonderfully, yet with certain pains I was paying that I was living in paradise.

Returning to my friendship with Miss W., she and I shared many wonderful experiences together in the Lord. She would tell me of all her enlightening times with the Lord in her humblest service to Him. She had a very close contact with Him evidently for everything was God to her, even nothing at times for she lived a very meek life.

By the way, I did find it quite hard to visit her so much, etc. for I felt very uncomfortable and also many times when I went over there I was wanting to normally be other places like the rest of the girls and boys, but I felt God wanted me to do this and that and I would try to follow my impressions of His guidance as closely as possible.

Here is the way it usually went: I would be impressed to do this or that as visiting, fasting, praying, denials, etc., and my first feeling towards it was null and void many, many times, but when I would follow through with many of these impressions I would later experience different types of what I call blessings—treats from the Lord for obeying and going that extra mile. It says the Lord loveth a cheerful giver and all I had to do was try out his Word and boy, oh boy, does it work if one remains patient, kind, understanding, and gives the Lord time to work. Actually I strongly believe this is what helped me so much about God for He taught me through experiences that the longer the test, the wait, the job, the greater the joy that can be recompensed for the work of God. Also time gives God the best means and ways to express Himself very strongly, clearly, exactly, and lovingly. I believe also that I learned that if I would put myself in His hands without questioning, but only realizing that I was doing it because I loved God and Jesus for their love to mankind, so I would do this and that, *knowing* that sooner or later He would show me in some way or another whether I was going right or wrong. In other words I would look for signs from Him for it states: "*Trust* in the Lord and lean not unto thy own understanding. In all thy ways acknowledge Him and He shall direct thy paths." "*Faith* is the substance of things hoped for and the evidence of things not seen." "Ask and ye shall receive, seek and ye shall find, knock and it shall be opened up to you." Also, "If ye lack wisdom, ask of God and He shall give liberally and upbraideth not." "You know how to give good gifts and things unto your children, so even how much more so does God know how to give good things unto His children." "Blessed are peacemakers for they shall be called the children of God." So all in all I learned to have greater, faith, hope, and charity through this lady.

The main thing she had me question within myself was whether or not I really belonged to God. I said I didn't know but I had been confirmed in Church through standard procedures. I felt I had an experience with God, but I didn't know positively I was His or not. This is a Big question on my mind! Just really what it is to be born again for it states: "Ye must be born again—CONVERTED." Someplace in your life. I read in the Bible that "the law of the Lord is the conversion of the soul." So I hope that many people, like myself, if they haven't, will make their peace calling and election sure. I believe I have now, but my question is just what a human being must do. He becomes sincere, contrite and broken in spirit with a deep remorse for sins inherited and otherwise and then prays, and pays, and stays in Church ("forsake not the assembling of yourselves together") and reads the Holy Bible, and watches for God's reflective signposts and answers from your response to Him in faith, thus He should answer sometime. I believe I was taught that if one confesses with their mouth and believes in their heart that the Lord Jesus died for their sins; they shall be saved. And I have learned that shall means just what it shall mean. Shall do!

"But what does God love but a humble, contrite and broken spirit." So I believe also that an invitation is open to all who have been born again of the Spirit of God (John 3:35) and who faithfully obey and trust the Lord unto the end will be saved.

So she taught me to put the WHOLE armour of God on: Helmet of *salvation,* breastplate of *righteousness,* Loins girth with *truth,* feet shod with gospel of *peace,* the shield of *faith,* and the sword of the Spirit which is the *WORD OF GOD.*

All in all the years between '62 and '65 with Church, people and God were the three most inspiring years I've had in my life for during this period of time I've had such a variety of good experiences with God and man that I've learned the *significance* of love and life.

"What shall it profit a man if he gain the whole world and lose his soul."

In the follow up, L.V. was brought back to our unit after being picked up by the police and post office department for placing light bulbs in mail boxes just before Christmas. His highly technical religiosity continued until it dawned on me that placing the "light bulbs" in the mail box had latent sexual meaning. I explained this to him. He understood this. I also confronted him in an unusual way. I had a resident physician hold his arms behind his back and I told him I would "knee him" in the testicles since he didn't need them if he accomplished his main wish—to be part of the "Bride of God." As my leg went toward his crotch, his own *left* leg came up to defend his precious organs. I made notice of this. "Which leg is God's leg?" I asked. "The right," he answered. "See, you lie—you do want to make use of these organs in a normal way," I said (very thankful that this rough therapeutic maneuver had to be only a threat).

This incident plus another, in which he carried a two hundred pound wooden cross fashioned from railroad beams all day, softened his longings for his "phony, self-made" religiosity.

The words that have been used in descriptive psychiatry no longer contain just that which was once intended. Words such as schizophrenic, mental case, paranoid, psychotic, deterioration, mental deficiency, etc., are no longer objective. They are in the everyday vocabulary and contain the emotional explosiveness equal to that of "four letter words." These words are now promotive rather than descriptive and might mean:

1. I don't like you.
2. I can't help you.
3. I don't want to understand you.
4. You bother me.
5. You are dirty, no good.
6. You should be destroyed, confined, incarcerated.

All this makes a mental examination by a trained psychiatrist and the resulting diagnosis and recommendations, a highly personal and subjective experience more akin to a courtroom experience than to a scientific deduction based on Aristotelian logic.

From my own experience, many former patients in state hospitals have said that all that occurred was first confusion, and then learning the proper answers. There was no emotional rebirth but rather a learning of how to appear well enough to get out of the hospital with their now hidden or compartmentalized crazy thinking still intact.

I have learned that patients learn to give you what you ask for. If I am rushed or not too sensitively alert because of fatigue, I don't get sensitive feelings from a person, but the stereotyped diatribe that everyone recognizes as this particular person's "mental illness," a defensive cover-up to his real feelings. If I am sincere, and "in tune" I may be rewarded by a flood of feeling. In other words, if one asks for "craziness or concreteness" one gets "craziness." If one asks for normal behavior, a show of useful emotion and appropriate talk follow. Labeling a person with a fixed diagnosis doesn't allow for the mood swings and changes in affect that can occur in some persons from hour to hour and in others from day to day. This swing is especially noticeable in patients who are in active treatment.

While I was working in the state hospital I often had a secret chuckle to myself during morning diagnostic staff meeting. For example, there was the 15 year old girl who had been labeled "Schizophrenic reaction, acute, undifferentiated type" at admission ward conference one month previously. I saw her for about an hour a day, five days a week. Although not yet completely well, this day she exhibited a markedly different and puzzling picture to the staff. She answered all questions with reasonable acuity and had a quietly pleasing calm with a sense of humor. The Superintendent finally pinned her with "Temper Tantrum—adolescent type" a diagnostic label that didn't appear in my diagnostic manual. "She simply couldn't be schizophrenic because schizophrenics simply do not show remission in one month's time" the aged Superintendent concluded.

Let us mention another dilemma, which represents legal confusion.

S.W. is a twenty-four year old draftsman of Italian origin who admittedly shot his wife to death. He admitted doing this but when his lawyers and parents met with him to plead guilty, he refused. "I want to deliberate my case before twelve people (in this case all women). Let them determine if I am guilty . . . if I had a right to do what I did." Finally he was persuaded to plead guilty by his parents and defense attorney. However, on the witness stand, under cross-examination he admitted no guilt, exhibited no self remorse and denied any memory of the actual time of the shooting. When asked by the district attorney "How do you know you killed your wife?", he stated, "They say I did."

Three physicians, all board certified psychiatrists, said that he was legally insane at the time of the shooting, that is, he didn't know the difference between right and wrong. All testified that at present he was legally sane. All three examinations were of one sitting, between one and three hours duration. I interviewed the man about seven times for approximately seven hours. One interview was conducted under the influence of Amytal Sodium, 7½ gr. and Methedrine 20 m.g. His reaction was quite unusual. Mr. W. became quite labile in emotion, alternately shouting and then speaking softly. The interview was permeated throughout with shades of homosexual overtones. He mentioned wanting to kill the neighbor. This neighbor was the wife's supposed lover. He saw his wife alternately as an angel before she met this neighbor, and as a devil or evil person, afterwards. As an example of the homosexual talk he said, "I must get out of here. If I stay here, I don't know what I will turn into." He said, "The woman I shot was evil, she was not my Sophie." And then he would shout, "I shot my Sophie because she would not let me grow a muzzie." Mr. W. at this time sported an Italian organ grinder type of mustache. In talking about his in-laws, he stated that his father-in-law cheated on his mother-in-law. He said his father-in-law once said to him, "I don't give a shit for you, your wife or your son." The patient said he loved his mother-in-law, and "I would marry her myself." It was interesting to note that when he called his wife the night of the shooting he said "Sophie please come home, my ass hurts." He mentioned that at the time of the shooting, his wife was giving his son pills at night. He didn't like this and suspected that she was poisoning the son and himself. Referring to how he felt at the time of the shooting, he said, "I felt possessed—there was somebody inside of me—a devil—I had no control of myself—I lost all control. There was no control in my fingertips."

About one week after this interview he said he felt much better. It was a great relief to get all of this off his chest. But he would alternate in his statements. Privately he would say to me that he wished he had gotten help before the murder, that now, with what he knows he would perhaps have defied his religious upbringing (strong Catholicism) and sought a divorce or left home. Murder wasn't worth all his suffering. Yet, on the stand, under the pressure of cross examination he would become more defensive, hedge and feel that he was right in what he had done. It is obvious that this man still has "crazy" thinking. Would it again thwart him to the point of taking another human life? Should he be living in the community? Should he be made to pay his debt to society? Should he have treatment? Is he all right? These questions make an accurate diagnosis necessary. The classical descriptive diagnostic system has failed in this area. Unfortunately real self-reflection by us professionals, comes too late. How often do we read in our newspapers of a violent crime committed by an "ex-mental patient." In this particular case, I was the only one of four examining psychiatrists who stated this person should get continued psychotherapy in a closed surrounding. The defense attorney, because of his desire to have his client acquitted on a charge of involuntary manslaughter, refused to call me, his own expert witness, to testify.

Here is yet another example, less dramatic, but in its own way equally perplexing. This session is with a patient who has a very intact delusional, paranoid system. This is the second interview. He has at present obtained a job in the Post Office. He is thirty-three, single, and had worked as a teacher, but had to quit work because of the overpoweringness of the delusional system. I use this to illustrate that his paranoia has maintained itself almost completely separate from his emotional life, and only recently had become involved with it so that it incapacitated him. He has had this particular thought disorder since he was approximately six or seven years of age.

(Patient arrives for session. Some talk about how the roads are.)

Therapist: How've you been doing? Did you get yourself a job, or what?

Patient: I got myself a job, see. That's the big problem. I got myself a job that would require me to work five days a week. And, uh, the only day that I'll be able to come here is on a Saturday. I mean, will this be all right with you?

Therapist: Let's see . . . We'll have to let you know. Isn't there any day —what about a Wednesday?

Patient: The hours I'm going to work on this job are from three to twelve. If the hours were the other way around—and I don't have too much to say about it, because it's for the government —I'm going to work for the post office.

Therapist: What are you doing there? Did you start . . .?

Patient: Well, I'm going to lug mail, be a mail handler for a while. This is only temporary until I can get into something else.

Therapist: Did you start yet?

Patient: I haven't started it yet. I start the 27th.

Therapist: Oh, I see, it's a week away, yet.

Patient: It's a week away, yet.

Therapist: Well, how've you been?

Patient: Well, I've been all right. I mean, I'm still overshadowed by this
           idea. I still, uh, now I mean I can go out and I don't have any
           trouble in doing things. I can got out and have breakfast, and
           things like that. And carry on normal functions, but this is
           always in the back of my mind. It's always there. No matter
           where I am—in a restaurant, in a bus station, waiting for a bus,
           or whatever I do. I got all my faculties, I mean, about any-
           thing I do, but this is always present. For some reason. I don't
           know.

Therapist: So you know that it's a thinking disorder, then. You're pointing
           to your head. So you know it's a thinking disorder. You know
           that's what it is. Now, how did it come this week?

Patient: This week? Well, I was thinking about what you told me about
           this masturbation, you know—causing a prostate condition,
           and I got scared of that, and I was thinking about that at night,
           while I was asleep. I lost a little sleep the last couple of nights
           over that.

           (The therapist had stated a simple medical fact. Without ejacu-
           lation, prostate secretion would store up, causing stasis and
           possible prostate infection.)

Therapist: Well, did you jerk off—were you able to masturbate?

Patient: No, I didn't. I was afraid—I was afraid because of this fear that
           I got. You know. What I was told when I was a young kid.

Therapist: What did they tell you?

Patient: They told me it was harmful to your health, your physical con-
           dition.

Therapist: And I told you the opposite.

Patient: You told me the opposite.

Therapist: So you don't know which way to go now.

Patient: No.

Therapist: You're sort of tied up. What went through your head? I'm a
           doctor, you know. Whoever told you that before was not a
           doctor. Did a doctor tell you that?

Patient: Oh, you mean did a doctor tell me that it was going to be
           harmful?

Therapist: Yes. That masturbation was harmful.

Patient: Well, that one doctor that I mentioned in Long Island diagnosed
           it as an anginal syndrome. He said that it was due to an over-
           strenuous masturbation.

Therapist: He told you that?

Patient: He told me that. I guess it was a minority opinion.

Therapist: It certainly was a minority opinion. Well, you know that.
           Haven't you read up on it?

Patient: I've read up on it. I've heard reports on it.
Therapist: I mean Dr. Crane—all these doctors in the paper. They mention that. That say it's not harmful, don't they, huh?
Patient: Sure.
Therapist: I think you'll find more doctors today who think the way I think. I know because you speak to urologists, specialists in kidneys and prostates. They'll tell you that.
Patient: How long is the period of time that it takes to develop a prostate condition? Due to not—uh——
Therapist: It gradually creeps up on you. For instance, in the service—overseas—they saw a lot of that. There were no women around. A great many men have a great fear of masturbation. It's not a rare thing. A lot of them have been told what you were told as a kid. They were told this sort of thing, so it depends. Some people are more susceptible than others.
Patient: Uh huh.
Therapist: It can build up and you can have an acute infection like you have a sore throat with pus, and it gets swollen up like a balloon. That can be very painful. And dangerous. Or it can become a chronic thing. Which becomes irritating—you can't urinate at night properly. You have to get up at night—things like this and this type of thing that I was thinking of with you. You may even have it—why do you think you have it?
Patient: Well, I have to—when I urinate—I have to urinate a few times during the day—but it feels that all of it doesn't come out. And I asked the doctor that I went to, a physical doctor, about— when was it—about—let's see—about three months ago that I went to him and I says to test me for prostate. He came up with nothing. He says you haven't got no prostate trouble. He took a urine test and says you have no prostate trouble. That's why I asked you what would be a length of time involved—maybe uh—
Therapist: Well, that's good that you don't have it, but you could develop it.
Patient: I could develop it.
Therapist: Sure. You may be one of the lucky ones. But, it may hit you— you may get cancer, too, early. The possibility of chronic irritation—cancer of the prostate, which is a bad thing too. It can happen. I don't know, but all I wanted to say that it was normal and I wanted to stress the illness. As a physician. Now what about this thing with the eyes—how's that coming out?
Patient: Well, I find myself watching people with brown eyes—you know watching them constantly to see what their signals would be, you know.

Therapist: Who do you have your eye on mostly?

Patient: Oh, my brother, my father, outside people who have brown eyes.

Therapist: Well, usually you single out someone in particular—now who do you have, who do you single out mostly—now don't kid me.

Patient: My brother, my brother.

Therapist: Your brother, he's the guy you're watching. How often do you watch him? Do you watch him all day long?

Patient: Not all day long—just around the house. I watch him at night, you know, when he's watching television and at the supper table.

Therapist: What was the diagnosis at the state hospital?

Patient: It was schizophrenia.

Therapist: Was he paranoid—do you know what paranoid is? (Patient says No. Therapist says did he think people were after him.)

Patient: Yeah, he used to think that, he told me he used to think that.

Therapist: Who did he think was after him?

Patient: I don't remember.

Therapist: Did he ever flare up in the house and think that someone was after him.

Patient: Oh, yeah.

Therapist: Who did he flare up at?

Patient: Well, he flared up at my father.

Therapist: What did he say?

Patient: Well, when we were young kids—I don't remember—there was a lot of violence though between my brother and my father. This was when it first came on him, you know, when he first got sick years ago. We were both little kids, I remember it though.

Therapist: How old was he?

Patient: He was about fourteen at the time his sickness came on.

Therapist: Do you remember whether there was something with the eyes too?

Patient: That I don't recall—I don't believe so. His was mostly a fear that people were after him.

Therapist: For what, do you remember?

Patient: He just thought they were going to get him for some reason— do physical harm to him.

Therapist: Does he worry about that now?

Patient: No.

Therapist: Does he confide in you? Does he tell you what's on his mind?

Patient: Not too much, not too much.

Therapist: Does he know how you feel about the brown eyes?

Patient: He knows how I feel, he knows that.

Therapist: What does he do about it?

Patient: He just tries to humor me about it—he tries to tell me it can't be so—he says it's nonsense. His response is academic, you know. He tells me I'm out of my mind.

Therapist: Tell me what you think about it—what do you notice about him?

Patient: Well, when I look at him I see that he's the leader of these groups I was talking to you about, you know, these groups of people. That's why I look to him for the sign—to see if things are good or things are bad, you know.

Therapist: How did you find out that he was the leader?

Patient: I didn't find out—it just occurred to me that he might be the leader. Nobody told me directly.

Therapist: Why did you single him out?

Patient: Well, because he's got brown eyes.

Therapist: Well, why him over your father?

Patient: Well, my father is the head of a group too.

Therapist: Oh, I see—there are several groups?

Patient: There are several groups.

Therapist: Which is the worst group?

Patient: My brother's groups—they're the roughnecks.

Therapist: They're the ones that can hurt you.

Patient: Yeah.

Therapist: Tell me what you do to sort of appease these groups—do they tell you what to do? Do they signal you on what to do or what?

Patient: Well, in order to overcome what they're doing I have to do something to overcome it. I have to persuade the other groups of people that I'm good with them in order to repudiate the group that my brother belongs to and that's where the communication comes in. I have to communicate with those other groups.

Therapist: Are the other groups all brown-eyed?

Patient: No, maybe blue-eyed or brown-eyed?

Therapist: Are the other groups on your side?

Patient: They are neutral depending upon the communication that I make with them.

Therapist: So you're the go-between.

Patient: Yeah.

Therapist: So you're the sacrificial lamb, the one that gets on the chopping block?

Patient: Yeah.

Therapist: Now are these two other groups fighting each other?

Patient: No, they're more or less allied with each other—they are friendly with each other.

Therapist: They are, eh?

Patient: You mean my father's and my brother's groups?

Therapist: And the other groups.

Patient: Oh, no. They're two groups within the whole organization. One is vying against the other.

Therapist: Who are the two main groups which are vying for power?

Patient: Some groups have brown-eyed people, one group has brown-eyed and blue-eyed people in it and the other group is mostly brown-eyed people and they are constantly vying for power.

Therapist: How come these brown-eyed people mix with the blue-eyed people?

Patient: Well, one is sympathetic to the other. The brown-eyed group of people are sympathetic to the blue-eyed people; they understand each other.

Therapist: Are these brown-eyed people weaker than your brother's group?

Patient: They would appear to be, yeah.

Therapist: What makes them weaker?

Patient: Weaker, eh, weaker in what they've accomplished—weaker physically possibly.

Therapist: Are they weaker because they are kinder?

Patient: They're kinder, yeah, they're more understanding.

Therapist: Does this make them weaker in your mind?

Patient: No. It doesn't make them weaker in my mind—it's just what they've done—in other words they've accomplished less physically and otherwise than the others.

Therapist: Can you prove this—that they've accomplished less?

Patient: Well I can't prove it materially—only make-believe.

Therapist: Through your mind?

Patient: Through my mind, yes.

Therapist: In other words, if I said "show me" you couldn't do that.

Patient: No.

Therapist: In other words, this whole thing then is imagination or a thing of the mind.

Patient: It's a thing of the mind, yes.

Therapist: Sounds to me like a bad dream.

Patient: I wish it would come like a dream and go away like a dream but to me it's a real thing—it's here. Like I say I can go out and do things like others—go to places, this and that but this is there—it's in my subconscious and when I have free time it starts to build up.

Therapist: Other guys might have pleasant dreams, dreams about the present and future—about what they're going to do but you get this thing.

Patient: I get this thing, yes.

Therapist: Would you say it's an obsession, or what?

Patient: I would call it an obsession—I am obsessed with this.

Therapist: I can see it's weighing heavy on your head. Was there a time when you didn't believe it?

Patient: Oh, yes, there was a time. There was a time, and I have to go back to be specific—before ten years old. When I was about ten or eleven that's when all this trouble started.

Therapist: When you go back can you think of anything that might have caused it?

Patient: Yes, when I go back to —— let me think hard now. When I was about eleven years old I began to masturbate quite heavily and I was censured for it and told that it was wrong, and things like that. I noticed that I was starting to mature faster than the other kids. I noticed that I was getting hair here and hair on my arms and it seemed to sprout out quicker than the other kids and this made me self-conscious. I'd be afraid to go in public—was afraid people were watching me. This started when I was about eleven and this is when these groups began to crop up. Everyone started to belong to a certain group.

Therapist: Do you think the two things might be connected?

Patient: Yes, I think so.

Therapist: The masturbation and . . .

Patient: And the groups.

Therapist: Is it because of the masturbation that you wash your hands so . . .

Patient: This washing of the hands I think is because I'm mostly afraid of the hepatitis that I just got over.

Therapist: That didn't come on . . .

Patient: No, that didn't come on when I was small. That's something recent. I started it because I just got over hepatitis.

Therapist: You didn't have this before?

Patient: I didn't have this before.

Therapist: Well it must be related—you told me last week about washing semen off your fingers.

Patient: Yeah, it might be subconscious.

Therapist: You do understand the subconscious and can appreciate it.

Patient: I've read about it, yeah.

Therapist: You know then how this can influence your mind and can drive you crazy.

Patient: My biggest asset, I guess, and I differ it from some other people is that I can go about everyday chores, I can hold a job, a responsible job and I know, I know for a fact that this is not so yet I can't erase it from my mind—I can't get it out of my mind—it stays in my mind and this is what I call subconscious.

Therapist: Does it ever get so overpowering that you can't distinguish?

Patient: It's never gotten that bad.

Therapist: Then you never really went out of your mind then?

Patient: No. It hasn't gotten that bad but it has gotten so bad that I
could not stop thinking about it—it became an obsession and
it's never gotten so bad that I wouldn't know the difference
between right and wrong—but I can't stop thinking about it.

Therapist: Would you say that you're crazy—are you that crazy?

Patient: (Laughs) . . . I would say I'm a little crazy, sure.

Therapist: Why?

Patient: Well everybody is a little mentally ill isn't that so? I mean is
mentally ill to an extent.

Therapist: Where do you draw the line?

Patient: Well I would call this a serious thing—this is serious but I
wouldn't say it was insane. I wouldn't classify myself as insane
—I would call myself disturbed—very disturbed. I think that
my problem is serious.

Therapist: Do you have a fear that you may go insane?

Patient: Oh, no, oh, no. This has never bothered me. I have feared this,
that if this continues, it could cause physical ailments.

Therapist: Like what?

Patient: Like heart trouble, trouble with the nervous system.

Therapist: Did you ever think you could develop something in your head
like a tumor?

Patient: Yeah, I've thought of that.

Therapist: How does it come out?

Patient: Well, like it has occurred to me that suppose I just wanted to
escape this thing, suppose I wanted to try to completely cut
this off. I know that it's there, right? Alright, I have to go out
and start doing my everyday job, this and that and this of
course which is away from this idea—I fear that there will be a
conflict—such a severe conflict that the jar would be so extensive if I stop abruptly that it would cause a tumor. In other
words if I suddenly try to stop thinking about this and yet
it's still there that there might be a confrontation there.

Therapist: Between what?

Patient: Well, between my brain cells and this, this force.

Therapist: Describe this force.

Patient: It's a force of like a dream—when you lie down and you're
dreaming about something. It's like when the dream over-
powers you in your sleep—you don't know any different. That's
the force of it—I mean the power of being hynotized.

Therapist: You mean where you have no control—you're subjugated.

Patient: Yeah, where you have no control.

Therapist: Has that ever happened—has that point been reached at
times?

Patient: No, but it has happened that when I would try to communicate with these people I would try to do it in the open—I mean in a bus or a subway station and I would be standing there making these contortions and people would look at me—I mean it's gotten to that extent—but I didn't draw it out—I would stop—I mean if I realized people were looking at me long enough I would stop.

Therapist: What kind of contortions?

Patient: Well, when I make a communication I have a certain muscular rigidity in my body—I tense myself up.

Therapist: Is it sitting or standing?

Patient: Well, it could be in any position—I just tense myself up—holding my body tense.

Therapist: Do you make a fist then?

Patient: Most of the time, yeah.

Therapist: Can you establish a communication right now? Do you find it necessary?

Patient: I don't find it necessary now.

Therapist: Did you on the way up here?

Patient: I thought of it, yeah.

Therapist: Did you do it?

Patient: I didn't stop the car to do it.

Therapist: All right, who did you have to do it with?

Patient: I had to do it with this weaker group I was talking about. I had to get them to understand that I was not inferior.

Therapist: Now what brought this about—what made you want to do it?

Patient: Just a general impression.

Therapist: Did you feel inferior?

Patient: Yeah, I felt that I had not made the right communication before this. That I was in the doghouse more or less until I would make the right communication.

Therapist: Were you in danger, feeling anxiety, a lot of anxiousness?

Patient: I wasn't tense in any way. I would call it an apprehension—a distant fear. I was apprehensive.

Therapist: Did you feel it had something to do with our talk today?

Patient: No.

Therapist: All right. Was your brother involved—-his group?

Patient: His group was involved, yes.

Therapist: Tell me about it.

Patient: His group was at the helm or at the head of these other groups.

Therapist: How did they show themselves—this group?

Patient: They look alike. Their identity is similar—in other words when a person was a twin well they look alike so they belong to the same group.

Therapist: What's your brother like?

Patient: Well, he's dark complexioned—he looks like my father—he takes after my father—he is about my height, he's downstairs. He came with me today. I guess his features resemble mine but he's darker—he's like my father—well, that's about it.

Therapist: And all these people look like this.

Patient: Well some of these people look like him—they've got his eyes.

Therapist: What do his eyes look like?

Patient: Ordinary brown eyes.

Therapist: Does he have eyes like yours? You have sort of bedroom eyes. Have women ever told you that?

Patient: Bedroom eyes? What do you mean by that?

Therapist: Well, what women call bedroom eyes—sexy eyes.

Patient: (Laughs) . . . I don't think I've ever been told that, no.

Therapist: Maybe you haven't been around too many women—you've been with some.

Patient: I've been with some—not as much as I should, of course.

Therapist: O.K. How are you making out with these sexual ideas? What's come up this week?

Patient: Nothing much—nothing in that respect. I have had a fear about this prostate because to be frank with you I've gone several months without any intercourse and without masturbation.

Therapist: Have you been thinking about doing something about it?

Patient: I was thinking about masturbating. I don't have any direct contacts with women right now. I haven't been dating regularly.

Therapist: You want my order to go ahead?

Patient: (Laughs) . . . Well, if it would help, I mean, I don't know . . .

Therapist: Well, if I issue an order it has to be done, that's it.

Patient: Well, I guess so—I guess I would have to have some kind of authorization.

Therapist: Well, would you want it in writing?

Patient: (Laughs) . . . It sounds ridiculous, I know.

Therapist: I didn't say it sounded ridiculous—do you want it in writing or do you want it verbal?

Patient: No, I want it verbal.

Therapist: All right, I want you to do it twice a week—tonight, this is Saturday and then Wednesday. Now that order must be obeyed for safety and health reasons.

Patient: (Laughs)

Therapist: What are you laughing at?

Patient: It sounds humorous the way you put it.

Therapist: Well, I don't think it's funny—it's an order and that's it. Now if you want I'll record it in City Hall with the Government. Do you want me to do that?

Patient: What do you mean with the Government?

Therapist: I'll send a memo to Washington through your department—the Post Office . . .

Patient: You'd ruin me, why should you do that?

Therapist: Well, I don't want to do that, I'd rather not. But I have connections in the department—the Post Office Department—and I could do that—issue the order through work but I'd rather not. Can you follow it this way? Is this enough?

Patient: This is sufficient, yeah.

Therapist: All right, good. (Long pause. Nothing on tape.) What are you thinking?

Patient: I was just thinking how it sounds so humorous—you know, the way you were going to send it through channels—official channels.

Therapist: If it has to be done we'll do it.

Patient: I want to ask you something. I recently recovered from hepatitis. Now I have this friend who goes with this girl—he says she is a nice girl. He says he wants to fix me up with her. If it comes to the point where I want to have sexual intercourse with that girl do I have to fear the fact that I've had hepatitis? It's been about seven months now since I've recovered.

Therapist: You haven't had any recurrence of symptoms? Do you feel well?

Patient: I feel all right.

Therapist: Go ahead, then.

Patient: Then there's no chance of me—you see when I went to the doctor he explained it to me like this, he said—when I had the hepatitis they were giving me blood tests every two weeks to determine the amount of points of hepatitis that I had in my blood. Now I started with 900 points and they brought it all the way down to 57. Now he told me that 45 is normal, but the last few weeks that I had the blood tests it remained at 57 but he said even though it remained at 57 I could consider myself cured. He said I'll always have a certain amount of points in my blood but it's all right.

Therapist: Yes, but that's only a test—to determine if you're well depends on how you feel.

Patient: Oh, it hasn't come back—I feel strong and my appetite is good.

Therapist: Is that what you're concerned with—spreading it? No. I don't think you have to worry about that. What was it? Infectious?

Patient: It was infectious, yes.

Therapist: How did you get it?

Patient: I don't know—I'm trying to figure it out. As a matter of fact, when I first got it the doctor was trying to trace back different things I had done in order to determine how I got it. He asked about infections, seafood, things like that and he can't come up with how I got it. I was going to a psychiatrist who gave me a lot of medication—he gave me a lot of different pills—and he gave me a B-1 injection.

Therapist: Was it infectious or was it serum? Some hepatitis comes from drugs.

Patient: Oh no, it was infectious.

Therapist: Infectious comes from a virus. Serum hepatitis comes from a needle or something like that—it's carried in the blood.

Patient: Oh, yeah. Now everywhere you go they use disposable needles. So, when I first got it he said where were you, what did you do, what did you eat and like that. They reported it to the Board of Health and they sent an inspector around to discuss the things that I did but they never arrived at the source of the thing. I could have gotten it through any way, maybe a contact, maybe the medication that this doctor was giving me who knows? Maybe it affected the liver.

Therapist: I think you'll be all right now. O.K. What other points have come up?

Patient: Supposing I want to live normally, now. Supposing I want to do my job and live like anybody else and that thing is there. It doesn't annoy me to the extent that I'm tortured by it but it's there. What do I do? Do I live with it?

Therapist: Yeah, you can live a normal life, why not?

Patient: In other words, you live with it.

Therapist: Maybe no doctor ever told you this but I'm going to tell you the secret of the thing—how to get rid of it. To get rid of it you have to force yourself to get involved with life. The more you get involved in living life, the less you'll have need for this.

Patient: I see what you are talking about.

Therapist: Because then you'll have control of your subconscious mind and you'll be happy and this thing will disappear.

Patient: I gotta be more involved with . . .

Therapist: With people and with life. In other words, take your mind off this to find out what's really going on in the world. Women are important.

Patient: They have to become a part of my life, right?

Therapist: I think so—you have problems with women—strong problems. I think you have to fall in love.

Patient: I would agree with that. I was in love a couple of times but it was circumstance. I mean the girl didn't like me. It wasn't reciprocal.

Therapist: That's not good—real love is when you dish it out it comes back to you.

Patient: Yeah, you get something in return.

Therapist: Yes, that makes you feel on top of the world because then you got it made, you're on a two way street—not a one way street.

Patient: When it's one way it's no good is it?

Therapist: Then there's tension—it builds up—it's aggravating—you can't work—it's anguishing—you don't get any cookies that way.

Patient: I find that the more I'm with people the safer I feel. Maybe that has something to do with what we're talking about. The more I'm with people, the less this has a grip on me. Even if it's just chewing the fat with someone.

Therapist: Do you mean right now it's not there?

Patient: No, right now it's not there but I feel safe from it—I feel safe and secure from it. It's just in the background. How does this start anyway? I mean why do certain people group up normally and why does this have to happen to me?

Therapist: What do you think?

Patient: I come back to this sexual thing. I think the roots of all this trouble are sexual. The masturbation when I was young—I overdid it—that's what I come back to.

Therapist: You can't overdo it—you can overdo the anxiety in your mind—but you can't overdo masturbation. You can only come a certain amount of times—that penis can't be stimulated too much—it just stops—it goes dead—it can only go a certain amount of times so that can't hurt you. So it really goes back to your thoughts. Your illness, sickness or whatever it is was developed for a reason—to protect yourself from something—from getting hurt. Now what are you trying to protect yourself from?

Patient: I was trying to protect myself from being self-conscious when I was young. I built this up—that's one reason why I built this up.

Therapist: Explain that.

Patient: In other words, when I started to get hair on my arms and started to get more masculine than other kids I imagined that they were looking at me all the time and I built these groups up to fight that thinking that if I belonged to an acceptable group then I wouldn't have to worry about them looking at me. That's one possibility.

Therapist: What's another?

Patient: Well, that's the biggest. I can't think of any others because that's what I was really concerned with—people staring at me.

Therapist: You mean because you were changing?

Patient: Yes, because I was changing—I was afraid of it.

Therapist: Did you think you were changing into a monster?

Patient: Yeah, yeah, almost.

Therapist: I wonder why that is? Do you still fear it?

Patient: No, it doesn't bother me now.

Therapist: Would you rather be a child or a woman or something?

Patient: Well, I'd rather be a child—I think everybody would.

Therapist: What age would you like to be?

Patient: I'd like to go back to childhood—about 10 years old.

Therapist: When it all started . . .

Patient: When it all started.

Therapist: You want to start all over again. Do you feel ten at times?

Patient: No, I couldn't feel that now. I didn't realize it but I had it made at that age. I wish I could go back but you can't—you can't turn anything back.

Therapist: What was it like?

Patient: It was like paradise. I didn't have these things on my mind. I got along with the other kids at school. I had few enemies, did my work at school, had a good appetite when I came home. Then whammo, all of the sudden all this started. Up until that time it was beautiful and I don't know what happened. I had this fear of masturbating. I felt guilty and I became more guilty. When I started to get pimples on my face and I started to get older-looking, I feared that this was a result of the masturbation.

Therapist: Were you ever in love with your mother?

Patient: No, no.

Therapist: Didn't you ever have a desire for her?

Patient: No.

Therapist: Tell me what she was like.

Patient: Well, she's the administrator type. You know, she's a good home supervisor. Looks after things—very businesslike I guess you could call her, but affectionate, very affectionate.

Therapist: Is she sexy?

Patient: No.

Therapist: Did she ever have another man?

Patient: No.

(Session ends with discussion about Saturday appointments as patient has found a five-day-a-week job. Therapist agrees to try to work something out for him on Saturdays.)

What is wrong with this person? He says he is not insane; but that he is disturbed. He doesn't need to be confined; he can work, but he is tortured and unhappy.

In other parts of this book I have attempted in different ways to describe what underlies the symptomatology of the mental disturbance, disorder, or weakness or whatever it may be.

Just as it is wrong to cling to old ideas or phrases or terms that no longer describe a condition adequately, it is equally wrong to abandon a tried descriptive system and leave it all to complete anarchy.

For instance, Szasz states: "It is customary to define psychiatry as a medical specialty concerned with the study, diagnosis and treatment of mental illness. This is a worthless and misleading definition. Mental illness is a myth. Psychiatrists are not concerned with mental illnesses and their treatments. In actual practice they deal with personal, social and ethical problems in living." [3] Is it right to advise a person, acutely disturbed, confined to a hospital, who calls you from the hospital (as a psychiatric authority) to get a lawyer? Or is it better to evaluate his call for help at a different level (as was suggested by one psychiatrist) to make clear to him that his need to leave the hospital will not free him from persecution? The persecution is from within, not without. No authority, at this time, has the right to say or even imply that people with "mental" trouble are not ill; that they are normal, that there is nothing wrong with them. Eventually, the behavior of such people will become so bizarre, that attention *must* be drawn to them.

Whatever the mental disturbance is, it must first be evaluated from within and only after this can it be truly evaluated outside oneself. Rarely is this the order of procedure. However, if this becomes the procedure—as is necessary—then it is safe to see the condition for what it is. And it is no ONE DEFINABLE SCHEMA. IT IS NOT A DISEASE, yet sometimes IT IS LIKE A DISEASE. It is not just medical (as cardiac, cancer, ulceration, neurological disorder) but involves social and ethical problems in living. Yet it shows itself in all of these problems. A professional can only get the *feel* of what it is by being intimate with it. This might mean living with it at times. It may mean having it in yourself or in your family—or both—and it always means having treated it or, if you choose, bringing it to a successful conclusion.

Rather than relying on the classical descriptive method (a system that is unworkable in treatment) a method of diagnosis based on psychological development, neurologic development, and incorporating the concept of regression will be presented. Along with the concept of regression, there will be a discussion of the hallucinatory phenomena, the employment of new words to describe feelings, surroundings, and the psychotic episode. There will be a discussion of the human soul and its relationship to diagnosis. It is hoped that this will provide a regenerative as opposed to a static understanding of a person, patient or client. This in turn will introduce a human quality into diagnosis. (Rather than the classic distance introduced by terminology such as schizophrenic, manic depressive, or character neurotic, it is hoped that these new terms will enable the therapist and patient to have a mutuality of feeling.)

Then again, I do not think it time yet to completely abandon the old diagnostic manual of psychiatric disorders—but only, perhaps, to inject it with life—perhaps with a transfusion of warm, human blood.

I. Neurological Organization—Its Function in Diagnosis

All systems of diagnosis are based on observations of the person's behavior. Very few, if any, attempt to explain or incorporate why a person behaves in the manner that he does.

It is easy to see how a medical model has been accepted until this time as the means for diagnosing functional disabilities. An acute and chronic brain disorder shows emotional symptoms; the same emotional symptoms that may appear in a functional illness. For instance, a diabetic may show symptoms of psychotic depression, withdrawal, auditory and visual hallucinations. With the restoration of proper metabolic balance through the use of insulin and electrolytes, the symptoms may clear entirely. A person afflicted with Aziemer's disease (pre-senile senility) may show symptoms of vagueness, loss of time and space relationships, depression, hallucinations. Unfortunately, due to increased arterial clogging and reduced blood flow, the condition is progressive. With cranial neoplasm, one may see symptoms of paranoia, severe headaches, insomnia. Drug toxicity and overdoses are often mistaken for functional psychoses, that is, psychoses with no physical cause. All these brain disorders will show cause and effect in some somatic disease process. To complicate matters even further, many functional acute and chronic psychoses, behavior disorders, childhood autism and idiopathic epilepsies shown known neurological-like symptoms that respond to known psychotherapeutic techniques.

It thus became easy to reason: If organic brain disorders show emotional symptoms and have known causes, then the so-called "functional disorders" must have a similar medical disease cause and effect—but we do not have the microscopes, the chemical reagents or the diagnostic tests to find the germ, the cell, the missing ingredient. This is one way of thinking. There is perhaps another approach. This approach assumes that all psychotic or neurotic behavior has its representation in normal development. Let us use an example. An extremely anxious girl hears and listens to someone's voice: to her comprehension, it isn't a voice, but a real person—because in fact the person is real but she won't accept the fact that he isn't really speaking to her because he hasn't been in her presence for months. She listens, his voice tells her what to do, for instance, to go outside, to talk to a certain person, to eat, not to eat, to stay awake, not to go to the bathroom. She also defecates in her pants and urinates on the couch. She doesn't bathe, comb her hair, or socialize. She shakes involuntarily, stutters, and repeats in perseverative way. One might diagnose her as: Schizophrenic reaction—catatonic type, but say that she exhibits hebephrenic and paranoid features. Long hours might be spent for the sake of descriptive argumentation but it would not draw the therapist closer to the patient. In fact it might do just the opposite.

But, if one might see her hallucinations as meeting the need of a frightened young child for protection—and theorize that perhaps all babies hallucinate after birth, one might begin to sympathize and understand. Her incontinence might then be compared with the incontinence of a baby—her confusion, her lack of concentration, her repetition, her problems with eating as problems comparable to a developing child. Her shaking, blurred vision, unsteady gait, drooling, swallowing and talking difficulties may then be seen as difficulty with bowel training, much like neurologic regressions that coincide with neurologic lags in development seen at certain early age periods.

Understanding Early Neurologic Development

The concept of neurological organization as it pertains to man contains the following elements:

1. It is the result of sequential ontogenetic neural development.
2. The progression is cephalad through the spinal cord, medulla and midbrain, until it involves the cortex.
3. The uniqueness of cortical involvement in man is that it results in lateralization of function (dominance).
4. Lower level function must be complete and intact in order for higher levels to develop and function properly.
5. If neurological organization is incomplete due to delay or disturbance in the ontogenetic progression, the individual will exhibit a problem of mobility or communication or both.

The brain needs stimuli from the environment to develop normally. Thomas says "as a consequence of the hierarchical development of the brain, the environmental influences of early life are of crucial importance for the development of neurological organization." [5] This holds true even if the brain has been injured during gestation, at birth or after birth. And so it is logical medically to institute therapeutic programs, designed to improve neurological efficiency by emphasizing both the sensory and motor factors, which evoke the most efficient development of neurological organization during infancy.

In the study of neurological organization in the people of primitive cultures of Brazil and of South and East Africa, it has been concluded that these people do not have complete neurological organization. All the tribes studied showed sensory deprivation of some form in infancy. [4]

The chart and related theories of neurological development are especially helpful in understanding gait disturbance, strabismus and speech disturbances found in childhood autism. It is also helpful in understanding transient neurological abnormalities often found in the most regressive stages of mental illness. It is also helpful, although not fully explaining the somatic delusional symptoms and body distortions and organ emphasis often seen accompanying the more regressive mental dysfunctions.

It also makes it reasonable to review mental dysfunctions as "like an illness" if not as an illness.

Recent work by MacLean has shown that area of registration of primal emotions may be in the limbic system.[6] He says the split between the lower mammalian parts of the brain (that are necessary for life) and the highly developed neomammalian brain may be the cause of psychosomatization. For instance, eating to sustain life, and eating as related to another human that involves the problems of externalization and love.

II. Psychological Organization and Development

"There is a film in front of my eyes that prevents me from seeing, my mouth is dry and I hear the voice listening to everything I say. It is coming from the refrigerator. I have a feeling of having to murder someone. Perhaps I need a doctor. I must have a cold."

To the uninformed, this talk would be unusual. To a psychiatrist it probably would be a clue. If added to a history of what has happened to this man within the last ten years—that is, a procession of admissions to veterans hospitals and state institutions with no improvement but instead retrogression, it would enable the physician to diagnose this patient as: "Schizophrenic reaction, paranoid type, chronic, severe."

This patient is getting well at Delaware Valley Mental Health Foundation. His mind has become organized to where he can read, understand and apply what he has read from a book on psychology to himself and other patients. He is driving a car, talking about all his feelings; in essence he is waking up from a 10 year old dream. It is truly a miracle to his mother and even to professionals. To me it is simply a matter of understanding what feelings he is trying to convey. For instance, if one remembers that all infants have a film before their eyes until approximately 6 weeks after birth, all infants probably hallucinate and that they see their own bodies as outside projections before they have a semblance of self, this patient's remarks become more understandable. His bedroom door faced the refrigerator—and this was the first thing he saw each morning. A refrigerator is used for storage of food and its motor exudes warm air and pleasing sound. Symbolically it could arouse the sensory-motor feelings of hunger, nursing and the warmth and protection of motherhood. The dry mouth was never made warm and moist. Frustration produced rage and murderous thoughts and finally apathy.

It was Freud, himself, who first opened the door to regression and then a developmental understanding of "neuroses." To my way of thinking, his greatest contribution to diagnosis has been his understanding of instinctual erogenous zones.* These are:

1. The Oral Stage
2. The Anal-Sadistic Stage
3. Urethral eroticism
4. The Phallic Phase
   Boys—castration complex
   Girls—penis envy

The Oral Stage is the stage of utmost importance in the diagnosis of the more severely disabled or regressed individuals: those labeled psychotic. Perhaps the most important feelings to understand, surround the phenomena "eat and/or be eaten." Earliest identifications or unions between human behings surround eating another human and being eaten by that person. The fear of oral pleasure and the subsequent denial of any wish for this basic erotic human right is the very cornerstone of human suffering. Unless one can mix blood, sweat, tears and sensations with another individual he will not begin to understand what it is to be human. A person only begins to become a better human by increasing this assimilation. Right at this moment, I am thinking of one patient I am treating who is afraid to make this union. Her whole body continues to suffer with guilt, torment and anxiety. She stubbornly clings to hallucinations, complicated false fantasies and bed wetting, defecating and denial of body sensation. (The skin is part of early oral period sensation.) The reason she gives her mind is that I am married, (the therapist), and so she cannot love me. At first she could accept me as a father, but now there is too much feeling in her genitals. This has only created more guilt. If she is to recover, she must deal with all of this.

All pleasure begins in the mouth and then extends downward. This is of diagnostic importance, especially in a partially treated case. For example, patients, grossly psychotic, confused, disoriented, may, in treatment, accept oral pleasure, anal pleasure, urethral pleasure, phallic pleasure and then go out into the world. The patients can work successfully, take care of themselves, but they are not whole because they have not worked through genital love or real love. They have appeared well but were not whole. Once again they break down with the same complex of symptoms and indeed look very sick, perhaps as sick as when first entering treatment. However, very quickly (sometimes in a matter of days) the psychosis will disappear and they will begin to work on understanding real love—solving the problems in the genital zone. Frequently after this, the result is the ability to marry and live in union with another person.

* For more detail concerning erogenous zones, one is referred to THE PSYCHO-ANALYTIC THEORY OF THE NEUROSES, Fenichel, M.D.; DEVELOPMENT OF INSTINCTS, INFANTILE SEXUALITY, pp. 61–83, W. W. Norton & Co., Inc., New York, 1945.

The Construction of Reality in the Child

Piaget has interpreted child development in cognitive rather than in instinctual manner. Understanding Freud and sometimes borrowing from him, Piaget has nevertheless provided us with a constructive model that has become extremely valuable for the "groping in the dark" work that must be done to reconstruct a personality. The seeds of psychosis are sown early, and once the "crazy patterns" are melted away or worn down during treatment only a shell of a human remains. All in all, in most cases, a reconstruction of reality has to occur.

In autism, it is even more crucial. Instead of a breakdown at puberty, the instinctual upheaval, it occurs at one and a half to two years of age, the crisis of cognition.

Stages of Universe Construction (Piaget)[7, 8]

SENSORY-MOTOR   Assimilation—in the beginning, the individual utilizes (takes in) the environment to nourish what heredity left him (his acquired schemata), sucking, sight, prehension (methods of assimilation) need objects. Whenever objects are introduced (accommodation), there is a conflict between the assimilation and accommodation. However, this conflict is small at first, i.e., for proper nourishment the object must be an extension of the subject. Thus at first the subject (infant) is egocentric. All the universe is an extension of himself. Intelligence develops by the incorporation of an aggregate of permanent objects connected causally and there is a connection and nonseparation of infant and object. Gradually through intelligence (coordination of his intellectual instruments), he discovers himself in placing himself as an active object among the other active objects in a universe external to himself.

Assimilation is conservative and tends to subordinate the environment to the organism as it is; accommodation is the source of changes and bends the organism to the successive constraints of the environment. Accommodation must prevail, for a change of accommodation allows a continuous flow of new assimilations. When they are in conflict, i.e., an assimilation can't accept a particular accommodation (mindful that there is a natural conflict) there occurs a breakdown. The external world and self remain dissociated to such a point that neither objects nor spatial, temporal, nor causal objectifications are possible.

Eventually assimilation and accommodation become interdependent. The growing child becomes interested in novelty or play and pursues it for its own sake. Thus, this play becomes interesting, invites more research and needs new matching accommodations. This leads into close mutual dependency with the development of reflective thought (age four to five). There is also a mutual dependency of assimilation deduction and experimental techniques.

Intelligence begins neither with the knowledge of self nor of things as such, but with knowledge of their interaction and it is by orienting itself simultaneously toward the two poles of that interaction that intelligence organizes the world by organizing itself. Accommodation to another's point of view enables individual thought to be located in a totality of perspectives that insure its objectivity and reduce its egocentrism. Co-ordination of sensory-motor assimilation and accommodation leads the individual to go outside himself to solidify and objectify his universe to the point where he is able to include himself in it while continuing to assimilate it to himself.

Imitation is the outgrowth of accommodation. By representing the image of the object (that is what the infant feels is the object), the infant in-teriorizes it. At first reflective movements of the mouth spread to sur-rounding areas. He thus becomes aware of his mouth, nose, ears and cheeks. He imitates gestures such as hand to face movements, prehension or grasp and then sounds such as "Ma, Ma" and even a smile. For instance, putting a finger to one's nose, nose puckering, are ends in themselves and are imitations occurring as early as seven months. Interest in one's mirror image occurs at approximately one year. At one year and four months a child can imitate something it has not seen for hours or days. Piaget says the object perceived externally is replaced by an internal model. With the development of language at around 18 months, true imitation through symbols, images and propositions occurs. Here is the beginning of con-ceptualization, mind work in the infant. This is extremely important as it coincides with the beginning of the autistic breakdown (the condition labeled as childhood autism).

Interiorization of images continues to become more complete between the ages of two and five. Thus, monologues and soliloquies continue to grow in scope. Failure in interiorization of images results in exteriorizations in later life such as projections and paranoia.

Imitations of objects such as aeroplanes, refrigerators, give life to these objects. This occurs before animal or human imitation. From two to seven representative imitation develops spontaneously, often being unconscious because of its ease and egocentrism, whereas at about seven or eight it becomes deliberate, and takes its place in intelligence as a whole. Sensory-motor intelligence, which during the first two years coordinates perceptions and actions, and thus makes possible the construction of the notions of permanent objects, practical space and perceptive constancy of form and dimensions, continues to play a fundamental role throughout the rest of the period of mental development and even in the adult stage. Although it is outstripped, as far as general control of behavior is concerned, by con-ceptual intelligence which develops the initial schemas into rational opera-tions, sensory-motor intelligence nevertheless remains, all through life, the essential tool for perceptive activity and the indispensable intermediary between the perceptions and conceptual intelligence. At about seven or eight, progress is threefold:

1. Imitation of detail with analysis and reconstitution of the model object.
2. Consciousness of imitation—a dissociation of external elements from what belongs to the ego.
3. Discrimination—now imitation is used only as an aid to the fulfillment of the needs inherent in the child's activity. Imitation can now be called reflective, i.e., controlled by intelligence as a whole.

Piaget acquaints us with the child's game playing and the importance of games in the mind development. He mentions three types of games:

1. Practice games (first month of life)
2. Symbolic games (second year onward)
3. Games with rules (four to eleven and throughout life)

Practice games are without symbols, make-believe, or rules, and are especially characteristic of animal behavior. For instance, a kitten running after a ball of wool doesn't have to think the wool is a mouse—it thus is just a simple game, with no make-believe or pretense.

Symbolic games employ representation and their functions deviate from mere pleasure of mastering reality. Games with rules necessarily imply social or inter-individual relationships. It is implicit in the game's sanction or penalty. Constructional or creative games are games such as hobbies. They are done for fun and no remuneration and so are not actually classified as work as they have no set schedule.

Symbolic games decline after the age of four because the more the child adapts himself to the natural and social world, the less he indulges in symbolic distortions and transpositions. Instead of assimilating the external world to the ego, he progressively subordinates the ego to reality.

In 1896 K. Groos * was the first to see play, not as a mental wastebasket, keeping children from homework, but as a phenomenon of growth, growth of thought and activity. However, Groos, like Freud, failed to understand the cause of unconscious symbolization. Freud said there is symbolism because the content of the symbols has been repressed. Groos said symbolic function exists because the content of the symbol is still beyond the child's reach.

M. Klein, S. Isaacs, Searl and others have shown the similarity to children's dreams and their play. If one can see the similarity of children's play, dreams and psychotic behavior (living in the "dream world"), it can be understood how psychotic content has meaning and that the psy-

---

* Comments from K. Groos, M. Klein, S. Isaacs and Searl, obtained from Piaget's *Play, Dreams and Imitation in Childhood*. (Norton, N.Y. 1962.)

chotic thought process is similar to the developmental egocentric assimilation of children's thought. It, also, does not proceed by logical concepts. The paralogical talk of psychosis should not be considered in its literal sense, but as metaphor, not unlike the context of poetry.[9]

Conceptual thought proceeds through sensory-motor intelligence as the child matures. There are several basic differences that initiate conceptual thought. Sensory-motor intelligence seeks only practical adaptation, that is, it aims only at success or utilization, whereas conceptual thought leads to knowledge as such and therefore yields to norms of truth. Conceptual thought involves socialization, it involves cooperation, and another person to verify truths. It thus becomes rational.

Samples of patients' expressions will be presented throughout the book to illustrate how recognition of levels of conceptual thought may pinpoint a similarity in a stage of normal childhood development and in levels of thought development in psychotic patients. These patients, in actuality, have "matured" to adulthood, but have never developed reflective awareness and cognitive thinking stable enough to exist in reality as we know it.

During the Victorian age, enlightenment toward the viewing of man's affliction took a new turn. All of man's thinking as evolved through history, has acted as a pendulum, swinging from one extreme to its opposite. In the 1890's, Freud in psychology began to see mental processes and symptoms not as ends in themselves, but as interrelated to the essence of man's psyche itself. The symptoms were not the affliction, they were only the outside signals of an inner conflict. It was the total organism that was involved in a conflict. Neo-Freudians smugly ignored reality conflicts and social everyday life, and the four or five time a week refuge in the dark room, and comfortable couch of psychoanalysis became to many a dream; like defense or escape from the world. Recently, men such as J. Wolpe, B. F. Skinner and H. J. Eysenck revived the Pavlovian techniques of conditioning and evolved the behavioristic school.[10] Debunking psychoanalysis and Freudianism, these men once again see man as a laboratory specimen with a set of symptoms. With shocking techniques and deconditioning techniques the neurosis or "bad habit" is eliminated. High rates of cure (78–95%) are claimed. Both these extremes of looking at man have robbed him of his soul and his dignity.

In the Victorian age, medicine went through similar changes. The causes of diseases were unknown and treatment was more mystical than scientific. Large potions of toxic medicines, each given to remedy a different symptom, were used. It took reformers such as Flaubert (early 19th century) and A. T. Still (1890's) to voice objection. Flaubert was a nihilist, objecting vigorously, but dying without his voice being heard. A. T. Still, like Freud, offered an alternative theory and a treatment technique.[11] Although a medical physician, he founded the school of Osteopathy. His theories about the body being a central and total organism

that can muster from within the knowledge to resist outside disease mal-
functioning was not dissimilar to Freud's understanding of the psyche.

Physical Diagnosis of Emotional Disturbances

Somatic changes take place in mental dysfunctions. No laboratory tests
are necessary to find these. They become extremely important aspects of
the *physical diagnosis of emotional disturbances.*

Most visible are changes in expression or body carriage. Birdwhistle and
others have studied gestures, hand movements, and postural approaches
in interpersonal exchanges.[12] It is significant when a woman strokes her
hair, raises her arms over her revealing her breasts, or crosses her knees.
Stroking of one's Adam's apple, folding one's hands or placing one's
hands in the form of the letter O have significant meaning. (I have found
that the Adam's apple is the key to the throat and stomach and is
stroked when a person is extremely hurt inside.) The O is like a presentation of one's mouth and denotes a receptive or taking-in mood.

There are pseudoparalyses that simulate real paralyses due to intra-
cerebral hemorrhage. There are musculo-skeletal changes that produce
pain similar to pain of coronary occlusion, but due to psychosomatic
tensions. How many hysterectomies are performed annually because of
vague abdominal and pelvic pains accompanying psycho-pelvic disorders?
The proctologists have a field day exploring the dark and odorous problems of the rectum. But their scopes are not long enough to reach the
brain.

Wilhelm Reich describes how word language frequently functions as a
defense against the real expressive language of the "biological core." [13]
Reich reminds us that the somatic disturbances of hysteria do not correspond to the anatomy and physiology of muscles, nerves and blood
vessels but to emotionally significant organs. Pathological blushing, for
example, is usually restricted to face and neck, although the blood vessels
run essentially lengthwise. Similarly, sensory disturbances in hysteria do
not correspond to a certain nerve path, but to emotionally significant
regions of the body.

A study of pantomime is helpful in understanding gestures. (Thus, the
next section of this chapter on diagnosis will be devoted to the work of
Francois Delsarte, the father of French pantomime.) Genevieve Stebbins,
in 1902, wrote about the work of Francois Delsarte, the father of French
pantomime, in *The Delsarte System of Expression.*[14] "Let your attitude,
gesture and face foretell what you would make it sell. . . . Expression
of face precedes gesture, and gesture precedes speech." Delsarte says:
"The above law illustrates the relation of pantomime to speech. It is a
very important one considering the true language of emotion, the verbal
and the pantomimic. The latter is revelatory of the true man; while the
verbal is more or less artificial. It takes many words to say what a single

look reveals. Gesture is the lightning, speech the thunder; thus gestures should precede speech." Some of Delsarte's findings describe my feeling in some detail.

It is well known by modern men working in kinesics, such as R. Birdwhistle, that gestures, just as dreams, may be the royal road to the inner mind of man. There are many conditions of so-called mental illness where there is no speech and it is only the appearance, the looks and the gestures that will determine the diagnosis of childhood autism, catatonia, etc. Delsarte divides the human body into three zones.

1. The head is equal to the mental or the intellectual zone.
2. The torso or body is equal to the moral or volitional zone.
3. The limbs are equal to the vital or physical zone.

An example of each one of these comes easily. The common expression, "he has no head" reminds us that the head corresponds to the mind. The torso contains the two great motive organs of the body, the lungs and the heart. Volition pertains to the will, the desires, the love of the being. The limbs are equal to the vital or the physical.

Now let us divide the head into several divisions:

Zone A. The frontal or mental zone. All this refers to various degrees of illumination: blindness or darkness or brilliancy in reference to the intellect. Such expressions as "a clear sighted man" depict one whose understanding is clear. We "look into" a subject: we "see" a reason.

Zone B. This is the buccal zone which is equal to the moral or the will zone. The buccal is the cheek and the nose. You have heard the expression "a keen-scented man" or one who has keen perception. A nose refers to the will or desire. You have often heard of the Roman nose denoting conquest or cruelty, a Greek nose depicting ethics and beauty, the Turkish nose, sexuality.

Zone C. Zone C is the mouth which is a vital zone. This also includes the chin. It represents touch, taste and sound.

Let us similarly divide the torso into three zones:

A. The thorax is the mental zone. The lungs inspire, aspire and expire.

B. The epigastric is the zone that expresses love. The heart beats quicker in excitement, slower in fear or horror. Gestures in this area all have to do with love.

C. The abdominal zone represents more material or physical instincts. Gestures from this section are vulgar or sexual.

Delsarte divides the fore limb into three zones:

A. He mentions that the hand emphasizes the expression of the eyes. The eyes are mental. When we look toward an object, the hand points. We talk with the hands to the deaf and dumb. We write with the hand. We draw, play and work with the hands. It is indeed an agent of the brain.

B. It is often said that the elbow is the soul of the arm.

C. The upper arm is the power force. For instance to strike out with the shoulder.

Now let us divide the lower limbs:

A. The foot is like an agent of the mind. For instance, tapping the foot. It makes gestures similar to the hand. It advances, retreats, stamps and kicks.

B. The lower leg is the moral area of the lower limb. To kneel is an expression of reverence, love and obedience. This is the subordination of the will to others.

C. The upper leg or thigh is the area of the will. For instance, the first impulse of the leg in walking should be felt in the thigh.

"The shoulders are indeed a thermometer of passion," says Delsarte. He says this because he feels the shoulder intervenes in all forms of emotion. It is a measure of heat, of intensity, of passion and of sensibility. For instance, the uplifted shoulder. In one subdued, the shoulder is down and he is hunched. Delsarte dwells on the wrist and the open hand. He said the wrist is an element of power.

Delsarte went to the statues of antiquity, especially in ancient Greece, and studied posture. For instance, in standing, when the strong leg is back, its knees straight, the free leg in front, the knee also straight, the position represents antagonism. The sentiment is defiant irritation. He shows the walk as quite significant. Observe an actress as she walks. She plants her foot with bent knee, using the knee as a spring—a soft, sinuous step, a panther-like effect, very effective in its proper place as an expression of controlled force, secrecy. "My knees sink under me, help or I die!" the despondent, despairing walk of frustration seems to exclaim.

There are laws, according to Delsarte, that influence emotion in the body. For instance, the law of altitude states every positive emotion rises, negative emotion falls. In the law of force, conscious stress assumes weak attitudes, conscious weakness assumes strong attitudes. This is true spiritually as well as physically. In the law of motion, excitment or passion tends to expand gestures, thought or reflection tends to contract gesture, and love or affection tends to moderate gesture. Thus passion tends to extreme expansion of the muscles, thought tends to extreme contraction of the muscles, and affection tends to a happy medium of activity of the muscles. The bonds of passion and reason and affection constitute the divinest emotion of being and produce the most beautiful modulations of manner in the body. There is a law of reaction and it states, "every extreme of emotion tends to react to its opposites." For instance, concentrated passion tends to explosion—explosion to prostration. Thus the only emotion which does not tend to its own destruction is that which is perfectly poised. The law of extension states, "The extension of a gesture is in proportion to the surrender of the will in emotion."

Primitive man, like a child, reached forward for that which he desired and drew back from that which he feared. He expanded to sunshine, he contracted when cold, he felt wide-awake, well, dominant when upright; he felt weak, sleepy, sick when prostrate. He saw the circles of the heavens and horizons and so when the sun was up, he reached upward to it and found that there was good and light and warmth. He raised the arm in an expanded circle, and so the meaning of exultation crept into the movement, as his first worship was for that which he could not reach—the sun.

He thought it lived, for it moved; and all things on earth that moved lived.

Naturally sun, moon and star worship was the first religion. Man glorified himself by sweeping the circle of the ground where he lived. When he lifted his arm and brought it down, it crushed that which was weak and so became later a gesture of dominance. Dominance, of the affirmative, of the yes; and again it was the line of his own erect figure. But when he threw a sharp stone at an upright tree and brought it low, it lay as he did when sick, asleep or dead, and the action became the great no, the negative. The burden he threw from him took the oblique line, otherwise it would have crushed his feet, and so figuratively we throw burdens off obliquely. He crouches obliquely from what he feared, and threw the hand up to protect and shield himself, and so the gesture.

When his sacks were full, they swelled at the sides, and thus the gesture of the outside quartered circle meaning plenty, the inside one, fineness and delicacy, originally was made to show a want of plenty.

He scooped a stone and made it hollow for his first dish, hence the undercurve for well-being and happiness, for shortly he who had a dish was well-to-do and had something to put in it. The uppercurve was a cover put over to protect his game or soup, and so grew to mean possession, secrecy, and thus the great law of correspondence was God's law from the first.

And today we use in the expression of sublime emotion, the same motions that primitive savages evolved as pantomime to express the first simple necessities of his nature. That they are true today is because the mental, moral and vital natures correspond.

Birdwhilstle described early development of language where in expression it gave man more impetus to make himself communicative and meaningful. Desmond Morris, in his book, *The Naked Ape*,[15] describes grooming actions seen in moments of aggressive tension. For instance, we scratch our heads, bite our nails, stroke our earlobes, rub our chins, lick our lips or rub our hands together in rinsing action. These actions all become ritualistic and we have this in common with our ancestors the apes. Morris states that domination is the goal of an animal's aggression, not destruction nor murder and basically we do not seem to differ from other species in this respect. Morris also describes grooming in medical care. He says in order to understand this it is essential to distinguish between serious and trivial cases of indisposition. In the case of trivial ailments, the medical symptoms reflect a physical problem that has taken a physical form, rather than a real physical problem. Common examples of grooming imitation ailments, as we can call them, include coughs, colds, influenza, backaches, headaches, stomach upsets, skin rashes, sore throats, tonsilitis, and laryngitis. The condition of the sufferer is not serious but sufficiently unhealthy to justify increased attention for him from social companions. The symptoms act in the same way as grooming imitation signals releasing comforting behavior from doctors, nurses, chemists, relatives and friends. Morris states that the heartbeat is similar to the beat of the womb and is a sign of protection in the animal and a sign of security in the young.

Erik Erikson has described Eight Ages of Man describing the development of the human in the social sphere. Let us take each of Erikson's eight ages of man and see what meaning they may lend to a developmental view of diagnosis.[16]

I. BASIC TRUST VS. BASIC MISTRUST   Basic social trust occurs between mother and infant when the infant finds more and more pleasure in his waking hours that give within him a sense of inner goodness. It shows itself in the ease of his feeding, the depth of his sleep, and the relaxation of his bowels. Basic mistrust shows itself in a continually raging infant unable to cope with his urges.

II. AUTONOMY VS. SHAME AND DOUBT   At this stage outer control must be firmly reassuring. The infant must come to feel that the basic faith in existence, which is the lasting treasure saved from the rages of the oral stage, will not be jeopardized by this about face of his, this sudden violent wish to have a choice, to appropriate demandingly, and to eliminate stubbornly.

III. INITIATIVE VS. GUILT   Here a child appears "more himself," more loving, relaxed and brighter in his judgment. He is in free possession of a surplus of energy which permits him to forget failures quickly and to approach what seems desirable (even if it also seems uncertain and even dangerous) with undiminished and more accurate direction. Initiative adds to autonomy the quality of undertaking, planning and "attacking" a task for the sake of being active and on the move, where before self-will, more often than not, inspired acts of defiance.

The danger of this stage is a sense of guilt over the goals contemplated and the acts initiated in one's exuberant enjoyment of new locomotor and mental power: acts of aggressive manipulation and coercion which soon go far beyond the executive capacity of organism and mind and, therefore, call for an energetic halt on one's contemplated initiative.

IV. INDUSTRY VS. INFERIORITY   Here the child masters "entrance into life." Past infantile hopes and wishes must be forgotten, while his exuberant imagination is tamed to the laws of impersonal things. Here he develops the fundamentals of technology—the child becomes ready to handle the utensils, the tools, and the weapons used by the big people. The child's danger, at this stage, lies in a sense of inadequacy and inferiority.

V. IDENTITY VS. ROLE CONFUSION   Youth begins. At this stage one is concerned with who he feels he is as compared to how he looks to others. The result, if ego identity, is an accrued confidence that the inner sameness and continuity prepared in the past are matched by the sameness and continuity of one's meaning for others.

The dangers of this stage are role confusion. When this is based on a strong previous doubt as to one's sexual identity, delinquent and outright psychotic episodes are not uncommon.

VI. INTIMACY VS. ISOLATION   This is the fusion of one's identity with others. It is a readiness for intimacy, the capacity to commit oneself to concrete affiliations and partnerships and to develop the ethnical strength to abide by such commitments, even though they may call for significant sacrifices and compromises. Its counterpart is isolation, a destruction of forces and people who are essentially different than oneself. This is the beginning of prejudices.

VII. GENERATIVITY VS. STAGNATION   Generativity is the ability to generate one's energy in teaching the young. Its opposite is boredom and stagnation.

VIII. EGO INTEGRITY VS. DESPAIR   Ego integrity involves the ability to continually develop mature philosophy, order and meaning to life.

Its opposite is despair, failure and breakdown of identity with the awful feelings of hopelessness.

Erikson has given us another way of looking at man's development. Arrests in development help us to understand personality level fixations that accompany every mental breakdown. More accurate diagnosis will be the result.

I. The Use of New Words and Terms in an Effort to Reach a More Accurate Diagnosis

Just as the old words of diagnostic category such as schizophrenic, manic depressive, neurotic and psychotic are no longer useful—there are in turn new words that have become useful in understanding patients' feelings.

A person may feel more dead, like stone, more unreal than real, differentiated and separate from all others. He may feel filmy, foggy, floaty or transparent; he may bend with the wind, be blown from here to there. He may feel amoebic with pseudopods flowing in all directions. "Spongy," "robot-like," "snow-flaky" are other words frequently used by patients. All of us humans, during our daily life, are in and out of a dream world that separates the normal from pathological. It is only a matter of degree. This is such an essential part of diagnosis that I intend more detail on the phenomena of hallucinations later in this chapter.

Laing characterizes three forms of anxiety manifested by the "onto-logically" insecure person: engulfment, implosion and petrification.[17]

A. ENGULFMENT   In this, the individual dreads relatedness as such, with anyone or anything or, indeed, even with himself, because his uncertainty about the stability of his autonomy lays open the idea to his dread that in any relationship he will lose his autonomy and identity. Engulfment is not simply envisaged as a liabe-to-happen willy-nilly despite the individual's most active efforts to avoid it. The individual experiences himself as a man who is only saving himself from drowning by the most constant, strenuous, and desperate activity. Engulfment is felt as a risk in being understood, in being loved, or even simply in being seen. To be hated may be feared for other reasons, but to be hated as such is often less disturbing than to be destroyed, as it is felt, through being engulfed by love.

The anxiety of engulfment expresses itself in different ways—almost always around the mouth. The fear of being "swallowed up" is most predominant. Disturbing feelings occur in childhood autism. Hands of the child in the therapist's mouth, growling, swallowing and biting noises and motions seem most disturbing to these children. Fears of choking, losing one's breath are engulfment-like disturbances referred to the throat-lung apparatus, that is in such close proximity to the upper gastro-intestinal tract. (The stomach is a sack for food, the lungs are sacks for air.) Other frightening feelings are the fear of being buried, being drowned, being caught and being dragged down in quicksand.

Fire, a flickering of one's inner desires for warmth, may become out of control, devastating, destructive. Aroused feelings of warmth, confusing, may indeed provoke feelings of anxiety. Coldness and dryness are easy but not intense heat or moisture. Feelings of being on fire, especially around the ears and face,* may be alarming for a chronically sick person to deal with.

B. IMPLOSION is the awesome feeling that at any time, any second, all the ego one has (or supposedly has—and it may be only slight) will be destroyed. The result will be an awful nothingness. I have worked with patients so threatened that even a sudden change in body position was enough to threaten their very existence.

C. PETRIFICATION AND DEPERSONALIZATION a particular form or terror, whereby one is petrified and turned to stone. There is a dread of this happening, a dread of the possibility of turning or being turned from a live person into a robot, an automaton, without personal autonomy of action. It is also a magical act whereby one may attempt to turn someone else into stone by "petrifying" him.

Depersonalization is a means of dealing with others when the other person becomes too threatening. One makes oneself irresponsive to another's feelings either deliberately or automatically (commonly called unconsciously). A wall exists between one's own feelings and the other person. This feeling makes one's body numb, floatable and ethereal.

---

* Flush reaction described in chapter on Subnormal Mental Functioning, Chapter XII.

The feeling of world ending catastrophe, destruction of everything around, with the eventual destruction of oneself, is another common feeling approaching psychosis. It is a feeling before tottering over the border into hallucinatory psychosis or into suicide.

Embodied or Disembodied

Most people feel they began with their bodies and will end when their bodies die. Such a person is embodied.

People who are unembodied (and this probably occurs in most people at stressful times but in some people all the time) are detached from their bodies. They have never achieved a state of incarnation.

In an unembodied person, the body is felt more as one object among other objects in the world, than as the core of the individual's own being. The body is felt as the core of the false self. Such a divorce of self from body deprives the unembodied self of direct participation in any aspect of the life of the world that is mediated exclusively through the bodies' feelings, perceptions and movements. The unembodied self, as onlooker at all the body does, engages in nothing directly. It becomes extremely crtical of body activity and gives way to false, disembodied intellectual mentality that cannot get its "hands into things."

II. What Does Sanity Mean

Father Thomas Merton, poet, philosopher and renowned monk at the Trappist Monastery in Gethsemane, Kentucky, wrote the following entitled "A Devout Meditation in Memory of Adolf Eichmann." [18]

> One of the most disturbing facts that came out in the Eichmann trial was that a psychiatrist examined him and pronounced him perfectly sane. I do not doubt it at all, and that is precisely why I find it disturbing.
>
> If all the Nazis had been psychotics, as some of their leaders probably were, their appalling cruelty would have been in some sense easier to understand. It is much worse to consider this calm, "well-balanced," unperturbed official conscientiously going about his desk work, his administrative job which happened to be the supervision of mass murder. He was thoughtful, orderly, unimaginative. He had a profound respect for system, for law and order. He was obedient, loyal, a faithful officer of a great state. He served his government very well.
>
> He was not bothered much by guilt. I have not heard that he developed any psychosomatic illnesses. Apparently he slept well. He had a good appetite, or so it seems. True, when he visited Auschwitz, the Camp Commandant, Hoess, in a spirit of sly deviltry, tried to tease the big boss and scare him with some of the sights. Eichmann was disturbed, yes. He was disturbed. Even Himmler had been disturbed, and had gone weak at the knees. Perhaps, in the same way, the general manager of a big steel mill might be disturbed if an accident took place while he happened to be somewhere in

the plant. But of course what happened at Auschwitz was not an accident; just the routine unpleasantness of the daily task. One must shoulder the burden of daily monotonous work for the Fatherland. Yes, one must suffer discomfort and even nausea from unpleasant sights and sounds. It all comes under the heading of duty, self-sacrifice, and obedience. Eichmann was devoted to duty, and proud of his job.

The sanity of Eichmann is disturbing. We equate sanity with a sense of justice, with humaneness, with prudence, with the capacity to love and understand other people. We rely on the sane people of the world to preserve it from barbarism, madness, destruction. And now it begins to dawn on us that it is precisely the sane ones who are the most dangerous.

It is the well-adapted ones, who can without qualms and without nausea aim the missiles and press the buttons that will initiate the great festival of destruction that they, the sane ones, have prepared. What makes us so sure, after all, that the danger comes from a psychotic getting into a position to fire the first shot in a nuclear war? Psychotics will be suspect. No one suspects the sane, and the sane ones will have perfectly good reasons, logical, well-adjusted reasons, for firing the shot. They will be obeying sane orders that have come sanely down the chain of command. And because of their sanity they will have no qualms at all. When the missiles take off, then, it will be no mistake.

And so I ask myself: what is the meaning of a concept of sanity that excludes love, considers it irrelevant, and destroys our capacity to love other human beings, to respond to their needs and their sufferings, to recognize them also as persons, to apprehend their pain as one's own? Evidently this is not necessary for "sanity" at all. It is a religious notion, a spiritual notion, a Christian notion. What business have we to equate "sanity" with "Christianity"? None at all, obviously. The worst error is to imagine that a Christian must try to be "sane" like everybody else, that we belong in our kind of society. That we must be "realistic" about it. We must develop a sane Christianity; and there have been plenty of sane Christians in the past. Torture is nothing new, is it? We ought to be able to rationalize a little brainwashing and genocide, and find a place for nuclear war, or at least for napalm bombs, in our moral theology. Certainly some of us are doing our best all along those lines already. There are hopes! Even Christians can shake off their sentimental prejudices about charity, and become sane like Eichmann. They can even cling to a certain set of Christian formulas, and fit them into a Totalist Ideology. Let them talk about justice, charity, love, and the rest. These words have not stopped some sane men from acting very sanely, and cleverly in the past . . .

No, Eichmann was sane. The generals and fighters on both sides, in World War II, the ones who carried out the total destruction of entire cities, these were the sane ones. Those who have invented and developed atomic bombs, thermonuclear bombs, missiles; who have planned the strategy of the next war; who have evaluated the various possibilities of using bacterial and chemical agents: these are not the crazy people, they are the sane people. The ones who coolly estimate how many millions of victims can be considered expendable in a nuclear war, I presume they do all right with the Rorschach ink blots too. On the other hand, you will probably find that pacifists and the ban-the-bomb people are, quite seriously, just as we read in Time, a little crazy.

I am beginning to realize that "sanity" is no longer a value or an end in itself. The "sanity" of modern man is about as useful to him as the huge bulk and muscles of the dinosaur. If he were a little less sane, a little more doubtful, a little more aware of his absurdities and contradictions, perhaps there might be a possibility of his survival. But if he is sane, too sane . . . perhaps we must say that in a society like ours the worst insanity is to be totally without anxiety, totally "sane."

III. The Phenomena of Regression

Regression may be defined as the re-emergence of modes of mental functioning which were characteristic of the psychic activity of the individual during earlier periods of development. Kris regarded regression as a primitivization of function.[19] Arlow and Brenner apply this concept to the functioning of all parts of the psychic apparatus, to the instinctual drives of the id, to the modes of operation of the ego, and to the demands of the superego.[20] This definition and concept of regression stresses the importance of maturational and developmental processes in shaping the form and function of the psychic apparatus.

It is important to emphasize four essential features of regression:

1. Regression is a universal tendency of mental functioning.
2. Primitive forms of mental functioning linger, and may exist side by side with more mature forms of activity, whether the condition is pathological or normal.
3. All forms of regression of so-called functional (non-organic) origin are transient and reversible.
4. Regression is not total or global. It affects particular aspects of the instinctual life, of ego or superego functioning, rather than the whole of either. The functions it does affect are affected differently.

Freud wrote in 1915 ". . . the development of the mind shows a peculiarity which is present in no other developmental process . . . one can describe the state of affairs, which has nothing to compare with it, only by saying that in this case every earlier stage of development persists alongside the later stage which has risen from it. . . . The earlier mental state may not have manifested itself for years, but nonetheless, it is so far present that it may at any time again become the mode of expression of the forces in the mind, and indeed the only one, as though all later developments had been annulled or undone. This extraordinary plasticity of mental developments is not unrestricted as regards direction; it may be described as a special capacity for involution—for regression—since it may well happen that a later and higher stage of development, once abandoned, cannot be reached again. But the primitive stages can always be reestablished: the primitive mind, is, in the fullest meaning of the word, imperishable." [21]

Piaget in "The Construction of Reality in the Child," mentions how regression appears in connection with each advance toward a new level of mental functioning.

All normal people can and do exhibit regressive behavior, both in acting out and in thought, especially in fatigue, in times of stress and even in periods of daily living. In fact, without this, life would be boring, dull and concrete.

Regression is the sweet pool of warmth wherein the creative artist can bathe and refresh himself. It is the method by which he can break the routine and restore the intuitive and cognitive processes necessary for his creativity. When this ability can be initiated by a person, it is called regression in the service of the ego.[26] With this goes a flexibility of personality —an ability to incorporate more primitive methods of functioning at will. In music, humor, in play, in sex, and in the art of psychotherapy—even in the art of living, such ego regression is vital.

One patient put it this way . . . "I crave for the good feelings of being a child again, the pleasant memories, but they do not come. There is only the feelings of falling asleep." When one can recall these good feelings, including deja vu—this helps to form a constructive solid base. It is most important to know that regression is not permanent, that it may come and go according to the patient's symptoms.

For instance, patient A may be defecating and urinating in bed in the morning, hallucinating the voices of the world destruction and indeed look very "schizophrenic"—but that evening may play basketball, score 20 points and perform satisfactorily in sexual relations. Of course, this is an extreme, but I have seen it happen. Whenever this does happen, even the most astute of descriptive diagnosticians is confused. Regression alone does not measure the degree of "sickness." The amount of sickness is measured rather by the persistence and intractibility of the regression. When looseness, as was just mentioned, occurs, it is usually a sign of movement toward health.

Primitive forms of mental activity are persistent and may exist side by side with mature forms of mental functioning. As the personality matures, these primitive ideations may still be present, and be of frightful natures. However, they do not dominate, but rather remain more and more in the background.

Many regressive thoughts do become alarming and provoke much anxiety in an observer faced with the task of making an accurate diagnosis. This is rightfully so, for there thoughts may contain ideas of violent aggression—of murder, or rape and may take on ghastly proportions. Some of these thoughts come out in close confidence, uttered by the most respected of individuals. A small proportion of threats are carried into action. It is only acute clinical judgment and perhaps therapeutic skill that may make the difference between furtive thought and foul deed. What determines the severity of the psychic illness is not the depth of the regression at a particular moment, but rather its persistence and the surrounding conflict.

Drive regressions in women show themselves in envy and bitterness toward men, competitiveness, and in regressive thoughts such as ripping men's penises, attaching them to their own body or "snatching" men's penises with their vaginas. This aggressiveness in women does not provoke the anxiety in society that it does with men—so it can easily pass into higher developmental personality levels. The desire for a penis can become the key to "understanding men" and men's ways. It can be the impetus for higher education and logical reasoning.*

However, with men it becomes a very serious problem. When a doctor (now a patient) says, "I saw the knife lying in the dissection room and had the desire to plunge it into the back of Dr. X, my colleague," people shudder. Who wants to ask why? No one bothers to realize that Doctor A. is expressing a passive-homosexual father prototype regressive thought. Before this he was obsessed with religion and turned all aggressive and sexual thought within himself. He couldn't work and was diagnosed as a paranoid schizophrenic. By showing no anxiety, I gave him courage to express first homosexual ideation, then incestual thoughts (he wanted in the worst way to have intercourse with his sister). These thoughts allowed his warm blood to flow and the ideas later developed into actual sexual deeds with other women. If I had become alarmed, it might have led to real violence or psychosis. How many of our men in prison are really victims of these thwarted and misunderstood early drive conflicts? Why are most of our prisons filled with men, not women?

Let me further illustrate other regressive expressions. These are only samples of secret thoughts of "sick people" and the way they have found to express certain feelings. It is important to view these with open minds. They are an effort at fluid development rather than definitive signs of diagnostic categories. Regressions are usually in specific areas rather than global. Only in total personality catastrophe are they global in nature. Examples of Regression:

1. Are you my mother? You are not my mother. You have breasts as an older man, when I saw you in a bathing suit. You are as my father.
2. I am ashamed to show my face in the morning. My mouth is extremely demanding. It doesn't allow my ears, my eyes, or my mind much fun.

---

* Cheers to Woman's Liberation—Too long women have lived a double life. Too repressed and frightened to express their own individual and collective identities. Oh what deceptions have been fraught on us men! But was it not of our own doing? Was it not our poor capacity to tolerate an honest, equal, and different opinion. Let us take another look and on our knees beg, "Oh woman, please liberate us men."

3. I was feeling good and relaxed but then I heard some construction going on in my mind. (The patient was describing in concrete terms constructive thoughts, new ideas that frightened him and that he couldn't handle.)

4. My mother told me I can't have my cake and eat it too. (The patient was expressing her hopelessness in trusting people and being betrayed, and also her utter frustration in building any life for herself.)

5. People from high society—from another planet, get me for something I did on that other planet. (I do not feel part of this world, I am suffering from my relationships with people during my early childhood.)

6. My real parents are in Japan, I'm Japanese—I have amnesia. (Translated: he might be saying I do not feel at home; I have no home base; I don't trust my early memories. In fact, I am trying to block them from my mind.) This boy was a Protestant white American of early pioneer ancestry.

7. I am Adolf Hitler; I killed all the Jews. My mother was a German. (Translated: I hate myself for all the hate I feel inside of me. I can't handle it.) (This boy's mother has German ancestry but he was brought up in the influence of his father's Scotch-Irish Kentucky heritage.)

Regressions involve all areas of the personality. Illustrated were ego or identity regressions (Who am I?—I'm not the same person I was); Superego or bad conscience regressions (Adolf Hitler—these represent regressions to more primitive guilt, magic control rather than use of judgment); and id or impulse regressions (murder and incest impulses).

Regressions are closely related to perceptual disorders. In regression, the mind uses phantasies, hallucinations, death feelings, nirvana feelings and extrasensory modalities and magical gestures in an interpretation of inner feelings that were never admissible to the conscious personality— even as a child. They are thus misunderstood, confused and distorted in conception. Malingering or feigned illness is actually a regression. Here a person assumes a degree of physical sickness because of a greater fear, the fear of implosion or complete destruction which is frightening.

IV. The Hallucinatory Experience

A discussion of the hallucinatory experience is, perhaps, important here for several reasons. At present, in the diagnosis of emotional illness the presence of the hallucination distinguishes the severe mental illness from the less severe mental illness. Most clinicians would state, positively, that the presence of hallucinations is enough to label a person severely mentally ill. There has always been an aura of mystery surrounding the hallucinatory phenomena. It is the feeling of this observer that the presence of hallucinatory phenomena has caused an *over-evaluation* of the degree of illness in any particular patient.

Hallucinations have been defined in one of two ways: one, separate and excluding illusions, and two, including illusions as a form of hallucination. For instance, Will, Arnold, Esquirol, and Darwin separate hallucinations from illusions.[23] Will says "by hallucination I refer to the occurrence of perception now commonly reported as auditory or visual, but at times involving other sensory modes without there being apparent a relationship between that experienced and observed phenomena in the immediate environment which might serve as stimuli." It is my feeling, and that of others, such as M. Aubanel that all hallucinations are more similar to illusions than otherwise—that is, although for the moment the hallucination may be based on a false perception, most often the perception that it is based on had a forerunner and an actual or real identity.[24] Thus, the significant difference between an hallucination and an actual illusion is one of matter of degree of perceptual awareness rather than a complete separation into two categories. DeBoismont was perhaps more definitive in his definition.[25] Giving the symptomatology of hallucinations and illusions, he defined an hallucination as the perception of the sensible symbol of the idea; and an illusion as a false appreciation of real sensation. However, at this point I feel we are dealing with fine sensibilities which are not clinically important.

Statistics

In an international census in the 1890's, William James in the United States, Marillier in France, Von Schrenck-Notzing in Germany did a study and found that 3,271 out of 27,329 people, or 12 per cent, admitted hallucinations when asked the question "Have you ever, when believing yourself completely awake, had a vivid impression of seeing or being touched by a living being or inanimate object or of hearing a voice; which impression was not due to any external physical cause?" [26] Fifty-two per cent of those questioned were between the ages of fifteen and thirty, they were equally divided between male and female. In another study done on 14,000 consecutive out-patient admissions to the children's psychiatric service of the Harriet Lane Home (under the age of fourteen), hallucinatory episodes are on record as less than 0.4 per cent.[27] About one third of the hallucinatory episodes occurred in children who were not psychotic. Most of these children had been severely deprived; beliefs and superstition and mystical experiences were part of the culture in which they had been reared. The hallucinations seemed to represent symbolization of fears; reassuring voices of idealized parents; projections of unacceptable impulses; fear of punishment from an externalized conscience; and germatic representations of religious or superstitious preoccupations.

GENERAL DESCRIPTION OF HALLUCINATIONS: Generally, there are two main types of hallucinations. a. protective or pleasant, or b. hypercritical or hostile. The hallucinatory system experience itself is very complicated and although these two main types are easily distinguishable clinically in an ordinary person's hallucinatory experience, most often the system includes both pleasant or protective and hostile and deprecative or hypercritical hallucinations side by side.

The Tibetan Book of the Dead in the section called Chönyid Bordo, the section on visions, illustrates the hallucinatory experience in a religious sense.[28] The Chönid Bordo has two sections that relate to visions of the human brain: 1) Seven Peaceful Deities; 2) Eight Wrathful Deities. In essence this is a description of peaceful or pleasant hallucinations and the bad feeling or deprecating type of hallucinations.

Hallucinations coexisting with a sound state of mind include hallucinations of sight, hearing, smell, touch, taste and a combination of all the senses. Perhaps all hallucinations begin in the state of sanity. For instance, Isaac Newton, after having looked at the sun for some time, saw an image of the sun in a looking glass with much surprise, and on directing his eyes towards the dark part of the room, saw a spector of the sun reproduced bit by bit until it shone with all the vividness and all the colors of the real object. At first, this might be considered after-image phenomena. But it could be considered as hallucination, recurring whenever Newton went into the dark.

Many well-known people throughout history have described their hallucinations and none of these people has been charged with insanity. For instance, Benvenuto Cellini, when imprisoned in Rome by order of the Pope, thought of taking his life. In his prison cell his sufferings increased. "I was not allowed a knife so I contrived to place a thick plank of wood over my head, and drop it in such a manner that if it had fallen upon me it would instantly have crushed me to death. But when I put the whole pile in readiness and was just going to loosen the plank and let it fall upon my head, I was seized by something invisible, pushed and terrified to such a degree that I become almost insensible. Afterwards, reflecting on what it might have been, I took it for granted that it was some divine power—in other words—my guardian angel. At first I dreamed that God had saved me but as my sufferings continued and I once more was faced with suicide, the invisible being that had prevented my laying violent hands upon myself came to me, still invisible, but spoke with an audible voice. It shook me, made me rouse up and said, "Benvenuto, Benvenuto, lose no time. Raise your heart to God in fervent devotion and cry to him with the utmost vehemence." [29]

The astronauts, when placed in the weightless and stimulus-free environment during their training for flight began to hallucinate. During the attempted rescue of several coal miners caught in a mine some years ago, I remember the search continued in vain filled hope because one of the miners kept hearing a voice he thought was that of his comrade in a nearby compartment. When digging continued, no compartment was found.

Hallucinations Involving Insanity

In insanity, reason is abandoned and the hallucination is obeyed as a magical force or direction. The healthy parts of the personality surrender completely. It is perhaps advisable at this time to describe what might cause a human to suffer such an affliction. One must again explore the beginnings of insanity. This has been done several times in this book, once using the contemporary terms in this chapter of implosion, estrangement, etc., and again in the chapter on the analytic treatment of schizophrenia, the Isakower phenomenon.

Let us now explain it in yet another way. Perhaps it all starts with strange, unequivocal threatening body sensations from within. Leary, in his book about the psychedelic experience, describes the symptoms of ego loss before the "Clear Light" is seen.[30] Commonly reported physical symptoms include:

1. bodily pressure, which the Tibetans call earth-sinking-into water;
2. clammy coldness followed by feverish heat which the Tibetans call water-sinking-into fire;
3. body disintegrating or being blown to atoms which they call fire-sinking-into air;
4. pressure in the head and ears, which Americans call rocket-launching-into space;
5. feelings of body melting or flowing, as if wax;
6. tingling in extremities;
7. nausea;
8. trembling or shaking, beginning in pelvic regions and spreading up towards the torso.

Leary says: "These physical reactions should be recognized as signs heralding transcendence. Avoid treating them as symptoms of illness, accept them, merge with them, enjoy them." After the ego loss comes the second period, the "period of hallucinations," as described by Leary.

It is known that hallucinations caused by a toxic overdose of drugs are mostly those of the fear and dread of dying. Leary and the Tibetans recognize these feelings and tell their participants to enjoy these feelings, rather than fear them. The next sensations would probably be those of pleasant hallucinations. This would approximate the feeling of Nirvana.

In describing the pleasant hallucinations as seen in insanity in my practice, i.e. in patients who have been diagnosed as schizophrenic; hallucinations without the use of drugs, I have gathered the following reactions:

"I didn't mind listening to the voices. I just sat around. It was pleasant. Before I knew it, I was completely absorbed by it. It was a whole way of life and I didn't realize it but life was passing me by. I would get up in the morning, imagine and dream. It was pleasant enough unless I looked out into the outside world. After a while it became impossible to be a part of the main stream and then when people got on my back it became unbearable."

Another patient described the beginning of her psychosis this way:

"I was unhappy, fearful of the world and frightened. I would lie in my room and imagine elephants on the wall. After a while my imagination became keener and I would actually see them. It was a pleasant respite from everyday life. But then the elephants came and I couldn't hold them back. They came in thundering herds. It became extremely frightening and I no longer had control."

Modell sees the voices as identifications of former loved persons, principally the parents, who in some unexplained way are fused to the self.[31] These voice objects function as parents in terms of giving advice and being a source of prohibitions and also in gratifying wishes stemming from all stages of infantile development. They are constant objects and the patient is the center of their world; this fulfills a fantasy that the child is the only object of the parents' world, a fantasy that defends against the reality of separation and relates to the early diadic mother-child relationship.

The early wish is fused in content to a wish in the latter oedipal period by the patients' hallucinatory experience of partaking of or sharing in parental intercourse. Perhaps the hypercritical or hostile aspects of the patient's hallucinatory experience come later, with the prodding of the superego and the guilt associated with this period. It is this phenomenon that cause the person to rage, sometimes endlessly, twenty-four hours a day, with no sleep or rest. Perhaps it is a throwback to the time right after birth when no object relationship was formed in this world and its first form shows constant anxiety and stress. Case AB recalled his hallucinatory experiences and they are recorded herewith. This boy exhibited sheer terror during his hallucinatory experience. Now out of the psychosis for two years, he does not want to recall it because none of it was pleasant but only sheer terror.

Case AB—A Patient's Description of Hallucinations

Code: Cindy—patient's wife
         Steve, Betty, Irv, Tom, Allen, Jake—family therapists

"The voices started the day I left your office after a session. The voices were of everyone that was here working particularly your wife, mother and father, my sister and brother and Tom. Friends of ours—Sue and Bob, Ted—he was in the Marine Corps with me. In my mind these people were not helping me but making me worse to send me to a state hospital. When I was in bed at night the voices were worse. First thing I heard was Betty and her husband having intercourse. I heard my wife Cindy having intercourse with Steve, Ray and Jim. Cindy taught Jim how to do it. I heard Cindy's parents signing papers to send me to Byberry (a state hospital). There was Cindy, her parents and Betty and her husband. The voices kept up night and day.

One day I was coming out of the house over here and the voices told me my father was dead and I believed he died up here. That's why I left my wallet downstairs in the office because my father said it was my best friend. My father had a heart attack in the upstairs. And that's when I came running upstairs in the attic like a nut.

There will be voices and hallucinations. I would see Cindy, my mother and my uncle Joseph at different times. They were trying to decide whether it was going to be Byberry or the state hospital where my uncle Joseph works. I also heard uncle Joseph's wife Irene and their daughter Fay trying to decide. One time I heard Cindy talking and playing the piano in the recreation room. One tap on the wall meant Cindy, two meant you.

In my bed at night in the red barn I believed they had some kind of system hooked up so they could talk to me. Mostly when you, Dr. H., would go away. I heard Dr. F. I believed they had an electrical system to freeze certain parts of my body. Every night I heard voices up there. Cindy's voice, yours, Dr. F.'s, Jake, Mary, Ray. Whenever I went out anywhere with Betty or her husband, I heard voices in the car. I heard Cindy, Steven, Betty and husband talking about me, to crack me up completely and get rid of me once and for all. I heard voices when I was out on the boat. Wherever Irv took me he spread the word around. They wanted to drown me. I heard your voice at the bank telling Irv when—instructing him what to do. One night in bed I heard Cindy's voice from outside. From Jake's and Ed's and yours. Cindy was supposed to be the bait so the rest of you could get me. The voices and hallucinations were so real I left the room that night because if they were going to fight me, I was willing. Let's get it over once and for all.

As far as the time I tried to leave, I just wanted out of this place. I trusted nobody. The voices got to the point where if they weren't talking about my case they just kept saying over and over, "Put him in a jacket," or "You're going in a jacket." I realize Irv and Betty were new and I didn't like being used as a guinea pig. I had bitter feelings there. I heard the voices in Riverton in the different stores. Irv took me in. The people would talk about my life. How I was wasting everybody's time and money."

One hallucination is as follows:

"Mary, Betty and Irv changed the size of my clothes. They did different things to destroy them. They took my ring and gave me another that looked almost the same. I used to look inside the ring where the initials C. W. were and kept thinking it meant "Cindy wait until I get better." For instance, when Dr. H. left I thought he left me to anybody who wanted to take care of me. I thought they had a system to hurt my ears because they would ring. I heard buttons click off and on to make it louder or softer. I heard my parents come up to see Jake and Mary. They talked about how I was and what was there left to do with me. It got to the point if I looked outside or went anywhere the signs were changed to put me off the track so I couldn't get out of here. I believed everyone in the world was against me. I had nobody to turn to. The day I left here I heard my mother's voice over in the red barn. I heard your voice from your office saying, 'Wait, I'll be back. I'll get him back.' I didn't believe I was going home. When I did go home to my parents the voices went with me. The first night home we slept in my brother's room. I heard Steve, Ed and some others saying they had Cindy's ring. Steve said he picked it up somewhere and that's when I thought the change was made. I believed that Cindy, you and my mother wanted to send me to Coatesville (the Veterans' hospital). My dreams were bad. I dreamed about distorted people or Byberry. I woke up one night and started choking Cindy. I thought it was somebody coming after me. I screamed. When we had intercourse I could hear Irv telling me I couldn't satisfy my wife. I could hear my mother telling my father that we were having intercourse and she said, 'He still loves her—if he touches her again he's going to the hospital.' When I would tell Cindy I loved her I could hear the voices telling my mother what I said. After Cindy left there was not another word about her.

When I laid in bed and heard my parents mention you, I would shake my head back and forth till I couldn't hear your name anymore. When my mother asked me to go see you I pleaded with her. I didn't want to see you again. I used to lay and look at my rifles and plot how I would kill you, Ed, Irv and Jake. The voices kept up until about the second week of November. It was four months and three weeks before I left the house to go downstairs. I heard your voice when I took a shower with Cindy. If I rubbed her back the voice would describe it—I would look out the window and see people I knew. Phil was in your jeep and you were coming to get me. I'd go back into the bedroom. One time when me and Irv and Betty were riding through Brownsville we passed Sue and Ed and they had white hair and looked real old. They were laughing at me. The end of November I took the dog for a walk that's when I knew I came out of it. The ringing in my ears never left but I overlooked it. After that my family worked on me. I asked about my wife one day at a meal. My mother started crying and said she'd rather not talk about it. After that they worked on me to get a divorce. And at that time I wanted to find Cindy and see if she was all right. Still in the back of my mind I wanted to ask you why the certain things happened up here. I wanted to get back at you some way.

I heard voices plotting to beat me up. They would go to you. First Tom (brother-in-law) wanted to tie me up. They would tell you what they wanted done with me. They would take turns beating me up. They wanted different parts of my body. Tom, my sister, Jake, Ed, Irv . . . they would want my face smashed in or my arm or leg broken. I don't know which person wanted what done. It's been so long ago now.

Another day down Riverton's shopping center we ran into your wife. I said 'hello'. After we left I could see her pointing at me saying, 'He's paranoid'. The voices read my mind, everything I thought about. Another voice, I heard Betty tell Cindy how to have intercourse with me so that I wouldn't enjoy it. I would get no pleasure from it.

The voices took over. No matter where I'd go, what I said, or what I'd do, they were with me constantly. They would criticize or make it wrong. It made it hard for me to talk or sleep or do anything. When I was in the strait jacket at the barn, somebody told me I was going to be shot. Tom, Allen, Bob, Jake, Ed were in the field. I got to the point where I'd dare them. I stood at the window for a half hour. I just stood there. As far as hallucinations go, I thought people were masquerading themselves, to trick me. Another time in the car with Irv and Betty going through Falls River, I believed people would follow me. This one time I saw Cindy and her father following us. Somehow they got ahead of us. Then I saw her standing on the sidewalk as plain as day. Her father was sitting in the car. One time me and Tom (another patient) were sanding a desk out back and he (the voices) was making fun of me. It was twenty-four hours a day. One time in the bedroom I kept looking down at the floor. The more I looked at it, it looked like an ant. I picked it up. I was a piece of black string. Things never got better as I stayed up here. They just got worse and worse and worse. It got to the point where I thought I was going to have a mental disorder for the rest of my life. Whenever I would go out on the boat, my legs would hit the cold water and I'd seem to be more awake than usual. The girl that used to come here every day and go out on the boat with us I believed that Cindy would talk to her and she would tell Cindy what was going on here. I used to lay in bed at night and listen for Cindy to come around. The way I was treated up here still bothers me. The therapy that was used on me was no good. When I did come out of this I remembered most everything and anything that was said and done."

HALLUCINATIONS THAT ARE REALLY ILLUSIONS   This is perhaps an extremely common (it may be the most common) type of hallucination because it is based in reality. Perhaps a great deal of chronic degenerative schizophrenia of the so-called hebephrenic type has hallucinations of this variety. Recently, for instance, we had a patient who would look out of an actual door of a house that was part of our clinic, and see a person come out of that door. He eflt that M. told him, "Dr. Honig hates you." He would also look at the refregerator and hear the voice of W. T., a therapist, saying "Grow up, grow up". In actuality it was the motor that was humming, but he gave it a human expression. It was indeed an illusion but it was not corrected by reason and the patient believed it completely.

Esquirol, in his *Memoire Sur Les Illusions,* has said: "One which appears to us as most characteristic, of the distinctive factors between illusions and hallucinations is the absence in hallucination of any external object while the presence of a material object is necessary to lay the foundation of an illusion.[32]

HALLUCINATIONS SEEN IN MELANCHOLIA OR DEPRESSION   These are simple hallucinations similar to those experienced in childhood. The patient may see things at night, simple things; for instance, a tiger biting at his toes. These frequently involve hallucinations of engulfment. They include hallucinations that are found in imbecility, idiotism and cretinism.

HALLUCINATIONS SEEN IN DELIRIUM OF ALCOHOLISM   These are mostly visual hallucinations and are well known—the so-called "pink elephants."

IDEAS OF REFERENCE OR THE HALLUCINATIONS OF PARANOIA   Ideas of reference would be classified as hallucinations because they are a matter of degree. We find that the patient thinks that people are talking about him. A seventeen year old Jewish patient recently complained that he was prohibited by his parents from going with any other girl but a Jewish girl. He had a crush on a petite Irish girl whom he had asked to the prom. His mother and a Jewish teacher admonished him for this. Soon after, he became depressed, extremely suspicious, had a glaring look in his eye, and began to think that the other pupils in school were talking about him as he walked down the hall. Soon the ideas of reference became all-consuming: he could not concentrate on his school work, he remained out of school, and when he looked at the television set he thought that the people on the set were laughing at him and calling him "queer."

HALLUCINATIONS IN NIGHTMARES, IN DREAMS   Improvement is shown when hallucinations are confined to dreams and do not occur in the waking state. At first this may be extremely upsetting—the same hallucinatory phenomena that occur during the day occur during sleep. The patient actually hears voices as if they are real and may even respond to them. Nightmarish accusations may occur during disturbed sleep. Dreams were ordinarily considered different from hallucinations because they were made up only of the day's residue and had no continuum as did hallucinations.

HYPNOGOGIC AND HYPNOPOPIC STATES   Included are the hallucinations as precursors to epileptic seizures. They may be hallucinations of smell, taste, or voice and are usually considered part of an aura. A similar type of phenomenon occurs in the hysterical states. Hallucinations occur in fugue states and amnesics.

THE SO-CALLED SIXTH SENSE OR HUNCH   This is an impulsive type of response, an extra-sensory perceptive response which is a modification again of hallucination. Also in this classification may be included those states of extra-sensory perception which might be hallucinations or illusions occurring under the hypnotic trances.

CRAZY THOUGHTS   Strange thoughts, thoughts with impulsive feeling, day dreams, are distorted perceptions that might be classified in the hallucinatory schemata.

CONFABULATIONS—REPETITIVE TALKING TO ONESELF   These again are impulsive in nature and not directly ego controlled.

HALLUCINATIONS IN ECSTASY OR ECSTATIC STATES   These are hallucinations of visionaries such as Joan of Arc and Swedenborg. They may occur with a great deal of religious fervor.

HALLUCINATIONS OF SOMNAMBULISM OR SLEEPWALKING   A patient may walk while in the trance state.

HALLUCINATIONS OCCURRING WITH FEVER OR SICKNESS IN DISEASE These are mostly visual but can include all other senses.

HALLUCINATIONS OCCURRING WITH CHEMICAL IMBALANCE DUE TO ELECTROLYTIC IMBALANCE   These are usually corrected by restoring the proper metabolism. They are temporary in nature.

Some Theories of Hallucinatory Experiences

Hulings Jackson said that hallucinations differ from corresponding thought in the intensity of neuronal discharge, which leads us to conclude that hallucinations result from pathologically strong discharges.[33] Jackson proposes that strong discharge results from elimination of a controlling force, either in the normal dissolution of sleep or the pathologic dissolution of cerebral disease. In more modern terminology, this amounts to the proposition that dreams and hallucinations result from the elimination of an inhibitory process. One known fact is that visual hallucinations are more prevalent in drug-induced psychoses and that auditory hallucinations are more prevalent in functional psychoses. Another phenomenon was noted by Freeman, the neurosurgeon, who originally proposed that the prognosis for psychosurgery was better in patients who were still reacting to their hallucinations and showing anxiety because of them, than in patients whose hallucinations were of a stereotyped nature, and who neither reacted to them nor admitted to them except on close questioning or through the medium of their very close relationship with the doctor.[34] (Not unlike prognosis with psychotherapy.)

It is known that extreme fatigue will cause hallucinations. DeBoismont described visual hallucinations that accompany blindness.[35] In experiments done with volunteers who were subjected to sensory deprivation in a tank type of respirator, seven of twenty-eight developed hallucinations. All seven had visual hallucinations, three also had tactile hallucinations, none had auditory hallucinations. In experiments done with loss of sleep, it was discovered that sleep loss leads to increased frequency of misperception. In many cases the subject seemed convinced of the reality of his false perceptions and in these cases we labeled them hallucinations. In these experiments it was found that hallucinations developed out of at least two kinds of subjective events: illusions and dreams. Sigmund Freud postulated that at a very early stage the infant under the pressure of an instinctual need, hallucinates its gratification by recalling the memory trace of an earlier experience of satisfaction.[36] So, according to psychoanalytic theory, hallucinations are in essence a regressive mechanism of early infancy. In this theory it is not necessary for language or organized and learned response to be present. All that is necessary is that the perceptions can be recalled.

Kolb described the hallucinations of touch and pain found in the absent or amputated limb.[37] Fisher describes the distortion and disorganization in body image boundaries found in hallucinatory patients labeled schizophrenic.[38] He attributed this to a literal expression of confusion of what is inside and what is outside and the reflections of the vagueness of their boundary organization. Fisher states that there is good evidence that in states of disorganization the individual becomes highly concerned about his body integrity. The body image organization which he has built up to deal with body experience is often seriously disrupted. He becomes alarmed at the consequent altered variety of his body experiences and is aroused to the possibility that his body is suffering radical transformation or damage of some kind. Within the setting of such alarm, he may therefore find the projection of symbolic representations of his body and colorful hallucinations to have reassurance value. That is, by populating the exterior world with rather autonomous symbolizations of his body, he can defend against catastrophic sensations of body dissolution. The autistic reduplication of himself out there may support the schizophrenic in his attempts to find some proof that he is not about to lose his body identity. At a more primitive level, the same mechanism can be observed in patients with organic brain pathology who lose the functional use of a body appendage, for instance, the hand; and react to the loss by hallucinating the presence of a third appendage which is not disabled. A new illusory body part is attached to the body to counteract sensations of body image breakdown. It is almost universal that in a hallucinatory patient the projective drawings of a person have no representation in a figure sense.

Functions of Hallucinations

In the discussion of the value hallucinations may have for an individual, we have license to speculate. First of all, it is known that hallucinations are universal, therefore their function must be universal. If they are a regression to an early infantile level of maintenance, then they are somewhat like physiologic comas, in that they reduce the organism to a state of bliss or rest to prevent it from dissolving or exploding or being disembodied or being swallowed up. Thus the hallucination prevents something violent happening to the organism. This would explain many things about hallucinations. For instance, it would explain the tenacity with which patients hold onto their hallucinations. It would explain why patients lie and cheat and when under stress will not reveal the fact that they are indeed hallucinating. The hallucination represents a maintenance of a lower level of life needed for survival. It would also explain the panicky feeling that occurs when hallucinations are disappearing. In other words, it is as if the patient has almost lost a part of his own body with the loss of the hallucination. There are probably other functions of hallucinations. If they are a psychological feeding mechanism, then they do supply needs that are substitutes for the patient's inability to meet these real needs in everyday life. They represent symbols of reality and not reality itself. They have communicative value, either directly or through interpretation, because they are symbolic of representations of past and current interpersonal events in the patient's life. Hallucinations serve to maintain a symbolic contact with other people. They then become a counterbalance to isolation and social death.*

But this does not explain the hypercritical hallucination or the anxiety evoked or elicited in the majority of hallucinations. Is the hypercritical hallucination the archaic mind's attempt to keep the patient in line, a set of rules such as we all must live by in reality? Why must a person suffer great pain? It is this great pain and this great anxiety, like a thorn in the side, that enables us to treat patients and to help them recover from hallucinations. Perhaps the hypercritical aspect of the hallucination is a flaw of nature, as nature does have flaws, in a perfect Nirvana—the one flaw that might enable a person to come back to reality and give up this total symbolic way of life.

Why don't patients relinquish their hallucinations quickly if they are so painful? It is because the hallucinations are a complete way of life, hard won, and represent part of a total commitment to a life of unreality. It was Percival who said it was when he knew the hallucinations were deceiving him that he knew he must rid his mind of them. Is the treatment directed only to hallucinations? I don't think so. I think we treat the person and give him the reality he needs, we give him the comfort and the integration and organization of body, ego and mind. When this is accomplished the hallucination will disappear by itself because there is no more need

---

* One of the last hallucinations to be held on to before giving up the hallucinatory process is a somatic one—involving the umbilicus or belly-button. Patients may even feel "the pain of the umbilicus being severed."

of it. Frequently patients will say that they gave up their hallucinations because they finally saw through the falsehood and lying of the hallucinations—the hallucinations were trickery—they fooled them—it really did more harm than good.

V. The Human Soul and its Relationship to Diagnosis

I looked on my right hand, and beheld, but there was no man that would know me; no man cared for my soul. I cried unto Thee, Oh Lord, I said, Thou art my refuge and my portion in the land of the living.

PSALM 142

One might wonder how a discussion of the soul is relevant to a chapter given over to the diagnosis of mental illness. I can think of many reasons why it is relevant and these reasons will be explored in the bulk of this section. To generalize, however, it might be said that man does not, nor has ever accepted the belief that the very, very end occurs with the death of his body. Complete annihilation is hard to swallow.

The very basis of natural law states that matter cannot be created nor destroyed, only changed in form. From the earliest times this has led man to experiment with his feelings and then with his thought. No matter how bad his day, he looks forward to a night's rest and then if he sleeps and all is well, he is reborn again to a new day. So the life process continues. It continues forever in man's mind. Perhaps all mental disease or discomfort is a result of a fear of utter annihilation or soul death. Perhaps psychosis is a biologic compromise to preserve the soul.

It may be that all men are spiritually gifted or endowed but it is not the majority who feel it, enjoy it and understand it. One needs bread and air to live, but so do the animals. This is the nature of protoplasm. Practical materialism as an end itself has never been enough for man; but neither has any religion, body of science, philosophy, political therapy or psychology quenched his thirst for more knowledge. He stands not still, but is almost in constant turmoil, with only brief moments of peace of mind. Is not this proof that man is also soul?

Carus defines the soul of man as not only the faculties he possesses at present, but the ideals to which he aspires; it is the direction of his energy and the goal of his endeavors. But perhaps we should turn to prehistoric history, because man's understanding of his soul has changed with the development of his personality.[39]

In the early days of mankind, it is obvious that death would be, in the great majority of instances, violent and premature. Such death, occurring in the vigour of manhood, when bounding energies are most active, would almost of necessity lead to the conclusion that the unfinished life would be continued elsewhere. In this way, man probably originated more or less general expectation and belief in a future life. Just as later, when man lived in civilized communities, he had to suffer so many injustices and unequal hardships that he found comfort in the belief that a man's personality does not cease with the grave. Such belief in immortality was probably fostered for the influence it had on the conduct of man. Prehistoric man imagined that in his dreams something left his body, and that this something returned to his body before he awoke. He noticed that in his dreams he appeared often to be far away, or other people seemed to come to him, and since he knew by experience that his body never moved, his perfectly natural explanation was that it was something which inhabited his body—a spirit, a natural shadowy image of himself—which could go out and return again. This spirit he at first identified with the breath of his body, since the dead man no longer breathes. It was also natural that he should think that the spirit does not die with the body, but lives on after quitting it; for although a man may be dead and buried, his phantom figure may continue to appear to the survivors in dreams and visions. There existed a duality or separateness of body and soul . . . the spiritual part of man was believed to have a life of its own, continuing after the death of his body, and even existing before his birth.

Man developed a concept of good and evil. There would be a good society for good men such as the "happy hunting grounds" of the American Indian. Evil would be dismissed to realm of darkness and despair. The degree of hope in an after life seemed to be in proportion to his problems on earth, but religious sects incorporated this into systematic beliefs. For example, the ancient Egyptians believed that the present life was a mere preparation for existence beyond the grave.

Plato (427–347 B.C.) ascribed personal immortality to the soul. Each soul had an existence of its own. Plato was an adherent of metempsychosis or the transmigration of souls. Hippocrates interpreted dreams. In the dream state, he said "the soul acts freely; it is no longer disturbed by sensations, for the body sleeps."

In its earliest days, Christianity attached value to the individual lives of the most wretched and outcast of mankind. For the slave and his master there was one law, one hope, one saviour, one judge. Sympathy was shown to the unfortunate and forgiveness to the guilty. To the needy, the charities of the faithful were freely given. Love, to the Christian, was the supreme principle in practical life which brought with it happiness and virtue and every other good. The Christian exalted faith above knowledge, and defined it as an act of self-surrender to the word of God but he taught that the supreme happiness is not of this world; it is another life to come. The faith in that belief takes the form of another virtue, namely hope. Thus we have faith, hope and charity as the three great Christian virtues.

New doctrines of justice and love were taught. The personal virtues of humility, charity and resignation received a new interpretation. True happiness could not be attained by victory over our enemies, but by victory over ourselves; not by success in life, but by a pure and holy life; not by the esteem of men, but by the approval of our conscience. The spirit of compassion, self sacrifice, devotion and unselfishness was enjoined. The moral virtues were transformed to a loftier character; chastity became holiness and vice, sin. Altogether, Christianity presented the world with higher and purer notions of the nature and destiny of man than had been held before. The Christian religion gave men something to live for, and something to die for. It supplied mankind not only with the ideal of excellence, but with a powerful motive for conduct, presenting it with an object of both fear and love. It thus gave rise to a higher discipline of the affections, of the inner life of man. And, by so doing, it produced those saintly types of character which it is impossible not to admire.

Unfortunately, beginning with Paul, with more organization and acceptance, the Church lost its sackcloth and ashes.[40] It no longer championed the individual, and like many dogmas before and since, which sought power over man's mind and control, lost its intended purpose. Man continued his search for answers. "Submit to the guidance of the church while you live, or you shall go to Hell when you die" fell on deaf ears.

Another great factor contributing to man's enlightenment was that astronomy, by its discoveries, upset man's notions both of the heavens and of the earth. The heavens, which had been regarded as the visible dwelling place of the gods, were resolved into the immensity of an airy firmament in which imagination could no longer fix the home of supernatural beings; and the earth, the sole stage of life and history, was transformed into one of the smallest parts of the boundless universe.

Descartes (1596–1650) conceived the souls as the fixed and immutable something from which all thoughts, feelings and acts of volition emanate. Perhaps dualism or a separate soul, mind and body was first challenged intellectually by Spinoza (1632–1677) who said the human mind is the *idea* of the human body; it represents all that takes place within the body. Spinoza said the emotions and passions perish with the body, but the human mind cannot be destroyed with the body.

Herbert Spencer (1820–1903) reversed the trend. He wrote the first psychology without a soul, "The Principles of Psychology," and so he might be considered the forerunner of the rationalist and psycho-scientists of today.

Although modern psychology, especially psychoanalysis, with its rational explanation of unconscious acts, has greatly contributed to diagnosis, the area of the spirit has entirely eluded rationalization. Scientific explanations for such concepts as transmigration of souls, transformation, mystification and reincarnation do not give satisfactory answers. Immortality, as a goal of man, has resisted harnessing.

There are several cold facts:

1. Before a person has reached the deepest forms of human despair—that is psychosis—or before attempting suicide in our Western culture, he has tried religion and it has failed him. There still may remain "spooky religiosity," a turning of religious phrases in a magical manner, but faith has disappeared.

2. When a person begins to recover from a severe mental illness, he detests any slogan that has anything to do with "mental health."

3. There has been no religion, philosophy, mysticism, political ideology or any belief that has quieted man's thirst for "soul searching." Psychology has not answered all of man's need for faith.

Suicide continues to flout all attempts at its cure. Grief defies intrusion.[41, 42]

Speaking of despair, Kierkegaard says it is not true of despair, as it is of bodily sickness, that the feeling of indisposition is the sickness. By no means.[43] The feeling of indisposition is again dialectical. Never to have been sensible of this indisposition is precisely to be in despair. The majority of men live without being thoroughly conscious that they are spiritual beings. Those, on the other hand, who say they are in despair, are generally such as have a nature so profound that they become conscious of themselves as spirit, or those who by the hard vicissitudes of life and its dreadful decisions have been made conscious of themselves as spirit. Either one or the other, for rare is the man who is truly free of despair. Without understanding spirit, it is impossible to understand despair. If there is nothing eternal in man, he could not despair.

Belief in a soul defies *psycho logic*. Yet what is the alternative . . . soul Death?

Suicide, to those who commit this act, is the only way left to live forever. This sounds like nonsense. It is non-sense in that it is not rational. It is performed to preserve immortality or soul life. All suicide notes leave the element of sleep with waking up, life in a hereafter or a feeling of ultimate rebirth in a new form (transformation, reincarnation). Not one really faces death. Death cannot be faced except with a feeling of full life. So death without fear can only be faced with great maturity, gained by the very few.

Perhaps we might use the phrase "irrationality" as does Otto Rank, to describe the nonlogical aspects of the human mind.[44] Rank uses the term to define man's struggle against adjustment and conformity. This not only includes the biological but his need for spiritual perpetuation. Perhaps it arises from a deep-seated need to be the only one with the universe. Rank sees psychopathology as the inability to express irrational forces within oneself spontaneously. This puts the special burden on both the diagnostician and the therapist of understanding the irrational as a weak attempt to express individuality and need for acceptance.

Once again this brings up the unanswerable question "Is love enough?"

McNeil has stated: "Even today we have fresh practical lessons to learn from the Gospels and Epistles in the matter of the cure of souls. We see here more vividly than elsewhere that the cure of souls is never merely a method, even a method derived from a doctrine, or a task for certain hours in the week, but that it involves both the faith we live by and all our daily activities and contacts." [45]

The concept of universality of soul and body brings up the question once more of delegation of authority. In the age of the dualistic concept, the theologians jealously guarded their territory as having jurisdiction over men's souls . . . in those days this was synonymous with men's mind. The body was the province of the physician.

But what of today? Certainly the theologian has lost his place because the dualistic concept no longer holds true. Man is a composite of body and mind. But does the physician do any better? In most cases, his representative, the psychiatrist, falls short. In an attempt to be scientific, he is forcing man's mind, and, to him, this means his soul, if he will accept this concept at all, into a medical-biologic framework of non-individuality. Man is being reduced to a biological formula—and it makes *rational sense*. But something floats out of the test tube into the air. It is the soul, everlastingly ethereal.

Oh where has faith gone? Will it not be destroyed forever by constant false or even honestly wrong promises? Do we not see it result in our mentally sick human beings?

References

[1] Leary, T. THE PSYCHEDELIC EXPERIENCE. New Hyde Park, University Books, 1964.

[2] Brossard, C. "Revolutionary treatment of the mentally ill." LOOK MAGAZINE. p. 30–39, April 5, 1966.

[3] Szasz, T. S. THE MYTH OF MENTAL ILLNESS. N.Y., Hoeber-Harper, 1964. p. 1–15.

[4] Green, L. J. "Functional neurological performance in primitive cultures." HUMAN POTENTIAL. *1(1)*:17–18 (1967).

[5] Thomas, E. W. "The validity of brain injury as a diagnosis." 9–17.

[6] MacLean, P. E. FRONTIERS OF PSYCHIATRY. (1967).

[7] Piaget, J. PLAY, DREAMS AND IMITATION IN CHILDHOOD, N.Y., Norton, 1962.

[8] ———. THE CONSTRUCTION OF REALITY IN THE CHILD. N.Y., Basic Books, 1954.

[9] Simpkinson, C.; Fine, H.; Pollio, H. THE POETIC FUNCTION OF THE METAPHOR IN PSYCHOTHERAPY. University of Tennessee, Memphis.

[10] Hunt, M. "A neurosis is just a bad habit." REFLECTIONS. Merck, Sharp and Dohme. *2(4)*:2 (1967).

[11] Still, A. T. FOUNDER OF OSTEOPATHY. Waukegan, Hunting Pubns., 1925. p. 20–22.

[12] Birdwhistle, R. INTRODUCTION TO KINESICS. Louisville, Univ. of Louisville, 1952.

[13] Reich, W. CHARACTER ANALYSIS. N.Y., Orgone Inst. Press, 1949. p. 370–90.

[14] Delsarte, F. A SYSTEM OF EXPRESSION. N.Y., Stebbins, Werner, 1902. p. 70–372.

[15] Morris, D. THE NAKED APE. N.Y., McGraw-Hill, 1967. p. 199–215.

[16]2Erikson, E. CHILDHOOD AND SOCIETY. 2nd ed. N.Y., Norton, 1965. p. 247–244.

[17] Laing, R. D. THE DIVIDED SELF. London, Pelican, 1960. p. 43–78.

[18] Merton T. "A devout meditation in memory of Adolf Eichmann." REFLEC-TIONS, Merck, Sharpe & Dohme. *2(3)*:21–23 (1967).

[19] Kris, E. PSYCHOANALYTIC EXPLORATIONS IN ART. N.Y., New York University Press, 1952. p. 303–318.

[20] Arlow, J. A. and Brenner, C. PSYCHOANALYTIC CONCEPTS AND THE STRUCTURAL THEORY. N.Y., Intnl. Univ. Press, 1964. (Journal of American Psychoanalytic Assn. Monograph #3).

[21] Freud, S. "Thoughts for the time on war and death." COLLECTED WORKS. London, Hogarth, 1957. v. 14, p. 273–303.

[22] Kris. *op. cit.* p. 173–188.

[23] Will, O., Jr. HALLUCINATIONS IN THE SCHIZOPHRENIC REACTION. N.Y., Grune and Stratton, 1962. p. 174.

[24] Aubanel, H. ESSAI SUR LES HALLUCINATIONS. Paris, 1839. p. 13–47.

[25] Brierre de Boismont, A. J. F. ON HALLUCINATIONS. Translated by R. L. Hulme. Columbus, J. H. Riley, 1860. p. 35–74

[26] Parish, R. HALLUCINATIONS AND ILLUSIONS. London, Scott, 1897. p. 275–76.

[27] Eisenberg, L. "Hallucinations in children." In: West, L. J. HALLUCINATIONS. N.Y., Grune and Stratton, 1962. p. 172.

[28] Leary, T. *op. cit.* p. 20–30.

[29] Brierre de Boismont, A. J. F. *op. cit.* p. 76.

[30] Leary, T. *loc. cit.*

[31] Modell, A. "Hallucinations and psychic structure." In: West, L. J. HALLU-CINATIONS. N.Y., Grune and Stratton, 1962. p. 172.

[32] Esquirol, M. ILLUSIONS OF THE INSANE. London, Liddell, 1833. p. 5–21.

[33] Jackson, H. SELECTED WRITINGS. London, Hadder and Staughton, 1931. v. II, p. 198–199.

[34] Feinberg, I. "A comparison of the visual hallucinations in schizophrenia with those induced by mescaline and LSD-25." In: West, L. J. *op. cit.* p. 74.

[35] Brierre de Boismont, A. J. F. *op. cit.*

[36] Freud, S. INTERPRETATION OF DREAMS. VI. N.Y., Basic Books, 1955. p. 326–327.

[37] Kolb, L. "Phantom sensations, hallucinations and body image." In: West, L. J. *op. cit.* p. 239.

[38] Fisher, S. "Body image boundaries and hallucinations." In: West, L. J. *op. cit.* p. 255.

[39] Carus, P. THE SOUL OF MAN. Chicago, The Open Court Pub. Co., 1831. p. 382–431.

[40] Hollander, B. IN SEARCH OF THE SOUL. N.Y., Dutton, 1920. p. 1–100.

[41] Fromm, E. PSYCHOANALYSIS AND RELIGION. New Haven, Yale, 1958. p. 4–87.

[42] Freidman, P. ON SUICIDE. N.Y. International Universities Press, 1967. p. 24.

[43] Kierkegaard, S. FEAR AND TREMBLING AND THE SICKNESS UNTO DEATH. Garden City, Doubleday, 1954. p. 151–157.

[44] Rank, O. BEYOND PSYCHOLOGY. N.Y., Dover, 1941. p. 323.

[45] McNeill, J. T. A HISTORY OF THE CURE OF SOULS. N.Y., Harper, 1951. pp. 320–321.

CHAPTER IV

Etiology and Prognosis

A chapter about cause and effect and efforts at prediction of outcome of treatment should be interrelated and interwoven with thoughts about diagnosis. Theoretically, we find out what is wrong, i.e., diagnosis—then its cause (etiology), and give its chances for cure (prognosis), i.e., is it worth it to try? Then knowing what is wrong, its cause, its chances for cure—we go ahead and treat the problem.

A. Etiology

I will leave the bulk of theoretical discussion on the causes of mental illness—especially psychosis, to those who have written textbooks on the subject. In fact, I must admit at this time that I do not know *the cause.* I prefer to say there are many factors involved and that each case is different. Because of our ability to live with the pathology, we are enabled to supply the necessary ingredients for a healthy change in behavior. Then, by examining what we have done, we may speculate what had gone wrong in the person's "bringing up."

We do look to the environmental upbringing. This does not mean that we ignore other factors such as (a) heredity, the nature of a person's Mendelian genetic structure, (b) birth injuries or deformities, (c) chemical imbalances and diseases.

In our method of treatment we cannot correct heredity, and at this time I do not know anyone who can.

Certainly, any correctable deformity should be fixed, if possible, because it can have an influence on the psyche. Patients are sent to plastic surgeons, orthodontists, etc., etc., but these are allied external factors—and are not directly involved with the nurturing, communicative and educative processes of growing up.

In my work, I concentrate on early mothering. This has more therapeutic implications that etiologic implications. I am not interested in placing blame on mothers. Certainly their guilt is heavy enough. Observations of psychotic patients with parents who have raised them most often show more direct emotional involvement with mother than father. Perhaps this is only because mother has us first—in infancy.

The feeling of mother is deeply imbedded. Adopted children seem always to have a problem about this. No matter how hard the adopting parents try, the child may reject their kindness to seek out something less rewarding. I remember interviewing a 30 years old man who had run away at age five from a perfectly warm and affectionate home provided by his new parents and never returned. He went, admittedly, looking for his biologic mother. He never returned to his adoptive home. He also never found his mother.

One thing might be established. Psychosis is a completely systematized way of life substituted for real human living. To force a person to such extremes, one might imagine the confusion, fear, and human disappointments to which they were subjected.

In childhood autism, the withdrawal from the world occurs at one and a half or two years of age. Oh, what pure hell must have occurred in those formative years!

Is insight important? I feel that emotional insight is. Frequently one might say, even most often, a person recovers and never knows what made him well. However, a "feeling" knowledge of the unconscious mind always accompanies recovery. If it is not there, the patient is always in danger of regression. That is, the patient must not only develop the "right instincts" about life but must reinforce these "right feelings" with thoughtful disemotionalized self reflection.

All in all, recovery rate is unpredictable. Many cases which seemed deeply discouraging at first interview have never ceased to amaze me several years later. They had achieved a fruitful life beyond anyone's expectations.

Once the symptoms of illness have appeared, pure unadulterated maternal love is not enough to change behavior. By then a defensive system against intrusion has already been established. It then becomes a battle of wills to see who is stronger, the mother or child. Unfortunately it occurs *too early in life*. The child is not ready to be on top, but the mother is too weak. She reacts with great guilt. This makes the problem worse and she yields further.

Because of the weakness of mother's force, her ambivalence and indecisiveness, the infant soon develops a feeling of omnipotence ". . . you are indecisive, you do not know, therefore I know more than you . . ." A psychotic patient may say, "I have ruined the world. I have infected everyone. I have the whole world inside of me."

In his experiments on baby viewing, Harlow felt maternal instinct was not hormonal. He states that there is every reason to believe normal mothering facilitates heterosexual development in rhesus monkeys. In the chapter on Subnormal Mental Functioning I have shown how maternal love can influence neurologic development.

What is the nature of maternal instinct? Where does it come from: Is it important? If so, how important? What is its effect on personality development? Is its absence responsible for psychosis (or all emotional illness)?

Perhaps in an answer to these questions, Harlow states: "Infants raised by live mothers were more advanced in social and sexual behavior than infants raised by surrogate mothers in a controlled play-pen situation. The mother's role is not entirely clear, however, because in a more stimulated playroom situation, surrogate-mothered babies have shown normal social and sexual behavior." [1]

It is a fact that a deeply injured brain cannot fully benefit from even the strongest of maternal instincts. I have seen severely brain-damaged children remain retarded in neurologic and psychologic development (probably physiologic as well) because of a sucking instinct undeveloped until age two. The children enjoyed fondling, touching and cradling but there was no sucking instinct as yet. The babies were spoon fed. This might support Harlow's hypothesis that touching, holding and cradling are more basic needs than are those of the mouth. I have found this true in the treatment of childhood autism where forced cradling and forced sucking are used as techniques of treatment.

In a therapeutic relationship it can be demonstrated that:

1. A latent maternal instinct can become active and strong as a result of therapy: The first sign of renewed interest in life by mothers in therapy is more interest and concern for her children. A single girl may become maternal toward her therapist. She may want to feed him by baking cakes, etc. One male patient I am treating is busy "mothering" a whole brood of baby chickens.
2. Role of Father: Any instinct in humans is easily thwarted. A jealous, demanding, annoying husband can affect the flow of "milk" from mother to infant. The mother is dependent upon the father and if she doesn't feel secure with him this may affect the infant. However, a woman with a strong maternal instinct creates an environment where there is no stress or interference with her ability to nurture her child.

Harry Harlow's experiments with monkeys shed a great deal of light on the possible etiology of emotional illness.[2, 3, 4, 5]

"Maternal behavior in the rhesus monkey is characterized by sequential states designed as attachment and protection, ambivalence and separation or rejection. During attachment and protection, the earliest phase, the mother has close physical contact with the infant and responds to it positively, holding it close to her much of the time and restricting its free locomotion in large degree. Negative responses such as rejecting some of the infant's approaches and punishing it for encroachments gradually appear. These mark the start of the ambivalence stage characterized by positive and negative responses to the infant. Usually physical separation occurs—usually with the birth of a new infant."

The feeling of "mother" security is deeply imbedded in the brain, perhaps in the brain stem itself. Can the therapist ever replace mother? Not completely perhaps, but enough to effect a personality change. For instance, a patient who had been in treatment for two years and with whom I had made deep identification, suffered a severe cerebral concussion and skull fracture after being struck by a motor vehicle in front of my office. In a semi-coma she called for me, saying "Al, Al, don't leave me." Apparently I had replaced her "mother" as a deep source of nourishment and comfort.

In turn, one might say that a new-born infant with normal sucking instinct is ready to *cement a foundation with a human being*. Since psychosis can perhaps be described as a set of behavioral responses in reaction to the awesome and terrifyingly empty feelings occurring within the organism, possibly its cause lies in the organism's lack of a "cementing bond" or security with another human to ward off the appearance of psychosis.

The Myth of "Mother"

The everlasting need for mothering, with its image of a great warm woman with large flowing breasts is one of the myths embedded in the phylogenetic unconscious of all humans. In infancy it is a necessity, because it is not the man who has the maternal milk. In adult life this myth persists in the belief that a warm breast or mother is the only thing necessary to cure the emotionally ill. But the nurturing process in emotional illness goes beyond the biological.

A warm, healthy breast is not all that is needed to produce a great human being, yet because this myth is embedded deep within the unconscious, the need must be satisfied in a symbolic way as part of the treatment. The mother surrogates working in our units, just by their physical presence meet this need. Perhaps touch, feel and the differences between the sexes are so basic that to learn about a woman one must "be a woman" i.e., incorporate a woman. (Take her inside of self.)

In the final analysis it is a myth, for men therapists can be gentle, understanding and motherly—and may be capable indeed of understanding women even better than another woman.

Later, in therapy, the patient must learn through insight that one's mother is only human, indeed, possibly less equipped emotionally than is the patient himself. For example, a female patient was lying with her head in my lap sucking the folds of skin on my abdomen through my shirt. She kept saying, "Oh, how I wish you were a woman!" Others, when the need arose saw me as a woman with large breasts.

The Sick Symbiosis

Throughout the text there are paragraphs alluding to, describing and illustrating the unholy, interdependent relationship between parent and child. This is especially so in Chapter VI, Anxiety in Schizophrenia, and Chapter VIII, Negative Transference and Psychosis. Let us now label this unique relationship. I have called it, "The Sick Symbiosis."

Because no "child" patient can get well or become a total whole person unless the parents give up their need to suck or nourish from this child, the sick symbiosis is included as a recognizable entity. It is something to be looked for at first interview, and something to be reckoned with all through treatment. In every case of psychosis, or "nervous breakdown" the patient is debilitated, thus becoming dependent on someone else. This other person (or persons), usually close family, has thrust upon them responsibility for caring for the patient physically, emotionally, financially and usually legally. The family, therefore, must be included. In most of the treatment cases, the family says "Doctor, here is my boy or girl—go to work; call me or tell me when I can call you. . . . I'll pay the bills, you do the treatment." In these cases, the parents have already worked through their interdependence (it had been there at one time). Here the only problem is the patient himself. It is not these families that I am writing about. In perhaps ten percent of the cases, the parents have remained caught within the sickness of the patient.* Here is truly a family illness. There will be progress with the patient only after there is equivalent freeing work with the family.

Margaret Mahler in 1952 and 1960 postulated three normal phases of ego development.[6]

1. Autistic period—from birth to three months.
2. Symbiotic phase—from 3 months to 12—18 months.
3. Separation-individuation phase—up to 36 months. Follows symbiotic phase.

Mahler states that "the intra-uterine, parasitic host relationship within the mother organism must be replaced in the post natal period by the infant being enveloped, as it were, in the extra-uterine matrix of the mother's nursing care, a kind of social symbiosis." The first orientation to external reality arises when the infant becomes aware of the fact that his satisfaction depends upon a force outside of his own body. The autistic

* The sick symbiosis probably occurs in all families—with or without a patient to some subclinical degree.

child is described as one who emotionally never perceives the mother as a representative of the outside world.

Through inter-reaction with the mother in a massive interchange of body feelings—of taste of her milk, smell of her body odor, feel of skin, sound of her voice, thump of heartbeat and rhythm of her breathing, the baby absorbs, assimilates, and digests enough of mother for a separation individuation and the resulting identification of self.

This process is an ever repeating and fruitful nourishing process throughout the life cycle.

A failure at separation-individuation causes a mutuality of dependency, then a too early rejection of the mothering figure with an illusion of omnipotence. It is as if the infant would say "you are not my mother . . . I am your mother." Surrounding this brittle symbiotic omnipotence are vast ideas of paranoia and projection of one's own feelings. There is no separation of I and Thou (mother and self). Confusion and panic pervade the child because there is a great dread of invasion, penetration and engulfment with eventual annihilation.

Threats to the organism produce anxiety and attempts to restore the feeling of oneness with the symbiotic partner. Repeated failures or partial satisfactions result in chronic object hunger. What follows is a return to autism with no affective awareness of other human beings and no realistic contact with the environment. Hallucinated and fantasied objects, or partially deluded objects, substitute for real emotional exchange.

A complete repression of the bad object with all the aggressive impulses turned inward may result in suicide.

Symptoms of Symbiosis in the Patient

The patient, because of past experiences, is hardened to the eventuality. To herself or himself he says "Yes, I am in treatment: I am safe here. I can rest, play and even have therapy. But it is all a game. Mother holds the cards. If she wants to (and she does) and when she wants to, she will take me out of here. All your efforts are useless child's play. Don't say I didn't warn you. So don't be upset when it happens." All this is expectant and implicit in the therapist's relationship to the patient. However, the patient may deny that his mother *bothers him*.

A female patient may say "I do not want my mother dead, Dr. Honig, I love my mother." The mere announcement of a parental visit will completely devaluate all the understanding between patient and therapist and restore the original mother-child symbiosis. You, then, as therapist (unconsciously perhaps as father) are immediately negated and destroyed. Oh, how often I wished for legal action that might forbid a parent to interfere with treatment at this time!

The patients may hate themselves for their dependency and all their life process may be absorbed in energies to "make themselves free." This is especially true when they sense a feeling of being closed in an engulfment. A sense of omnipotence pervades.

Then, in utter frustration, they may do just the opposite—run toward the overpowering object with great anxiety—when they look at the outside world, and other people . . . then give up in utter frustration.

Examples of Patient Reaction

I. Fear of engulfment may show itself as:
   a. Asthma, difficult breathing, air hunger, fear of swallowing.
   b. Claustrophobia, fear of crowds, fear of driving.
   c. Generalized stiffening, tightening, muscle guarding.
   d. Not eating, not using the bathroom (fear of going down the drain).

   All of these symptoms or any of them may turn into its opposite.

II. Omnipotence of Self—Since Mother and Self are not separated they are often "two peas in a pod." The patient may see himself as all powerful and mother, too, as all powerful.

   Example: "Dr.—You say I'm crazy—well, I think you are crazy." (Patient really believes this because he has reinforcement of his thinking by mother's thinking.)

III. Maintenance of Symbiosis can be shown in following patient reactions:
   a. Patient—"I love my mother, I need my mother. My mother is my whole life, Doctor."
   b. Disdain for men, devaluation of the father by both patient and mother.

   Rejection of male therapist . . . Overevaluation of female therapist.

Symptoms in Mother

Aggressiveness, invasiveness, penetrating, blundering, impulsive, bold, instrusive, insensitive striving. Outright lying or the use of words for personal gain is quite common. Gutter-like behavior or animal-like behavior would surprise the uninformed.

This type of person plays none of society's games by the rules. Yet often outwardly such a one is a picture of respectability, social order and conformity.

For a reason I cannot yet explain, even to myself, I have noticed symbiotic relationships in most all of the young teenage "drop out and turn on" drug users. But here, interestingly enough it is the parent of the opposite sex that is involved. To escape the almost obvious incestual relationship, the youngster "drops out," that is, runs away from home and "turns on"—creates chemical Nirvana—a beautiful childlike or dreamlike existence. This is all a defensive action against emotional catastrophe or breakdown. The following is a letter illustrating my point:

February 6, 1968

Dear Doctor Honig,

After coming to see you on Saturday I gave the whole matter of Edward a lot of thinking and have come to the conclusion that I am now giving you notice that I want Edward released from your hospital. I know my son to well and feel that it is now the time to take his crutch away and make him walk on his own. (Edward had been with us only 2 months.) Edward must some day go out on his own and now is the time. I really feel that with 3 or 4 visits to a Doctor a week and being home it will be good for all concerned because I really cannot afford to keep him there any longer, I don't feel that it is fair to myself and my family. The bit of money that John and I were saving was for our future years and we together worked very hard and I don't think we can afford to clean ourselves out. Edward's ideas have not changed and never will in order to be a man he must have the responsibility of one not being coddled. The way I feel is he can come home and be treated by a doctor you recommend and go to school and work to keep busy. There he is too idle and from his appearance has become very sloppy and not caring. Our visit to Edward have not become a pleasure they have become more of a burden and it has cost us more than we can afford. With us he has a good home, good food and would get the care of another good Doctor. If we lived closer I would board him home and have you care for him but that is impossible. I'm sure with the winter coming it will be hard on all concerned Edward cannot stand the loneliness of the woods. I would become more nervous making the trip back and forth and my husband and I would be sure to break up our marriage. So I have spoken to John and told him how I feel and weather [sic] he agrees with me or not its to [sic] bad. I and my family have had to do without things to keep Edward in your hospital because we are not rich but we are comfortable and would like to stay that way. Between the Hospital bill of $1,400.00 a month and our expenses of going to see you there and calling I'm sure Edward can see a Doctor here 4 or 5 times a week and I'd still be ahead. As far as you are concerned you are tops but as far as Bill and Mary (family therapists) I have my own feeling about them. So in ending my letter I want to say thank you for all you've done and please don't try to change my mind because I know you cannot and if John tries he will not have any wife or family because I will sell my home and move far away from all of my family. I am tired of giving I want a little respect and care from my children. When Edward comes home Thursday it will be for good.

Again I say thank you for all you've done. And please understand and give me the name of a Doctor here.

Mrs. L.

Fortunately, I was able to spot the deep symbiosis and save this case. The mother realized how she used her boy to cover up both her own emotional frustrations and her unhappy marriage. She agreed to psychiatric exploration for herself. Here is a letter dated one month later, written by the same woman:

March 12, 1968

Dear Doctor Honig,

 I've read the book you told me to read and I honestly don't understand it all but some has reached me. I know Sunday when John and I were there I must have sounded awful like a spitfire. I'm really a gentle person at heart please forgive me. I have also been very rude to you and you are a fine person. I seem to have a knack for hurting people. As for my son Edward I don't want to call him or speak to him any more and I don't want to force myself on him. He must grow up alone. I realize now I've never grown up. I'm still a child in lots of ways. When I told you I dreamt of lambs I was wrong they were sheep and I must have been little Bow [sic] Peep. And as for the burnt matches. I guess I wanted to burn my bridges behind me. You would know better than I. All I ask of you in the future is to help me along the way and maybe you can do that through Edward. John is a good man in his own way and maybe I should pity him. He may be more lost than I. You asked me to write to you once I hope you won't mind if I did again. I hate to call you and bother you. Your life is already to [sic] busy without my troubles but I feel I can talk to you. That I've found a friend (God knows I need one). Please let me know about Edward and if because I had to sign him into the South Wales Hospital I may have to sign him out. But I won't see him. I would like to call Bill and Mary at home to ask about his health but not talk to him. About my mother I'm really not as disturbed as I thought I'd be. I'm glad I'm alone and John and I had a talk this morning. I've decided to hire a maid again. So if I want to go and have a day for myself I won't feel guilty that I left my mother to stay at home. I'm going to do all the things I've wanted to do. Like going to New York City and anywhere I please with no ties. I'm only having one problem. No one can find any domestics I may have to run an ad in a Philadelphia paper or maybe you may know of an agency by you in your town. If you can help me I hope you will. If you don't have time I'll understand. Let me know about Edward and when he'll be released from the hospital Doctor. Thank you for everything you've done for Edward because I have to admit you've helped him a great deal.

A friend,
L.

However, in two cases, I was not able to save the patient. Strangely enough, in both cases it was the father who became the interfering agent —the one unable to stand the separation and individuation of their child.

 One father invaded our treatment unit, against advice, and without other medical opinion whisked out his 30 year old son in a great show of rescue (where the patient didn't want to be rescued). The father even had a physical fight with one of our male family therapists. He admitted that if his son got stronger he was afraid this same son might kill him.

In another situation, with a 30 year old unmarried daughter, it was the father again who became anxious. A daughter blossoming into a woman became too much for him to handle. A hatefilled relationship between himself and a wife, who herself had been mentally ill, would have to be faced if the daughter was no longer a problem. This presented obvious problems and forced interference. He seemed to feel it was better to have the problems of a mentally sick daughter in a state hospital, with all its social sympathies, than to face his own misery. Truthfulness doesn't always win out.

B. Prognosis

It is difficult to predict the future. It is almost impossible to predict human behavior. Yet a therapist is asked to do this every day. Families who are about to lay out large sums of money need more than blind faith to see them through. However, faith is more important than any statistics about the number of cases cured. When science fails, faith is all important. Science today fails in prognosticating cure or failure.

I make no promises of cure. I state the truth as plainly as I see it, i.e., lay my cards on the table, then let the family make the decision. I remember one epileptic girl, age 15. . . . I had a great feeling that I might be able to help this girl—but I refused to make a promise of cure. The father was enthusiastic, even placed a week's deposit to insure that we would take his daughter's case. The mother, however, had great anxiety dreams about her daughter dying here in an epileptic fit. So the mother won out, and the girl didn't come for treatment. By the way, the girl herself was quite eager to be a patient. I took someone in her place, another epileptic, and he recovered.

One never knows. I have had the most violent, abusive and agitated patients, some who had been this way for years in restraint in state institutions, calm down, work well in therapy and make excellent useful citizens. All the work was done within one of our family units.

Other patients fooled me. A facade of wellness prevailed. It was only a facade and early interpretations sent them into a full blown psychosis. They had appeared more well than they actually were. If a patient has a brittle ego, and there is an underlying psychosis, it doesn't do any good to play "therapy games of patting on the back" ego type support. The patients must face their "insides." The aim is to make people strong and not to do "patch work."

I have confidence that even if treatment is interrupted for some reason, the gains we make will hold. I have seen this happen with patients who come back in acute distress some years after they left treatment with me. They look "just as sick" as before—but in a week's time they reintegrate. They had used the old "psychotic" defense structure to protect themselves in the outside world, but it wasn't permanent.

Vegetation or stagnation over many many years is not good. If one doesn't keep up with one's peers one loses a great deal. If withdrawal goes on for too many years, prognosis may be affected.

Lobotomy, insulin, or electric shock are insulting to the brain. Rarely do I transfer a patient to another therapist. In psychosis, the communication barrier might be so difficult for a patient that I believe the therapist who has learned to understand the patient *should see his case through*. He must realize the death-life struggle of psychosis—and what the patient has given up in making an attachment to him—a *human being* (not just a doctor)— choosing this over the psychosis.

Generally, age can be a factor. A teenager may recover much faster than a person past 40. But this is true in all recovery processes.

References

[1] Harlow, H.; Harlow, M.; Hansen, E. W. THE MATERNAL AFFECTIONAL SYSTEM OF RHESUS MONKEYS. Madison, Univ. of Wisconsin, 1958. p. 255–281.

[2] Harlow, H.; Rheingold, H. MATERNAL BEHAVIOR IN MAMMALS. N.Y., John W. Ley, 1963.

[3] Harlow, H.; Cross, H. A. OBSERVATION OF INFANT MONKEYS PERCEPTUAL AND MOTOR SKILLS. Baton Rouge Southern University Press, 1963. p. 22.

[4] Harlow, H.; Harlow, M. "The effect of rearing conditions on behavior." BULLETIN OF THE MENNIGER CLINIC. *26(5)*:6–12 (1962).

[5] Harlow, M. "The nature of love." AMERICAN PSYCHOLOGIST. *13*:673–685 (1958).

[6] Handelsman, I. "The effects of early object relationships on sexual development— autistic and symbiotic modes of adaptation." In: PSYCHOANALYTIC STUDY OF THE CHILD. v. 20. N.Y., International Universities Press, 1965.

CHAPTER V

The Therapeutic Process

Is there such a thing as a "therapeutic process"—a series of actions or operations conducive to an end? Or is treatment haphazard and successful by chance alone as the anti-psychiatry movement would have it? Will people get well by themselves? Do we have a right to intervene in someone's mental processes? If we do, will intervention benefit the person?

To assume a concept of mental illness forces us to assume a concept of mental health. Relative mental health can give way to mental illness; so too, mental illness can become mental health.

Personal motivation is perhaps the most important factor in the psychotherapeutic process. Without it, behavioral change is doubtful. People can and do get well by themselvees. But in severe mental illnesses, such as psychosis, childhood autism, paranoia and antisocial behavior, the psyche is anti-motivated with regard to a conscious desire for change. I believe it is possible, under certain circumstances, to motivate a mentally disturbed individual to change in behavior. This action I call "finding the key to the case."

But although the person is suffering and wants both relief and a feeling of well-being, he may feel it is too late to change. Most often this is unconscious resistance, for example, in chronic depression. Here a patient's ruminations about hopelessness are easily seen to be non-reality based. But just as often the feeling is based on seemingly real factors. These factors might include age, extended length of illness, physical incapacity or lack of interested people wanting the patient well. An interested person may be defined as a non-professional who will live with him, love him, want him or need him, such as a wife, or close friend, once he can live on the outside. In cases without an interested person, motivation becomes a difficult task.

There is a part of everyone that wants to improve or become better. This part, however, is not as large as that seeking immediate relief of discomfort. When a therapist can deliver immediate relief for suffering, he is acclaimed a magician by thankful patients, his public, and even his own mirror. But this relief can be a double-edged sword because the intricacies of personality problems make the therapeutic process more like the handling of different types of reality problems.

Each set of these problems is a new living experience for the one who has been mentally ill; each new reality conflict poses the threat of relapse into the world of withdrawal, helplessness, fear and frightening imagination which is called psychosis. However, once the illness is exposed and the patient sees what it was really like, there is no turning back. There would be no pleasure in illness.

After bizarre behavior disappears, the therapist faces the problem of "bringing up" an overgrown baby.

Such was the problem which developed in the treatment of a twenty-three year old married woman who had delivered a baby dead of hyaline membrane three months previously and since then had been psychotic. Her symptoms? Lying around the house, feeling she was rotting away (indeed, she smelled), and hallucinating.

When this woman came to our unit she immediately regressed into catatonia. I had to force-feed her. She once ran from her room shouting, "Mother, Mother . . ." (Her mother wasn't there.) Two weeks later she was free of the fright and remarked about it:

"I thought Jane and Joe (the family with whom she was living) were cannibals. I was to be shot; my head was to be cut off, ground up and eaten. Even mother was to partake in the feast."

"Do you still have these feelings?" I asked.

"No."

"Where did they go?"

"I don't know." (God had been kind to her. She had no recollection of the terror she recently experienced.)

The psychosis was gone but the patient now walked around like a mere little girl, a wide-eyed child, knowing little of the affairs of everyday living. She had a four year old boy of her own who was wild and overbearing. She cringed when she thought of going home to face him.

Essentially, the therapeutic process has three parts: nurturing, communication and education. Although all three parts of the process go on simultaneously this is the natural order of occurrence.

Nurturing

Nature intends the psychosis to ward off the severe anxiety present. But here the illness fails to achieve the intended purpose. Instead, the psyche is subjected to the discipline and regimentation of the rigid psychotic system—the false reality. In place of the hoped-for peace of mind are terrifying hallucinations and a constant battle for equilibrium—continually self-defeating.

A psychotic patient I treated said, "Everyone, my husband, my mother-in-law, says it's all in my mind. I know it isn't. I have some horrible physical disease."

"Is it cancer?"

"It's worse than cancer. I'm dying. I have no strength, I ache all over, my face, my hands, my feet are cold. I hurt. I'm dead. I have a terrible discharge from the vagina."

This patient was dehydrated with a fetid odor to her breath and skin. What she said was essentially true. She was suffering from the physical effects of mental illness. Primarily, her complaint was *chronic exhaustion* with dehydration. This complaint was secondary to the mental conflict, but at this point was primarily the illness. Before she could understand her psychosis, her physical needs had to be catered to.

Nurturing consists of catering to the patient's oral demands and pleasures. A selfless, all-giving person must attend every need of this fragile being. This "mothering" is done at first by one person, usually the "mother" in the therapeutic unit. It is custom-styled to the individual's need—(much like good hotel service)—food, warm bathing, powdering, clean sheets and maid service. When needed, privacy and closeness and tenderness are given. The patient is encouraged to feel that someone who cares *is always on hand.*

The nurturing process softens the hard "knots" and thaws out the coldness and anger. To describe the extreme, it is possible to become too chronic because of too much "bad treatment" such as isolation, incarceration, vegetation and electric shock. It can be too late to reverse the process. The nourishment needed is more than is humanly possible to give. The "hurt" to the psyche has been irreversible.

It is rewarding to feel one's lifeblood flowing into another's veins and see the glowing effect. But it is frustrating to work until exhaustion overtakes one and finally see the glow appear, and then to see it gone by the next visit because of too much chronicity. Fortunately, time and good treatment will reverse most psychotic syndromes. Patients in treatment for twenty years have continually improved over this twenty year period. At present, I am working with one man who only after five years in a unit, is acknowledging that there might be something wrong with him.

THE COMMUNICATION PROCESS The intense, one-to-one, nourishing process continues between the all-giving "mother" person and the patient until the need for it is satisfied. This happens with the first equilibrium in the patient's psyche.

Now he wants to be alone at times; he wants to move away from the nourishing person. Perhaps this reaction can be compared to that of the infant who wants to feel the presence of its mother but also wants to enjoy its own autoeroticism. Where there was once only havoc and extreme anxiety, there is now relative calm and introjected security.

A therapist can easily forget how difficult it was getting the patient to this point. This was just such a frailty of mine 14 years ago when I first began treating psychosis. Feeling jubilant after overcoming the gross, moribund symptoms of the illness, I would send the patient to a more orthodox psychotherapist for follow-up treatment. My own schedule would be free for a new case and the dramatic work necessary. Perhaps my motivation was the feeling of having done the impossible.

But in committing this error of judgment, I ignored the very basics of human attachment—the very reason for the patient's change of behavior. This change happened because of the family therapists' work, my own sweat and blood, and the subsequent attachment to the family milieu environment. A miraculous change had occurred—perhaps within weeks or months, but the patient was far from well. Indeed, he was psychologically a weak, helpless infant *willing to be* subdued and accept our help.

Now, there is a rule at the Delaware Valley Mental Health Foundation. It states that in the treatment of psychosis a patient whose treatment has been successful with one therapist will, under no circumstances, have a change of therapists. (This rule may not necessarily apply in the treatment of neurosis.) There is a reason for this rule. Much communication is necessary because a great deal of the patient's personal understanding must still be accomplished. Communication and nurturing occur simultaneously. Explanation and interpretation of the psychotic feelings are part of the nurturing process.

If the person is confused, emotional impact is understood more than are words. In a state of confusion, truth is more symbolic and paralogical than earnest and sincere. For this reason play-acting and role-playing are done. For instance, saying "Ah, shut up, stupid voices" is more meaningful than is a long explanation of the merits and demerits of hallucinations.

A disturbed patient is frightened of his feelings. Is not a child? To what will children respond? Certainly not to the logical, methodical conformity of the so-called adult world. Making the greatest impression on children are clowns and animals, or the playful, the imaginative, the exaggerated, the gruesome and the monstrous.

However, the meaning and substance of the message must be conveyed to the patient without buffoonery and loss of dignity to either party. The patient is ill. He wants, instead of his illness, his own wellness. He wants answers. He wants someone wise and strong to lead him from the engulfing forest. The responsibility of leading his patient from the forest demands of the therapist a deeply personal commitment—the art of therapy. When flowing smoothly, this art of therapy is as rewarding to the therapist as is any creative expression—writing, painting, music. And when flowing smoothly, the communication evolved is deeply beneficial to the patient. It is intuitive, and oftentime assumes a babbling, nonsensical, baby talking rhythm. To the outside observer it may make no sense, but it is soothing and curing to the sick mind.

I have heard therapists say that all psychotherapy is merely an educative process. As far as I am concerned, psychotherapy is a communicative art. It is true I follow a rigid standard of protocol; certain facts about the unconscious are taught to the patient. But this "education" is done through artistic communication.

Rigidly entrenched anal traits must be fought with more than "just talk." A.P. is an 18 year old male patient who lived in one of our units and attended high school in town. His affability and friendliness are superficial; underneath the pretense is a sullen, obsequious, sloppy, indolent boy who is allergic to the discipline of hard work. In school he does well in those subjects taught by favorite teachers. Otherwise he brings no books home. The family therapist who accompanied him to school sat with him during lunch hour. It seemed A.P. had the habit of eating double lunches—those he brought with him and the ones he bought. His weight was approximately two hundred pounds and he easily gained ten pounds in one day.

Talk about his falling grades had made no impression on him. Finally the family therapist, at wit's end, went to the boy's locker, made him take out his books and announced that each subject would be checked. Though angry, A.P. made no retort. As a result of the action, the boy was able to answer in class, talk to his classmates and actively participate in school activities.

Method of Communication

The therapist accomplishes the art of communication through his own resources and human energy. Pictures show graphically, probably better than words alone, different phases of the art of therapeutic communication with psychosis.[1] When the patient is no longer threatened from without, his anxiety lessens and he will sometimes say he is in a state of suspension. He is. Receptive and somewhat comfortable, he will continue to take nourishment from the environment but will be dependent on the primary therapist for movement.

The family therapists' role will now be one of support. They will, if all goes well, become the patient's "buddies". The "rescue operation" once primarily on their shoulders, will now take place within newly formalized therapeutic sessions with the primary therapist.

At first support and nourishment were most needed; during the stage of mass confusion and disintegration of the ego (impending doom) attacking the defenses was secondary. Now it is just the reverse.

EXAMPLES OF COMMUNICATION   The more regressed the personality structure, the greater the communicative needs of the patient. In chronic schizophrenia, communicative needs and nourishing needs are identical. In rut depression with psychomotor retardation great amounts of energy must be expended to move the patient from the depression, and this energy must be expended verbally. With a catatonic patient, verbal techniques may fail and preverbal techniques work.

As part of the communicative process, I will sometimes have as an auxiliary therapist a person whom the patient knows and trusts. Here I will communicate with the patient through this "third party". In the full transcript of Edgar, I used first the mother, then the father, to communicate with the boy.

As the patient becomes stronger, he often feels that the therapist is "siding" with the parents and attempts to go his own way. When he is under attack this way, it is essential that he have someone to talk to. Someone at the Foundation will become the "good mother." It is best to keep it within the Foundation family because rarely does the outside world know or even want to know how to care for someone who had been this ill.

Communication with autistic children and with those who have developmental brain lag—mental retardation is quite interesting. I usually hold one of these children on my lap on a first visit until he relaxes and becomes limp. Using a bottle, I attempt to stimulate oral desires. I feel that early oral deprivation (possibly due to late development, poor sucking or brain damage) and misunderstanding of the baby's needs result in his turning away from human contact. This in turn can lead to the development of autism, mutism, or non-speech. This mal-development can be counteracted by forcing human contact; proper patterns of learning can be reestablished.

Communication is one to one—patient and therapist. When the patient is strong enough, he will want to disengage from his symbolic breast or teacher (therapist). What was once blind love, faith, adulation, is now mistrust! What else have you done for me but hurt? Ambivalence develops—positive feelings, then negative. This negative transference is an attempt to escape the therapist. But secretly there has been an attachment to another nourishing object—husband, wife or is it lover? This attachment has provided the patient with strength to fight the antagonist (the therapist). He may even plot revenge and destruction. (More detail will be found in the chapter on Negative Transference and Psychosis, Chapter VIII).

If the therapist ignores his patient's negative transference, the patient is left weak, suspicious, and without insights. The therapist must stand up to the barrage and fight back with truth, proving he can tolerate any outbreak of his patient's emotions, reason and logic.

Waking from the Nightmare and the Problem of Aggression

> *In my name shall they cast out devils—*
> MARK 16:17

The medical profession as a whole, and the public, must get used to the psychiatrist dealing as boldly and decisively with the sick mind as the surgeon deals with the sick body. Just as the surgeon has the tools for murder but does not murder, so the psychiatrist has the tools for perversion of behavior but uses them for healing.[2]

Anna Freud states: "Aggression, destruction, their expressions and their development are as much in the center of interest for dynamic psychology now as the development of the sexual function was at the beginning of the century." [3]

When facing aggression, resourcefulness is the key. Probably nothing else but an exhaustive study of ancient religious practices, such as magic, ritual and exorcism, offer as much refreshing material about the unconscious and open previously locked doors of therapeutic treatment of the psychosis. To substantiate this theory, Boisson says: "The progress of medical science, the discoveries relating to abnormal aspects of psychic life, have removed possession from the supernatural plane to one that is open to investigation. The frontiers of what cannot be known are therefore not eternally fixed." [4]

Simultaneously the psychosis displays itself in both (a) feeling and (b) ideation. The psychotic feeling is the true psychosis. Included is the anxiety, described by Freud, Sullivan and myself, that is dread, assuming life versus death proportions.[5,6] This dread is accompanied by tremendous oral craving and tension. At times, there are cutaneous and anal cravings. But the dread, and oral feelings are always present. The ideation defensive structure is the form in which the feelings present themselves. They represent attempts at restitution and homeostasis—ranging from hypochondriacal preoccupations with body organs to compulsive mannerisms, hallucinations, delusions, projections, daydreams, and catatonic states.

The psychotic feeling may embody the general chaos that precedes suicide or is witnessed in catatonic excitement. Or there may be isolated pockets of psychotic feeling—noticed only in times of stress.

These manifestations have caused some observers to conclude that neurosis and psychosis are basically the same illness—differing only in degree. Psychotic feeling may be compared with the latent content of a dream and the psychotic defenses with the manifest content. It seems to be a total alarm reaction to stress.

SOME NOTES ON THE THEORY OF AGGRESSION Freud, in his first theoretical formulations on the subject of aggression, *Three Contributions to the Theory of Sex,* centered his attention on the development of sexuality and the vicissitudes of psychic energy attached to the sexual impulse.

Impulses of an aggressive nature—manifestations of destruction or cruelty—were treated as components of sexuality. Aggressive impulses were considered derivatives of a drive for sexual mastery. Later, Freud postulated the existence of two primary drives—libidinal and aggressive. Being a drive, as is libido, aggression has an impetus, source, aim and object. Aggression is often expressed in activity, but absence of activity may itself be an expression of aggression. (Passive-Aggression)

Rage has the imprint of pregenital expression, orality, and, most often, anality. The basic aim of aggression is the total destruction of an object. If thwarted, damming of libido occurs. Aggression must then be released in substitute formation or sublimation. Freud states that libidinal drives are transformed into symptoms and aggressive components into guilt feelings.

Aggression may be modified by (1) displacement to other objects, (2) restriction of the aims of the aggressive impulses, (3) sublimation of aggressive energy, and (4) fusion with libidinous elements.

Aggression can be discharged by fight or flight. It may be internalized against the self, as in suicide or in the formation of the superego. For the latter, neutralization of the aggressive energy must first take place. Sadism entails discharge of aggression and destruction of objects. Pleasure is its additional characteristic. This is achieved not only by the aggressive discharge, destruction, but also by pleasure occurring at the infliction of pain and the suffering and humiliation of others.

In an infant, there exists the "frustration-aggression" hypothesis. Lack of pleasure produces frustration and aggression. As the child grows, he becomes dissatisfied with his aggressive reactions to frustration. Both his ego and his superego disapprove of aggression turned outward. The aggression is internalized, contributing to an increase in guilt feelings. As the aggressive and libidinous drives become neutralized, their expression is socialized. The aggressive drives are directed to useful pursuits by the ego.

RELATIONSHIP OF PSYCHOTIC FEELING TO AGGRESSION   Anna Freud, in writing about the management of aggression, has stated: "Efforts to control these pathological states of infantile aggressiveness by force, and efforts, with all the means used in upbringing, to urge the child to control his destructiveness are found to fail. The appropriate therapy has to be corrected to the neglected, defective side, i.e., the emotional libidinal impulses will follow automatically, and aggression will be brought under the beneficent influence of the erotic urges." [7]

In management of the psychoses, manifestations of the illness may appear which are different from those occurring previously. Instead of showing obvious anxiety and search for help, the patient may become indolent, sullen, preoccupied, dreamlike, and hallucinatory. He is generally dull and quiet, withdrawn, tight, resistive—he is aggressive in a passive manner.

He resents being aroused from his lethargy. If questioned, he gives a malevolent and superficial answer. An overwhelming force within him seems to demand his restraint. It seems that he fears an internal explosion bent on destroying him. Because of his attribution to the external environment of death wishes, mental acuity suffers. The result may be further disorganization; shallowness of affect; decreased intellectual function; loss of orientation to time, place and people; impaired judgment; and memory loss. The *picture is often diagnosed as organicity.* There are elements of depression present, without outward mourning or agitation. There may be compulsive repetition and obsessive ruminations, extreme obstinacy, and immobile stubbornness. Accusations may be stated—people trying "to get something from me"—and the desire to destroy them. This condition has been observed even in our own treatment units, which with twenty-four hour intensive care, we consider to be the ideal protective environment. To add to the problem, tranquilization and other medications seem useless. Electroconvulsive therapy, giving initial relief, may add to the severity of the problems, producing post-shock confusion and other organic effects. We have discovered that with this complication the use of the psychotherapeutic technique called *direct confrontation* * gives gratifying results.

DIRECT CONFRONTATION OF RESISTANCE: ITS COMMUNICATIVE VALUE
Direct confrontation is a therapeutic technique employing "straight from the shoulder" verbalization in an attempt to overcome resistance. To be effective, the verbalization must be clear, concise and meaningful to the patient. Therefore, it must bear direct relationship to his thoughts or actions at the time of confrontation. Usually conducted in the form of an attack, it arouses the patient's hidden anger, hostility, or other negative feelings.

In direct confrontation, it is advisable to have assistants present to reinforce and give impetus to the main therapist's words. (These assistants are usually the family therapists.) With a successful confrontation, penetration into the defenses occurs. Anxiety, rejection, and loss of love and self-esteem result as libido shifts from narcissism to objects. The assistants, in explaining to the patient the reason for the attack, support the patient when the main therapist leaves.

Direct confrontation should be avoided with an ambulatory patient (non-resident patient) until a positive relationship has been established. Intuitively, the patient must realize the extent of the therapists' solicitude and the benefit of the attack. In direct confrontation, the therapist, by words alone, must exert an unusually large amount of energy to overpower the resistances. For example:

Therapist: She's mad, tape, she's mad. (Talking to tape—patient asked to have sessions taped.)
Patient: I am mad, and I'm going to pull my hair out—
Therapist: She's pulling her hair, tape, she's pulling her hair—(talking to tape). She's getting real hot and sexual over her hair!
Patient: What're you trying to say?
Therapist: I'm telling you, you don't know what sex is all about—that part of your life seems to be cut off.
Patient: You're full of shit!
Therapist: You couldn't know—You're as bad as Joe and his epilepsy— you and your hair.

* Frequently, I substitute the term direct intrusion for direct confrontation.

Patient: What makes you say that?

Therapist: Because I know the feeling one gets when one pulls one's hair.

Patient: No you don't—it's entirely different. You have no basis for this—you don't know what I'm feeling.

Therapist: You don't know what I'm feeling either. Just like Jean said to Joe when he had an epileptic attack—mine are worse than yours.

Patient: Do you pull your hair?

Therapist: Yes, I pull it out by the white roots.

Patient: What white roots?

Therapist: You don't even know what that is. I've studied hair under the microscope.

Patient: (Angrily)—I've done it, I've done it.—I don't see any bald spots on you. Just like sex—you have to do it, not just read books.

Therapist: Look tape, she's contradicting herself—First she tells me to stop pulling my hair—now she says I've never done it!

Patient: Do it, Do it!—Pull your hair (Loudly, angrily and frustratingly).

Result: Patient seemed happy, her eyes were bright, and she thanked me and went back, told the family therapists she loved me and began to bake a cake.

Theoretical Formulation of Direct Confrontation

The goal of direct confrontation in psychotherapy is the overcoming of resistance. If a technique is effective, one or more of the following psychological principles is at work.

1. Omnipotence. The therapist, assuming an aggressive possition, is seen as an omnipotent figure. The patient is deliberately forced into a position of passivity and dependency, similar to that of parent and child. It is thought that this type of relationship must be established early in the psychotherapy of schizophrenia, much as the mother must take the hungry infant and force it to the breast.

2. Ambivalence. There is an attack on ambivalence. The therapist establishes himself as the object to be reckoned with. He forces the transference, with all its emotional forces, to himself. He lets the patient know that therapy, more than just an intellectual exercise, will entail a high degree of emotional exchange.

3. Anxiety. By forcing attention to himself as a flesh and blood human being, the therapist dissipates anxiety. At that moment, the patient is able to forget his imaginary threats. It is impossible to think of two different things at once; the therapist makes use of this simple fact. With this provocation, the patient is unable to hallucinate, daydream, or act in an unacceptable manner.

4. Stimulation of the body's own instinct of self-preservation. Psy-

chotic individuals feel themselves flowing in all directions (much as amoebae). They do not feel solid boundaries. They cannot protect themselves against attack. Thus, attack by the therapist forces the patient's own instincts of preservation to awareness, with accompanying ego integration.

5. Prevention of further regression. By compelling mobilization of ego defensive forces to deal with the real threat (the therapist), further regression or disintegration of personality is prevented.

6. Stimulation of erotogenic feelings by forcing the flow of libido outward toward warm objects.

7. Enhancement of positive relationship. By expanding energy to control the patient's aggression, the therapist conveys to the patient that he really cares for him.

8. Provision of outward controls of the patient's aggression where judgment fails and reasoning power is not developed.

9. Forcing awareness of reality, so that the patient becomes aware of his own self and his separateness and an acceptance of such follows.

10. Furtherance of identification through identification with the aggressor.

11. Use of aggression in group surroundings to cause embarrassment, shame, chagrin. These are healthy, socially acceptable feelings, showing an awareness of others.

12. Relief of guilt by allowing the patient's aggressive feelings to be superseded by the more powerful display of the therapist's anger. We believe this is only one of many reasons why direct confrontation is successful therapy. Many people have dismissed use of direct confrontation techniques, citing this reason as the only explanation of their effect. Such reasoning shows scant knowledge of the unconscious.

13. Threat of loss of love, so that the patient will sublimate his infantile aggression through neutralization. The expressed aggression then becomes socialized.

Freud described erotogenic masochism and the conflict between the sadism of the superego and masochism of the ego. There is reason to believe that in psychosis there is a great need to suffer pain and distortion of the pleasure principle. The guilt in psychosis is strong. This is probably why psychotic patients tolerate and even seem to enjoy direct confrontation.

Psychoanalysis, in theory and practice, is verbal communication between therapist and patient. Psychotherapeutic techniques have been extended not only to the neuroses but to children and the psychoses as well. With this effect, new emphasis has been placed on preverbal communication. Frank states: "It seems clear that the child's reception of verbal measures is predicated in large measure upon his prior tactile experience so that facial expressions and gestures become sign and symbols for certain kinds of tactile communications and interpersonal relations." A person who is emotionally disturbed while holding or carrying an infant may communicate that disturbance to the infant through tactile contacts just as a calm, relaxed person may soothe a disturbed child, by holding him, with or without patting. The close, tactual contact of being held firmly apparently reassures a child. And further, it cannot be too strongly emphasized that the infant when disturbed emotionally usually responds to patting or even vigorous, but rhythmic, slapping of the back with increasing composure. In an older child this patting may awaken him or keep him awake, but it puts an infant to sleep. This age difference offers some support for the assumption of an early infantile sensitivity or need for rhythmic tactual stimulation which fades out or is incorporated into other patterns or becomes quiescent until puberty." [8]

Catatonic schizophrenia is considered by many observers as the deepest form of regression. In many cases of catatonia, the patient withdraws from all contact. In this phase, referred to as "catatonic mutism or rigidity", the individual moves and talks minimally, seeming to comply with a maternal superego command: "Be still; be quiet; be dead. Then I might love you."

In these cases, direct confrontation through verbalization is unsuccessful. The patient, so regressed, may respond only to preverbal communication— some form of tactile stimulation. Entering the psychosis is of paramount importance. Many observers have speculated on the means of doing this.

When a child begins exploring the world, one of his basic experiences is learning to respect the inviolability of persons, places or things. This involves curtailment and prohibition of tactile experiences. The child is forbidden to touch what is adult-defined as inviolable (persons, property, sacred places, forbidden objects). Often painful punishment blocks his approach to these inviting objects, until he perceives them as untouchable.

The schizoid and schizophrenic personalities exhibit early in life resistance to accepting the ideas and concepts of culture. Early denial of tactile experiences, or inability to establish and maintain tactile communication upon which conceptualization can be built, may account for their action.

Little has been written about direct confrontation of resistance through physical means. When a therapist, several years ago, reported an incident of face slapping, his colleagues angrily spurned him. Bacon states that Rosen frequently will "enter into the psychosis" and attack the patient physically, inflicting minor violence but displaying magic evil.[9] He is transfigured in the patient's mind as the "personification of the violent and evil power of the persecutory super ego."

Early medical authors, such as Rahses and Valescuse de Taranta, have described physical treatment, including infliction of pain, as the therapy of madness. Cooper states, "Cases may and do occur where bodily punishment becomes indispensable, in order that the body may feel what the judgment cannot comprehend." [10]

Flagellation is a common means of exorcising spirits by believers in spirit possession. They regard this method as most rational and consistent with their beliefs. As a discipline, flagellation has a long history. King Solomon stated, "He that spareth his rod hateth his son; but he that loveth him chasteneth him betimes." (Proverbs 13:24) Petrarch remarks, "Correct your son in his tender years, nor spare the rod. A branch when young may easily bend at your pleasure." [11, 12]

Because of vast abuses, corporal punishment has almost disappeared. Shoving it back into prominence was the State of Delaware controversy. There a judge sentenced a young, repeated offender to twenty lashes in the public square. Crying and cringing with fear, the boy stated he would rather be imprisoned than whipped. [13]

It is reasonable to suspect that infliction of physical pain in the treatment of psychosis might revert to the abuses of the past. But one fact is obvious. If a therapist courageously controls a patient's aggression, the patient is grateful.

At the Delaware Valley Mental Health Foundation we have developed methods to handle this passive hallucinatory dream or nightmare—like aggression when words have failed. The simple baby bottle, filled with sweetened warm milk will provoke the most unusual and violent responses.

Examples: M.V., a 28 year old hallucinating woman was extremely agitated and walked around imagining how it would be to be married. She finally had settled for the most regressed of our male patients and had even adopted his last name as hers. Numerous attempts to expose her ridiculous ruse with verbalizations failed. "He can't support you. He is of a different religion; it won't work out." "Look, he can't even read." "When he sits here, he ignores you." Interpretations such as "All these men represent breasts (mothers) to you" were meaningless. But the simple bottle was another story. She fought the sucking, spilled the milk, bit off the nipple. She cried, "I am a woman, Dr. Honig, I am a woman." (She finally realized she wasn't a baby, but a woman.)

With another patient, the use of a dunce cap in the form of a bag on the head, and isolation from the group, reduced the symptoms to absurdity.

Recently the use of reducing machines and myotonic stimulators have proven effective. They are relatively harmless, but their effects on a hallucinatory or delusional patient are extremely rewarding. One patient, who had delusions about her sexual organs and who was extremely guilt-ridden about a baby she had delivered, had the stomach girdle hooked to her abdomen. As her muscles rhythmically contracted and relaxed, she cried: "Dr. Honig, don't take my sexual feelings away. Oh, oh! I don't want to die." She had attempted suicide by taking lye when she was pregnant and apparently was reliving this episode.

What about the actively aggressive person? A berserk human is frightened, fearful of the physical harm he may inflict on another. We hear reports of the raving destructive psychotic tearing apart the hospital ward or living unit. Without intervention, his power and fear increase. If physically subdued and restrained, he frequently falls asleep, much like a contented baby. With an unreasoning patient, sedation in the form of medicine will not accomplish the same quiescence.

Every therapist working intimately with the psychoses has experienced a physical attack from a psychotic patient. Forced into battle with the patient, the therapist must prove his courage and ability to control the aggression without harming his patient. Once the patient is subdued, these occasions effectuate a closer relationship between therapist and patient, resulting in clinical and reality-testing improvement.

Our policy is a simple one—*meet aggression with aggression*. At the Delaware Valley Mental Health Foundation we find it better to keep a patient, only when all other methods have failed, in a strait jacket with leg cuffs (to prevent kicking and running). The patient is contented that his aggression is controlled and he may eat and stay with his therapeutic family. Cold isolation and side room techniques (cells) are non-therapeutic. One family spent a Saturday evening entertaining a minister and his wife and children with one of its patients so secured. Although wrapped up in this strange apparel, he was able to participate in all the discussions.

The Educational Procedure

True understanding never tires of interminable dialogue and vicious circles; it trusts that imagination will eventually catch a glimpse of the always frightening light of truth. The educational process in psychotherapy evolves from the theories of social structure and education. To understand its application within the framework of family milieu therapy, one must consider the very basic social structure itself—the family.

Hobbes, in the seventeenth century, perceived society as evolving from "a state of nature in which men unrestrainedly endeavor to destroy or subdue one another." Rationally perceiving the perpetual insecurity that results, men enter into a social contract and establish a common power to protect them from one another's aggressions by restricting the use of force to this power only.[14, 15]

Dennis H. Wrong writes "Human conduct is totally shaped by common norms," or "institutionalized patterns." Sheer ignorance must have led people who were unfortunate enough not to be modern sociologists to ask, "How is order possible?" A thoughtful bee or ant would never inquire "How is social order of the hive or ant possible?" The opposite of that order is inconceivable when the insect's instinctive endowment insures stability and built-in harmony between individual and common interests.[16]

Human society is not essentially different, although conformity and stability are maintained by non-restrictive and non-instructive processes. Man began to live in groups for individual and common interests. Freud says "Love was one of the founders of culture". Man discovered that genital love gave him his greatest satisfaction; it became a prototype of all happiness to him. Therefore, he must have been impelled to seek further happiness along the path of sexual relations and to make genital erotism the central point of his life.[17]

But by doing so, he became dependent on a part of the outer world— his chosen love object. He thus exposed himself to powerful sufferings upon rejection or loss of the object through death or defection. To protect himself from this suffering, man has become independent of his object's acquiescence by transferring the main value from the fact of being loved to his own sense of loving. He then protects himself more by attaching his love to all men equally—thus avoiding the uncertainties and disappointments of genital love by turning away from its purely sexual aim and modifying the instinct into an impulse and an inhibited aim.

The love that instituted the family retains its power; in its original form it does not stop short of direct sexual satisfaction, and its modified form (aim-inhibited friendship) influences our civilization. Genital love forms new families; aim-inhibited love forms friendships which are culturally valuable. Positive feeling is promoted from father and mother, parents and children, brothers and sisters. The family unit, hothouse of birth, growth and development, forms the unit of protection against outside forces. I have found this social structure to be the most ideal arrangement for development of all three phases of treatment.

In our therapeutic family units, the structure is flexible and mobile. At first, it represents an integrated unit against outside forces such as the community because the patient's needs demand this. But as the patient grows, the treatment requires relaxation of family autonomy and directs the patient toward the therapeutic community and finally the outside world. Friendship and the all-embracing love of others becomes the essential theme; it is taught as the highest aim of man. It is the "modus operandi" of the Delaware Valley Mental Health Foundation.

Since the father of the "house parents" works at home in the therapeutic family structure, more love is directed into the family. (The husband works outside the home in most families and "home work" is left to the woman.)

In the primitive unconscious, individual love (narcissism), love between two individuals and love between blood family members are subordinate to aggressive instincts against another. However, in the family milieu treatment, a new gratification is recognized—devotion to others. This devotion, growing out of man's aggressiveness, is aimed toward the therapeutic community and humanity itself. *Not every person has the strength of character to participate in this type of life.* But it is ideal and within its daily workings, economic and social scientists might discover a cure for man's social ills.

Another chapter, entitled "Anxiety and Schizophrenia",* describes the

---

* Anxiety and Schizophrenia, Chapter VI.

void present in a human being's personality upon disappearance of the psychotic system. Because these people have never experienced daily living, they do not know *how* to shop, cook, purchase, drive, mow the lawn, talk to people, read, add, fish, use makeup, stay alone or clean a house, garden, swim, catch a ball, use a camera, etc. Either they have never learned or they have forgotten. Often their style of dress takes them back to the era they lived in when last well—perhaps twenty years in the past.

Then again, strong character defects such as stealing, lying or violent outbursts may persist. I have found this acting-out behavior and character defect more often than the simple "near neurosis" (Neo-neurosis) that Rosen sees after psychosis. All in all, it is quite obvious the patients suffer from a lack of being "raised."

Do defects in character represent a form of mental illness? Eric Fromm says: "In order that any society may function well, its members must acquire the kind of character which makes them want to act in a way they have to act as members of society or of a special class within it. They have to desire what objectively is necessary for them to do. Outer force is to replaced by inner compulsion and by the particular kind of human energy which is channeled into character traits. As long as mankind has not attained a state of organization in which the interest of the individual and that of society are identical, the aims of society have to be attained at a greater or lesser expense of the freedom and spontaneity of the individual. This aim is performed by the process of child training and education. While education aims at the development of the child's potentialities, it has also the function of reducing his independence and freedom to the level necessary for the existence of the particular society." [18]

Fromm continues: "Today we come across a person and find that he acts and feels like an automaton; he never experiences anything that is really his; he experiences himself entirely as the person he thinks he is supposed to be; that smiles have replaced laughter, meaningless chatter replaced communicative speech; dulled despair has taken the place of genuine pain. Two statements can be made about this person. One is that he suffers from a defect of spontaneity and individuality which may seem incurable. At the same time it may be said that he differs little from thousands of others who are in the same position. With most of them, the cultural pattern for the defect saves them from the outbreak of neurosis. With some, the cultural pattern doesn't function and the defect appears as a severe neurosis."

I want to stress the necessity of proceeding from the origin of neurosis to the origins of the culturally patterned defect and finally to the problem of normality. The goal implies that the psychoanalyst, while concerned that the neurotic individual readjust to his individual society, also must recognize that the individual's idea of normality may be in conflict with full realization of himself as a human being. It is the belief of the progressive forces in society that such a realization is possible—that the interests of society and the individual need not be antagonistic forever. Primitive cultures are rigid and statistically controlled; our culture is dynamic and manifested by social change.

The Application of Social Theory to Process

The confused, ambivalent, disassociated sick mind needs a solid structure of conformity to grasp. This conformity must include the primitive elements necessary in the beginning of any new and growing life. One must give the essential elements of sunlight, warmth, water and rich soil for the development of a new plant. These elements must be delicately balanced. There must be protection from outside forces and general acceptance of the disturbed person. These elements, blended in the beginning of the re-educative process, engender good feelings within the sick individual. These feelings include peace of mind, warmth, freedom from anxiety and a general "blissful" state throughout the body.

People often describe this blissful state as "being reborn." Once the "key" to the case is found, i.e., the essential ingredients necessary to produce improvement, a repetition of these ingredients will eventually create within the patient a sense of being "filled up."

When the patient is filled up with his individual healing potion, new demands are made upon therapy. Up to this point complete instinctual gratification has been given (within limits, of course). I am strict in not allowing sex play between staff and patients or patients and other patients. In the first case, it is a direct violation of incest, parent-child or therapeutic symbiotic teacher-pupil taboo. It is not allowed between patients simply because it is not the cure, for the reason that they are inpatients and most such affairs are exposed as Brother-Sister incest themes. We are not against love. Too often patients attach themselves to each other in a pseudo-love, a sinking symbiosis that is a reestablishment of their old sick family relationship. It does not allow for the separation and individuation they really need. Now the patient is ready for exposure to the cultural demands of our society.

This exposure presents an extremely difficult step in therapy. The patient has become ill through a misunderstanding of the delicate balance between culture and instinctual gratification. He is burdened with hostility and frustration because of what has happened. His misunderstanding of cause and effect evokes negative feelings toward the therapist.

Expecting too much too soon may re-precipitate the illness. The therapist must then win the patient a second time, a more difficult task than the first time. Great care is exercised to make it unnecessary. This principle is extremely difficult for lay people to understand (especially parents and family). Seeing the sick individual reasonably well, they want to remove him from his protective environment and may even seek to end his therapy. As everyone involved in this work knows, the sick person is kept buoyant by his nourishing environment. He needs to "take in" much more of this environment to have the healthy and strong personality that will enable him to face "out-side world" stresses.

In his presidential address before the American Psychological Association in New Haven, 1899, John Dewey stated, "the adult is primarily a person with a certain calling and position in life. These devolve upon him certain specific responsibilities which he has to meet and call into play certain habits. The child is primarily one whose calling is growth. He is concerned with arriving at specific ends and purposes—instead of having a general framework already developed. He is engaged in forming habits rather than in definitely utilizing those already formed. Consequently he is absorbed in getting that all-around contact with persons and things, that range of acquaintance with physical and ideal factors of life, which shall afford the background and material for the specialized aims and pursuits of later life. He is, or should be, busy in the formation of a flexible variety of habits whose sole immediate criterion is their relations to full growth, rather than in acquiring certain skills whose value is measured by their reference to specialized technical accomplishments. This is the radical psychological and ideological distinction, I take it, between the child and the adult. It is because of this distinction that children are neither physiologically nor mentally describable as 'little men and women'." [19]

Freud, attempting to shed light on the psychological process of re-education by formation of what he called the EGO-IDEAL ways, "the ego is the heir to the original narcissism in which the childish ego found its self-sufficiency; it gradually gathers up from the influences of the environment the demands which the environment makes upon the ego and which the ego cannot always rise to; so that a man, when he cannot be satisfied with his ego itself, may nevertheless be able to find satisfaction in the ego ideal which has been differentiated out of the ego. In delusions of observation the disintegration of this faculty has become patent and thus has revealed its origins in the influences of superior powers and above all, of parents. But we have not forgotten to add that the amount of distance between this ego ideal and the real ego is very variable from one individual to another, and that with many people this differentiation within the ego does not go further than with children." [20]

To Summarize

Although the work of "breaking" the psychosis is dramatic, exciting and contains the elements of rescue, it is the slow, tedious, day to day learning in the living units that is really the strengthening work. A psychotic patient must be given a true re-education to life in order to survive in the outside world.

References

[1] Brossard, C. and Herron, M. "Breakthrough in psychiatry—revolutionary treatment of the mentally ill." LOOK MAGAZINE. April 5, 1966.

[2] English, O. S. "Clinical observations on direct analysis." In his: DIRECT ANALYSIS AND SCHIZOPHRENIA. N.Y., Grune and Stratton, 1961. p. 15.

[3] Freud, A. "Aggression in relation to emotional development: Normal and pathological." THE PSYCHOANALYTIC STUDY OF THE CHILD. Vol. III/IV, p. 37–42 (1949).

[4] Bouisson, M. MAGIC: ITS HISTORY AND PRINCIPAL RITES. N.Y., Dutton, 1961, Ch. 7.

[5] Freud, S. "Loss of reality in neuroses and psychoses." In his: COLLECTED PAPERS. London, Hogarth, v. 2, p. 280.

[6] Sullivan, H. S. THE COLLECTED WORKS. N.Y., Norton, 1956. v. 2, p. 104–139.

[7] Freud, A. *loc. cit.*

[8] Frank, L. K. "Tactile communication." GENETIC PSYCHOLOGY. #56, p. 209–255 (Nov. 1957).

[9] Bacon, C. L. "The Rosen treatment of the psychoses from the viewpoint of identity." In: English, O. S. *op. cit.* p. 62.

[10] Cooper, W. M. A HISTORY OF THE ROD. London, Reeves, 1900. p. 204.

[11] Nevious, J. L. DEMON POSSESSION AND ALLIED THEMES. London, Redway, 1897. p. 270.

[12] A HISTORY OF FLAGELLATION. N.Y., Medical Pub., 1924. p. 193.

[13] "Mother begs mercy for her son—says he fears whipping post." PHILADELPHIA BULLETIN. Nov. 16, 1962. p. 15.

[14] Arendt, H. "Understanding and politics." PARTISAN REVIEW. 20:392 (1953).

[15] Parsons, T. THE STRUCTURE OF SOCIAL ACTION. N.Y., McGraw-Hill, 1937. p. 89–94.

[16] Wrong, D. H. THE OVERSOCIALIZED CONCEPT OF MAN IN MODERN SOCIOLOGY. N.Y., Random, 1956.

[17] Freud, S. CIVILIZATION AND ITS DISCONTENT. London, Hogarth, 1953. p. 69–70.

[18] Fromm, E. INDIVIDUAL AND SOCIAL ORIGINS OF NEUROSIS. N.Y., Knopf, 1948.

[19] Dewey, J. PHILOSOPHY, PSYCHOLOGY AND SOCIAL PRACTICE. N.Y., Putnam, 1899.

[20] Freud, S. GROUP PSYCHOLOGY AND THE ANALYSIS OF THE EGO. N.Y., Liveright, 1951. p. 69–70.

CHAPTER VI

Anxiety in Schizophrenia *

I would like to reflect at this time on the anxiety that is seen in schizophrenia. My intention here is to encourage a practical, as opposed to, a merely theoretical interest in the immense suffering in schizophrenia with a hope that such an interest will lead us closer to the therapeutic possibility of offering psychotic patients a decent measure of relief.

Reviewing the literature on anxiety in schizophrenia, I came across a panel discussion held almost two decades ago. The panelists, some of them leaders in the treatment of schizophrenia, were theorizing on the origin of the anxiety that was so universally found in schizophrenic patients. All of them being clinicians, they rightfully thought that if they could elicit a single dynamic concept for the origin of their patient's anxiety, which was the cause underlying the symptomatology, this concept would lead to more successful therapy. Although most agreed that the schizophrenic's symptomatology was an expression of anxiety as well as the defense against it, marked disagreement remained as to why the anxiety existed in the first place.[1]

One panelist said that it was because of the patient's latent hostility; another because of fear of separation; still another because of the widespread diffusion of libidinal feelings. A sense of loneliness because of the inability to communicate was also mentioned. My personal belief is that all that was said is essentially true, but that no patient would benefit to the maximum, therapeutically, unless the therapist had a more basic understanding of the patient's language that expressed his needs, for only

---

* Schizophrenia is used here not as a diagnosis, but rather as a convenient word that exemplifies all severe mental suffering. A person, labeled in many different psychiatric categories, may feel a sense of identity with the subject matter herewithin. Paper originally published in Psychoanalysis in 1959.

such an understanding brings the therapist into direct, therapeutic contact with the underlying anxiety.

Clinical Application of the Method

The Delaware Valley Mental Health Foundation itself is structured but not in the usual rigid manner. The guidelines are broad, and therefore not easily understood by the mind that must be told constantly what to do. Each and every patient eventually must find himself (or herself) in his own way. Each therapeutic family has autonomy, only superseded by the medical director's authority. This autonomy is used to allow the individual patient to do "his thing."

The importance of being able to do one's own thing cannot be overemphasized. To get well, an individual must invest his libido into *one thing,* no matter how absurd it seems. This "thing" or program must allow for undisturbed (by other people) problem solving and mastery. It is not unlike children who, in growing up, build a whole world around dolls, stamp collecting, model airplanes, and the like. One patient did nothing all day but lift weights. However, he became an expert in the subject of body building, even to the point of deciding whether to open his own gymnasium. His parents never understood his need or its function—and felt that which was really the opposite of reality. That is "If only Freddy would throw away his weights he would get well."

Another patient staked out an area of Clinic ground to raise chickens. He built his own coops, fences, and tends to them like a mother hen. Alas! It has paid off with fresh eggs for breakfast.

Yet another has a car engine block and tackle, hanging from an apple tree, ready to be placed in a new chassis.

Once the foundations of life are cemented, room must be allowed for experimentation. For instance, one patient said that each day he went to school and came home he felt compelled to tell his mother everything that went on. Eventually he felt his mother was "stealing his mind." He had nothing of his own, he felt, and this was destructive. The chapters of this section illustrate different facets of experimentation *within* the therapeutic structure. Previous chapters described the structural framework.

Psychoses are rigid structures. No rigid structure survives long at the Foundations. When security is provided without total regularity, people become anxious because they don't know what's expected of them.

Different problems, such as anxiety, or mental retardation, are treated differently. Idiopathic epilepsy and mental retardation are still considered medical and neurological conditions. Perhaps a very biased neurologist might be angered before getting far into the chapter on epilepsy, because idiopathic epilepsy is considered here as an *emotional disorder.* To see subnormal mental functioning in this light no longer is viewed as nonsense, but not so yet with epilepsy.

At first a reader may be bothered by the repetition of situations where regression and direct confrontation are mentioned. This has been deliberately done for emphasis. Each of these two subjects is difficult to grasp. I have attempted to give them more clarity by illustrating different crisis situations.

Much is learned by problem-solving in a crisis situation. In fact, many observers have said Delaware Valley Mental Health Foundation is *crisis oriented*. This is only part of the story. Over and over, one can read into the story the hours of dedication. This is most of the tale.

The regression in schizophrenia is, in a way, similar to the fever and pain of an acute inflammation. Every practicing physician knows that the pain of coronary thrombosis means the heart is under great stress and life is at stake. He places the patient in complete bed rest until the pain subsides. I was taught in medical school never to whip a tired heart, and thus I look with chagrin on some of the techniques still being employed in the management of psychoses. I feel that there is a similarity in the regression of a schizophrenic to the pain of the acutely inflamed heart.

In psychosis, it is the patient's unconscious that has taken command and gives out the danger signals. Dramatically, as with coronary pain, the need to be rescued is paramount. There seems to be a method to this schizophrenic madness. The cry for help seems so like the cry of an infant for milk, that I have seen women visitors want to reach out to the most violent and thoroughly disturbed patients on the wards.[2] There must be a reason why the maternal instinct is stimulated in these women, and perhaps in this maternal response lies the reason the patient behaves as he does.

Watching the facial expressions recently of my newborn son before his feeding, I compared what I saw with the expressions and grimaces of some of my disturbed patients. The searching eyes, the keenly drawn up nose, the sucking lips and the tense moving neck are similar. I had one patient recently who could see only a white haze before her eyes (it is thought that babies can't distinguish objects for at least three months after birth). Another patient, when brought to my office, could not control the backward movements of his head so that he was compelled to look at the ceiling and make sucking motions with his mouth and tongue.

The warm glowing relaxation that comes over the baby's face after sucking the breast reminds me of the peace and warmth that comes over the patient's face when he feels at ease after being freed of his psychosis. The rhythmic nursing of the baby and the rhythmic therapy of the schizophrenic seem to me so naturally similar in affect that I have felt for some time more thorough investigation in this area might be illuminating. I feel there is a definite relationship between the anxiety in schizophrenia and the healing ability of a normal maternal instinct.

Perhaps it is well to start with a definition of anxiety. Freud states that anxiety is an unpleasurable feeling accompanied by motor discharge along definite pathways.[3] The discharge may have physical qualities such as flight, sweating, rapid heartbeat and incontinence. The discharge also has a prototype in some previous experience. Anxiety has a function in that it arises as a response to a situation of danger. The physical components of discharge were at one time the normal, useful reaction to this situation of danger. Rank, looking for the prototype of anxiety, attributed it to the trauma of birth.[4] Freud, in reviewing Rank's work, said that it could be boiled down to a single situation, that of feeling the loss of a loved object.[5] Thus, anxiety would be a reaction to the perception of the absence of an object. In the infant, Freud says, the danger situation is an increase of tension arising from non-gratification of its needs, a situation against which the infant is powerless.[6]

In The Problem of Anxiety, Freud mentions two types of anxiety, (a) ego-anxiety; (b) id-anxiety.[7] In ego-anxiety, the unconscious thought is displaced on a psychically less painful situation and the anxiety develops in relation to the secondary situation. This occurs, for example, in phobias and ideas of reference. Id-anxiety results from an idea that is repressed, which then results in an inhibition of motor discharge with subsequent manifest anxiety.

An example of ego-anxiety would be hallucinations where the anxiety is bound to an idea; thus, patient Marion would bolt the doors at night to keep out those who would attempt to get her, fearing that somehow she would disappear were they to find her. Later, in treatment, she said that her mother was only able to show maternal feelings toward her as an infant for brief moments. After that the mother would lose interest. However, when crowds of people were present, the mother seemed stimulated to give her more love. This, in later life, was transformed into the patient's need to have crowds of people around her. Here she would feel wanted, and assured that in this setting no one would lose interest in her. Her symptomatology was similar to the ego-anxiety Freud mentions where the anxiety is related to a possibly real situation such as real people coming after her.

With id-anxiety, the primary process is repressed, but due to some failure in ego functioning the unconscious permeates the ego. This occurs usually in sexual excitation which is inhibited, frustrated or diverted because of the ego's contamination by primary process. A stoppage of normal motor activity occurs, and the energy is discharged into anxiety. At first this is somewhat free-floating, as we often observe clinically, because the idea is repressed. This symptom marked the beginning of Marion's psychosis.

She had recently married, and for three weeks enjoyed the greatest happiness that she had ever known in her life. She was relaxed and felt like a woman. However, she gradually began to lose her sexual desire. First she became cold; then she developed symptoms of impending cancer of the lung which she claimed were due to car fumes. She refused to drive the car, became quite anxious, and said she couldn't live with her husband another day. She said if she could live with her college roommates (a large group of friends), she would be all right. Her husband refused her permission to live with her girl friends, and she finally developed delusions. These were (a) that she witnessed a murder on the street late at night, (b) that several of the men involved in the murder saw a light she had turned on in her room, when she heard a shot, (c) that they would get her because she witnessed the crime. Anxiety caused sexual inhibition. Discharge of normal sexual gratification had the following meanings: (a) An unconscious desire for the father. (The reader will notice that the symptoms are of the primal scene type.) (b) Unconsciously, intercourse with the husband represented intercourse with the father, which (c) brought up a fear of the mother, fears of destruction and disappearance instigated by mother. (d) Consequent death wishes toward the mother. (e) Tremendous repression of all this material which had slipped into consciousness, which resulted in inhibition of normal sexual discharge and free-floating anxiety. This id anxiety soon became ego-type anxiety because there had to be an idea (the paranoid delusion) to which the anxiety was attached. The patient said the free anxiety was unbearable. It gave her a feeling of going mad, something over which she had no control. The symptoms of the delusion gave her intrigue, excitement, imagination and dignity.

We can see that there is basically very little difference in actual practice between these two types of anxieties. They are closely related and even interrelated. A further example: another patient saw the most frightful black monsters and fought and yelled at them, thrashing his fists violently, trying to push through walls. The patient also had hallucinations. I saw him swat at something over his shoulder, saying that someone was poking him. He would turn frightfully pale and go into a cold sweat over things the voices were saying to him. He was deathly afraid of being destroyed.

The fear is of the unknown. I mentioned before that patients need to attach the affect they feel to an idea. Sometimes the idea is plausible in reality and sometimes not, but to the person experiencing the affect the idea they attach to it is always real, because they know what they feel is real. They erroneously conclude that the idea is also real.

Marion really believed that the people would kill her. She felt the affect of impending doom (extreme anxiety), and therefore the idea of the people getting her became just as real. In treatment it would have been silly for me to say to her, "Oh, don't bolt the doors and windows. This is your imagination." This would have made her even more distrustful of me. She would have concluded that I didn't understand her and wasn't really interested in her. Instead, I gained her immediate trust by going with her to the hardware store and buying the largest bolt we could find. By acting this out, it helped her to see that I accepted her the way she was. To accept her insanity was to accept her. Insanity was a deep-rooted part of her, perhaps to her even a somatic part. She trusted me more because I understood her and this enabled her anxiety to wane.

Quite recently, a patient, after being out of his psychosis for several weeks, said that he had a metallic taste in his mouth. I asked, "Does it taste like blood?" He said, "Yes." "Whom do you want to eat?" I asked. He talked about how as a child his mother force-fed him and yet, instead of gaining weight, he became emaciated. I want to say again that to the unconscious in infancy, food and love are really inseparable qualities and feelings. In infancy, with normal maternal feeling available, the qualities of food and love are associated because the mother is able to enjoy giving part of herself for the baby to eat. If the baby has her permission to eat her, he can also eat her food. This is probably the residue of the cannibalism that still exists in the unconscious of all of us. If this quality of the maternal instinct is absent, if the mother does not feel relaxed by the baby "eating her," there will be anxiety and feeding problems.

Another expression of anxiety seems to be most common in suicidal patients. It is very tightly bound to the self. There exists a tight union between the internal superego and ego. There is a paralyzing inhibition of motor action in this type of individual. I treated a thirty-seven year old female who was only saved from suicide when an alert brother-in-law, a physician, detected poison on her lips as she lay in a coma in her bedroom. The patient still had the symptoms of depression after four months of treatment with us. When I first began treatment she had been catatonic. In conversation with this girl about her mother, sister (or any mother-type figure), there was never any outward sign or signal of anxiety. She was very deceptive, unconsciously, in masking all facial expressions, movements or gestures that would be detectable as signs of anxiety. The only way I knew of her extreme pain was to feel her hands. Her palms turned a deathly cold. She was not even aware, consciously, of being anxious. I think that in the seriously suicidal patient there exists this tight binding or smothering of the ego's ability to seek outside help in some way, through some method of communication. The instincts of self-preservation are completely inhibited by the internalized object. These patients are even unable to seek solace in hallucinations. There is no way out except in death. I won this patient through carefully attacking the internalized object and then offering her myself as a real, comforting object. She is now living a normal life. I have not been so successful with some others.

When anxiety exists there is hate, distrust, negativism and destruction. There is none of the love that is felt in contentment. The ego feels threatened and will protect itself at any cost.

The creation of a phobia and the creation of the hallucination in schizophrenia have similar value to the ego; (a) It wards off the conflict centering about the infantile object, which is more threatening than the hallucination. (b) It helps to ward off anxiety connected with the primary object.

In treatment of the psychosis the process is reversed. The anxiety is again stimulated, the bind of affect and idea in hallucination must be broken. The therapist must make the interpretations necessary to show the effects of the "bad mother introject."

Of course, even the psychotic hallucination is a much less economic and more archaic way of dealing with anxiety than is the phobia. Because of this naivete, the schizophrenic is more amenable to treatment than, say, the phobic obsessive compulsive. Psychotic pain is greater and therefore the schizophrenic's capacity for transference becomes greater. Freud says that anxiety is the reaction to a situation of danger, and that it is circumvented by the ego doing something to avoid the situation and retreat from it.[8]

One might conclude then, that symptoms are created in order to avoid the development of anxiety; but such a formulation does not go below the surface. It is more accurate to say that symptoms are created in order to avoid the danger situation of which anxiety sounds the alarm. In the cases so far considered this danger was castration or a derivative of it. Castration in schizophrenia is an oral castration. This may be true in neurosis too. I am not sure of this aspect, but I am sure of it in psychosis. The anxiety did not give the schizophrenic girl I spoke of a moment's rest; day and night she kept her constant vigil, bolting doors, locking windows and surrounding herself with hammers, knives and other weapons to protect herself, for fear that someone was going to get her and kill her. She would accept no human aid, for she thought that no one would or even could protect her. She didn't sleep for a week because of her belief that "they" would come. One might think that she feared her mother would come because the mother knew that the girl had sexual desires toward the father. I'm sure that this is true, but such interpretations would have been meaningless to the girl, Marion, in the beginning of treatment. Much preliminary work had to be done first in the oral area.

Then, in the second month of treatment she was allowed to visit her mother. She reported having awakened in the night to hear a window opening in the room where her three-year-old niece was asleep, a room that had been hers when she was about the same age. She thought someone would attack her niece. Her impulse was to run in and protect the child. Telling me these events, she burst into tears, saying that she always had the fear that her mother would forget about her and leave her. Her mother's span of attention for anyone was only a few minutes. She recalled that she would lie in her dark room, fearful that her mother would not hear her if she cried.

There is nothing in any of this which contradicts Freud's theory of sexuality. I do believe, however, that in schizophrenia the emphasis is on oral castration. The threat to the instinct of self-preservation, and fears of castration probably occur in the budding ego, most likely during the first year of life.[9] I see in my patients a great deal of oral guilt. Sucking or eating is dangerous.* One mother, whose daughter was a paranoid schizophrenic, and who was herself a social worker, told me that she felt she had smothered her child with her voluminous breasts and that she had great difficulty in relinquishing her child. This tenacity of the mother was felt by the child and she interpreted it to mean that life would stop if she loved anyone except her mother. In fact, once a patient becomes strong enough to break away from this type of mother relationship, the mother often fights with great hostility, most often subtle, but sometimes quite overt. Here the therapist must support the patient with great power to make new relationships. Success here often determines the success of the total treatment. When I first began this work, I failed with two specific patients, because, I believe, I was unable to convey to the patients that I was strong enough to help them break this hold. Frequently, I see a patient who actually waits to get mother's permission to be able to relate to me as a therapist. Freud connected the fear of castration with the fear of death. "The situation to which the ego reacts is the state of being forsaken or deserted by the protecting super-ego by the powers of destiny which put an end to security against every danger." [10] I think that the anxiety the patient feels is much more painful than neurotic anxiety because reality is much farther away.[11] The unconscious is much closer to the surface. This anxiety has its prototype in feelings actually experienced with the mother during the nursing period. An anxious mother conveys much anxiety to the child. To an ego that is weak because of inexperience in living, this actually means the state of being forsaken or deserted by the new world. In psychosis, the patient resorts to a system that excludes human contact because the patient has learned through early experiences that there is no security in human relationships—thus, the difficulty in making contact with a schizophrenic and the building of a warm relationship between patient and therapist. The patient is not helped by lying on the couch. The distance felt where the patient cannot see or feel the therapist's presence is a barrier that can never be overcome by so-called "classical" analytical means.

Perhaps the first anxiety (to which Rank gives greatest emphasis) is the trauma of birth. The child is forcibly removed from the bath of the amniotic fluid, where the environmental temperature matches his own. As a baby's sensitive skin feels the air, the experience can only force the baby to feel that he is separate from the mother. But this is nature's way. The

---

* The talionic principle of the unconscious: if I eat, I will be eaten.

feeling of being alone in a strange environment is a world that was never known before. However, frustration produces growth. The mouth, lips, tongue and stomach displace skin as the primary areas of eros. If the mother has a sensitive maternal instinct—one that responds to the baby's needs— all goes well. The pleasure at the breast is greater than the pleasure of the womb. The baby can sense by its own feelings a responsive mother. The mother whose maternal feelings are warped will leave the baby unsatisfied and in need.

When Rosen says the schizophrenic is full of transference, he means that the schizophrenic patient is seeking out that feeling of oral gratification, a feeling that was absent in his early life.[12] This present seeking is ac- companied by the anxious feelings that existed before. It is a continuous searching for something that is needed—"milk" and strength to face life. But there is also an attempt to separate, because there exists in all rela- tionships between schizophrenic patients and their parents an unholy and unhealthy bond. Bowen has shown in his family treatment of schizophrenia that a separation of the patient from this triangle of mother, father and child is a difficult one.[13] The family relationship is a dynamic inter-de- pendent one. Change results in one member exerting stress on other members. Bowen has noted severe psychosomatic disturbances in the parents, when the patient begins to improve. In therapy I have found out that the extreme anxiety that exists with all thoughts of separation, is of life and death proportions. The demands by schizophrenogenic mothers upon their infants must be extreme. In the mother's anxiety about life, she must seek comfort in the infant as her protector. This itself, if one thinks about it, is crazy. I often interpret to a patient, "Your mother wanted you to be her mother." Certainly if any therapist remembers his state hospital days, it is obvious the patient must represent some kind of totem to the family. The weekly visits are handled with ritualistic exactness. It has always reminded me of the ritualistic visits of families to the cemetery to mourn over the grave of the dead mother and father.

Patients are peculiar in their behavior. They see their struggle as one of life and death. In their anxiety, I have seen them pray to light bulbs, raise their heads to the sky and make sucking motions and search the room for hidden microphones. In the beginning, they always resent intru- sion into the magic, trance-like state that exists between mother and child. They would even commit violence to prevent such intrusion. Even though hallucinations are a poor substitute for a real mother, they are still better than the anxiety of being empty.

I have had a few patients lately who have actually waited at a certain level without further improvements. They are waiting, I thought, for the mother to relinquish her psychological hold. I mentioned this previously. This may seem somewhat different from what Freud postulated in his theories of superego and introjected object, but the situation is really the same. In deep psychosis, unlike neurosis, the failure in development may be the failure to incorporate satisfactorily. In some schizophrenic families, the archaic mechanisms of personality are prominent, and the unconscious always remains close to the surface. The regression is so marked in these families that it is still predominantly at the pre-oedipal stage. There is little advancement toward normal solving of the oedipal situation in the latency phase. In these cases, which are fairly common in my work, one cannot ignore the family in treatment, or the treatment would be unsuccessful.

Treating the Anxiety in the Psychosis

Having treated many psychoses, I have been impressed with the quick relief patients get in the severest of anxiety states, when they feel the presence of a firm, warm, understanding human being. I vividly remember the first case I treated several years ago in the state hospital. The patient was a fifteen-year-old girl whose hands and feet were strapped to the bed, and restraining sheet was fixed about her middle. I heard her cry out something uninterpretable about God and that she was blind and couldn't see. She had been confused, assaultive, and hallucinatory before her admission and had been non-communicative and unable to swallow food for about a week. All this time she was confined to the bed. First, I told her that I loved her and would protect her from harm. Second, I fed her supper. Third, I released her restraints. And last, I interpreted her blindness by telling her that she was blind because her eyes were daggers that could kill.

She talked about how she wanted to kill her foster mother, an elderly asthmatic woman who had raised her since birth, when the patient was abandoned by her natural mother. The reaction was amazing. In one hour she was communicative, she was relaxed, and she slept most of the day and all that night. All the tranquilizers were unable to accomplish in one week what was accomplished in that single hour.

This has happened to me so often since, that I would like to find out much more precisely what it is that I supply, qualitatively, to relieve the psychotic anxiety in these cases.

I would like to mention another case with whom I worked at about the same time, which reinforces the thoughts that I have had. The patient was an eleven-year-old schizophrenic boy, so regressed that he only made sucking noises with his mouth, moved his hands ineffectually, and sat on the floor and rocked back and forth all day long. He was completely incontinent. This was the most regressed case that I have ever seen.

Twenty minutes a day for six months, I held him on my lap and rocked him, trying hopefully to imitate the behavior of my wife with our infant son who was then four months of age. I was struck by the similarity in mouth, eyes, and hand movements between this boy and my infant son. I thought that both boys' needs might be similar.

There was a change to normal feelings each time after I had held him. The coldness in his hands and the paleness and lifelessness in his face turned to warmth. He would become flushed, sweaty and more alert after these periods. He would eat and voluntarily go to the bathroom. All in all, the child benefited. He became toilet-trained and began to be more sociable in games with other children on the ward. I left the hospital, however, six months after the beginning of his treatment and could find no one else who wanted to work with this boy. The last I heard was that he had gone back to his rocking again, probably to remain this way for the rest of his life.

The experiences I gathered in this case I have never forgotten. They have convinced me that I am on the right track in treating the anxiety in the psychotic.

It is imperative that we discover more accurately the necessary essentials in treating a psychosis. Perhaps a nursing mother would recognize rather quickly the qualities that are similar in treating a psychotic and treating an infant. I learned from working with the boy just mentioned that the "feeding" necessary in resolving a psychosis must be similar in quality to the mental feeding the relaxed mother gives to her newborn infant. The work of Spitz [14] supports this thesis. I asked each of my recovered patients what role I had played that enabled them to get well. Invariably they said "mother." All that can be concluded is that the mother was the instrumental agent in early life. This does not mean that the father is not involved. The father is the primary feeder. He feeds the mother who feeds the children. All too frequently in these families, the mother tells me that the father leans on her and provides no support to her. However true this may be, it is none the less the "poor mothering" that is an early influence in the psychosis. Rosen has called this lack of maternal quality perversion of the maternal instinct. [15]

In treating psychotics it is important to remember that only after your patient is comfortable will the therapist's intepretation be meaningful. This means that the ultimate effort in therapy is to relieve the anxiety. It does little good to tell a drowning man that he is drowning without first throwing him a life preserver. To treat a patient effectively, the therapist has to discard his daily hourly schedule. To make the necessary contact, the doctor has to be prepared to sacrifice his time for the patient's well-being. The patient demands that he be more important to the therapist than the analytic procedure. I have had many schizophrenic patients formerly treated by analysts who made this mistake. Perhaps many failures with neurosis are also the result of following the rules of analytic procedure too stringently.

Since 1961, in severe cases, my patients have lived with analytically-trained families. Other patients may need assistance part of the day only, and can be treated in their own homes. Here, however, caution must be used. I now have one case; a post-partum psychosis of five years duration and over one hundred shock treatments. The patient began to recover, and when she awoke from the psychosis, the husband developed a full-blown paranoid schizophrenia. Treatment had to be stopped at this point.

When the tremendous dread disappears in schizophrenia, there emerges an unbearable loneliness. I have one patient with a tenacious psychosis of twenty years duration, with which I fought continually eight hours a day for a year. The patient became non-psychotic. Then one day he looked out a window and said to me, "Al, I feel terribly lonely." He withdrew once more, soon after this, into his psychosis and has remained there since. This feeling of loneliness is uppermost in psychosis. I believe that the anxiety, hallucinations, and delusions can be viewed in part as defenses against this terrible feeling. Freud recognized this fact when he said the situation which the infant appraises as "danger" and against which it desires reassurance, is one of not being gratified; it is the dread of an increase of tension arising from the non-gratification of its needs, a situation against which it would be powerless.

Freud and Rank have suggested that probably the first anxiety-producing situation was separation of some kind, either the birth trauma or actual separation from the mother. From working with very regressed patients I am inclined to add that even the anxiety felt while being carried in the mother's womb is traumatic. Perhaps the mother's psychosomatic tensions, too, may affect the infant in utero. Certainly more investigation would be worthwhile here. But what surely can be said now is that a mother may be with an infant and not supply what is needed. This creates anxiety in the infant and lack of faith in human contact, which is clearly evident in psychosis.

Of course, I must remind the reader that I have been using the terminology of the unconscious. Some psychotics see no conscious connection between their early infancy and their symptoms. Nevertheless, the infantile mother has been incorporated as a superego, and while there are varying degrees of incorporation depending on regression, in severe regression the superego is practically all mother.

The conversion of this kind of understanding by the therapist into practical treatment for the psychotic is no mean task. It is apt to require a total commitment. Recently, while on a consultation call, a group of new internes watched me treat a suicidal patient in her hospital bed. As the patient changed, almost dramatically, from a withdrawn, suspicious, dirty annoyance to the hospital staff because of her need for constant surveillance, to a helpful, assisting, nursing aid to other patients on her ward, one of the internes drew me aside and said that I was probably a remarkable actor. I replied that perhaps an actor is good only when he lives the part.

References

[1] "Provocation and manifestations of anxiety in schizophrenia; Panel discussion." BULLETIN OF THE AMERICAN PSYCHOANALYTIC ASSOCIATION. *6(4)*: 37–42, 144–148. 1950.

[2] Honig, A. M. "Analytic treatment of schizophrenia." PSYCHOANALYTIC REVIEW. *45(3)*:51–62 (1958).

[3] Freud, S. THE PROBLEM OF ANXIETY. N.Y., Norton, 1936. p. 70.

[4] Rank, O. THE TRAUMA OF BIRTH. N.Y., Brunner, 1952, p. 11–29.

[5] Freud, S. *op. cit.* p. 75.

[6] *idem.* p. 76.

[7] *idem.* p. 41

[8] *idem.* p. 65.

[9] Spitz, R. "Anxiety in infancy: a study of its manifestations in the first year of life." INTERNATIONAL JOURNAL OF PSYCHOANALYSIS. *31*:138–145 (1950).

[10] Freud, S. *op. cit.* p. 67.

[11] Sullivan, H. S. INTERPERSONAL THEORY OF PSYCHIATRY. N.Y., Norton, 1953.

[12] Rosen, J. "Transference, a concept of its origin, its purpose and its fate." ACTA PSYCHOTHERAPEUTICA. *2*:301–314 (1954).

[13] Bowen, M. SCHIZOPHRENIA AND THE FAMILY. Philadelphia, Conference held at Temple University Medical Center on Oct. 10, 1958.

[14] Spitz, R. "Anaclitive depression." In: THE PSYCHOANALYTIC STUDY OF THE CHILD, v. 2 (1947).

[15] Rosen, J. *loc. cit.*

CHAPTER VII

Pathological Identifications*

In all living matter, the process of identification exists. This is reason enough to believe that it is a basic procedure, perhaps innate. Its origin perhaps draws from the very nature of protoplasm itself.[1] Each generation repeats its kind through identification. In lower animals it is genetic and biological. In higher animals, including man, the process is also psychological.

Many have said that man's compassion to man is therapeutic. It is only during this century (since Freud), that attempts have been made to define scientifically how this compassion operates in treatment. Identification is certainly the core of this therapeutic process.

The Normal Process of Identification in Humans

Let us first review the normal process of identification. An infant is born with needs. We call these needs instinctual and say they derive from the unconscious. The ability to meet the infant's needs we define as maternal instinct. Freud states: "In the primitive oral phase of the individuals' existence, object-cathexis ** and identification are hardly distinguishable from each other." [2] When an object is cathected, it is with the full emotional impact of the id.*** This eroticization, which is directed at first only to the breast, soon encompasses the total organism. The person cathected is of course the mother or her surrogate. Spitz, Klein, and others, have emphasized this point.[3, 4] According to Freud, before identification can take place, the libido must be desexualized by a withdrawal from the object.† It then becomes centered again on the self. Thus through

---

* Originally published in British Journal of Medical Psychology, 1962.
** Charged with psychic energy.
*** The reservoir of psychic energy residing in the unconscious.
† Freud was the first to use oral indorporation, he said the ego "devoured" the object. He says this is a primitive cannibalistic form of identification.

regression, it becomes narcissistic libido. Through introjection (reinstatement of the object within the ego) the object remains within the ego. Identification may be the sole condition on which the id can give up its objects. The result is that the ego then assumes the features of the object; and says to its erotic id, "Love me. Look! I'm just like your former love (the object)". Identification is thus an ego function, one of those ego functions that gives mastery over the id.

In healthy identifications, sublimation takes place. The ego is able to relinquish the object as an object; libido is then turned back into primary narcissism; desexualized;* and the ego becomes stronger by absorbing that part of the object's personality into its own. Freud has said it forms that part of the superego called the ego ideal.[5] I think the ego ideal probably is more than a part of the superego, probably it is a strong part of the ego itself. These might be examples of healthy identifications: the son of a doctor identified with his father and became a doctor; a daughter identified with her mother and became a mother and housewife. In normal identification, the developmental stages in order are: (1) autoerotic, (2) primary narcissism, (3) partial object identification, (4) sublimated object identification.**

Pathological Identification

In the process of pathological identification the object is still eroticized. The amount of eroticization and the number of pathological identifications determine the degree of sickness. For instance, in an hallucinating Schizophrenic there is little healthy identification formed and the object must be magically fantasied. In catatonia the lack of movement, curling up posture, and so forth are reminiscent of the womb state. In the womb, before birth, little identification has yet been made. The lack of object attachment found in catatonic states has even prevented pathological identifications from forming. The instincts are strong and growth is fixated at the autoerotic stage. It is purely instinctual and automatic, and even one's own body is not known as an object.

Pathological identifications are formed from partial object cathexis. Whenever an object is eroticized, transference exists. The amount of transference (transference is an instinct derivative) is directly proportionate to the amount of eroticization that exists and inversely proportionate to the amount of healthy sublimation that has occurred. Theoretically this is so, but clinically speaking, I must say that I have never seen a person in

---

* Desexualization—neutralization of the sexual drive so that energy which would ordinarily be expended in immediate id discharge, is held up and made available to the ego for its various tasks and wishes.
** In further thinking about theoretical stages of development, I feel it might be helpful to the reader to compare autoerotic, here, to autistic as described in the "sick symbiosis." Also primary narcissism may be likened to the symbiotic phase as described in the same section.

whom complete desexualization of the object has occurred. A healthy personality is measured by the degree of sublimation. This would explain why Rosen has said that schizophrenia is accompanied by a high degree of eroticization.[6]

Let us now theorize on what causes pathological identifications. I have have said that identification is primarily an oral procedure. Regression takes place to the oral phase. Let us use a mother as the object, since in infancy the mother or mother substitute is with the baby most of the time. The infant has instinctual needs. When the lips are eroticized and sucking motions are made, primary narcissism or the stage of eroticization of the self already exists. Sucking motions have been noted even before birth. If the object, the mother, feels the baby's instincts with her own maternal instinct, the roots and pathways for object cathexis are formed at once and early. If the mother's maternal instincts are not flowing easily, the baby will feel this. Frustration will occur and there will be withdrawal of libido * from the object. No, or little sublimation occurs. All through life, through the process of transference, this instinct will seek satisfaction. If partial object cathexis has occurred, as in pathological identification, the instincts are still not satisfied but are able to seek out new objects more easily than if no object cathexis had occurred. In more severe psychosis, complete object withdrawal occurs. The object here may be hallucinated or projected through a delusion. Thus regression had approached to almost an autoerotic stage. The body is not eroticized as in primary narcissism. Clinically this is demonstrated in severe psychosis such as the catatonic and hallucinatory states. In paranoia, depressions, hysteria, obsessive compulsive neurosis, hypochondriacal stages and anxiety reactions there is partial object cathexis and so pathological identifications are formed. Of course, clinically, one sees mostly mixtures of all these states combined. So, if the mother has her own unfulfilled needs, she is not prepared to give herself to the infant. She is hostile and frustrated. I think that the degree of these feelings in the mother will determine the severity of illness in the offspring. Ignore constitutional qualities; it is known that some infants can get more from the source of supply than others. In children who have extensive brain stem damage due to birth injury, the sucking instinct may be delayed for months, or even up to several years. These children are spoon fed and remain subhuman emotionally. Even though some human warmth may be given through the skin in hugging, kissing and cradling, they remain subhuman until sucking is pleasurable.

CLINICAL EXAMPLES OF PATHOLOGICAL IDENTIFICATION   Let us review the process of identification again in the treatment situation. In therapy, in order to guide the patient's ability to have good judgment when identifications are revealed, the therapist must have a sense of what is pathological

---

* The energy that all instincts are endowed with.

and what is normal. For instance, J.B. is a 21-year-old male, a recent Art School graduate who had recently been sworn into the army reserve. Soon after, following consultation with his general physician, I saw him in a general hospital. He was hallucinating about God and talking to images in the room. He would shout, "Mom, Mom, where are you?" His face was twisted with anxiety. He was incontinent. His pajamas and sheets were wet. I answered, "Whom are you looking for?" This made him pensive and he turned his head in my direction, obviously noticing that I was in the room. I then asked him questions, purposely to focus his attention on me as the object. "Do you feel as if you are floating? Can you feel your body? Hold my hand!" He withdrew. I asked: "Does that make you feel queer?" He answered: "Yes, I feel like a little girl. Mom, Mom, where are you? My chest is swelling. My God! I have breasts! I feel I have to do something. There is something I must do immediately but I don't know what. God if I only knew." Then turning to me: "Please, do you know?" I answered him: "Yes, you want to be a woman, a mother, and nurse your baby!" He looked at me again. Obviously the answer had penetrated. There was a long pause. Then: "God I feel lonely, empty inside." I took advantage of several things that I knew about identifications to make these interpretations. The boy had an anxious, searching face. His eyes were wandering all over the room. He was at the earliest stages of psychosis. Depersonalization and estrangement had taken place. He was beginning to hallucinate an object. He reminded me of a wet and hungry baby in his crib. His cry for mother demonstrated something Freud had said: "First identification in earliest childhood will be profound and last- ing." [7] The boy had formed partial object cathexis and was trying to rebuild from the fixation point. However, when his mother, who was there with us in the hospital, came into the room, her presence was meaningless to the boy. *He still called for his mother.* Obviously, the object he was calling was an object cathected when he was an infant. My interpretations were meaningful to him. Through these interpretations I was more closely approaching his infantile object than was his somewhat bewildered and anxious mother who was there too. I was understanding his needs. I was becoming the early object—the infantile mother. It is interesting that at this stage, I have had patients see me with large breasts. His next statement was "I feel like a girl, I have breasts." This meant to me that he was projecting his mother on to himself. This was an early identification with his mother. *Before he could form an identity as a boy or man he had to identify as a woman.* This was a partial identification and a pathological one for him. In therapy, however, I recognized it as a normal developmental stage and accepted it. Suppose I had not said, "That's silly, you aren't a girl, you're a man." The statement, although correct, would not have soothed him because it would have shown disrespect for his basic feelings. The feelings in turn, reflected his unconscious needs. One can thus see how understanding the process of identification is important in therapy. His last statement, "I feel empty inside," showed his lack of healthy identification. My answer was, "I will fill you and you will be strong like me." So, in this one hour he had progressed from beginning hallucinatory psychosis to beginning identification with me, the new object. He would have to recathect me as the object, redirect all his libido on to me throughout therapy, before he could form healthy lasting identifications by the process of sublimation.

So far I have kept away from Freud's theory of the development of the superego. This has been done in order to eliminate confusion. Freud has said that superego formation reaches its apex with the passing of the Oedipus complex. Then again, Melanie Klein says that the superego sets in as early as the second half of the first year. There is no doubt that the superego is involved in the formation of a pathological identification.

Freud has stated: "The child's ego turns away from the Oedipus complex. The authority of the father, or parent, is introjected into the ego and there forms a kernel of the superego which takes its severity from the father, perpetuates its prohibitions against itself and so insures the ego against re-occurrence of the libidinal object cathexis. Libido trends belonging to the Oedipus complex are in part desexualized, sublimated, which probably happens with every transformation into identification; in part they are inhibited in their aim and changed into affectionate feelings." [8] So in a pathological identification there still exists a large part of sexualized object libido in the ego. Along with this remains a strong inhibitive superego. The superego prevents further satisfaction of the instinct with object. If sufficient in degree this (remembering the instincts necessary for the process of identifications are pregenital and mostly oral) will inhibit further identification. The object does not become desexualized, and little further sublimation is achieved.

M.L. is a 41-year-old divorcee whose case demonstrates the formation of a pathological identification that exists alongside a sadistic superego. She has been in therapy for three years. At first, being catatonic, she was treated in a hospital. Soon, she emerged from her psychosis and was able to live alone. Living in a friendly and noisy hotel, she prefers being alone and traveling alone. She prefers meeting people superficially and attempts to make her identifications this way. She rejects her family, her brother-in-law and older sister. The girl was raised in a German family before the war. The father was a banker and the mother concerned herself with flowers and afternoon tea. The woman is obsessed with proper manners and constantly talks about being brought up as a lady. She values people on these counts alone. She does not like scientists because they have bad manners. She wants to meet a young lawyer or businessman with a Harvard education. She, thus, would be sure of his good manners and proper attentions to her. Thus the object, her mother image, still is cathected, but in a degree to inhibit her movements and preoccupy her thoughts. A strong superego, in turn, punishes her, by not letting her vary from the internalized identification.

The strongest resistance to cure is the transference. Many people in therapy, almost consciously, it seems, will not give the therapist up as an object. The female patient will try to get the therapist into a genital relationship. The male patient will try to keep the therapist in a latent and ineffectual passive homosexual relationship. There seems to be no interest in the therapy, but only in the therapist. If it could be remembered that identification is essentially an oral, and certainly a pregenital process, the therapist must concentrate on ways to fulfill these pregenital needs without making the patient feel guilty about her genital feelings. The patient's seductive and sometimes amorous flattery is often hard to resist, as all beginning therapists know.

The following cases demonstrate pathological identifications with the infantile mother image as the object:

(a) J.D., a 17-year-old high school graduate, listened on television to news about the Berlin crisis and felt that President Kennedy wanted him to go to the White House to join his "unofficial family" of advisors. The boy was familiar with psychoanalytic concepts and offered his own interpretations. His reasoning was that Kennedy was the father of our country and that he wanted to be near his father figure. I was not satisfied with this explanation and I offered my own. I said, "You wanted to go to the White House because it offers the finest grade A milk." He grasped my equation of White House and white milk and became extremely anxious, fuming. "You think you know it all! You think that I'm looking for a mother." It was obvious that my interpretation had touched upon something basic. He was trying to ignore memory traces of a pathological identification of earlier life.

(b) Another patient, K.W., age 47, confided some of his thoughts: "I was thinking of a cow's udder in my rectum." In free association he continued: "I think I have tits . . . I think my wife isn't a good enough mother to my kids." On another day he said, in free association, "I want to suck your penis . . . I have a thought of my mother . . . I want to suck her tits; I see them with sugar . . . I was at a party last night . . . I thought of sucking other women's tits at the party—then I thought I had tits . . . I had a feeling I was losing my manhood." I answered, "It's obvious that you want to be a woman, a mother." I then said: "Before a man becomes a man, he has to be a woman."

(c) B.L. is a 24-year-old weight lifter. Almost all his thoughts are of his body. His desire is to be Mr. America. His weight-lifting occupies all of his energies. He is unable to seek gainful employment. His wishes are to win a Mr. America contest, then open his own gym. His mother once won a beauty contest when she was young. He has voluntarily shown me a picture of her taken at the time of the contest. In one session he said: "I visualize myself in intercourse, my stomach is out and it looks like a vagina. I can't get the feeling of a cock and balls below." At this time he was obsessed with the thought about his stomach muscles. He became depressed and said it was all to no avail. But, compared to my own, his stomach was very flat.

(d) D.M. was a 50-year-old pants presser who was having psychosomatic symptoms. "I have a kicking-like feeling in my abdomen." He was the only offspring so I asked if his mother had ever given birth and then lost the baby when he was a child. He could not remember but when he went home and asked his wife, she told him that his mother had lost a baby girl when he was three.

(e) E.W. was a 35-year-old auto mechanic. He remebered making mud breasts as a child. His associations follow: "My grandmother bumped her breast and developed cancer of the breast. My mother spent all her time with my grandmother and not us kids. Maybe this is why I have this chest pain."

(f) A.M. is a 19-year-old single female who has a delusion that she "lays air." She says it has come out of her rectum continuously since she was in the fifth grade. People avoid her because of the odor. On street cars and in public places she hears people whispering about her. There is no pleasure in life for her—but she cannot change. This is the punishment she must endure for committing her sin. She constantly clings to her mother, she goes everywhere with her, although there is very little other communication between mother and daughter. The mother is concerned with A.M., and although the father has been dead three years, and the mother is still relatively attractive, she cannot go out with men because of this great concern for her daughter. The mother is depressed, feels unworthy, and is greatly obsessed with cleanliness and odors about her own person. She, however, denies any responsibility for the daughter's condition and says that she loves her daughter and has told her so. One can see how the mother's unconscious feeling of unworthiness about herself has influenced A.M. The result is a feeling in A.M., that (1) Mother says she loves me and so she must; but (2) I feel a lack of something, a feeling of being unloved. (3) If mother loves me, it must be my fault if I feel this way. (4) It must be because I smell, that people react to me the way they do, and why I feel the way I do. Mother's concern with odors and smells has led to the formation of a pathological identification in A.M. with her mother.

(g) Another patient, B.W., age 32, married, had one child of seven and an adopted girl of five. The patient was suicidally depressed. She felt that she was "rotten inside"; she had had surgery seven times, including a hysterectomy at the age of 24. She was the last of five children and was born when her mother was 44 years of age. She had eczema since she was three months of age. Her earliest memory was of her mother saying: "I wish and pray that God may take you if this horrible rash doesn't leave." This was after one of her frequent journeys to one of many hospitals to have her eczema treated. In seven months of her previous analysis she had seven hospital admissions. The first three were for abdominal pain, nausea and dehydration, which her surgeon diagnosed as further adhesion formation. She had her first abdominal attack after the disappearance of her eczema at the age of 14. The analysis revealed that the surgical operations were a device by which she tried to remove the rottenness from her body. Gynecological examination revealed that she suffered from endometriosis. However, both before and after surgery, the pain was referred up under the costal arch in the gastroduodenal area. Somehow the feeling of being rotten was an oral incorporation and identification. She describes her mother as having been an excitable person who was of little help when she, while growing up, had need of a mother. Whenever she had a problem, instead of getting from her mother what she needed, she would end up consoling and comforting her mother lest the mother collapse. She recalls that only in hospitals and with doctors did she know a feeling of safety. It is interesting that she trained as an X-ray technician, worked in a hospital and when she married she persuaded her husband to go to medical school. The mother was weak and ambivalent. Her low self esteem was conveyed to her daughter at an early age, as if it came from the milk itself. Rotten milk produces rotten insides.

The next example shows how a pathological identification caused a loss of reality that almost ended in death.

(h) L.L. is a 40-year-old housewife, who one day told her daughter to put a plastic bag over her head. The 11-year-old child became frightened and the woman was admitted to a general hospital where I saw her in consultation. She was calling her mother and crying and was obviously in extreme anxiety. She thought she heard her mother calling her and telling her to join her. The only difficulty was that her mother had been dead nine years. She told me she had been lonely and empty. Her husband was an alcoholic. She had had an affair with a 30-year-old bachelor but her guilt feelings prevented her from continuing. Several visits later, when she was feeling better, she said she felt she had been reborn and that I was her new life.

(i) Women frequently identify with their fathers in a masculine way. This may be a very early identification, and may only be with an organ. Thus it is a partial object identification, which is pathological. Thus V.O., age 21, thought she had a large nose. She would get bursting headaches in which she felt that her eyes were popping out and her nose was swelling larger. Only a nose bleed relieved the pressure. The nose symbolized the penis in erection.

Summary

I have mentioned that in therapy it is necessary to distinguish a budding healthy identification from a fixed pathological identification. Actually both are partial object cathexes. However, the budding identification is flexible and will grow into a healthy identification while the pathological identification (unless worked with vigorously) will remain fixed.

In the process of growing up, object relationships may be treated in different ways. This way well serve as stages of growth of budding identifications. Melanie Klein has outlined this clearly. Abraham has also written on this subject.[9] Klein writes: "The nature of a child's object relations and character formations is very strongly determined by whether its predominate fixations are situated in the oral sucking or oral sadistic period. The introjection of a kindly mother leads to setting up a friendly father image, owing to the equation of breasts with penis. In the construction of the superego, too, fixations in the oral sucking stage will counteract the terrifying identifications which are made under the supremacy of oral sadistic impulses." [10]

In the relationship to objects, one may: (a) withdraw from the object and hallucinate it. This happens in severe psychosis. (b) Turn toward it with greater positive feeling. The mother image is split into good and bad objects. The mechanism of projection is used to accomplish this. Usually the bad object is projected on to the real world. This is a further step in object relationships. This occurs in paranoia. (c) Be abstracted, treated and controlled; as in obsessive compulsive neuroses. (d) Be railed against, depreciated, made to suffer with sadistic verifications derived from its suffering—as in depressions. (e) As the individual approaches the genital stage, he employs restitutive mechanisms and reaction formations of pity for the objects. This is accomplished only when the ego feels strong enough and secure in dealing with the object. In the therapy of psychosis we may see all stages develop, in the above order, with the therapist as the object.

In direct therapeutic intervention, or confrontation, several new rules are introduced to aid healthy identification formation. The therapist, unlike the classical psychoanalyst, offers himself as an object of identification deliberately. He does this by injecting his opinions and value judgments. The psychotic, as mentioned previously, is void of object cathexis, proportionate to the degree of sickness. First the therapist concentrates on the removal of the psychotic defenses ("the hallucinatory object cathexis").

The patient shows, by various signs, that the treatment is successful and that the therapist is being incorporated inside the patient's own body. The patient may vomit. I always interpret this as an ejection of the bad object. Symptoms subside. The anxiety lessens. The patient, who before felt depersonalized and had delusions of the end of the world, may say, "I feel reborn." Probably even before this he admits to feelings of emptiness and loneliness. If you ask him how he feels at this stage, he usually says, "sort of like standing still, I am waiting, I enjoy my visits with you—afterwards I feel better." This is ideal for therapy. The therapist is like the mother; his very presence represents oral gratification to the patient; incorporation and basic identification processes are at work. When the patient has had sufficient oral gratification to stop the hallucinations, his symptoms become anal in character. Then therapy is more classical in approach. Progress is slow. The work is tedious. Through the transference, old pathological identifications arise. The patient continually seeks out old object memories from the past unconsciously. He attempts to make the therapist act like his old objects. This must be pointed out to the patient. At this stage the patient may be working and living almost a normal life. Other people in reality have become objects of identification, where previously it had been the therapist and his assistants. Office visits may be regulated just to periods of anxiety "built up," or may be on a regular basis. I use both methods, depending on what the patient needs. But I do insist on follow-up treatment. If the patient is able to confide his pathological thoughts, in due time, with conscious effort, the patient may overcome his pathological identifications. The repetition compulsion makes progress tedious and it takes time for new identifications to form. It is most important in many cases to win over the mother (original object cathexis). If this can be done, therapy that might have failed, may have a satisfactory outcome. In normal growth of the ego (as in the growing child) partial object cathexes are continually being made. In the therapeutic process this occurs too. If therapy is discontinued, fixation will occur with the therapist as the object and a pathological identification may be formed. Time and frequent contact with the object are important for the formation of healthy identifications. When healthy identifications have been made with the therapist, the bond between therapist and patient becomes everlasting.

References

[1] Tinbergen, L., THE STUDY OF INSTINCT. London, Oxford, 1951.

[2] Freud, S. THE EGO AND THE ID. London, Hogarth, 1950. p. 40.

[3] Spitz, R. "Anxiety in infancy." INTERNATIONAL JOURNAL OF PSYCHO-ANALYSIS. *31*:138 (1950).

[4] Klein, M. THE PSYCHOANALYSIS OF CHILDREN. London, Hogarth, 1954.

[5] Freud, S. "The passing of the Oedipus complex." In his: COLLECTED PAPERS. London, Hogarth, 1953. v. 2.

[6] Rosen, J. "Tranference, a concept of its origin, its purpose and its fate. ACTA PSYCHOTHERAPEUTICA. *2*:301–314 (1954).

[7] Freud, S. "A case of paranoia." In his: COLLECTED PAPERS. London, Hogarth, 1953. v. 3, p. 300.

[8] Freud, S. "The passing . . ." *loc. cit.*

[9] Abraham, K. A SHORT STUDY OF THE DEVELOPMENT OF THE LIBIDO. London, Hogarth, 1947.

[10] Klein, M. *op. cit.*

CHAPTER VIII

Negative Transference in Psychosis *

A. A Fight with the Patient

It's a common expression among people to say "it's better to be hated than ignored." Another way it is said is "you know, love and hate are very close."

This chapter is a collection of negative experiences, confrontation with patients and exchanges, case histories and some whys and wherefores. I have always enjoyed the emotional exchange because it is human, alive and even thrilling. Sadly I must admit I have not always won—but I prefer to have the cards stacked . . . let's face it, in the long run, the patient and I are on the same side—fighting the same thing. If I win, he wins.

When dealing with patient's negative transference, the patient will naturally counter with aggression. Any change in behavior will be resisted at first. So, within this chapter there is a description of the fight with the patient. Once again direct encounter of the psychotic dream world is being emphasized, as it is repeatedly throughout the book. I know of no better way to present its method than by viewing it at various angles, in different practical situations. Perhaps this seems repetitious. This is done with purpose. It is hoped that each practitioner of the art of therapy may pick up something adaptable and usable to his own personality. Once the basic theory is understood, the application must vary with each individual therapist. Some may be more forceful, others more seductive. Each may produce good results.

One observer has stated that the literature does not clearly define transference—that there is no negative or positive—just transference. To this

* Originally published in Psychoanalysis and the Psychoanalytic Review, Vol. 47, #4, Winter 1960–61.

observer a patient expressing negative feelings is still expressing a need; like an angry baby who, not getting his way or for other reasons, refuses to comply with his mother's wishes.[1]

Regression or infantile-like behavior is observed in all psychoses. Symptoms of this phenomenon may include increased movements, dryness and tension around the mouth and a helpless dependent state in the patient—whether he realizes it or not.

The stronger a fixation, the easier will this regression be. Freud, to explain the theory of fixation, used the analogy of an advancing army in enemy territory leaving occupation troops at important points.[2] The stronger the occupation troops, the weaker the army marching on. The latter may meet an over-powerful enemy force—and retreat to those points where the strongest occupation troops were left. These points are the points of fixation. But in psychosis the old points of fixation no longer offer security; and in an attempt to re-locate this security regression may simulate the earliest infantile-like mannerisms.

In most cases it takes a "giant step" to precipitate maturity. In this step a person, experiencing emotions of aggressiveness or love for the first time, desires to have these feelings continue. This desire, coupled with the patient's basic unreadiness to achieve his desire, causes his regression. The giant step never occurred.

As I see it, this regression may be a natural phenomenon of the mind—a second chance, a rebirth. It may have a basic purpose, i.e., re-nourishment or retreat for strength. However, purposeless side reactions interfere because, as magnificent as is the human mechanism, it is also full of wasteful maneuvers and inefficiencies.

Negative transference must emerge in open battle between the therapist and patient. Without this there is always the danger of re-regression. Since negative transference is the knife that severs the umbilical cord, the negative remarks must constitute explosive emotion directed at the therapist himself. But this is only possible when the therapist has deep meaning to the patient. The atmosphere must be so highly charged it may take on life and death proportions. It is conceivable that the patient may feel it necessary to kill the therapist in order to live himself. Recognizing this danger, and in order to remove such thoughts from his patient's head, a therapist may well consider somatic treatment like electric shock. Or he may think of transferring the patient to a locked-ward institution far from the scene of his practice.

It is known that Schreber * made many accusations against Flechsig, his physician—from committing "soul murder" to throwing Schreber to

---

* Schreber was the famous judge and legal professor—a prominent fixture in the pre-Freudian Vienna. He suffered a paranoid episode and was treated by Professor Flechsig. The treatment did not end on a friendly note. Freud used the case to define and illustrate his views on paranoia.

attendants for sexual abuse.[3] Finally, leaving Flechsig's sanitarium, he sought another physician. He recovered from his illness and "spent eight years with my wife—years upon the whole of great happiness."

During those eight years I am sure that Schreber had feelings of admiration for his former physician because he freed himself and was able to make an independent and complete life. However if his feelings of dependency and inadequacy remained, it can be assumed he felt bitterness toward Flechsig all the rest of his days. In other words, he would never have resolved his negative transference.

This negative involvement is unlike the vague, hallucinatory psychosis where a paranoid persecutory delusion complex exists. In this, the person is extremely circumstantial and uninvolved in the therapeutic relationship. As such, he cannot be pinned down to facts. Some therapists, in working with this negativism, go to great pains to have the patients include them in their hallucinations and delusions—despite the dangers (participation in the psychosis).[4] In some ways my technique looks similar, though experience has taught me that patients continue to see the therapist as benevolent and loving so long as their need for support continues. Their passivity may go on even in the face of violent attacks on the psychotic system. But their negative feelings at this time remain hidden.

The negative involvement in negative transference is directed toward one person—the therapist. It is the patient's desire to hurt and destroy as he feels the therapist has done to him. At first there may be test remarks about the dirty floor, the patient may say "I hear your kids are the most ill-behaved in the neighborhood." Finally the patient, with fear and trepidation, lets the full volley of the storm emerge . . .

These negative outbursts can be quite alarming to the beginning therapist —especially if he has expended his own "blood and guts" in the patient's behalf. But it is just this dependency that the patient cannot tolerate and from which he is trying to free himself.

Therapists I have supervised during this part of therapy have exhibited extreme anxiety, anger, bewilderment or feelings of having been "conned" —that is, unappreciated. I have told these therapists to stay with their patients. The patient is not to be abandoned. Where one might easily be vindictive, one should remain calm and listen to the barrage, remaining uninvolved. Interpretations, common sense, and reason are the patient's greatest needs.

I have been called everything: a cheat, a Communist, a Nazi, anti-Catholic, anti-Semitic, a Kike, money-hungry, cold-blooded, a whore-master, not being a doctor, unethical, crazy, a killer, a bastard, a persecutor, a lecher and a jailor.

In desperation, I have searched in the literature for a way of handling an emotional charged negative situation. Such a search has been fruitless, Freud himself has stated "where the capacity to transfer feeling has come to be of an essentially negative order, as with paranoids, the possibility of influence and cure ceases." [5]

But my experience does not agree with this statement. If negative transference is essential to sever the umbilical cord, it must have the opportunity to express itself. It is best that this expression be verbal so that the patient will have the opportunity to change his ideas. To deter a patient from any physical aggression toward me in the heat of his negative outbursts, I always have present a male assistant, perhaps two. This action forces a verbal response from the patient.

Some of my earlier cases, because of mismanagement of negative transference, did not conclude successfully. There were varying circumstances; perhaps the main reason was my need to "shield" the sick member from his "destructive family." This action only antagonized the family. Since they felt I did not understand the problem, they would remove the patient from treatment.

Wanting to be all and everything to a patient, was indeed, expecting too much of myself. I usually refused parents visitation rights when the patient was in the throes of negative transference because I felt they would not understand the situation and would side with the patient against therapy. A therapist in 2,000 years of treatment cannot replace a patient's parents. He can only hope to replace their deficiencies. Most families want to be part of the treatment and I have found it best to let them.*

S.L. was a 32 year old unmarried male, a college graduate, and the son of an upstate department store owner. My assistants and I brought him to our unit from a reputable mental institution in the city. While in college the patient had interpersonal difficulties and his advisor recommended outpatient therapy. After six years of orthodox psychoanalysis, he began, in his seventh year, to have thoughts that he and his therapist were special agents for the state of Israel. He became extremely upset, couldn't sleep and began to telephone the analyst constantly. The analyst gave up the case; the patient was hospitalized under the care of another physician. Apparently his feelings continued and he was transferred to another institution and subjected to sixy hours of insulin coma.

Two years later he came under my care. At this time I would hire psychologists as assistants and rented houses in the country. Still hallucinating occasionally, he had gained over 100 lbs. since his insulin treatment.

Under treatment for five months, he lost eight pounds and seemed asymptomatic. He enrolled in school and began a Master's program in Education. He averaged B grades the first semester. After the start of the second semester, however, he told me the professor was teaching "Americanism"; and he couldn't tolerate it. He felt that the professor was trying to influence his mind with ideas that wouldn't fit with his ideas of world union.

---

* At the D.V.M.H.F. parents are included only with the consent of, and only at the time the therapist considers it to be therapeutic. There is no weekly "Sunday visit."

He became more anxious, and accused me of giving him nightmarish ideas. He talked aloud to his only refuge—a kitchen light bulb—and called me a queer, a Jew-Kike and a homosexual. If it took him fifty years, he said, he would get even with me. He walked all night making speeches; he was Attila the Hun, his mother had seduced him and cut off his penis. He eventually accused me of forcing him to become a teacher. What he really wanted to do, he said, was go to Israel and join the Israeli army.

This fragment demonstrates a patient in the throes of negative transference. Some might say it represents a re-occurrence of the original transference psychosis he had during the therapy with his first psychiatrist.*

The transference psychosis, with its essentially negative features, represented a wedge between the patient's desires to identify with me, his therapist, which eventually could result in real independence, and his fears of being destroyed if he "gave in." He expressed his struggle by wanting to discontinue his studies (he claimed this was my wish—not his), and go to Israel to start a new life.

It would have been extremely naive of me to give in to the patient's vague and erratic wish for independence. Although I respected his need to "be on his own" I saw how disorganized his thoughts were, and how filled he was with feelings of fear, anxiety and trepidation.

Unfortunately I did not get the opportunity to finish this case. The father, in great despair, broke into my unit one night and forcibly removed the boy to a state hospital. The father said at one point he was afraid his son would kill him; at another, he said the boy was getting worse and would eventually drain all his money. The father's action was accompanied by great anxiety on his part, and I had no opportunity for explanations. Perhaps, since it was the beginning of my practice, the parents sensed my uncertainties. Today, families seem to sense my greater patience and knowledge, and will often back me up.

The following case demonstrates negative transference in the form of hostile remarks toward the therapist. Diagnosed as paranoid schizophrenic —hallucinatory type—the patient had had previous hospitalization in a state institution, treatment with medication, and seeming remission.

Edgar C., a 23-year-old ex-sailor, had been in treatment with me for eight months while living at home with his parents. The following events came after a call from Edgar's mother asking me to tell his father (who had accompanied the boy to the office) to spend more time with the boy.

Background: Edgar, one night, got extremely frightened at home. He ran down to the Naval Air Base—leaped over the high barbed wire fence

---

* Transference psychosis may be considered similar to the transference neurosis observed by Freud, S, in "The Dynamics of the Transference" collected Papers, Vol. II, Hogarth Press, 1963. By "establishment of a transference neurosis" Freud meant that the repressed infantile instinctual conflicts find their representation in the relations toward the analyst. Therefore they do not need any other expression or at least do not need as many other expressions as before. The doctor is looked upon as a reincarnation of the parents and as such may provide love and protection or the opposite—threatening with punishment.

muttering his need for protection from "outside forces." The Navy called me in the middle of the night. Since we had no unit available we had to place him in a local hospital.

Home one week from the hospital, the patient defiantly entered my office, left the door open and cockily took a seat. His negative feelings were so obvious and theatening I felt he might cause me bodily harm. A male family therapist and another patient were present.

Therapist: Close the door.
Patient: No.
Therapist: You want it open?
Patient: (Defiantly) yeah.
Therapist: You want to start a fight?
Patient: Yeah, why?—You got these two guys here for, anyway?
Therapist: Why do I have them here? They were involved in your case before.
Patient: When?
Therapist: When you were in the hospital—if you don't mind.
Patient: I do mind.
Therapist: Bother you?
Patient: Yeah.
Therapist: You want to talk alone?
Patient: Yeah.
Therapist: O.K. guys (beckons to assistants to leave).
Patient: (Patient begins threatening remarks) I think you're treating my case by hypnosis.
Therapist: I'm going to bring them back.
Patient: No, I'm getting fed up with this shit.
Therapist: R. and M., come back (assistants return to room. Therapist is taking no chances with patient's aggressions).
Patient: What for?
Therapist: If you're going to talk crazy, I'm going to bring them back —I don't trust you.
Patient: I don't trust you either.
Therapist: One minute I think you're coming out of it, another minute you're in it— you want to fight?
Patient: I don't want to fight—just telling you what's on my mind.
Therapist: Guys (talking to others present) one minute he's normal, now he's on "hypnosis." He might start poking me again.
Patient: I never did that.
Therapist: Oh, yeah—the other day you were tapping me on the head. Now what's on your mind?
Patient: Nothing much, I'm just tired of coming here, sick and tired. I think you're taking my dad's money.

Therapist: And doing what—getting fat on it?
Patient: That's what it looks like to me.
Therapist: You're still hearing voices.
Patient: Yeah, I'm hearing voices. I'm sick and tired of it. You're treating me by hypnosis and you know it.
Therapist: You're still crazy. You conned me into getting you out of the hospital.
Patient: I never shoulda been in there.
Therapist: What are you hearing now?
Patient: Pretty damn bad whenever I go someplace *I hear your voice.* (transference psychosis)
Therapist: You hear my voice wherever you go? You mean on the water skis you hear my voice?
Patient: On radio, television, every damn place.
Therapist: What am I saying to you?
Patient: You're controlling me through hypnosis—so what's the difference.
Therapist: (raised voice) What am I saying?
Patient: You're asking me to do things, too.
Therapist: What do I want you to do?
Patient: I don't know. I wish you'd tell me to my face what you're doing.
Therapist: Don't you know what psychiatry is?
Patient: Yeah, that's your field—so why don't you treat me like any other person. How am I gonna get well when I wasn't even sick? (arrogant denial of illness)
Therapist: I'm going to treat you on the couch today. You want to be a neurotic—so I'll treat you like one. You ready to analyze?
Patient: I don't know what you mean—analyze.
Therapist: Lie on your back and say what comes to your mind.
Patient: I'll sit up. I ain't gonna lie down.
Therapist: Can you analyze sitting up?
Patient: I don't care what you call it. I'm sick and tired of this shit. (pause) What do you call analyze?
Therapist: Say what comes to your mind.
Patient: *I'd like* to do it.
Therapist: Can you?
Patient: I'm trying the best way I know how. If I lay down I'll go to sleep.
Therapist: O.K. sit up—say what comes to your mind.
Patient: O.K. I think someone is paying you off. Some broads used me, hypnotized me, running my life. I'm pissed off but I don't get mad anymore. I know hypnosis is being used. I don't care for it!

Therapist: Go ahead.

Patient: You control me—all over—wherever I go. My father and brother-in-law are talking with their hands. They never did it before. At Atlantic City, people making motions at me, I think someone's doing it. Shit like that going through my mind. I was the cause of all the Selma shit! (Selma, Alabama riots) You have people doing this. Maybe you're trying to drive it out of me this way. A guy sitting outside my house all hours with a dump truck last night. I got up for no reason at all. I think you said—no, I know you said, "I'm gonna make you eat your words." If you gotta do it through hypnosis, it's pretty bad. I didn't have thoughts like that—only since I came here. If you can't come right out and say it—yeah, I got a funny feeling in my head and I resent it. I think you're making a few bucks out of this by writing it up. (Patient knew I was taping the session.)

Therapist: You mean for a medical magazine.

Patient: Yeah, you've kept me in the dark about the whole thing. Just like last night I came from Jersey, Oh, God, this shit is driving me crazy. I don't know if people can communicate with my mind—I'll be goddam if it's possible. It's terrible! There were people on the steps—I was trying to figure whether they knew what I was thinking—I know, you think I got a guilt complex. You must have one, the way you jump around and mouth off. You know all this shit going through my mind—happening without my knowledge. I don't know any more. I want to ask you something. Suppose this was all possible—if someone could take advantage of people's minds—what would you think? You know, lots of things did happen to me—everything—since I went to school, parents said I was going to have a college education. Even when I took a shower, I hate the smell of sweat. I used to go home to take a shower.

Therapist: I knew a doctor who had to go miles and miles to his own toilet.

Patient: I had a habit going to a bar. Sat near a mirror—I hate people getting up behind me. Even when I went sledding I felt self-conscious if girls laid on top of me—maybe had something to do with sex; when I was younger I had a fat ass—I still do.

ONE WEEK LATER

Therapist: It's hot today.

Patient: I still get these ideas in my head. Somebody putting these ideas in my head. I want to know what's bothering me.

Therapist: It's projection—you can't stand the idea that these are your own thoughts. You can't accept facts; your folks put one over on you—you're upset.

Patient: I think you're upset—you might as well put a fuckin' mustard plaster around your head—as soon as you open your mouth you're fucking yourself. I hate to see someone taking advantage of someone else. I know it doesn't sound like reality but something is going on. Even priests and nuns tried to help me—everyone. I didn't know—lots of people I knew and met. A lot of ideas are coming into my head. It's like you said. I was ignorant. You're making an ass of yourself. You're trying to project yourself through me.

Therapist: You're not talking sense. Why are you telling me nonsense?

Patient: I ain't—I'm just telling you what's on my mind. I could go back to a wedding reception as a kid—6th or 7th grade—they were all shooting crap—I didn't know what was going on. Oh, another thing—I won't go any place with anyone. I don't like people takin' advantage of me.

The patient's utterances became increasingly hostile, then humorously hostile, then teasing as from a younger to an older man. Finally when another patient, an ex-Marine of similar background, sat in on his sessions, he seemed to feel more understood and eventually quieted down.

Severing the umbilical cord never happens in one clean sweep. Like chopping at a tree, the patient, with each new surge of strength, risks the nourishing and protective relationship with the therapist and hacks away. Success makes him bolder. At first he may have spoken of himself as "you" or "we"—now he uses "I". When the crushing effects of the severe superego or conscience are removed and the patient is getting "filled up", it is then he rebels. But this rebellion is always against those who have freed him. This is the hardest fact of all to understand.

Melanie Klein sees an infant's gratification and love directed toward the good breast. She says that destructive impulses and feelings of persecution and frustration are expressions toward the bad breast.[6]

Anna Freud says that negative feelings result when a patient has feelings of being engulfed or invaded by the analyst.[7] I have found this to be true. All psychotic patients who recovered and remained independently well were able to fight openly with me. By doing this, they were able to see (a) they would not be destroyed if they disagreed, and (b) their destructive impulses were not so dangerous as they first believed. Feeling and controlling the full measure of their anger, they were able to realize their relationship with me was symbolic. Since I had been in their life a relatively short while, they were able to see that I could not have been guilty of all their accusations.

Perhaps the theoretical aspects of negative transference can be expressed in a simple formula. This formula is: Negative Transference (N.T.) times Energy (E) = Self (S).

Unconscious *energy,* bound up due to fears of castration or annihilation, when activated through the expression of *negative transference* will always eventuate in a stronger *self* (ego).

The following clinical examples illustrate how the energy made available in explosive negative transference becomes available for greater ego growth.

One paranoid schizophrenic girl in this stage of treatment said "Your direct approach was wonderful when I needed pasting together. Now that I am an integrated person you are trying to suffocate me again." *

In more anger, she said, "You are a quack. I am going to a classical analyst." Newly married, she lived in a midwestern city with her husband who was a university professor. Three months elapsed. Since she was over the acute psychotic reaction and seemed very happy with her husband, I thought she could be transferred to another analyst. This man was supposed to be well versed in the treatment of psychosis. Now, however, I would have had her remain to continue treatment with me. She was ambivalent. As much as she loved her husband after a session and wanted to see him, she would criticize him. It is now obvious to me that she was still under the domination of the "bad breast" and not independent. In my early days of practice I was impressed with my ability to remove psychotic symptoms quickly. I have since learned that there is much work to be done if the patient is to be independently well.

To make matters worse, the analyst to whom I sent this girl sympathized with her negative feelings. To him it became a test between his indirect approach and my direct approach and the relative merits of each.

This patient stayed well for almost two years. Since she was a psychologist, she assumed a responsible position in a child clinic. However, her negative feelings were never adequately worked through. Once, on a visit East, she came to me. "After I see you, I am good for several days," she said. "Then when I realize I have to live my own life, I get aggressive and masculine."

Though extremely ambivalent toward me, she was under another therapist's care and I didn't want to interfere. She soon became psychotic and her family called me. Unfortunately, I was recovering from emergency surgery after an attack of appendicitis and had to transfer her case to a colleague. Six years have gone by; she has had two other therapists, has divorced her husband and is still psychotic.

B.T., a 34-year-old divorcee, was in a catatonic stupor when she first came to me. She had many electric shock treatments and over three years of hospitalization. One and a half years of treatment went by—the first eight months in a home-like environment. For the next six months she had a room in a local hotel, and was relatively independent. I saw her three times a week. However, in every session she was extremely angry and would complain about having been in the hands of psychiatrists. She seemed to make acquaintances easily—although deep friendships eluded

---

* I searched my mind to see whether I was unconsciously doing this. I come to the conclusion that I was not and hers was a transference reaction.

her. She was extremely surly toward older women and me. Perhaps she was unconsciously acting out her negative transference toward mother objects. When asked why she was so hostile toward me she answered, "I have to protect myself."

Her surliness continued for over two months. Then I brought her into contact with a third person—a young woman assistant who had recently given birth. The patient's hostility began to diminish. This assistant took the girl to her home; they spoke about babies and feminine things. The girl had found someone, a friend with whom she could identify. A "good breast" had come into her life with the kind of "milk" that was needed to help her achieve real social independence. I was no longer wholly "bad breast." I steered away from remarks that might once again provoke a "bad breast" reaction. However, it is true that, with some patients, deliberately acting as a "bad breast" enables them to achieve insight into their problems. But with this girl it wasn't the solution. She seemed too angry. She would allow me to see very little of her improvement—or even her better side. It was from others that I discovered she was working, taking evening courses and making rapid social improvement. She confessed to others she felt like Sleeping Beauty waking from a dream. To me, she remained sneeringly caustic.

A transference relationship is child-like. The therapist's relationship with a psychotic must be as playfully real as with children, and as symbolic as the classical transference relationship with neurotics. But when it assumes an essentially negative characteristic, the patient will condemn everything once thought accepted—from the doctor's unkept promises to broken appointments to off-color remarks. These things which are not taken too seriously by the therapist, are taken as absolute hurts by the patient. He is like a child and the therapist is his mother.

During the heat of the transference reaction the patient will not listen to interpretations concerning infantile relationships. It never fails to amaze me how, early in treatment and while the patient is more psychotic, direct interpretations seem to sink in. But perhaps half of this is due to his hunger for a good human relationship. If the therapy supplies this healthy interpersonal relationship, the patient readily accepts the interpretations.

At the negative stage, however, the patient is no longer interested in fighting with his own mother—who has long since ceased to be a challenge. In fact, there is little emotional involvement with anyone except the therapist. The patient's whole world centers around the therapy and the therapist. And it is an angry world! After coming many miles to see his physician, a patient may deliver a blistering attack. The more raw anger there is, the less coherent is the reasoning. With a great deal of hurt, there is an aura of great revenge. I can ask a patient "Why are you so angry at me?" "I have been in your life a very short while." Or I can say, "Look, I didn't hurt you. Why don't you hurt those who have?" But these phrases remain meaningless and the fight with the therapist continues—perhaps because the patient is less afraid of the therapist than he is of his own family members.

The therapist owes it to his patient to see the relationship through once the negative transference has ceased to be dormant. If he does not the patient will remain weak. Re-regression can occur. More often, there is angry negativism. It is transference and will come out with someone else if the therapy ends. Introduction of a third person may be of help—this other relationship becomes the nourishing buffer. With anger and resentment toward the bad mother come good feelings toward the good mother. One cannot live forever on hate, anger and revenge. The rage can be so great as to blind the patient and make him useless and out of touch with reality. He must be guided and protected.

If there has been psychosis, huge gaps will show in the personality of the patient. The energy most people consume in external social relationships is used by psychotics for inner defense.* But when the psychotic superego structure no longer exists, the mind is like a child's mind—open and impressionable with fewer restrictions and fixations. In many ways, the patient has been reborn. He has a second chance to learn about life—this time in a more permissive environment.

The techniques of therapy in this re-education period vary with types of behavior. In normal adolescence there is also rebirth—a breaking away from the old and an adaptation of the new. Thus, many of the treatment methods are similar to treatment of adolescents.

In our treatment, the therapeutic family unit remains home base; the patient ventures away quite cautiously at first. Much trial and error takes place. It is difficult to mature without the company of others having the same kind of growing pains. The therapeutic community works well in this area. It represents a small community within a large one. The family therapists' own children represent identifications because of their similar problem-solving. The patient learns he has many allies—any and all of whose resources are available to him.

Although he remains a member of the therapeutic community, the patient may request a room with someone else, possibly someone going through similar experiences. He wants to maintain the security of the therapeutic community while having the freedom of his own individuality. These actions minimize the intensity of the transference ** and help the unconscious take its rightful place in the human personality.

---

* The psychotic is involved in his own intrapsychic relationship rather than in an interpersonal one. "Malone" Concepts of Therapy with Schizophrenia, Lecture, Temple Univ. Med. School, Nov. 12, 1959.

** The patient must find some way to make peace with his or her castration and incestuous feelings. In latency, repression of sexual feelings occurs mainly because of the castration threat. In adolescence, the oedipal relationship becomes more genitalized and the incestuous threat becomes the most important one. In psychosis, because the patient has traversed both developmental periods, the feelings may occur almost simultaneously.

Probably the greatest reason why I insist on having the patient remain for a year after emergence from psychosis is that, like an adolescent, he is constantly seeking to learn from parental substitutes. The adolescent may reject his own parent image but form a crush on a teacher, a movie star, an athlete or a mirror-image of himself—another teenager. Very impressionable at this stage, he seems always to agree with the last person he's spoken to. The patient should be guided with care, and never made to feel that the therapist is controlling his actions or injecting moralistic judgment.

Is it necessary that a patient undergo intensive psychoanalysis after recovery from psychosis? If so, who should conduct this analysis? Can a patient be transferred to another therapist?

To me, situational analysis within the setting of the therapeutic family milieu is probably the best way to continue therapy after the acute phase of psychosis. The patient's behavior and reaction in situations is probably of more value to the therapist than a daily ritualistic free-association or dream analysis. True, the couch has its value—but only at times. I use it when I feel that a separation of patient's and analyst's thinking would be helpful. Many patients have told me that the remoteness felt when they lie down and I sit behind them causes intolerable frustration and anxiety. The heavy structural work with resistances and transference has been done during the actual treatment of the acute psychosis. Most of analysis has taken place within the framework of the psychosis.

Since analysis of children is somewhat similar to treatment of psychosis, one can borrow from its writings. Anna Freud said "analysis of children has to be very different from the analysis of adults because of the immaturity of the child's ego and because of his dependency on the environment." [8] Another reason for variation in therapy is that the child has just begun to develop a superego. He needs his parents and others to teach him right and wrong so that he may decide on his own set of values and build a conscience. When he enters a child's life, an analyst knows that, besides the analytic functions of interpretations and freeing of the ego from too much id-invasion thus clearing the way for sublimation and maturation, his role is also that of another adult who will be expected, at times, to direct and support superego development.

E. Geleerd says that the adolescent is definitely in need of an adult friend—one to whom he can trust and relate.[9] Very often the adolescent needs an adult as a sounding board as he tries out various ways of life. He also needs the analyst as a superego figure. Since he has to reject his parental figures, it is essential that he find a relationship in which he has sufficient trust and confidence.

A similarity also exists between the treatment of an adolescent and the final stages of work with a psychotic. An analyst cannot maintain absolute neutrality. He must get involved in the patient's daily living. He must be available if crises develop. To know his patient, an analyst must see his behavior in every situation possible.

Awareness and acknowledgement of self always bring to mind the question of cure. Unfortunately, this determination is often ignored in treatment of mental illness.

In Freud's first interview with a prospective patient he always asked, "Are you happy?" and "Do you enjoy your work?" Link includes the ability to work, play, love and worship as essentials to a full life.[10] Marie Jahoda says that as far as we can discover, there exists no psychologically meaningful and, from the point of research, operationally useful description of what may constitute mental health. Jahoda uses five possible criteria: (1) absence of mental disease (2) normality of behavior (3) adjustment to environment (4) unity of personality (5) correct perception of reality.[11]

I would add that Jahoda's description of cure is accurate. Perhaps, too, a person must also have a certain reliability or consistency of normal behavior.

Certainly in a deep-seated cure, there must be a clear feeling of self. Patients without this are always vulnerable to re-regression into psychosis. Spock thinks that an awareness of self becomes crystallized by age one year.[12] The child indicates his separateness from the mother in terms that say, "I have wishes in regard to what I eat, what I do, and my bowel movements." Fremont-Smith says that the awareness of self begins with the infant's rage toward an outside object—a milkless nipple.[13] It can be said that an awareness of self and a personal identity begin in infancy. The self is then nourished and permitted to grow through an understanding and trustful relationship with another human being. How often I have heard a psychotic patient say "This is what I believe—then after talking with my mother I question whether this is what I really believe. Then I think that I must be wrong—mother knows more about it than I do. I then become very frustrated and empty."

Any therapy directed toward self-identification must have a clear emotional meaning to the patient. It is only through such a trustful relationship with another human being—with a full range of emotion—that a healthy personality can emerge and continue to grow.

B. Ambivalence—Shaking Up a Person Forces Out His Anger

Emotional upheaval, rebellion and revolution are not the final solution to a sweet and happy life. A negative reaction might be a person's first attempt at changing a dependent relationship with another human being into a more independent and fruitful life. In the patient's fear of being "swallowed up," the patient may avoid contact with anyone. The new feeling of independence is prized as if it were a conquest of death itself. If psychosis might be considered a death-like condition, the human psyche does not remain in equilibrium long. It moves forward toward more independence, or regresses. I believe this feeling of independence is understandable. At this time, there will be no turning back to the old psychosis, the feeling of loneliness and isolation will force a person once more to seek a relationship of love. Although negative transferences produce independence, it is the positive transferences that produce the warmth and the true emotional feeling. The process of emotional growth is an alternation of one phase with the other—first negative, then positive.

A patient stays in this dependent position in the family because he or she believes this is the way the parents want it. The therapist, for example, faces a man or woman, the patient, the early or late twenties, and a greying mother and father, with an emotional situation that should have begun to be settled more than twenty years ago.

When the explosion arises, the therapist who has spent time with the patient's family, now understands why this explosion is necessary. Patients know that one way to break the therapeutic relationship is to ally parent-patient against therapist. All of the secrets of the therapy are told to the parents by a guilt ridden weak patient in fear and confusion. It is they, the parents, in the final analysis, who determine whether the therapy is to continue. Can a patient, who will go to such ends to destroy a relationship that has obviously helped him or her to at least gain some measure of independence, really be well? I do not believe so, because of the underlying dynamics involved.

AMBIVALENCE IN THE NORMAL GROWTH PROCESS In the normal mother-infant union, a mutually beneficial relationship is established. This relationship consists of the mother feeding the child both physically and emotionally. Each feeding produces in the infant new strength, resulting in new growth. This, in turn, forces a continual change in the one-to-one relationship. For whatever reason, if the initial mother-infant (new child) flow of energy, delicately balanced, doesn't continue, then frustration, fear, confusion and anger occur both in the mother and child. If the child has grown strong enough to seek out a new relationship, the damage may not be devastating. But if he is yet too weak, lasting damage can result.

For normal growth, the mother must give to the child the strength necessary to seek a normal relationship with a third person. In a normal family, this person is the father. Men and women, by their natures, are different, with different strengths and weaknesses. Generally speaking, the mother is gentle, more observant of small things, more conscious of interpersonal relationships, more tolerant of pain. She is also more prone to show her emotions. The father is physically stronger, quick-moving, less fearful and more adaptable to change. A mother should seek out these qualities in her husband and introduce them to her child. A good mother does. She is able to abandon the mask of omnitpotence and avoids accompanying feelings of guilt at not knowing all the answers.

In the child, as in the primitive, there exists ambivalence: aggressive and hostile feelings along with those of love. I consider it normal in the child—but the adult should have outgrown these feelings to a great degree. Freud, in all his writings, was puzzled about a separate aggressive instinct or drive.[14] He finally accepted this in his attempts to postulate a death instinct. If the aggressive drive is accepted along with the love drive, it can be understood how ambivalence exists in the growing child.

Marked instinctual ambivalence in the present day human being may be regarded as archaic inheritance. We have reason to believe that the part played in instinctual life by unmodified active impulses was, in primeval times, greater than it is today.

Freud continues, "Which do you love most, Daddy or Mommy?" This time-honored question accompanies the child through his whole life, whatever the relative intensity of his feelings to the two sexes. Normally, this opposition soon loses the character of a hard and fast contradiction—either, or. Room is found for satisfying the unequal demands of both sides, although even in a normal person, the higher estimation of one sex is always thrown into relief by a depreciation of the other." [15]

Freud states, "The libido follows the path of narcissistic needs and attaches itself to the objects which ensure the satisfaction of those needs. In this way the mother, who satisfied the child's hunger, becomes its first love object and certainly also its first protection against all the undefined dangers which threaten it in the external world. In this function of protection, the mother is soon replaced by the stronger father, who retains the position for the rest of childhood. But the child's attitude toward its father is colored by a peculiar ambivalence. The father himself constitutes a danger for the child, perhaps because of its earlier relation to its mother. Thus it fears him no less than it longs for him or admires him. When the growing individual finds that he is destined to remain a child forever, that he can never do without protection against strange superior powers, he lends those powers, the features belonging to the figure of his father, he creates for himself the gods whom he dreads, the one he seeks to propitiate and to whom he nevertheless entrusts his own protection. Thus his longing for a father is a motive identical with his need for protection against the consequences of his human weakness." [16]

Augmentation of allegiance without adequate expression of ambivalent feelings intensifies guilt which is normally present due to unconscious motivation. Ambivalence is a step between fixed pathological thought process and healthy thinking. Its presence serves to introduce doubt into a fixed delusional structure. Franz says, "A certain amount of ambivalence is universal, because the narcissistic nucleus of the personality 'hates' every loved object which depletes the ego's self-love." [17]

In mental illness there is a breakdown in (1) the nurturing process, (2) communication, (3) education. The genuine "feeding" process of "taking in" has ceased. Something unreal has been substituted for a genuine emotional relationship. If this happens very early in life, little feeling of identification as a human being occurs and a state of idiot savant or childhood autism results.

In mental illness, identification with the pathological defenses of the "mothering" figure masks the underlying turmoil. The ability to succor is crippled; maturation ceases. In its place is an arrest of the psychic development of the individual, usually even below that of the mothering figure. (The child is less emotionally mature than its own mother.)

If this lack of relating occurs very early between mother figure and infant, the presence of a third figure (father) does not relieve the situation. In a severe crippling psychosis, the mother and father figures have, themselves, never breached this communication break; that is, they have never achieved a higher level of communication themselves. If the lack of relationship existed before the infant's birth, usually the father is unaware of it. If he did recognize it, he was unable to break through to the infant constructively when it was born. The patient is hopelessly "stuck with Mother." Other siblings can become similarly involved in the bind.

In therapy, much the same situation may occur. The patient unconsciously seeks out and tries to reconstruct the familiar relationship, however devastating it has been to his psyche. He tries to recreate this one-to-one attachment with the therapeutic environment.[18] If he is successful, the therapeutic process becomes stagnant, the "taking in" has stopped and the patient's unconscious controlling defenses have the upper hand. The results are extremely frustrating to a therapist. The patient will take full advantage of the situation and try to destroy the therapy, even though he will be the eventual loser. It is assumed that he is doing this against his better judgment and that he cannot help himself.

The atmosphere is negativistic—the patient may become petulant, arrogant, and vitriolic in his language toward the therapist or the control may be more subtle. The patient may be unresponsive, stubborn, hard and fast, stonelike. More often the patient is politely agreeable and submissive, and in this passive state, refusing any further emotional response, controls the relationship.

All this can affect an ambivalent family who may harbor the same thoughts that their "sick" family member is overtly expressing. If because of finances or because of their own unconscious tensions (and in every case there is not just a "sick person" but rather a "sick family"), the family doubts the efficacy of the treatment procedure, they may quickly "rescue" their beloved.

Perhaps the therapist feels worst. I know what I go through when this situation arises. Nothing runs completely smoothly. Fortunately, now, the collapse of a case occurs less and less often than when I first started. I think I must be able to convince families of my earnestness and zeal. I may leave them with enough confidence that I understand what I am doing, so that they back me and not the patient, most of the time. This eases the situation, for often communication of their trust in me to their anxious "sick family member" helps to relieve his anxiety. For however tough, courageous, or cock-sure the patient may act, he or she is really fearful and frightened under the surface.

Let me say, as a therapist, what it all does to me. I do not feel well. I am cranky and demanding with my wife and children. I have thoughts of getting away—going fishing or something. But I know this will not help. I hate seeing the patient in therapy. I neglect my other patients and become preoccupied with the problems of this one case. It is all-consuming in my mind. All my other work suffers.

What has happened unconsciously is that the patient has directed a vehement, vindictive, life-and-death struggle attack on "bad mother." All the warm and good feelings are buried in all-consuming hate and revenge. If this continues, there will be a full return of all of the patient's symptoms including the fear and dread that may result in hallucinations. (One could almost hope for a return of ambivalence, for then at least some "taking in" occurs and is associated with positive feelings.) However, unless the negative feelings come to the surface, there will be no real therapy.

It is here that I have accepted the need for a third party. Others have written about the need for a third party. Stierlin and Searles point out that a temporary splitting (or diffusion) of the transference, by diverting it to persons other than the therapist, has a constructive aspect in terms of the preservation of the patient-therapist relationship.[19] Ideally, perhaps, this should never occur, but any therapist's tolerance of anxiety has some limit, and the schizophrenic patient's ambivalence may be, at times, too intense for the therapist to bear in a consistently sharply-focused state.

I feel that although the therapist may be trained to take the bombardment, it is the patient who cannot survive unless he or she has access to a third party who will become a supportive source of positive feeling.

HOW THE THERAPEUTIC FAMILY MILIEU WORKS WITH THE AMBIVALENT PATIENT   The Therapeutic Family Milieu is constantly challenged with crises centering around ambivalence. The patient at any one instant will make any one member into "good mother" and another into "bad mother." There is no delineation as to the age, sex, experience or professional status of the therapist. Sometimes, the patient's reaction is aided by provocation, and sometimes only by his own inner turmoil. Most usually, it is I who am placed in the position of "bad mother" because I am attacking the patient's defenses while the therapeutic family members are lending support. Sometimes, however, it is one of the family members who is doing the attacking and I get a chance to play the other role—that of "good mother." The patient (one might call him a refugee at this point) comes to me for a kind word, a bit of understanding and interpretation of behavior. Then sometimes all three of us, the two family therapists and myself, are unrelenting in our unified attack. The patient then goes to another therapeutic family for understanding.

All of this is extremely nerve-wracking. It is a constant challenge to security. But it is life-like and real. It forces the patient to make the decision for himself, and he can do this with reason. It gives the *patient* the choice.

As I have become more proficient as a therapist, I have also become more honest as a human being. This honesty has produced a confidence that is not toppled easily. It enables me to stand my ground with almost everyone and thus to give my patient rational reasons for his behavior. The patient will understand and, although attacked, he comes back over and over again for more interpretations of his behavior. With this procedure, he is unable to feel "smothered." He cannot easily "corner me", that is create the deadening "one to one" relationship the patient had with his own family.

Y.L is a 19-year-old female who dropped out of school in the ninth grade. For four years she stayed at home while her mother and father worked and her 16-year-old brother went to school. She was extremely phobic about seeing people and wouldn't let anyone in her room. She slept most of the day, and stayed awake all night. Her mother could reach her only by threatening to go away from the house permanently. As soon as the girl was admitted to the Foundation, her father and mother separated. The girl was depressed and felt empty and worthless.

In the following interview she tells how, by her passive resistance, that is—lying in bed, she was able to manipulate the family into a regressive non-productive, deadening relationship.

Patient: I am always trying to "cubby hole" someone. (patient speaks in a whiney, crying voice).

Therapist: Have you got Jim and Irene (therapeutic family) cubby holed?

Patient: No . . . eh . . . you know they are so different from my parents. I don't think they are like anybody I ever knew. I guess I don't know what to expect yet.

Therapist: And the natural tendency is to make everyone like people in your past—to the way your parents are because that is what you are most familiar with. That's what I'm going to challenge you on all the time. . . . The first thing I'm going to challenge you on is getting up in the morning. We made a rule the other day that you are to get up at 7—and already you broke it. So you got them (the therapeutic family) "cubby-holed" a little bit. Things can only get from bad to worse. You saw what happened with your folks. That was terrible, a disgrace—the level that you reduce them to. It can't make you feel good to do that.

Patient: No, it didn't—(patient continues to talk of her ambivalent feelings) . . . I am a mess

Therapist: There are a few guys around here that have their eyes on you—
there must be a better side to you.

Patient: Yes, sometimes I think that I'm two-faced. I am, you know . . .
Mr. Hyde at home . . . Dr. Jekyll on the outside . . . Dr.
Jekyll is the good one—right . . . the only time I really let
down my hair is at home—only after I went to the hospital—I
learned that I'm not the only one that has feelings and problems.
It's reassuring to know that. I used to think I was separate from
everyone else.

Therapist: You said ten minutes ago that you still feel that you are that
way.

Patient: Yeah, I don't think I realized it—I always used to be afraid
of hurting everyone else's feelings. I didn't think they could be
hurt as deeply as I could. Now people are more real to me.
My mother has improved a lot with Dr. Wade (her analyst).
She is concentrating on what she wants to do. You know—
feeling from the belly—instead of everything going thru the
head first. You know I've been so used to everybody calculating
—what should I do now to make her do this and that—it's
wonderful—the Shaws (her therapeutic family) aren't judging
everything I do—they are just letting me live—Jim, he's not at
all like my father—he's talkative—with my father the conversation sort of ends—it's an effort to have him talk.

Although it is at first nourishing, a close relationship between two
people can eventually become regressive. This is the time for introduction
of a third party. When this happens in the treatment of psychosis, as it
often does, there is limited relatedness and decreased gratification from the
relationship. The patient may become indifferent. The self-directed hostility
that develops may lead to a re-occurrence of original symptoms. This
hostility may show itself in weak passive aggressive acts, such as failure
to keep appointments, or in subtle destructive ways, such as a recent experience of mine when a patient escaped from one of my units with my
wife's car. If the hostility is not brought into the open, ambivalence continues, accompanied by anxiety and guilt. The result is intense frustration,
then regression. The ambivalence is an outcome of the patient's dependency
needs on the one hand, and his striving for individualization on the other.
In hallucinatory psychosis, the relationship exists with the hallucinated
object. Moments of quiescence and relative bliss may alternate with
moments of marked violence and anger expressed at the hallucinations.
These feelings must be transferred toward real objects. The patient,
because of the intensity of feeling and weakness of ego, cannot understand simultaneous feelings of love and hate toward one object. Therefore,
the presence of a third object is necessary. One therapist becomes the
"good" parent; another becomes the "bad" parent. This situation may

alternate. The one attacking the defenses is the "bad", the one offering support is the "good." Vilification of the bad object and support by the good object dissipate guilt and fear, strengthening the ego.

Rosen attacked the hallucinations by giving them objectivity.[20] Translating them as "bad mother", he and his assistants became "good." This method of "talking to the unconscious" works well in hallucinatory psychosis. It transfers interaction from within the patient to an outside object. Then, by interpretation and understanding, the unconscious becomes conscious. This method, however, does not work in the absence of hallucinations. Such vilification of a "bad mother" rarely makes conscious sense to a patient feeling the presence of real people around him.

Ambivalent emotional attitudes in young children exist side by side without interference. An eventual conflict between the two is often settled by the child displacing one of the ambivalent emotions on a substitute. This occurs in the development of an adult neurosis (or psychosis) where suppressed emotion may frequently persist for a long time in unconscious or conscious phantasies. Yet this opposition does not result in any proceedings on the part of the ego against what is repudiated. The phantasy is tolerated for some time. Suddenly, one day, usually as a result of an increase in the affective cathexis of the phantasy, a conflict breaks out between it and the ego with all the usual consequences. In the process of a child's development into a mature adult, there is more and more extensive integration of his personality, a coordination of the separate instinctual impulses and purposive trends which have grown up in him independently of one another.

J.B., a 37 year old female, hiding her fear of her older sister, tells her how beautiful her new hat is. This praise and placating continues until her sister "double crosses" her by agreeing with the therapist that she is not yet well enough to go home. She shouts, "What a cheapskate. You know you bought that hat for a dollar. Mother always said I had good taste and that yours was awful."

K.F., a 23 year old male, addresses me as "sir." Then he expresses his ambivalence by planting all the flowering bulbs in the garden after damaging the roots so they would not grow.

C. The Treatment of Tom: An Example of Negative Transference

Tom was first seen in October, 1964. He came to the office with his mother. When I first saw the boy, he was neither obviously delusional nor hallucinatory. Anxiety was prevalent. He was overtly friendly. Denial was an obvious mechanism of defense. There was a great deal of preoccupation with violence.

The youth obviously had only made very superficial interpersonal relationships. In early sessions he would brag about his ability to have the girls like him. He complained that men resented this and would attempt to get back at him.

His father worked hard at a butter and egg route and made $100.00

weekly. The mother was devoted to the boy. There was only a daughter, nine, at home. Because of the poor financial condition of the family, it was decided to establish a family unit in the home. The boy was to come twice weekly to the office and the mother was to act as the female mother surrogate or "mother figure" in the home. The parents seemed desperate to get the boy well. He had just emerged from the state hospital only to remiss into psychosis. The father was a powerfully built man. Although the son, too, was big and strong, I thought that if I could teach the parents what to do, the home could provide some therapeutic potential.

In the beginning, I was most impressed with the traumatic aspects of the accident as related in the history. The boy seemed guilt and anxiety laden. I decided on a course of sodium amytal interviews. No paranoia was evident and I didn't yet know of his previous hospitalization at the state hospital three months previously. (No one mentioned it the first weeks of treatment.) The onset of the acute phase of his illness and the history of his state hospital stay are summarized in the following report from the hospital:

Most of the history came from the mother who seemed to be unaware of the emotional illness of the patient and blamed what had happened on the accident which occurred one year ago. The mother told the story about his psychotic behavior many times, she told unnecessary details. She was very upset especially when she saw that the patient at times hollered at her and the patient did not want to see her anymore. The mother brought along with her what the patient wrote before he was admitted. The father is quiet with a domineering attitude toward the wife. The patient is the oldest son. He left school and went into the Navy for four years. He was honorably discharged in 1962. The patient took a job in a machine shop and was doing fine. In March 1963 the patient had a car accident, the patient was sitting in the middle and the two men beside him were killed. The patient was unconscious but the father does not know for how long. The patient was hurt on his left leg and arm. Patient refused to stay in the hospital. Patient seemed to change a lot after that. He had a quick temper and talked back to the mother, he forgot to see the doctor many times. He cursed the mother often, he stopped working and slept in the day and went out at night and came back around 2 or 3 A.M. Driving a car one time he was warned by the police because of speeding. Last month patient talked about different illogical stories, that he was hypnotized by some man, that he traveled around the world in one night and the government paid for him, he had a bank account in Switzerland. The mother told the patient to see the doctor but the patient refused to go. One night before admission the patient cried and stated that he was married to a girl named Bonnie and she was killed by him. The mother tried to ask him and describe to him that it was not true. This made the patient upset and he shouted at the mother to get out of his life and smashed his fist through the living room wall. On admission the patient was oriented for time and place. He was cooperative and willing to be interviewed. The attitude toward the physician is passively hostile and sexualized. Affect is inappropriate with unnecessary smile. Stated that his parents brought him here because of a drinking problem. Stated that he was high when he got drunk and he feels bad. The mother is always getting on his nerves. She nags (and) . . . (crys) which makes him blow-up in a temper. Patient stated that on March   he felt very high, he went out at night and did many things which he wrote on the paper. Stated that he wanted to be a writer. Patient denied remembering the strange things that he talked about the first time stating that he did not remember but later he admitted that he was hypnotized by a man in a bar who hypnotized him on purpose which he did not want to discuss. Stated that he was always dreaming and has difficulty in differentiating that which is real and that which is the dream because the dream is so real. He dreamed that he killed the woman. There are men who are trying to influence him in some way. Stated that he was in trouble because he went out with a married woman and her husband was after him. He felt that he was in this hopsital before when he was in the Navy after he jumped out of the boat. Patient rambled about this event.

Physical and neurological examinations were within normal limits. Impression: Schizophrenic Reaction, paranoid type.

The injections were stopped after five visits, when the patient began to tell his mother that they were making him feel strange. The patient was then seen in modified family therapy, that is, mother and Tom together. This continued for four months. The father never came at this time. It was hoped that the effect might be similar to that which takes place in our unit. Could a home environment that has provided the toxins for the emotional illness of an individual be reconstituted to provide the reverse—the nourishment for a rebirth?

The interviews herein are the tapes of some sessions from November to July, a period of eight months. Around May 13, the patient became extremely delusional and reacted to his hallucinations. In an attempt to escape the hallucinations, he climbed the fence to a nearby Naval Base in an effort to board an outgoing plane. He was confused and frightened and I was called by the Navy. Apparently, in his incoherent babbling my name was mentioned. This incident showed that there would be difficulty managing him at home and on May 13th he was admitted to the ward of a nearby private institution for a two week period. On June 1, 1965, his aggression subsided and he once more returned home.

Treatment continued at home, and within a month the boy seemed so improved that the mother thought she could go to the hospital for a much needed hysterectomy. She had bled profusely around her menstrual periods all during Tom's treatment but had kept silent. Exploratory surgery was recommended but she was unwilling to leave Tom at home alone. Now she thought that Tom was showing a closeness to his father that hadn't been present since adolescence. She was pleased with the change and went for her operation. It proved to be a mistake. Tom's father could not get close to him. He neglected to bring him for his appointments. Violent arguments occurred. Tom became secluded, stopped fighting with his father and became extremely paranoid toward his therapy. He was nice at home, obsequious and a "good boy"; however, in the office he was belligerent, abusive and threatening. Finally hospitalization was necessary. It was obvious that he was caught in a latent homosexual hostile negative transference. Living at home, he couldn't work out his problems.

This first interview is with mother, patient and therapist. At this time the patient was easy to talk with. His mother unburdened herself frequently during the interview, mentioning mistakes she had made in his upbringing.

M—mother   P—patient   T—therapist

M. This other boy had money to spend always. His parents have a business. He'd take different ones out and pay the whole complete thing, maybe it's just being good natured . . . (sob) . . . I don't know. I do know that Tom used to go with him a lot and then it seemed that several boys, whether they were jealous or not, they used to tease him about it. He made some remark about him and the boys said, aw, your just taken him for his money. But I don't know maybe the kid was just good natured. The last time the boy came to the house and he even knocked, I said, what's his name, I can't even remember his first name. He had a new car and everything, Harris, that's what his last name was.

P. You mean Harry?

M. Yes, Harry. I said, Tom, Harry is down here and he wouldn't even come down.

T. When was this? How long ago?

M. That was about last year wasn't it? The last time he came. Then he got married, to a nurse. I had a little talk with Harry. I asked him, "Had Tom borrowed any money from you?" He said, "Oh, no." I said "Now you don't take Tom out and spend all this money just for the fun of it, so is Tom borrowing it?" Well he sort of hedged around, young boy, never met me before. It was the first time I ever had him in the house. I told him whatever he owes you it he can't pay it, I said I'm willing to pay you so much at a time if he has borrowed any. The boy said, "Oh, I never expect anything back." Now, was there anything besides just taking you out?

P. No. Not that I know of.

M. Because this guy used to go out on the streets of Ferndale and pick different guys. He usually only took one fella at a time. Then they'd go down to Lemon Grove Park.

T. Your mother's again thinking about this queer thing? Was he queer?

M. He was a nice kid. Maybe he wanted friendship or something like that.

T. He got married. Is he married happily?

M. I only know he got married.

T. Was there any sexual thing between you and the boy?

P. No we just used to go out and pick up girls and stuff like that.

M. Well, maybe that's what it was. Maybe you could always pick them up a little easier . . .

P. You know, something's going on that I don't know about. I'm not in my right mind or something.

M. Yes, you're in your right mind.

T. Maybe you weren't in your right mind. You took that walk there, you weren't in your right mind then. You didn't know what you were doing. (pause) What are you thinking? (Here therapist gets the opportunity to once more bring up the "crazy" behavior of patient—to make the unconscious conscious.)

P. I'm just trying to figure out some of this shit.

T. Well come on start trying to figure it out. Do you still think that people are hypnotizing you?

P. I still think it has something to do with mesmerism, or whatever the hell it is.

T. Mesmerism—what do you mean by that?

P. I always thought if you're hypnotized or like that then you don't know what the hell you're doing.

T. You're wrong. I told you that. You always know what you're doing even when you're crazy. I've had a lot of crazy guys come in here but I never saw one walk through the walls instead of the door. Even if you're out of your mind there are parts of you that know what you're doing. There's always a part of you that knows what it's doing. Under hypnosis, you're in a trance . . . like you've got medication there . . . did you know where you were going or what you were doing?

P. Whaddya mean?

T. Did you know when you were under that drug? (When the patient first came in, it looked as if he was suffering from a traumatic neurosis due to his violent automobile accident. The first four visits were under amytal. At that time I didn't know the extent of his paranoia. It wasn't exhibited, but was hidden.)

P. I'd get these funny feelings.

T. What feelings?

P. I don't know felt like something in my head was getting fuzzy.

T. That's because of the drug. It's the same when you're hynotized and and feel a little fuzzy. This guy is all mixed up with this mesmerism. Were you hypnotized yesterday or mesmerized?

P. Not that I know of.

T. Are you being mesmerized during your treatment?

P. Not that I know of.

T. I don't like the way you say that! (attacking patient's suspicion)

P. Yeah, but I'm not sure of anything anymore, that's why I came here.

T. I don't like the fact that you're accusing me, in a way. You ought to know whether I'm hypnotizing you or not. Your mother's sitting here. Don't you trust her either?

M. He told me he wasn't sure.

T. Is she part of a scheme or a plot to do away with you?

P. I don't know.

T. I don't like the way you say that, "I don't know."

P. How should I know anymore. That's what I want to get. I want to get help.

T. You ought to know something, you've been coming here a couple of weeks already.

M. Doctor, the other time when he wanted his reducing pill and I got it out without the bottle and he said, are you sure this is the pill? I said yes.

T. You're still mixed up and what I call paranoid. You know what that means? You use fancy words like mesmerism, well I have some fancy words too. Paranoid means that you think people want to take advantage of you. Eventually it becomes the thought that you're alone in the world and everybody's against you. That's your attitude. I don't like it. I'm trying to help you not harm you. I don't like your attitude.

M. I think that's why I've had to explain so much and I've gotten into the habit.

T. It's affected your whole way of thinking. How long have you been that way? All your life? You think that everybody's trying to do you in? How can you have any friends? You probably don't. I don't think there's anybody that you trust. (pause) No wonder you're such a loner. You live in a world all by yourself.

M. That's what I don't understand, he's had so many friends.

T. I don't think he's ever had any real friends.

M. Could it be that he has tried to do so many other people in? Then he would feel this guilt. (Mother making an interpretation.)

T. Because he thinks that he's that way, he thinks everybody is that way. Is he that way? Does he try to do everybody in?

M. Well, there was this thing when he had it against Agnes. She was working and he used to borrow money from her and when he had money and she'd ask for hers back he'd refuse to give it to her. So I used to give it to her on the side. I knew that she wanted to be good to him and everything but she would say, oh, the heck with you, you should know better than to lend it to me. You know yourself that I have given you money on the side when you didn't have it just to keep you out of trouble. I know that if a boy doesn't have any money, he will get into trouble.

T. Well, if you're kookie, that's it. The fact is that you don't trust anybody. How can you love anybody? You feel separate, apart from people. You've been that hurt in your life that you can't get close to anybody? Maybe all that stuff that went on when you were a kid hurt you that badly.

M. I never denied him my love.

T. He certainly feels it. I don't know where it's coming from. I'm sure he felt it all his life.

M. I still say that this all started in the apartment because before then he was always so generous.

T. You mean there was a time when he trusted people?

M. Oh, yes and especially me. I know that for sure because he was great for birthdays and holidays. He was always the first one to save his money to buy me a present. But, after we moved to Ferndale he didn't even see me in the hospital and he was old enough to get in. The first time he bought so much as a card since that move was this last Mother's Day. He went out and bought me a card. He acted as though he was trying to spite us. Everyone bought him presents. I wouldn't let him go without presents. We never said anything but always wondered just what he had against us. He just turned after we moved to Ferndale. I kept up his car insurance when he was in the service. I wouldn't let it run out. I always gave money . . . all I could. I saw that he had things. That's why when he assumed this attitude that we weren't his parents and he wanted nothing to do with us . . . well, it hurt.

T. Sure, it hurt.

M. It hurt very deeply. At Christmas I bought him sweaters that I knew he'd like. Shirts, everything. Just a few months age he said, "I want one thing for Christmas and that's a motorcycle." I said, "Tom, we can't afford a cycle for you and if you realized that you wouldn't even have asked."

T. He's bitter about something. That bitterness has permeated him.

M. When he got his first car, we . . .

T. Whose car is that out there?

M. That's his.

T. Where did you get that car?

P. From insurance.

T. Where did you get the money to buy the car?

P. Insurance.

M. From the damage to the other car.

T. They don't buy you a new car. They give you as much money as they think it's worth or the damage is. Where did you get the money for the other car?

P. Which one's that?

T. The one that was damaged? Did you earn it or did it come from your folks or what?

P. Which car are you talking about?

M. The black convert.

T. Did you have a car before this one that was damaged?

P. Uh, huh.

T. Where did it come from? The black one, the one before this.

P. The white one. The white Ford before this.

T. WHERE DID YOU GET THE MONEY TO BUY A CAR? That's what I want to know.

M. The black convert. that you just thought was something out of this world. It meant everything to you.

P. Well, let me see . . . from you (referring to Mother).

M. Tell the doctor how. Did you get it all from us?

P. No, just the down payment or something like that.

M. Is that all? You don't recall everything? (Long pause.) Anything about when you were in the service?

T. Did you save your dough there? How much money did you put down on the car? How much did your folks give you and how much did you put down? What's on your mind that you can think of right now?

P. I just can't think.

T. Let's hear, what's on your mind that you can't think of? Let him talk. (Pause—patient became self-absorbed . . . as if he was hearing voices. I began to probe.)

P. I don't know, it's just confused now.

T. Come on, I want to hear all the confusion.

P. I don't know, it seems that my mind is real good, then all of the sudden . . .

T. When you say you're confused, it means you must be confused about something. Something's confusing you, what is it? What are the thoughts that are confusing? What are you thinking?

P. I'm trying to think of something but I can't now.

T. Is it what I was talking to you about before?

P. Like what?

T. Like you don't trust anybody—this mesmerism stuff? You thought that you knew all the answers too.

P. I don't follow you.

T. You had the whole thing figured out that you were hypnotized or mesmerized. Your whole mental breakdown, that was the reason.

P. I still don't know.

T. I'm tell you that you're wrong. You have had a mental breakdown. These ideas came into your head as part of the nervous breakdown.

In trying to explain the strange feelings that you had the confusion in your mind, you heard about this mesmerism and blamed it on that. You didn't think about a nervous breakdown, you thought someone was hypnotizing you. But I know a little bit more about the mind, that's my business. I've treated other guys who had the same ideas you do, they were being hypnotized or were hearing loudspeakers telling them what to do. All kinds of things, ideas about getting messages in various forms. These ideas were all meant to be the explanation of what was happening to them, they couldn't accept the truth, that they were having mental breakdowns. Didn't you meet other people in the State Hospital that had the same ideas as you?

P. I can't remember because of that dope we had so much of. (talking of tranquilizers at the hospital.)

T. Well, I've had hundreds of mesmerized cases or hypnosis cases. They all thought that's what was wrong with them. They all turned out to be nervous breakdowns. That's what you're going through. The quicker you understand it the quicker you'll come out of it. If you keep thinking that you're being hypnotized . . . it's a way of keeping you away from people and you'll go on being crazy.

M. He thinks he's completely alone.

T. What are you thinking now?

P. I'm trying to understand it . . . what you're saying.

M. At times he's told me that he must be completely crazy. I said no you're not and you will get better if you just face it.

T. I've had a lot worse than you. It's just that it's been going on a long time. Nobody sat down with you and tried to explain it to you. It'll just go on and on until you let what I'm telling you sink in. When you get a nervous breakdown, your unconscious mind takes command of you. It comes up and takes over.

T. Your mother seems to think you're more relaxed when your father's there. When he leaves you are more upset. Is that true?

P. Not that I know. I'm not conscious of it.

T. All right, then it must be something crazy. Some crazy thought in your head that keeps you awake. Do you feel that someone is going to get you? Is that why you stay awake at night?

P. If they are I don't know about it.

T. You think there's somebody after you. Who is it?

P. I don't know.

T. That you have to stay awake all night to protect yourself . . .

M. Last night . . .

T. What are you thinking?

P. I don't know, I'm just trying to figure out what the hell is going on.

T. Well, come on. Do you look out the window going to bed at night to see if anyone is out there?

P. I haven't looked out the window and stuff like that . . .

T. Do you think someone is after you to get you for something?

P. I don't know.

T. Do you think that way? Yes or No.

P. I don't know. I might have felt like that at one time or another.

T. I think that you still think that way.

M. Remember when you used to go down to New York on the weekends and that one time you came home with your shirt dirty and torn. You told me that someone had crashed the party you were at and there was a big fight and the police came to break it up.

P. Not that I remember.

M. Was anyone badly hurt that night?

P. Not that I remember.

T. Do you remember that incident?

P. No, I don't.

T. Who might be after you? Who did you used to think was after you? (long pause) Don't you remember?

P. No, I felt good until I got into that hospital.

T. Where, State Hospital?

P. Yeah.

T. If you felt so good, how come you wound up there?

P. I don't know.

T. These are the things you have to try to explain to yourself.

M. He put that blame on me.

T. They don't put well people into a hospital. They don't keep you there if you're well. They would have kicked you out in five minutes if you were well.

M. That could be what he's holding against me. Are you afraid that I'll put you back in there? I wouldn't have brought you up here to see the Doctor if I wanted to put you back there. I told you then that I want you well. I'd do anything to help you if you'd promise to go to a psychiatrist but if you kept on that way and wouldn't go to anybody you'd have to go there.

T. If you were so well they wouldn't have kept you there so you weren't well. Don't blame the hospital for your illness, it was going on long before then.

P. This must have been going on all my life.

T. I imagine it has been contrary to what your mother said. I think it's been going on all your life. It started when you were a little kid.

M. Not when he was a real small child I don't think . . .

T. The thoughts have always been there. Not as badly when he was young but they have been there. They usually are.

M. Not until he went from one school to another.

T. I don't think you were aware what was going on with your boy, if you want my honest opinion.

M. Yes, I do. But he says that my husband would come home and I would go out. That is positively false. I would never leave the children alone unless I had my sister's boy or daughter to take care of them.

T. I don't know. You still don't want to face the fact that maybe his childhood might have something to do with all this. Maybe that's what he holds against you.

M. Maybe . . .

T. If you were strong enough to admit that maybe there would be the possibility maybe he'd give in too.

M. All my life I feel I gave, gave in to him and that's probably the fault. I couldn't resist.

T. Giving in to him?

M. That's right.

T. That might be it too.

M. Maybe if I had let his Dad get him and beat him half to death— because I know what a temper my husband has . . .

T. The way you're talking . . . when you say things like that it shows that you really are angry.

M. It's true. I'm not angry at my husband—I love him or I wouldn't be here, but . . . .

T. Nobody wants you to take the blame. You want to blame yourself. Nobody wants to blame you but nobody wants to look at themselves and say well maybe I made some mistakes.

M. I've made mistakes.

T. If you can admit your mistakes maybe this guy can admit his.

M. But, but, if anywhere . . .

T. Look, if you go around trying to blame everybody else, he's going to continue to blame you.

M. But I know when my husband isn't drinking he's the best person in the world.

T. He's a good man.

M. He would do anything for Tom and he should know that.

T. You think you're perfect—you're a woman and he's a man—don't think he's going to give in to you.

M. I'm not perfect. I've made plenty of mistakes.

T. All right, let's try to figure the puzzle out. The past is the past. Let's try to get this boy well and if he's well maybe you'll feel better too. All right (to patient)?

P. All right.

T. I have got to go to Philadelphia. I'll see you on Monday. Do you like being alone for a couple of days?

P. No.

T. Why not?

P. I would like to start getting out and enjoying life.

T. All right a person should be alone at times, look at some books. Do you enjoy that? Is that why you've been withdrawn?

P. I don't know.

T. Or is it some crazy ideas in your head that you're trying to hide from your mother.

P. There must be all kinds of crazy ideas in my head.

T. Maybe so. You've still got plenty of crazy thoughts there yet.

P. Yeah.

T. Like what?

P. If I knew I'd tell you.

T. Try to figure them out. Are you ashamed to talk about them in front of your mother?

P. No.

T. Will you write them down over the weekend and we can talk about them on Monday. Let's get it all out of your head, all the crazy stuff. Maybe you'll be able to live a normal life and enjoy it.

M. Doctor, that is one thing he won't do. He won't write anything down like all those yellow pages he knows I gave them to that psychiatrist.

T. Will you write them down for me? Do you trust me?

P. Yeah.

T. All right, write them for me, you don't have to show them to your mother.

M. No, I don't want to see them.

T. I'm just going to keep them for you and me, that's all. You might find that your crazy ideas are no different from anybody else's. Maybe I had the same thoughts at one time from my nervous breakdown. Do you believe that?

P. Yeah, anything's possible.

T. That's right.

Shortly thereafter, because of pressure of increased bleeding and a probably unconscious feeling that Tom didn't need her as much— but needed father more—the mother went to the hospital for a hysterectomy. As it turned out, the boy reacted badly to the absence of his mother in the home—but it took a while.

It should be mentioned that the father is a giant of a man—about 260 lbs. and going three inches over six feet. Our patient is muscular and husky—probably 170 at 5'11".

First session with patient's father: present P—patient, F—father, T—therapist

T. How's your wife?

F. She won't be back for six weeks. The doctor couldn't take her uterus out because it has a tumor and it's pre-cancerous. They're giving her radium on Friday then in six weeks they'll take it out.

T. Did they test them?

F. Yes and the doctor said it looked better than he thought it would. (further discussion on wife's condition)

T. How are you doing?

P. So-so.

T. How's he doing?

F. I think he's doing darn good. I was just telling my wife, I can't see anything wrong with him anymore. (Interesting remark—certainly from the previous session, it was obvious that the boy was now able to fool his father about the crazy thoughts. The father was the weak one, less involved and the boy patterned himself after him.)

T. What do you notice that's still not right with him?

F. Nothing.

T. How have you been feeling about the hypnosis?

P. I had a dream about it last night. Someone was trying to hypnotize me and I was trying to get away.

T. Was it a man or a woman?

P. A man. It seems like I wake up at night. I go to bed between 11 and 1 and I wake up about 3 in the morning. Lately I go downstairs and get something to eat. I don't know why, I just do. Then I'm not really hungry.

T. Just to have something in your mouth.

P. Just to go downstairs. I have a habit of looking out the window.

T. To see if anybody is there?

P. Yeah.

T. You still have in the back of your mind that someone is out to get you.

P. Then I wake up in the morning, a little after 6 and go downstairs again.

T. What's the first thing that you do when you go downstairs?

P. Look out the front door.

T. Do you open the door?

P. No, I look through it.

T. Do you ever see anything?

P. No, well, I've seen cars parked around.

T. Do you connect anything up with you when you look out there?

P. No, I don't know what it is.

T. First you have to decide whether it's a real fear, whether there's something really to be afraid of.

P. I don't know.

T. If you're not sure yet then it means to me that you think there's someone that's still after you. When there is fear it's because there's guilt—something that you feel you have to be punished for.

P. Once I was accused by this guy. He said that I was driving the car that hit his son's car. His son was killed in it and I wasn't driving.

F. He'd had a few beers, the boy's father and said he was going to prove that Tom had driven the car.

T. The record would show your position in the car and that you weren't. Did you have to go to court?

P. No, this happened a long time ago. The whole idea pisses me off, though.

T. Guy got a little drunk and he missed his boy, I guess.

P. Yeah, but it makes me mad.

T. Don't be too hard on him. What else might there be that you're still hiding in your mind?

P. (A long silence)

T. You had a dream last night that a guy hypnotized you or something like that? How was he doing it?

P. I don't know, I was trying to get away.

T. One way that you can tell about being hypnotized is to give a post-hypnotic suggestion. Such as, look at the nails on your left hand ten minutes after you awaken.

P. Just talking about this makes me nervous.

T. That's because it's still on your mind. You won't be right until you get over this.
(Therapist is trying to clarify hypnosis for father's benefit—explaining the process of hypnosis.)

P. You said to me once that a person's brain can get messed up if hypnosis has been used on him.

T. To what degree? Tell me how you think your brain got messed up and I'll tell you if its possible.

P. I think that somebody hypnotized me and put thoughts in my head.

T. That's not so, simply because you can't put any thought into a person's head that they wouldn't ordinarily do. I know a psychiatrist in New York that I studied with who was taken to court because of this idea. He was treating a girl and the girl's parents accused him of putting sexual thoughts into the girl's head. The judge threw it out of court because he was aware that you can't put ideas into a person's head, that they had to be there to begin with. I think that we can apply some of this to your case.

P. In what way?

T. Because anything that you accuse someone of putting in your head was there always. It might have been buried but that doesn't mean that it wasn't there. What are some of the thoughts that you think were put there?

P. I can't be sure of anything.

T. How did you feel after you were hypnotized?

P. I felt . . . I . . .

F. Were you hypnotized or drunk?

P. I just remember feeling floaty. Like I wasn't myself.

T. That's when you were having your nervous breakdown, although you get that feeling when you are hypnotized too. I got that feeling when I was hypnotized but you'd know it Tom if you were. You have to concentrate very hard on it so you'd have to be aware of it because you'd want it to happen. Do you think that I can hypnotize you right now? I'm not going to, but do you think that I can?

P. I don't want any part of it.

T. I'm not going to but if you didn't want me to I couldn't. The reason that you don't know or aren't sure is that your mind isn't firmed up yet. You're still just a little off. Why do you go to the ice box at night when you say you're not hungry.

P. As an excuse I guess to go downstairs and look out the window.

T. Then you eat after that?

P. Yeah.

T. I think that the ice box is like a mother. It feeds you and protects you. What else?

P. I'm thinking about why I said that about the guy being after me?

T. (to Father) Did you ever threaten to cut his balls off with a knife?

F. Not that I know of.

T. Sometimes guys say that.

T. (to patient) Are you scared of him? (Looking at father)

P. Sometimes.

T. Did he ever threaten you that way?

P. Not that I know of.

T. That he'd cut your head or arm off.

F. I never said anything like that.

T. Are you feeling better each day?

P. I want to get up in the morning but I just roll over and go back to sleep. I just get disgusted all around.

T. With what?

P. Everything.

T. When you feel disgusted what comes to your mind?

P. I just think about all the chances I had to make something of myself.

T. Do you miss your mother?

P. I guess.

T. Is your sister coming over? Is she a good cook, as good as your mother?

P. She's good but she's young yet.

This is one of the final interviews. It illustrates vividly where the patient's difficulties and fears remain.

T. Did you have a good time last night?

P. Sure I had a good time . . .

T. Did you talk to anybody?

P. Yeah.

T. Did you feel like you were hypnotized?

P. Should I?

T. I asked you a question, did you?

P. I shouldn't have been if I was doing what I was doing.

T. You are so cagey, look how cagey you are.

P. What do you mean by cagey?

T. Cagey means . . . eh, slippery.

P. Do I look slippery?

T. It means also flippant with the mouth. (Changing the subject) I asked you a question. I'll ask you again. Did you feel like you were being hypnotized or mesmerized?

P. I thought we got over that.

T. Are you over it?

T. You gotta bring it up again, don't you?

T. I told you I'd continue to bring it up till I feel you are free of it. I don't know whether I feel that you're free of it yet because you're still very angry. You are belligerent and angry, when you have to fight with a poor kid like Mike . . .

P. Now I'm fighting huh?

T. Your mother said to me. "You'd better ask him to come up, he's starting to pick on Mike." She got frightened. (Mike is one of our family therapists who had gone over to Tom's house when Tom refused to get up in the morning and his mother couldn't get him to come to the office with her alone.)

P. Sure, I am, I am. . . . If I ever pick on the SOB it'll be more than what I just did.

T. I wouldn't stake on it, he's pretty strong.

P. He smells pretty strong.

T. Don't hit him because if you hit him I'm not responsible for what he does to you.

P. I'll have him come up here and have him work you over then.

T. He doesn't work me over.

P. He must, you seem afraid of him.

T. If I was afraid of him I wouldn't have him here. I'm more afraid of you than I am of him.

P. Oh, get off that shit will you? (pause) Who are you talking to, a two year old?

T. I'm talking to you.

P. Then why don't you act your damn age too. (silence)

T. Did you come around yesterday, did you call up?

P. No, I didn't come around yesterday. I had other things to do.

T. It's raining out.

P. It's washing away some of the shit.

T. You are so angry, can't you get over that? Do you know what you're so angry at, do you know what you're fighting?

P. You tell me this shit makes sense when I have to talk to you like that. What the fuck am I doing?

T. Watch your language.

P. You don't seem to watch yours when you jump around and go on your rampages around here.

T. How have you been feeling?

P. PRETTY DAMN GOOD!

T. How are your nerves doing? (silence)

P. How are they supposed to look?

T. How are you feeling?

P. I said O.K. What do you have the DTs or something? I'll tell you this is a goddamn shame my coming up here and spending my parents' money like this.

T. Their money and my time.

P. Yeah.

T. Listen a little bit.

P. What is there to listen to, what is there to talk about anyway? You stand there on your soap box all the time. I ain't got no reason to either. (silence) You talk about me putting my head back and forth and putting my hands up to my face. Well, what the hell are you doing? (silence)

T. I want you on the couch today so finish your cigarette, chew your gum and let's go.

P. I got plenty of sleep already today.

T. You're a cocky boy aren't you?

P. I got a cock and I use it when I have to.

T. Finish up and take the gum out of your mouth.

P. You can hear me with the gum.

T. I can hear you.

P. Then what does the gum have to do with anything.

T. I don't like chewing.

P. I ain't annoying you. If I am there is something wrong with you.

T. All that mouth, all the business with your mouth going on the cigarette and the gum at the same time. Then you talk too at the same time.

P. Is there a law against it?

T. Yes Law 360 regulation 781.

P. You just made that up didn't you?

T. It says, thou shalt not chew, smoke and talk at the same time.

P. Well you ain't God.

T. In the statute books of the State of Pennsylvania, Bucks County.

P. Don't ever get that in your mind that you're God. You sit in the goddamn chair and act like one and tell me you are God and all that shit. If you ain't off your rocker no one is. (silence) I ain't got no business being up here anymore and I ain't shitting. No business whatsoever.

T. How come every time you get upset you bring that up?

P. What do you want me to do, come up here for the rest of my life? Give you money just to shoot the breeze with you?

T. I'd like you to come up here once where you did that. Where you weren't hollering.

P. First I don't talk loud enough, then you can't hear me, then I'm smoking a cigarette and chewing gum at the same time, then I'm talking too loud.

T. I'd like to see you come up here once when I can talk to you man to man.

P. I know I'm a man. I don't know about you. Why are you hanging your head down now like that?

T. I'm thinking that maybe you're not as truthful with your thoughts as you should be.

P. You look like that damn duck down there hanging its head down. Even the ducks got his head up. Jesus Christ if I can't talk the way I want up here oh, hell. Excuse my profanity.

T. Taking the Lord's name in vain is profanity.

P. I excused myself.

T. I accept your apology.

P. I didn't excuse myself to you.

T. When you finish your cigarette come over for some analysis.

P. I just got up and I'm raring to go. You and your analysis, I feel better already you moved away from me.

T. Let's go.

P. What have you got on your mind?

T. Come over here.

P. I can hear you from here.

T. I want you on the couch.

P. Wait till I run into my real good friends. Wait till I tell them what a fuck you are. They'll laugh their goddamn heads off. What do you call them desert boots or booties? I forgot you call them booties. I've got shoes on my feet I don't know what you've got.

T. Whenever you're ready, come on over here.

P. I'm telling you what's on my mind, what more can I do?

T. You can come on the couch. You ain't telling me everything.

P. Screw your couch. (the argument about getting on couch continues)

T. If you don't get over here I'm going to take the next patient.

P. I don't care what you do, there ain't a damn thing wrong with me.

T. Are you going to get over here?

P. What's that supposed to mean?

T. I'm telling you I want you on the couch.

P. I know what it was, I must have insulted you when I told you that you were a little off your rocker.

T. Come over here and let's do some work.

P. Ha! You call that work you don't even know what work is. For as young as I am I probably have worked harder than you ever have in your life.

Get your fucken hands off of me or I'll throw you across this room.

T. Let's get to work. Get your head down.

P. My head's on the pillow, as close as I want it.

T. I want it on that pillow.

P. It's on the pillow. What are going to do fucker. I need an ashtray. You're hurting me more than you're helping, you fuck up. All right, I'm on the pillow.

T. I think that every moment that you're alive you have thoughts of sucking my dick.

P. Fuck you.

T. That's why you're not getting well.

P. You're so fucked up you must go home and suck your old lady out.

T. Let's not fight.

P. I ain't fighting with you, you're the SOB who pulled me over here. You're a damn mother fucker. What's wrong with you, you got problems of your own? Don't hand them off on me. If I want to smoke a cigarette and chew gum there ain't no damn law that says I ain't allowed to. I don't give a fuck who you are. I already told some SOB about you. The kind of fuck up you are.

T. Let's not fight.

P. I clip mine I don't know what you do with yours. ICK! GET YOUR HANDS OFF ME. DO YOU HAVE TO TOUCH ME, DO YOU??? IS THERE SOMETHING WRONG WITH YOU?

T. Can't you lie down? I think you bite your nails.

P. I don't. I clip them, see. See this???

T. Come here, let's see your nails?

P. You sick my poojam too. Want to see that too?

T. Why are you so nervous?

P. I ain't nervous. I think you're nervous the way you are sitting over there biting your goddam lips, playing with your face. I ain't got no time for you.

T. Lie down.

P. I thing you're so fucked up you're trying to have me treat you. I know what I think, I don't know what you think nor do I care.

T. I think you're dishonest with yourself.

P. If I am then I should be in jail. I ain't in jail.

T. They don't put you in jail when you're dishonest with your thoughts.

P. They ought to put you there.

T. Why are you so angry all the time?

P. I ain't angry.

T. You holler and curse all the time.

P. You talk like—you gotta go take a pee, you talk like a goddamn cunt. It's a piss!!! Same sack of shit.

T. Get down on the couch.

P. Are you going to play around with my cock again?

T. Get down on the couch! You've already wasted too much time.

P. Man, go get some other patient to play with, don't play with me.

T. Those thoughts of yours are driving you crazy.

P. Nothing is driving me crazy.

T. Do you know what sucking cocks is in the unconscious?

P. I don't want your problems so keep them away from me.

T. Do you know what a cock, a penis, is in the unconscious? Mothers milk. A cock is a breast in the unconscious.

P. It is?? IS IT?? IS IT??? You're a fucken liar too.

T. In the unconscious, since a man doesn't have breasts.

P. Do You? I don't want to find out.

T. A man does not have breasts so if a man wants milk from another man

P. He goes to the store and buys a quart of milk.

T. Listen to me, I'm talking about the unconscious. I think you are smart enough and if you weren't so nervous maybe you'd listen.

P. I'm never nervous, I'm nervous, I'm nervous (sing song)

T. Let your ears, head and neck relax, and try to keep your mouth quiet for a minute.

P. You stink.

T. Can you do that?

P. If you have to get money like this and have me come up here . . .

T. Do you know what I mean when I say that a cock is a breast in the unconscious?

P. A cock is what I've got between my legs. If you go down south it's a pussy.

T. What does he mean?

P. The Hell it ain't. You go down south and ask them what a cock is.

T. A pussy is a vagina anywhere.

P. I bet when you go down south a cock is a cock to you.

T. When a man wants another man's milk.

P. Oh,

T. Listen

P. I don't gotta listen to that shit. You have to tell me about your problems. Is that the way you feel? You have to put me down on the couch and play with my cock all the time.

T. I'm talking about your unconscious.

P. You're talking about yourself . . .

T. Trying to teach you so you'll understand. It's working with your mind.

P. That's what you call it, huh?

T. I'll explain it to you.

P. I ain't shitting. I better get a chastity belt when I come up here. I had the time of my life last night. Man I went all over.

T. You haven't told me about last night.

P. Fuck you. I'll fix you up with some cunt and she'll find out you're queer. I've seen dames all over. What's it to you. You're not my keeper. Why are you trying to act like one then.

T. If you're with a girl and chewing gum and smoking and talking at the same time . . .

P. If she's got a smelly cunt, I'll plug it up with chewing gum. I don't even waste my time. I tell them to get the fuck out.

T. Where did you go last night?

P. Let me see. I had four wheels under me. I was on a road. I went south. Does that help you any?

T. Why are you so upset?

P. I'm not.

T. I still think these homosexual thoughts are driving you wild.

P. Do you know what Homo is, it's a man! Do you know what sexual relations are, that's with a woman.

T. Homosexual is a relationship between two people of the same sex.

P. You aren't keeping me up here any longer if that's what you've got on your mind.

T. I think you have it on your own mind. I'm trying to explain it to you.

P. I told you, I'll tell you what's on my mind and I don't give a fuck what's on your mind.

T. I'm talking about your subconscious mind, the reason why you are so upset.

P. I'm upset all right, I know I am.

T. What's doing it?

P. I'm upset because I'm on my ass.

T. You're on the couch.

P. My ass is there, too.

T. You're upset and nervous.

P. I walked in here like any other person and you sat down and went off your rocker.

T. Look, Tom, you're not facing the truth or yourself.

P. I'm facing the truth.

T. Do you want to get well?

P. I am well. Damn well.

T. How can you be well you don't even know the source of your mesmerism.

P. I've been over that, I told you.

T. When you're running around harboring all these homosexual thoughts in your subconscious you'll be uneasy with everyone.

P. You really have trouble don't you. No wonder you sit there staring with your head down.

T. I'm talking about you.

P. Why don't you get off that subject. Want to play, go play some golf, and you can play with a ball while you're at it. There ain't a damn thing wrong with me . . . taking my parents' money. Can you think of any other reason that you've been keeping me here?

Soon after, the patient became more withdrawn; it was impossible to get him to come to the office except by force. He was then hospitalized against his will.

In reviewing my records about patients that were treated in their own homes, I find most success with depressive reactions, no matter how severe. Most success has been with treating a young husband or young wife— usually where there are young children. Here a new home, a new family has been established. The toxins of the father, mother, early infant relationships are bypassed. In severe psychosis for the most part, I find the imprinting of early childhood too difficult to overcome in one's own home. Treatment will fail at the most critical point—the birth of the *patient's own* individual personality. This is the reason for the creation of the *therapeutic family milieu*.

We use mental hospitals in emergency situations. When Tom became violent, he was placed in a nearby locked-ward mental hospital for two weeks. To keep him in one of our therapeutic units in this condition would have required the hiring of another male assistant. For the short time necessary, this was not considered feasible. He was hospitalized and two assistants went to the hospital each day and brought him to the clinic.

Most mental hospitals are antiquated, institutional and rigid in their rules. When Tom went to the hospital roaring hostile remarks about me and stating that I had hypnotized him, he demanded a new doctor, a staff doctor. His mother called me, very upset. It seems that one of the secretaries had picked up his words, related them to his mother, and added "You know, we don't like Dr. Honig either." The mother was angry and answered "I don't want anything bad said about Dr. Honig to Tom. If he is to get well, he must have complete trust in his doctor." On another occasion, my two assistants called me from the hospital. Tom would not go with them to my office, and I had to call the staff physician personally to have him order his attendants to help restrain Tom so he could make the seven mile trip.

Because of the understaffing, these hospitals do not provide the proper atmosphere for psychotherapy and the individual attention that is necessary to get a patient well. Unfortunately the family financial picture precluded Tom's admission to our therapeutic family milieu. He needed the deeply involved intensive care that we can give. Too much distrust and hurt had accumulated in his psyche. Because he couldn't come to live in the warm security of one of our units, he didn't get enough warm feelings within him to overcome his negative hostile feelings.

Several years ago, I became acquainted with a female therapist who, with an office at home, had been in private practice for 30 years. She became interested in psychosis and took into her home a 28 year old male schizophrenic. He had been described, in the back wards of a state hospital, as both violent and unapproachable and when he threatened her life, she called me and asked me to help her with the case. We added to her home a male schizophrenic, aged 36, with a history of chronic alcoholism and a female schizophrenic, aged 42, with two male assistant therapists. Each patient had an illness of 8 to 15 years duration. Each had been institutionalized and each had received electric shock therapy. Each of us assumed different roles—she the mother figure and I the father figure. (In the most regressed cases, this sexual difference is all that is necessary to form identifications.) In one instance, however, the character structure of the therapist was more important than the simple fact of one therapist being male and the other female. When the female therapist complained to the male patient about his excess time in the bathroom and usage of too much hot water, the patient became angry, ran out of the house and came to me saying, "M." is like my father, always harping on me. My mother was always permissive and my father constantly angered me with his shouting." Eventually I found the patients relating to me as "nourishing mother," and I concluded that a person's sex was not important in the role of therapist. The ability to do therapy is the ability to give love and a male therapist can have good feminine or "mothering" identifications that enable him to do this part of the job adequately in all but the most severely regressed cases. In other words, the nurturing in therapy is more abstract and symbolic and is, in fact, a sublimated and highly technical type of mothering.

Experience with these three cases has been unique and rewarding. They have given me the opportunity to observe and work with ambivalence as never before.

D. *The Calculated Risk*

How much control should a therapist exert over a patient's behavior? Obviously, after a period of "oral" feeding, of nourishment, communication and education, a patient must be able to try what he has learned in the outside world. But when is this point reached? No one can answer this for sure. A guideline that I use happens just as much unconsciously, that is without my total awareness, as it does consciously, with full awareness. When a patient is standing still, seems bored, and further interpretations seem to reverberate like echoes in a stone canyon, it is probably time for some amount of "acting out" or participation in the outside world by the patient. Often this results in great success, sometimes in partial success, but sometimes what happens might be considered to be more harmful than useful.

The psychotic patient's freedom of movement is being challenged, today, as never before. This is probably because of the mass murders and destruction that readers see in newspapers daily. Some perpetrators are described as "ex-mental patients," and others have been exposed to psychiatry in some way, either by examination or therapy. The public is frightened and pressures are placed on mental health workers to be more discriminating in their decisions. If we are not careful, the backlash may result once again in an end to the open door policy.

Obviously without freedom to move in the outside world, recovery cannot occur.

Fortunately most patients give warning when they have uncontrollable urges of sucide or homicide. Our living units, docile and peaceful homes, at a moment's alarm can be turned into fortresses of defense against aggression to ourselves or others. Knives and pills are locked up, heavy screening quickly will enclose previously opened windows and the personnel are all alerted.

Even the completely maximum security unit has not proved a deterrent to the person completely intent on self destruction. Bed sheets, light sockets, head banging, all have become effective ways of self destruction. I'd venture to say that our family milieu therapy with its intense personal care and ability to reach a patient and make them feel better, human restraint, has been more of a deterrent than any forceful restraint. Certainly, this has been so with many patients we have had who attempted suicide before coming to D.V.M.H.F.

We are well prepared for the *impulsive passionate aggressive attempt* that is NOT planned, but is done on the spur of the moment. Because our whole treatment is crisis oriented, everything is of life and death proportions. Here are a few illustrations:

B.W., aged 29, is a husky male, psychotic since early adolescence and prone to violent outburst to counteract feelings of impotence and infantile helplessness. While visiting a zoo one day, he gazed through a cage at a pack of wolves and said, "I think they ought to put me in a cage." "You've been locked up for 12 years," I answered. "It didn't work. Only brought out the beast in you. At some point, you and I must take a calculated risk."

L.A., a 22-year-old female, has been in one of our units for six months. At present, she talks of going to New York, becoming independent and taking care of herself. She blames her 10 years in and out of mental hospitals on "not getting away from mother like all my friends did." She says this left her dependent, hopelessly inadequate and depressed. She secretly bought a waitress' uniform. She had an appointment with state rehabilitative services about a future job. Instead of keeping this appointment she fled to New York City. Eighteen hours later, at 2 A.M., she called to say she was all right. She had not slept in two nights, but she had been working almost continually. Then there was another 24 hours of silence. Another call—this time she announced she was getting tired. She was going to a friend's house to sleep. There we picked her up.

When she came back, after three days, she had $50.00 and she was happy. She looked and talked with greater strength. She was better. However, her feet were placed in leg restraints; she could walk all over, but not flee (unless she really wanted to—others had cut these leather bindings).

In these bindings she paraded around. But the bindings were there for a reason. They were to be her roots, her beginning toward building a "Home Base." This security she never had had in her previous treatment.

But sometimes we cannot predict behavior as well as we would like.

For example: Jack, an 18 year old, had been psychotic since 14 and in three sanitariums. After five months in our unit, it was felt that Jack should resume his education in the local high school. (It is clinic policy to take advantage of all community social and educative facilities. This way the clinic is integrated into everyday living and not an isolated integer.) I had a meeting at the beginning of the year with all of Jack's teachers and Jack did well for the first semester. Then as warm weather came, all hell broke loose. He began raiding teachers' pocketbooks, taking money and charms and mostly giving them away. He fancied himself Robin Hood. He was arrogant with men teachers and became so intolerable that he was asked to leave school two weeks before finals. Fortunately, the school permitted him to take the finals with his class under the watchful eyes of one of the family therapists. He passed his school year, and also fortunately, the police were kept out of the matter!

This patient began acting out his unconscious conflicts within the community. It got to the point where the rules could not be stretched to accommodate a "sick" individual. The community reacted with vindictiveness, punishment and expulsion.

In this case it became the community that expressed its negative feelings.

References

[1] Freud, S. "A case of paranoia." In his: COLLECTED PAPERS. London, Hogarth, 1953. v. 3.

[2] Freud, S. INTRODUCTORY LECTURES OF PSYCHOANALYSIS. N.Y., Liveright, 1920.

[3] Rosen, J. "Transference." INTERNATIONAL JOURNAL OF PSYCHOTHERAPY. 2:301–314 (1954).

[4] Rosen, J. DIRECT ANALYSIS. N.Y., Grune and Stratton, 1953. p. 18–19.

[5] Freud, S. "The dynamics of transference." In his: COLLECTED PAPERS. London, Hogarth, 1924. v. 2, p. 204.

[6] Klein, M. "Origins of transference." INTERNATIONAL JOURNAL OF PSYCHOANALYSIS. 33:433–438 (1952).

[7] Freud, A. PSYCHOANALYTIC TREATMENT OF CHILDREN. London, Imago, 1947.

[8] *Idem.*

[9] Geleerd, E. R. "Some aspects of psychoanalytical technique in adolescents" In: PSYCHOANALYTIC STUDY OF THE CHILD. N.Y., International Universities Press, 1957. v. 12, p. 263–283.

[10] Link, H. C. THE RETURN TO RELIGION. N.Y., Macmillan, 1936. p. 37–51.

[11] Senn, J., ed. CONFERENCE ON PROBLEMS OF INFANCY AND CHILDHOOD, SYMPOSIUM ON THE HEALTHY PERSONALITY. N.Y., Josiah Macy Fndn., 1950. p. 213.

[12] *idem.* p. 287

[13] *idem.* p. 288.

[14] Freud, S. "Instincts and their vicissitudes." In his: COMPLETE PSYCHOLOGICAL WORKS. N.Y., Macmillan, v. 14, p. 131.

[15] Freud, S. "Case of obsessional neurosis." In his: COMPLETE PSYCHOLOGICAL WORKS. v. 10.

[16] *idem.*

[17] Alexander, F. DYNAMIC PSYCHIATRY. Chicago, Univ. of Chicago, 1952.

[18] Scheflen, A. "One to one relationship." PSYCHIATRIC QUARTERLY. 34:692–710 (1960).

[19] Stierlin, H. and Searles, H. PSYCHOTHERAPY OF SCHIZOPHRENICS AND ITS REPERCUSSIONS IN THE HOSPITAL STRUCTURE. N.Y., Basic Books, n.d. p. 269.

[20] Rosen, J. DIRECT ANALYSIS. *op. cit.* p. 18–19.

CHAPTER IX

Existence as Self

"The man who cannot despair ought not to live; it is despicable to sur-
render like a coward."

GOETHE TO MUELLER

It has been 15 years since I first began the treatment of the psychoses. This is not a long time, but because the method used has been called revolutionary and unique, I feel qualified to speak openly about my experiences.[1] The basic theory has its origin in Freudian orthodoxy, but all in all it is eclectic. This is also true for the techniques of the therapy I use. It was long ago, while still a general practitioner, that I concluded a medical or classical psychiatric approach to the mentally ill produced little results, and so I abandoned it. I am not alone. Most young physicians entering the specialty of psychiatry are thinking this way. So are the psychologists, social workers, and other professionals. However, it is the laity that clamors for a breakthrough—a refreshing approach.

St. Elizabeth's, the Federal Hospital in Washington, D.C., has drastically reduced the amount of shock treatment they previously used. Norristown State Hospital, where I received some of my training under Dr. Arthur P. Noyes, abolished its insulin unit ten years ago, kept the same personnel and changed over to group therapy. Drug research, as yet, has produced no light on the cause or effect of mental illness. In fact, in overdose it has produced neurological deformity. Radiation is being used to destroy tracks and pathways of the brain, but this is only a more highly specialized way of doing old and useless brain surgery (lobotomy).

But can we, who have allowed ourselves to be labeled psychoanalysts and psychotherapists, sit back smugly and feel that we have all the secrets of the mind safely in the palms of our hands?

Let some unanswered questions be directed to Training analysts and supervisors at the Psychoanalytic Institutes.

1. Why are so many candidates, physicians, psychologists, and other professionals, all with proper academic qualification for admission as psychoanalytic students, rejected with the answer that they do not have suitable temperament for this work?

2. What is the percentage of patients accepted for psychoanalytic study and treatment? Why are the others rejected, many with the comment that they would not be good candidates for psychoanalysis?

3. Why is there so much controversy about the beneficial effects of psychoanalysis?

4. Why, especially among the medical practitioners and the lay public, is there so much scorn heaped upon the practitioners of our specialty? A favorite remark is that psychoanalysts "occupy their own white ivory tower."

Apparently, to many people, there is much to be desired, both in theory and practical application.

It is no longer appropriate to remark (with one's nose in the air) that Freud wasn't interested in therapeutic results and that psychoanalysis was meant only as a theory to better understand mental functioning. To say this shows a serious lack of knowledge about a method of obtaining scientific data in clinical science.

It is no longer appropriate to heap upon a discarded waste pile, with a smug shrug of the shoulders, the many seriously ill, borderline, and actually psychotic patients and say that psychoanalysis was never meant for these people.I remember talking several years ago with my highly esteemed teacher, Professor Theodore Reik, and asking him earnestly about Freud and his own experiences with psychoses. His answer to me was quite frank, but also quite disturbing: "I know little about psychosis and Freud did not work much with these people."

At that time, some 15 years ago, I had been working for a year with psychotics in the state hospital. My therapeutic effects, although not startling, made me feel that in psychoanalysis there lay an understanding and perhaps a cure for the psychotic mind. In several cases, the simple application of psychoanalytic theory, through an interpretation of behavior in unconscious terms, produced dramatic results. The classical techniques could not be employed however, in treating a patient pacing the floor, stark naked, praying to God for forgiveness, or a statuesque mute catatonic, or a woman sitting clucking like a chicken.

In Freud's and Breuer's "Studies of Hysteria" Freud shows the evolvement of theory from therapeutic treatment.[2] I feel that most of these patients, Anna O., Emmy Von N., etc., were probably psychotic and inasmuch as he was successful, I feel that Freud's gift was primarily as a therapist. It was only through this delicate and sensitive opening up of the patient's mind that he could have gathered his material for his libido theory and theories of sexuality. Since his observations came from his clinical skills in uncovering the mind's layers, Freud had to be a skilled therapist, whether he wanted to be or not. It is simple to see the pattern in psycho-sexual development when treating a psychosis. Anybody treating or observing the treatment of psychosis, would not be honest if he did not believe in the Freudian concept of psycho-sexual development of the personality. This is the cornerstone of psychoanalysis.*

I know the failures of psychoanalysis, personally, with psychosis and its borderline states. Because I know the men who failed with these cases ** were well trained teachers and practitioners of psychoanalysis of the neuroses, I feel that the failure is not a personal one, but one of method. Psychoanalysis has just not developed enough knowledge of early life (the first year) and has not formulated techniques to deal with this knowledge and apply it to patients.

How would an analyst deal with a neurotic whom he had been analyzing for two years, four times a week on a couch, who suddenly became paranoid, threatening, violent and abusive? What about the girl who suddenly withdraws further and shows signs of silent hallucination? What about the pregnant mother perched on the rooftop so confused and disoriented that she feels her body is not her own and that the world is in a turmoil and coming to an end? Consider a self-accusatory depressed, hopeless man, wringing his cold and clammy hands with futility, who says "Nobody can help me," and then threatens to shoot himself in the stomach. He says he is sinful and there would be much relief in the world if he would end his life this way. These were all patients I have treated successfully. All are well and living normal lives today.

Heinz Hartmann, in one of his articles, stated, "Methodological development of analysis would mainly rest on the work of analysts, themselves. One would hope them to be prepared for this additional task." [3]

He writes about the difficulties in communication in the preverbal period of life. He mentions the contributions of the child analyst toward an understanding of this preverbal period.

In my experience, the preverbal period is best understood by the study of psychosis. I have stated before that psychosis has its origins in the human relationships of the first year of life. The baby gathers its strength and optimism from its early contacts with the mother.[4] If the infant's basic needs are not met, growth will go on superficially, but psychosexual development becomes arrested and fixation at an oral dependent level takes place. Somehow, it reminds me of a rubber band that is being

* Many men, since Freud, have contributed other named theories as supposed oppositions to psycho-sexual development. Whether the therapist follows Reichian, Rankian, Adlerian, Jungian, Piagetian, Cybernetics, Dianetics or even the theories of a witchdoctor in Africa, the eventual concept varies little.
** See Chapter VI.

stretched. The point is reached where the rubber band can be stretched no longer and it snaps back to where it started.

The reasons for the developmental arrest are not all known. It is probably caused by internal tensions in the mother, preventing her from relating in a maternal way to the infant. The reasons for this can be numerous. It may be due to the baby's inborn inadequacies (e.g., brain damage at birth), to external pressures in the home, or to mental illness in the mother. I believe the final story rests in the interpersonal communication of feeling between the mother and baby. If it is there, there will be growth— if it is not there will be fixation.

Some of my patients have told me of the unbearable loneliness that they cannot tolerate. I feel that psychosis occurs to relieve this loneliness. This is why I have said that psychosis is a complete way of life. It is a system to avoid loneliness but also to avoid human contact.

If the thinking were done in adult terms, it might be in these terms: "Look around the world is large and full. Surely there is a place for me. I can find love and recognition somewhere." But the psychotic individual is tortured.

There are also elements of guilt at work here too. This, I feel, is what causes the rubber band to snap back. Whether these elements come from early life as Melanie Klein states, or later on, as the more orthodox Freudians believe, I cannot answer. I know however, that every patient feels extreme guilt about receiving this oral emotional gratification from *anyone except the mother,* or a figure similar in personality to the mother. It is this guilt and subsequent ambivalence between instinct and superego that plays a role in causing psychosis or suicide. A psychotic man, torn between incest and oral needs, told me he tried "everything but intercourse" to try to get his mother to want him. You see the magnitude of these problems when oral and oedipal problems intertwine.

I have also mentioned another facet of this problem: the mother's gratification and need to keep the child infantile. There will always exist an unconscious fear on the mother's part that this child will leave. Patients told me they felt that if they got well their mother would die.

Freud himself meddled in family life when he felt it necessary. Certainly with little Hans, he tried to rearrange the family constellation, and it is said he attempted to mate a female patient with a man she loved.[5]

The analyst who deals with psychotic and borderline states must not ignore family dynamics. In studying myth, folk tales and rituals, I wondered what had become of the ancient customs of human sacrifice. Perhaps the one who has become psychotic is a sacrifice that is necessary to keep the rest of the family functioning.

To forsake one's total absorption with one's inner feelings as the ultimate of existence is a major task. This is especially true for the individual who has emerged from a psychosis. Indeed what is needed is to fit oneself into a pattern of real daily living. In one's inner phantasies the world can be as exciting as one wants to make it. To adapt oneself to a real world where one can be adored, noticed, respected, appreciated, wanted and loved in the true sense is not easy.

Many observers have described two types of schizophrenia. They are (1) reactive and (2) process.[6]

The reactive type lived normally, was essentially happy, reacted well with the outside world—then suddenly had an acute breakdown. With the right treatment (in most cases, all that may be necessary are the proper interpretations, temporary separation from the outside world and self reflection) these people are able to go back, live, and be better than ever before in their lives.

The process type person had always been a problem. Daily life was always painful, existence had always been borderline. These people have been like turtles, always the ego emerging just a little from its shell of isolation—always again ready to withdraw. Terror, loneliness, shyness, a secret world of phantasy have always been present. In most, problems in living made parents or school authorities seek professional consultation while they were very young. Many were labeled as childhood schizophrenia. A poor school record, manneristic behavior such as stereotyped rocking, speech problems, facial expressions and bluntness of affect with a lack of interest in everyday affairs, have caused a diagnosis of borderline intelligence or retardation, in some cases.

These patients all lack spontaneity, imagination, aggression. They are very dull people to be with. They do their routine tasks well when told what to do. Most are compulsive, ritualistic and may have some similarities to what Abraham calls "anal characters".[7]

I see the problem in a dynamic way. I find these people withdrawn and with no self confidence or social grace. I, too, recognize their anality. They have never experimented. Might it be that experimentation begins with accepting and handling feces? A baby who handles his feces is able to feel them, smell them, taste them, and begin to mold them. These people are afraid to make a move for fear it is not perfect. There is an old saying "every dog can smell his own." Perhaps the sense of being, of existing, begins with feces.

There is little room in our competitive world for individuals who have once been psychotic to experiment. Treatment of this phase has been neglected badly until recently.

True, more sheltered workshops and half-way houses are being created. The treatment must be spontaneous and individualistic. New adjunct therapies such as art therapy, the dance, poetry therapy and music therapy attempt to bring out the individual. Work gives a patient confidence, especially if he earns money. But with each experimental move, more of the individuality emerges. This is psycho-sexual development and it is slow.

The release from the psychotic world has been a hard-won victory in therapy, but the patient is cautious. In most cases, against his will, he has put trust and faith in a human being again. Yes, the therapist has won the patient's confidence, but he is only one person. There is a memory of all the deep hurts that the patient has experienced in the past. The therapist, family and Foundation must not relinquish responsibility. There is no doubt, as many patients have told me, that when self-esteem is low, every rejection is multiplied.

The progress is from (1) psychosis, to (2) trust in the therapist; but the biggest test is yet to come, (3) functioning in the outside world.

Rejections are frequent in the outside world and rewards are hard-won. There is give and take. The therapist must prepare his patient for this. I have mentioned in another chapter that being a permissive mother-like person is only one phase of therapy—therapy in a protective environment. At this point, the therapist must feel confident that the work in the protective environment has satisfied the oral starvation that existed in the psychosis, and he must show this confidence to the patient. In most cases, as psychosis begins, it starts with a feeling of impending doom, a picture of darkness, and thoughts of the world coming to an end. The world symbolizes mother. This is an interpretation from the unconscious, but it also represents reality. Everything in the external world seems to be ending. Because of internal stress, the external world collapses but the patient must find his place in the real world before he can entirely believe this. Now the external world again must take the place of the mother surrogate, or the therapist. This is a trial and error period. I know of one patient who could stand no contact with his reality. He had been psychotic since the age of 15 and he was now 28. The balance between psychosis and real feeling was a very delicate one in his case and he would interchange one for the other almost instantaneously. When he thought of himself in his place in the world, the darkness was too much for him to face. He had lost 13 years, his brothers were married. He regressed again, probably never again to make the effort to recover.

Another patient told me "the outside world is my only problem" as he recovered from his psychosis and began preparing himself for a teaching career. It was a bigger bite than he could chew, and after spending several years in institutional confinement, he regressed into the psychosis again. I think this phase of therapy is very important and taxes the therapist's ingenuity as much as does the management of the deep psychosis.

The trend in all patients' thinking is to return to home and mother, hoping things have changed. Patients soon find out that no change has been made at home, and the repetitive pattern of behavior of the other members of the family may cause varying degrees of regression. I have worked with many families at this stage. Sometimes a patient continues to improve in this environment and does not need to seek another way to solve his problems. In other cases, dissidence is too great at home and the patient finds out that to survive he must move outside his original family.

The therapist must be tolerant. He has to allow his patient to experiment by trial and error and to guide him; but he must not do things for him if the patient is to find his way as a person.

Soon it is successful. The proud and in-the-beginning hesitant, "I" begins to emerge. "*I* like things this way," "This is the way *I* think about it." And the patient, with pride, defends his own point of view. It can be seen now that the work had not been in vain.

I discharged one patient who I felt had enough understanding about the unconscious to try an effort at home. She could hardly wait. She had been catatonic and was enthusiastic about beginning life anew. A few visits with her parents at the unit had been well controlled and went successfully. Despite my warning that her parents had not changed, she clung to her enthusiasm, sure that everything had changed at home. She had changed, so they must have.

The first month was quite revealing to her but she developed some of the old defenses. They had not changed but she was determined to stick it out. Gradually, she became quite hostile and stubborn and then outwardly aggressive toward the mother. The parents, as they had done before, said that this was a return of the psychosis and desperately wanted to get rid of her (in the worst way), especially since some of the things she was saying they admitted were true. Once before, while the girl was like this, they persuaded a well-known psychiatrist to give her shock treatment. She was in a "manic-depressive psychosis," they said, though no symptoms of mania existed (no flights of ideas, etc., were seen). *This was frank emotion,* and true feeling emerging, although it was hostile, I agree. I was in danger of losing this case. The girl trusted me and I think only her tenacity in meeting her appointments kept her on my rolls. She explained that the hostility was the only way she could deal with the mother's verbal attacks. She had to protect herself now and be tough if she was to survive. She became stronger, she no longer needed this protective armor and there was more peace at home. The girl, however, knew she had to leave the environment because the mother's attacks were incessant and would probably wear down even the strongest of minds, eventually.

The development of a healthy personality in chronic psychosis is slow and tedious. It is much like the growth and development of a child. One does not give up a piece of pathological behavior without a firm feeling of strength, using healthy reactions to replace the sick behavior. For instance, a symptom such as hair pulling (I am treating a 21 year old female who pulls out her hair, eyebrows and eyelid hair by systematic removal), is a substitute for a great many normal human emotional responses. An active hallucinatory system is similar.

George Herbert Mead, the 19th century social psychologist, used the terms "I" and "me" to describe the development of self.[8] To Mead, the "I" is the response of the organism to the attitudes of others, the "me" is the organized set of attitudes of others which one himself assumes. The "me" develops before the "I". "Me's" development of attitudes might similarly be compared to the development of positive identifications. The growth of "me" might be the "Home Base" cemented within the patient through the therapeutic process. The patient is literally "enthralled" or "in love" with the therapist and is open and receptive to all of him. It might be compared with the early mother-child nursing relationship. Imprints of the others' attitudes imbed themselves deeply in the mind.

This is the forerunner of the development of the "I". The "me" and "I" make up the self. Intrapsychically, it is a constant battle. To avoid anxiety and catastrophe, one part of the mind tries to maintain the status quo. It seeks equilibrium and security. This part of the mind must be constantly challenged if growth of "I" is to continue. This challenging is done by parents, teachers and friends with children. It is the job of the therapist in treatment. Sometimes it is insurmountable. In some people the defense against basic dread or anxiety taxes the basic core and they fight with every instinct of preservation to maintain security. If we look at the patients' side, perhaps we would not blame them. Each giving up of a part of psychosis leaves an empty void that can once more be filled with loneliness and terror. It was this emptiness that fostered psychosis. Day after day of loneliness, with only slight gains in reality, seem to make it all not worthwhile.

There are some cases where total human involvement is not enough to overcome resistance. One may break through for a few minutes, and then there is sheer exhaustion. The defenses return very quickly, and one does not have the human effort to sustain another attempt. One is satisfied with a slight rationalistic "wearing down" of the defenses. If only one had a powerful drug in this case.

LSD * and other hallucinogenic type drugs might give some promise in this area in certain cases.[9] One often feels that if the patient really let go he would actually be destroyed or would disintegrate or disappear. Certainly the patient feels this. But, as therapists, we cannot accept this as being anything more than our own inadequacies and we must search for new tools beyond our own frail human resources. There is a need for something here. Therefore it will come. *I have just written about an insoluble problem. Most that I meet are solvable.*

---

*Perhaps LSD and similar "consciousness expanding drugs" work best with those who are not "mentally sick" or psychotic, but rather those who have a normal, well intact mind that seeks new perceptions and feelings. Perhaps it works by showing the individual he does not have to fear "letting go."

Childhood autism is an example. The child in this state only recognizes his self, nothing outside. But this self is dead. When he is given clay, he smashes it with his fist. If one is successful in entering his world, he becomes YOU. Everything is the therapist. He is the therapist and he begins to emerge as the therapist works. Once opened up, he takes in from his mother (who must be worked with), and others. One five year old boy I am treating is now "Batman". This is his total, all-consuming identity.

The Emergence of "I"—The Area of Total Commitment

Kierkegaard called schizophrenia "the sickness unto death".[10] It was Kierkegaard who also said "pooh-pooh" to the manifesto that "the less we are involved in a given situation, the more clearly we can observe the truth." The fact that a therapist participates in a total way and in a real way does not necessarily cloud the field. Conversely, without total participation (Sullivan called it "participant observation"), one does not allow the patient to let go. Total participation is not necessary for the "me" formation, i.e., one can copy or imitate the attitude of others. This does happen to some degree in the failures of psychoanalytic analysis. An example is the patient who has a good intellectual understanding of himself as a result of analysis, but no true emotional insight. However, for emergence of the "I", total commitment by the therapist is necessary. Total commitment by the patient will then follow.

What is the "I"? According to Mead, the "I" is the source of all that is new original. We do not passively adapt ourselves to the reactions of others, but we actively create new relationships to other individuals. Because of the "I", we live in a constant state of growth, in which fresh perspectives are continually being created.

By its own struggles with its insistent difficulties, the human mind is constantly emerging like the chambered nautilus, into enlarged new worlds of greater promise.

The world of interpersonal relationships is in a continual state of flux, a continuous interplay of "I" and "me". This goes on in each individual, it is hoped, in a wonderful ballet. Where it is absent there is fixation, stagnation, and human sickness.

The Value of the Crisis

In the psychotherapy of the psychoses one must, with imagination, create crises. Oxford theologian Ian Ramsey has stated that socialization has immunized man against the wonder and mystery of existence. "We are now sheltered from all the great crises of life. Birth is a kind of discontinuity between the prenatal and post-natal clinics, while death just takes somebody out of the community possibly to the pre-recorded hymns at the funeral parlor." [11] The psychotic, chronically ill, has shielded himself from the normal crises of life—probably because of the utter frustration and failure that reality brought him. It is well known that crisis precipitates change.

Despair and the Cleansing of the Soul

Nietzsche said, "The thought of suicide is a great consolation; by means of it one gets successfully through many a bad night." [12]

In the separation of "me" and "I" there is despair. Eventually the point of ebullience of *me* is reached. It is the false "I". The wearing of another's personality no longer produces social magic. One sees this in utter blackness. "I am really nothing" results in anguished breath-sucking despair. There is no suicide in despair. It is different from depression. Depression is emptiness and nothingness. Despair has life. There is a "me". There is separation and loneliness. There exists the search for freedom and separation from the human herd and its unwritten laws. And it will come with greater "I".

But it is not insane; it is not wild; there is no loss of reality forever— just momentarily. The pain at that moment is too great. One can only suffer it. And then it is gone. Suicide and death are cheated. There is a true rebirth, a true cleansing of the soul.

Despair: A Personal Battle with the Problem

As I sat listening to a Symposium on Suicide (held at the Benjamin Franklin Hotel in Philadelphia—American Psychological Association Convention, Sept. 1964) I felt unusually drawn to the remarks made that morning. I felt a strange feeling as I listened. It was of infinity, of mysterious aura, of buoyancy, of unity with air and space. We psychiatrists call it depersonalization. For some reason, the subject made a deep impression.

The evening before, I had returned from a month's camping trip with my family. On such trips I have always found complete peace and rest in the outdoors. A unity with nature and freedom from the burdens of responsibility at the same time. (Perhaps my wife would have liked to spend her vacation another way; but seeing me happy seems more important to her.) The trip had been wonderful, and I had mixed feelings about returning to the rigid demands of my practice again.

The evening of my return, I went over a paper previously prepared which I was to give the following day. I was on a symposium, "New Frontiers in Psychiatry", and my presentation was called "Ambivalence in the Therapeutic Family Structure." As I read it and attempted to cut it to fit the fifteen minutes that I was allotted, I had little real feeling for my material. Instead there was a feeling of futility. My offering was meager, where the others would be full. There was none of the self-satisfaction which I had experienced after reading the first draft back in June. I was obsessed with finding a funny, interesting, opening remark to catch my audience.

The next day I walked in the rain to the hotel where the symposium was to meet. I was soaked when I arrived and spent some time in the men's room drying out. I walked into the meeting room nonchalantly, five minutes early—and was immediately greeted by the Chairman. He looked worried lest I fail to arrive. All the others were already seated on the rostrum.

The audience soon filled the room. Dampness and overcrowding prevailed. People were standing quietly but impatiently. It was obvious that another, much larger room was needed. We moved again. Soon, this too, was filled to capacity, and people began to sit on the floor leaning against the walls. I was to be the last speaker.

Each speaker read his paper and there was the usual applause. I felt a sense of power and importance as I gazed at the audience. There were many friends among the strange faces. It was at that moment that I decided to discard the text that I had so dilligently prepared and to talk extemporaneously.

I began well, but then I seemed to run out of words. Soon I was handed the five-minute slip by the moderator. This I took as a sign that they wanted me to stop. I knew I had been bad. All I had said consisted of praise for my teacher—with a few inconsequential remarks about my own work. I failed to realize that each panelist had received the same warning. But I wanted to end the talk, to sit down and withdraw into myself. The audience seemed to me to be a mass of cold, angry faces. I thanked them and sat down.

No one came up to tell me how well the paper had been presented. All my friends remained silent. Only my wife asked, "Why didn't you read the paper?" "I don't know," was my reply.

It was then that I felt all those feelings which had been building steadily since the five-minute warning. They came flooding in upon me. I felt darkness, heaviness and smothering. My feeling of insignificance became a feeling of nothing at all. I became frightened . . .

There was some relief in self-accusation and belittlement. "I am no good. I never was."

That night I paced and talked out loud in the bedroom. I spoke half to myself and half to my wife who was trying to get some sleep. I knew I was upsetting her, making her angry, but revenge was part of my intent. When I had asked her how the talk had been she answered "Terrible, people were laughing at you. You looked tense and stage frightened."

I do not blame her. She had been hurt and robbed of a sense of pride in my delivery. She was getting back at me.

But her misunderstanding of my feelings that had now become despair was another blow. I didn't sleep that night. The day repeated and repeated in my mind and each time it was worse.

Suicide was never so strong in my mind. It was only a matter of the best way. Shooting seemed best. Perhaps only the verbal revelation of my plans gave me the strength to stop there. *It was awful.*

On the third day, despair was still there in the morning. Yesterday was better by the time afternoon came. The self accusation and inward direction was lost in the physical labor of fixing my daughter's horse stable.

Things were bad again the next day. The previous night my father dressed me down by saying, "you would have been better not to present yourself at all than to make a fool of yourself. You did the Clinic no good." There was restless sleep at night and I remember shouting, "Officer, Officer!" I vaguely remember a mob chasing me with a rope. Lynching! I was running for my life. It seemed like a dream, but was it real?

The next morning was the worst. I didn't want to get out of bed, but I knew if I didn't I'd slip deeper into this. The ideas of being no good would become more fixed. It seemed to be too easy. I remembered some of my patients who allowed themselves to be passive in the face of these feelings. I arose with difficulty, put on a track outfit, and ran a mile.

I recall that I am now in my office. It is Labor Day and all is quiet. If I did not sit down and write, I feel the feelings might soon be lost. I am feeling better once more, and when I feel better, I feel more whole and stronger than I've ever been. I feel more real too.

How long this despair will continue, I do not know. A little is still here.

But, I will not kill myself, for I know this would be really the end. It is not the happy moments of life—but physical pleasures that keep me alive. However they seem meaningless to me right now.

Such are the recollections of despair, remembered.

It is flirtation with death and the breathtaking experience of change of emotion that I want again. My own unknown. I know that only *by staying alive* will I experience this again.

It seems to me that in order to magnify our range of feeling, each one of us must experience this inner death and life many times. I feel sorry *for those who have gone by their own hand,* no matter how great they once were.

The Subject of Will

> *The will to overcome an emotion is ultimately only the will of another or of several other emotions.*
>
> NIETZSCHE

The subject of will is an important subject, if one is to consider existence after psychosis, because in all psychosis there is a disability of will. Somewhere along the line there has occurred an ever widening split between the will and the object of will. Enough frustration of this sort results in complete deadening of the will. Perhaps this is the salient feature of chronic psychosis.

But what causes the death of will? Can the flame be rekindled? To live there must be a will to live. This is different from breathing. Breathing is an instinct. It is usually effortless, but if one holds one's nostrils and mouth shut, then there must be a fight for breath. This takes psychic determination. Will is awakened. To feel this will re-emerge, can give a person faith.

What kills will? Certainly the imposition of a stronger will has an effect. This is an outside force resisting one's will—pushing it down. There also must be inside factors at work.

Man's inability to understand all his emotions such as guilt, anger, grief, melancholy, exuberance, revenge, bearing pain, inflicting pain, fear, anxiety, loneliness, love, and sexual passions has forced the crippling of his will. This very writing is again an aid to understanding another factor of man's emotion. . . . The very fact that he has lost his will, for if one is to regain one's will, surely one must know first that it is lost. If man accepts the position of supreme authority, as does a physician or a psychiatrist, he must honestly be trying not to destroy faith by his treatment. The loss of faith is antecedent to the loss of will.

What Does It Mean—God Is Dead?

What part does God play in the emergence of the human personality? Certainly, in a mentally-disturbed individual there is little understanding of God. Instead of understanding there is "religiosity", compulsive ritualization, but little faith. But the empty churches and the threats of a rising Godless society have caused all the world's philosophers, clergy, psychologists, and laymen to wonder what Nietzsche meant in the end of the last century when he said "man's soul has gone stale."

Man's quest for God takes place in a series of stages:

1. *Forced absolute Deism.* . . . This usually takes place during his emerging years, from five to thirteen, where the idea prevails (at least in America) that it is good for children to "get religion." In their will is our peace" cries Dante in the Paradise, genuflecting before the throne of God. The forced teachings of good and evil, heaven and hell, become tied in with the growing child's emotional feelings toward the adult world. In the weak, where strong guilt prevails, religion becomes the unwitting ally to mental illness, religious delusions and hypocrisy—all things that it, itself, had hoped to avoid in the saving of souls.

2. *Revolt into freedom.* . . . Freedom means a separation from the human herd and its laws, including the laws of God. According to ancient tradition, Daedalus glued together wings of wax and feathers and soared toward the sun. Why did he do it? Presumably, because for him the act of liberation from this earth on which he was forced to live . . . even a liberation lasting the briefest of moments—represented the greatest possible measure of freedom.[13]

3. *The denial of God's existence.* . . . The stronger young minds are able to break away—deny God's existence and call themselves Atheists. Joshua Liebman says, "like many of my colleagues, I have wrestled with a

number of these non-believers in the dark night of their souls, attempting to reassure them with such rational comfort as I might command. But for years I hit my head against the stone wall of their imperviousness to logic. Gradually I have come to see that all the rational arguments used on many atheists and agnostics are futile because words do not, and cannot, touch the real causes of their disbelief. I wish to suggest that these causes stem from the sufferer's own inner conflict, aggression and cruelty, projected upon the larger canvas of the universe. Somewhere in the crucial years of his development, in some very important area of his life, his parents let him down catastrophically. In his unconscious, he condemned them as untrustworthy and faithless. Disbelief in life, skepticism about humanity, the denial of God—all sink their roots in the soil of emotion long before exposure to courses in philosophy and science." [14]

4. *Agnosticism* . . . a doubting of the Old Deism but a desire not to close the doors on a concept of God. This is a beginning of a need for something—a floating search.

5. *The belief that God is nature.* . . . In the bosom of mother earth one can find security, peace and love. "I have heard it said that a man can only work himself free from gloom, self-torture and despondence by observing nature and letting his heart go out to other men. Even the slightest knowledge of nature in any of her aspects and any real attack of her problems, as a gardener, say, or a farmer, a hunter, or a miner, will take us out of ourselves. The forces of the mind are turned on real objects, genuine things, and little by little we win the greatest satisfaction, clarity and knowledge of which we are capable." [15]

6. *Humanism* . . . *the finding of faith.* Does one find faith if one finds love? The answer is probably yes. What about Karl Barth's warning that "a God found in human depths may be an imagined idol."? [16] But is this not a paradox? Does not one have to taste, sample and understand humanism to feel it oneself? And how else is it possible but with deep and involved contact with another human being? If we kill the old God, we do it because his own impotence has reduced us to an unworthy nothingness, from the depths of which all our own dignity is lost. *He is dead,* because he has *denied our existence.*

Man cannot have a soul if his very existence is denied. Before man can look for his soul, he must know his body. He must understand his instinctual responses and all the emotions within himself. This, all totalled, represents his humanism. This he can *only* learn by borrowing other human beings' humanism.

The New Concept of God

One cannot find a concept of God in luxury and security, but only in the catastrophe of exile, where one's world has been shaken to its foundations. There is a time where one finds one's own humanism. Man has then found himself and he no longer has the deep quest for identity. He has felt despair, he has survived catastrophe (perhaps many times), but there still is a need for something greater than himself.

Can man accept a God that is limited? Yes, but only in the sense that this God accepts man's individual identity. Man's new concept of God is a feeling that is as individual as each man is himself. It is deeply personal. The feeling is strong and indestructible and man will protect it until the last moment of his existence. He wants it to live after he dies. Perhaps this is really soul—a warm, humanistic organism that knows life by its own feelings and is content within.

References

[1] Brossard, C. "Revolutionary treatment of the mentally ill." LOOK MAGAZINE. p. 30–39, April 5, 1966.

[2] Freud, S.; Breuer, J. STUDIES IN HYSTERIA. London, Hogarth, 1957. p. 160–161.

[3] Hartmann, H. "Comments on the scientific aspects of psychoanalysis." In: PSYCHOANALYTIC STUDY OF THE CHILD. N.Y., Intnl. Universities Press, 1958. v. 13, p. 135, 145.

[4] Abraham, K. "Oral eroticism and character." In his: SELECTED PAPERS. N.Y., Basic Books, 1954. p. 399–400.

[5] Freud, S. "Analysis of phobia in a five-year old boy." In his: COLLECTED PAPERS. London, Hogarth, 1925. v. 3.

[6] Fine, H. J.; Zimet, C. M. "Process-reactive schizophrenia and genetic levels of perception." JOURNAL OF ABNORMAL AND SOCIAL PSYCHOLOGY. 59:83–85 (1959).

[7] Abraham, K. *op. cit.* p. 370.

[8] Desmonde, W. H.; Mead, G. H.; Freud, S. PSYCHOANALYSIS AND THE FUTURE. N.Y., N.P.A.P., 1957. p. 31–50.

[9] "LSD" LIFE MAGAZINE. 60(12):40–46 (March 25, 1966).

[10] Kierkegaard, S. "The sickness unto death." In: Bretall, R., ed. KIERKEGAARD ANTHOLOGY. Princeton, Princeton University Press, 1951.

[11] Ramsey, I. "Toward a hidden God." TIME MAGAZINE. 87(14):85 (April 8, 1966).

[12] Nietzsche, F. THE PHILOSOPHY OF NIETZSCHE. N.Y., Random House, 1954. p. 88.

[13] Hlasko, M. "The protest dies." REFLECTIONS (Merck, Sharp & Dohme) 1(1):12–17 (March–April 1966).

[14] Liebman, J. L. PEACE OF MIND. N.Y., Simon & Schuster, 1956. p. 24–60.

[15] Goethe, J. W. von. THE WISDOM OF GOETHE. N.Y., Carlton House, n.d. p. 36.

[16] Ramsey, I. *op cit.* p. 82–87.

CHAPTER X

Further Notes on Therapy

"The use of steam, electricity, wind, water and other involuntary forces in nature is dependent upon the intelligence of an engineer. Our subconscious power cannot function without its own engineer—our conscious technique. It is only when an actor feels that his inner and outer life on the stage is flowing naturally and normally, in the circumstances that surround him that the deeper sources of his subconscious gently open, and from them come feelings we cannot always analyze. For a shorter or longer space of time they take possession of us whenever some inner instinct bids them. Since we do not understand this governing power, and cannot study it, we actors call it simply nature." [1]

Although the above quotation comes straight out of a basic textbook in acting and not from the vast storehouse of psychiatric literature, it has a great deal of application to the psycho-therapy of schizophrenia.* Treatment techniques stem from the unconscious resources of the therapist who uses them. It is the skillful manipulation of one's tools that makes the artist. Although the tools of the art of therapy are intangible, they are there to be used. They might, perhaps, be better understood by the actor, the comedian, the used-car salesman or the witch doctor. For all these people use the resources of the unconscious as does the psychotherapist. The actor's skill finds expression in the spoken word and body movements or verbalization as opposed, say, to the written word of the poet, the painting of the artist, the cabinet of the cabinetmaker or the surgery of the surgeon.

The treatment of schizophrenia has a long history of growth. This growth has been in three dimensions. Although in most cases each of

* Schizophrenia is used here as a catchall for all psychoses of known non-organic origin.

these has developed independently, they are all of equal importance in treatment.

Humane Physical Care

Pinel freed the inmates from the chainings in the Bicetre at the time of the French Revolution. Similar changes occurred in both England and America about the same time. Perhaps the greatest innovation can be seen today in a small community of 15,000 in Belgium. For over 900 years the mentally ill from all over have been accepted in the Belgian Church of St. Dymphna and its annex, the "sick room", and then placed in the community of Gheel in the houses of the villagers.

Similar "family care" colonies, on a smaller scale, can be found in Holland, France, and Germany. Tradition and religion helped the villagers of Gheel, Belgium to survive severe damage during the last war. Because the village was located near the Albert Canal, it suffered severe bombing. The original "sick room", where the lunatics were kept as far back as 1462, was completely demolished in the battle between British and German forces. Homes also were destroyed and many patients and villagers died. Before the war in 1939 there were over 4,000 patients living in village homes; now there are 1,400. Breakup of families and their ties and economic neglect of patients on the Government's part has caused a further reduction. I have visited Gheel and have seen the good effects of family care when a patient lives "as a guest" with a strong wholesome family.

But Gheel is a state institution. Poor pay has reduced the staff to a pitifully low skeleton crew. Other than good family care, there is little else in the way of treatment of the illness. And so although this one *essential ingredient* of good therapy is present, it is not enough in a great many cases. There are many old schizophrenics who have been in homes for over 40 years, well cared for with their own rooms. But their illness is still present, and it has left them peculiar and isolated. They are guests but not real family members—not by their own or anyone else's choice. They are victims of the "devil" that has never been exorcised and that has slowly paralyzed them.

Therefore, although humane care is essential, it is not enough by itself. Understanding of the "devil" is perhaps just as important.

It is reasonable to assume that a scholar with access to the records of the ancient Greek, Chinese and Indian civilizations probably could find evidence of man's early concern with self-awareness and self-enlightenment. Reflection would have led him to create the need to infer from has direct experiences that some of his mental processes go on without his immediate awareness of them. Whatever he might have called these hidden mental processes, they would be in essence the same as what we today call *unconscious mental processes* or the *unconscious*.

If we deny the existence of the unconscious (which seems to be the sophisticated attitude of some psychologists today), we are shutting the curtains on the hard-won enlightenment developed over 2,000 years of Western civilization. We are doomed again to an age of mysticism, fear and darkness. This time there will be no renaissance or rediscovery.

However, if we accept the existence of the unconscious fully, mankind may open itself to an unexpected renaissance, not "moral" but biological and human. Human dignity will be preserved. The unconscious mind is the expression of the life process in each individual. If there is a God, he must speak there. If there is a healing power, it must operate there. If there is a principle of ordering in the life cycle, its most powerful manifestation must be found there.

Comprehensive analytic theory must today encompass without bias all relevant philosophical and psychological school of thought about the unconscious. Freud's greatness lies not so much in his particular ideas as in the fact that he compelled the race to face the problem of finding an adequate concept of the unconscious mind. He showed, once and for all, that the unconscious is so powerful it cannot be neglected.

The development of a theory for understanding mental processes can become most complicated. But if one builds his theory around the understanding of the unconscious, what might have resulted in a mass of psychological jargon representing everything from orality to thought process, can instead follow a relatively simple path. In the face of irrationality, one must find faith.

An understanding of what we, today, call the unconscious has developed through Western civilization side by side with man's self-awareness. Man has always fought himself and his tendency to prefer his own personal conception of order as final or universal, but this exists through literary history. We know that ideas of the unconscious date back at least to the early 1700's. The writing of Wordsworth and Coleridge in the early 1800's show it as an adjective and in the 1650's in both German and English literature it was used in noun form—as *The Unconscious*. The idea of applying the developing objective knowledge of unconscious processes to provide a technique for treating pathological mental conditions first appeared about the end of the 18th century. The first systematic professional efforts to base curative procedures on theories about the structure of unconscious mental processes were made 100 years later in the last decades of the 19th century.

Whyte says, "Measured against the importance of such knowledge and techniques, the 50 years and more which have passed since these attempts began, and the high hopes placed on them, it is unfortunate that no self-improving psychological methods of permanently curing grave mental conditions have yet been established." [2]

One psychologist told me that in over 100 cases followed for more than five years, similar results were obtained regardless of the school of psychotherapy. All her results show that the patient was no better than before treatment. . . . But perhaps all is not lost. Irrationality will not prevail. The world will not come to an end.

A History of the Unconscious [3]

Galen (A.D. 130–200), the Greek physician and philosopher, is credited with the recognition that we make unconscious inferences from perceptions.

St. Augustine (350–430), the great Christian philosopher, was impressed as Plato had been with the power of memory.

St. Thomas Aquinas (1224–1274), said: "I do not observe my soul apart from its acts. There are thus processes in the soul of which we are not immediately aware."

Jakob Boehme (1575–1642), was a German shoemaker and a mystic. To him God was "underneath" not "above." God is nature.

Writers of the 16th century were beginning to show, if not an understanding, at least an awareness of mental life. Cervantes (1547–1616) with Don Quixote and self delusions and of course, Shakespeare (1564–1616)

> My mind is troubled, like a fountain stirr'd;
> and I myself see not the bottom of it.

and Macbeth:

> Canst thou not minister to a mind diseased;
> Pluck from the memory of a rooted sorrow;
> Raze out the written troubles of the brain;
> And with some sweet oblivious antidote
> cleanse the stuff'd bosom of that perilous stuff
> which weighs upon the heart?

Doctor:

> Therein the patient
> Must minister to himself.
>
> (Macbeth, V, iii 44)

Descartes' (1596–1650) reflections on his dreams, and Spinoza's (1632–1677) stressing of unconscious memory can be found in the writings of philosophers of this period.

Later, in the period of 1670–1730, there were Audwath, Leibniz, Vico, Shaftesburg and Kames. Kames was the first to use the words "conscious" and "unconscious" to characterize awareness and nonawareness in relation to particular mental functions.

Rousseau (1712–1778) showed some understanding of basic force when he said "the true and primary motives of the greater part of my actions are not so clear to me as I have for a long time imagined."

In the later 1700's professional psychology had already begun. Herder (1744–1803) wrote about "knowing and feeling." C. P. Moritz (1757–1793) founded a journal of Observational Psychology in 1783 which contained articles such as "Strength of Self-Consciousness" and "Walking Dreams" and "Strange Behavior without Consciousness." F. A. Mesmer (1733–1815) claimed to achieve permanent cures of mental illness by overcoming consciousness through the use of "animal magnetism."

The German Philosophers Fichte, Shelling, Hegel, Schopenhauer and Nietzsche developed the conception of the unconscious mind as dynamic principle underlying conscious reason.

Langerman (1768–1832) published "On a Method of Diagnosing and Curing Morbid States of Mind" (written in Latin) in 1797. In this work he developed the thought that many physical diseases were of psychological origin and stressed the need to treat these by psychotherapy.

One of the greatest discoverers around 1800 was J. W. Goethe (1749–1832). Goethe, the poet, said "Man cannot persist long in a conscious state, he must throw himself back into the unconscious, for his root lives there." It was he, too, who said that sometimes the only thing that kept him from committing suicide was the ability to flirt with thoughts of that act.

Ego psychology had its beginnings with the Danish philosopher, Kierkegaard (1813–1855). Kierkegaard: "Despair, viewed so that one does not consider whether it is conscious or unconscious. . . . If the self is not true to itself, then it is in despair, whether it knows it or not." [4]

There are men who influenced Freud directly but are little known. C. G. Carus (1789–1869) was a German physician and friend of Goethe. Many of Carus' works were found in Freud's library at his death. Carus stated in one of his works on "The Psyche," "The key to the understanding of this character of the conscious life lies in the region of the unconscious." [5]

Europe, and now even America, were influenced by mental process thought. Between 1870–1880, there were many writings about the unconscious, human physiology, instinct, will, ideas, reflexes, sexual love, feeling, morality, metaphysics and even probability theory. In Europe there were W. B. Carpenter, C. F. Fleming, A. Schmidt, E. Colsenet, E. Hering, Laycock and S. Butler. In America were Janet, Oliver Wendell Holmes and W. James.

There were the writers and philosophers, F. Nietzsche, and F. Dostoevsky.

If one might review this long history of the evolvement of ideas, one can see that the intellectual climate was ready for a Freud and his theories of psychosexuality.

The third part of history, has thus developed. I have described the evolvement of (1) care of the patient, and (2) theory of the unconscious.

The third factor important in the management of mental illness is (3) the techniques of therapy.

Techniques of Therapy following along with the Physical Care of the Mentally Ill

At first the treatment of the mentally ill was in the hands of the elders of the tribe, then the judiciary and those responsible for law and order took over. Frequently the mentally ill were subject to the same harsh treatment as was given law breakers. In medieval days they were subjected to the tortures given criminals and political prisoners.

However, with the idea that the mentally ill were possessed by the devil came the beginning of humane care and the development of techniques of "exorcism." For, if one could be possessed, one could be freed. The job of exorcism or removal of the illness became the province of mystics, witch doctors, and then the clergy. Not until the Age of Enlightenment in the early 1800's, did the medical profession influence techniques of therapy. At first physicians applied the tools of their trade. Their patients were sick and attempts were made to make them well. Diet, fresh air, medicaments, rest, nursing care, were all ingredients that were used. Patients were isolated from their toxic environment and removed to the hospitals. This was the time of centralization and the development of large city-like institutions.

For those who did not respond to the average means of treatment, more severe shock treatments were devised. Ice cold plunges in lakes and streams, needle showers, typhoid fevers and the more sophisticated insulin and electric shocks became the methods of choice. The surgeons entered the picture and prescribed operations to cut "pathways" which changed behavior. The new pharmaceutical companies employed biochemists who developed medications to tranquilize the mind.

There has always been a segment of the medical profession which attempted to influence the mind through non-physical means. These men have devoted themselves to furthering the use of a psychology to change behavior. They have always employed the ploys or "bag of tricks" of the medicine man, mystic and witch doctor, the man of the theatre, the court jester. They have borrowed from the poets, the writers and the philosophers. With the advent of psycho-sexual theory and speculations concerning the unconscious mind, they were able to explain more thoroughly to themselves, their colleagues and their patients, what they were doing.

Those who have contributed to the understanding of schizophrenia are worthy of mention:

Emil Kraepelin (1856–1926) is the first name of great importance. He adopted the French psychiatrist Morel's term, dementia praecox, and concluded after a comprehensive study of thousands of patients that a "state of dementia was supposed to follow precociously or soon after the onset of the illness." He thus doomed his patients as far as prognosis went, even by his terminology, for one who is demented can never function normally.

Kraepelin divided his patients into three groups: (1) the hebephrenic, (2) the catatonic and (3) the paranoid. His descriptions of hallucinations, delusions, incongruous emotivity, negativism, and stereotyped behavior are both accurate and brilliant, and it must be concluded that his organic and metabolic approaches still exist today in modern psychiatry as chemical approaches to mental disease. In all fairness to Kraepelin, it might be said that he later changed his views about dementia in schizophrenia. His organic theories were more accepted than his views on psychology. Critics feel that Kraepelinian psychiatry, in fact, held back the progress of the understanding of schizophrenia because of the tenacity with which his views were upheld. Zilboorg writes "the system of Kraepelin appears to have become a thing of the past as soon as it announced its own birth in 1896." [6]

Eugene Bleuler (1857–1939), the famous Swiss psychiatrist, is actually responsible for the name "schizophrenia," referring to what he called the "splitting of the various psychic functions." Bleuler concentrated on the processes of the thinking disorder itself, and thus dealt a blow to the organic approaches of Kraepelin. He described the disorder of the process of association, which to him was the most important characteristic of schizophrenia. He also described autistic behavior and ambivalence. Later, Bleuler was influenced by Freud, and used Freud's concepts of symbolism. In his book he mentioned that mental causes probably produced the symptoms of the disease, but that he could not dismiss organicity as the cause. He thought that perhaps a toxin was responsible. [7]

Adolph Meyer (1866–1950) reopened the psychologic approach to schizophrenia and this disorder became one of the major interests in his life. He wanted to study each patient from the beginning of life, in order to find all the factors contributing to the patient's condition. He called his approach psychobiologic, bringing into play both the beginning biologic and the psychogenic environmental factors. His philosophy may be considered one of the early dynamic approaches. Meyer said psychotherapy in schizophrenia was "negative and rarely clearly positive."

Carl Jung (1875–1962) made several important contributions to schizophrenia while he was still a colleague of Freud. He was the first to apply psychoanalytic concepts fully to schizophrenia. He said that it was an emotional disorder causing abnormal metabolic changes inflicting physical damage on the brain (psychosomatic). Jung was a philosopher and a thinker; his work on symbolism and the unconscious will still apply to the understanding of human personality. [8]

Paul Federn (1871–1950) was the Viennese contemporary of Freud who became most interested in the psychoses rather than neuroses. Federn contributed knowledge of depersonalization and estrangement. He also said: ". . . firstly, psychotics are still capable of transference; secondly, one part of the ego has insight into the abnormal state (he was thus the first to believe the psychosis could be cured with psychoanalysis); and thirdly, a part of the personality is still directed towards reality." [9]

Sigmund Freud (1855–1939) contributed greatly to the understanding of the schizophrenic psychoses although most of his theory was written not from personal involvement with his patients but from the writings of others. His interpretation of the Schreber case is a classic in the study of paranoid psychosis. He helped to replace the concept of deterioration with the concept of regression. Many of his concepts that have been applied to neurosis also apply to psychosis. His contribution is so great that the treatment of schizophrenia and other functional psychoses can be called in essence, analytic treatment. Freud, himself, felt that transference was not applicable to psychosis because of the negative withdrawal of the schizophrenic. It was others, through the application of his theories, who proved him wrong.

In the 1930's and early 1940's there were isolated cases of treatment of psychosis in the literature.

Sechahage worked long hours and many years with one patient.[10] Fromm-Reichmann did likewise on the wards of a private sanitarium.[11] Harry Stack Sullivan's sensitive way of describing emotional feeling has always made me want to understand the man even more. His emphasis on interpersonal relations causes more self-reflection and emphasis on the intrapsychic structure than he himself would have conceived as important. Actually, Sullivan made the psychotherapeutic treatment of schizophrenia his life's work.[12]

I readily acknowledge the influence of Freud, Sullivan and Rosen on my own work. The reader has found reference to them throughout this book.

All human beings cross the same barriers in the rise toward maturity. If one believes this, it is hard to believe that any emotionally disturbed person can really be diagnosed as hopeless. It is better to think in terms of maturation arrest, and fixation points, rather than chronicity or incurability.

In man's zeal to apply new found scientific theories and medically sound instruments to the treatment of the mind and soul, he had stepped with a heavy foot. There is little in today's literature about the effects that electric shock may have on brain function. Does electric shock cause brain damage? Although I have treated patients who had previously received electric shock treatment, who seemingly showed no ill effects from their electric convulsive therapy, and who were responsive and alert, I have also worked with patients who had 100–200 electric shock treatments and were dull, slow witted, rock ribbed, immovable and resistive. They were dead inside; burned out. I hate to say anyone is hopeless and perhaps somewhere, at some time, someone can help these people. The use of electric and other shocks is dying out.

Larsen and Vraa-Jensen have found brain damage following such electric shock.[13]

Oxygen saturation experiments done at Ohio State in 1955 showed the oxygen saturation of the blood after shock was below average normal functioning levels. Jacoby concluded that many complications and deaths were due to anoxia.[14]

Perhaps my harshness against electric shock and those physicians who use it is too strong. But even recently I was reminded of another complication of electric shock. A family got in touch with me about their 24-year-old son and brother. The father passed away two weeks ago and the mother had just come with the brother and daughter from California. They were grief stricken. (This son and brother felt that the house was wired and that his food was poisoned.) Two years ago he was hospitalized and then went into a catatonic-like state. The mother said over the phone "the doctors had to resort to electric shock; it was the only thing that brought him out of it."

But they were fearful to have me come over. The boy was deathly afraid of doctors. He was afraid, too, of electric shock. The daughter did not trust the doctors in the East, even though I told her I did not use electric shock and I described fully our live-in home treatment of mental illness. She was determined to go back to California . . . and this is what she did. It was as if no electric shock was given in California.

This *dread* of electric shock is certainly a complication. Perhaps, in some cases, it is what sustains a person at a level of comparative "wellness"— a reminder of what might reoccur if regression took place. In those poor unfortunates who do regress, the fear of this traumatic experience keeps them from reaching out. It only adds to their impoverishment and inability to establish a relationship.

Treatment with Schizophrenia

He who engages in the psychotherapy of psychosis must have both a theoretical formulation and the tools of operation. All through my years of practice I have attempted to further my understanding of the unconscious. Such understanding is essential for correct insight into the patient's expressions, utterances, and movements. It is basically the other person's feelings that one must understand. It seems obvious that if someone else understands us first, we are then able to understand ourselves. If the therapist has such knowledge of the unconscious always in mind, psychotherapy can never be dull. It is only the blocks within ourselves that make it dull. Something in us refuses to give way and we cannot communicate with, or understand the patient. I have always tried to recognize this and so have never ceased analyzing myself. At first I would go to an analyst (there were four who influenced me, three men and one woman) . . . and then I had my wife . . . and myself . . . and my patients.

One must throw himself into therapy with great involvement and then withdraw when the situation ceases to become dynamic. It is the aim of therapy to produce change. There should be no stagnation. There are no set rules to follow. There are books that describe techniques of therapy. They are good to read, but each has been devised by an individual therapist to fit his own personality. Every new therapist experiments with the techniques of his teacher, until he feels confident enough to devise his own, using his own personality resources. Just as the actor must use his emotions to move an audience, and yet have complete control of his emotions, the therapist must know his own unconscious reactions. The patient does not give the therapist time to learn his part. The therapist must be alert to understand each breath, gesture, movement or verbalization that the patient may have.

To the patient, who feels it is his life that is at stake, therapy is always a battle. Any change in equilibrium produces great anxiety. This anxiety is painful but necessary. It is a step in between. In order for it to be present, the patient has had to give up something (usually a symptom). It is like a leap over a large chasm between two mountain peaks. What is to be obtained must be conceived as being better than one has had.

There is not much that the psychotic really has that is real . . . this is why if a therapist persists, he can really win the patient. With the very sick, a therapist must have the patient a complete captive. For this reason, a controlled therapeutic environment is best. It represents the utmost security and warmth. The therapeutic home does reach the deep unconscious. It has the mother in her own nest and so can provide the ultimate. However, it provides an uncontrollable rivalry with the real parents. Sometimes this becomes so intense that a patient is snatched away by the real mother (who has influenced the father), with violent jealous hostility. If this occurs before the patient is ready, it is bad for the patient.

In treatment, I have always tried to pick out the one main defense the patient may use that day, and hammer at its irrationality. Sometimes this has meant great demands upon my time, perhaps seven or eight hours at a stretch (with coffee breaks). Time is a good substitute for understanding. Time will produce a closeness and warmth that will wear down the defenses. This requires intensive involvement and commitment of the therapist, who knows that simply being with someone else—even sharing the same bed—does not produce a close relationship.

As I said, each case has been important enough for me to keep myself free from any blocks. At our clinic there are always other therapists with whom to consult. I myself do not have to go back regularly to the analyst's couch as I did during the first eight years of practice.

In brief, the therapist must battle the patient's psychotic defenses and destroy them.* He must also offer his patient a real person, powerful, secure, loving and understanding enough to save him from his anxiety and his psychosis. This first contact with reality should be taken seriously. It is a binding and a lasting one. It must be respected and continued. It is better to let the apple ripen and fall naturally from the tree, than to pluck it violently while it is still unripe.

The therapeutic home and therapeutic family are the home base. It is they that provide the environment with warmth, emotional support and security. Therapy continues all during the waking hours and the environment is constantly dynamic as long as it is needed.

Bateson has noted that the mother is the child's first contact with reality and all subsequent interpersonal relationships are experienced in terms of the reactions of the baby toward its mother.[15]

In therapy, one does not win the patient from his real mother. Biology is stronger than psychology. First and early imprints are everlasting. The therapist joins the good in the patient's mother and allies with it. When the patient is strong enough to repudiate his own mother, he will be strong enough to let go of the therapist (and it will be the latter who will be dropped first). Those already parted from their mothers have the easiest time, but few psychotics have done this.

Rosen has repeatedly stressed the oral contact in the verbalizations of schizophrenia. In regression, the patient unconsciously attempts to re-experience the feelings that were felt in the womb before birth.[16] The feelings are of the warm fluid, restful sleep and growth without effort. Since it is no longer possible to return to the womb, an enclosed shell of his own is constructed—an unrealistic wall that protects him from reality.

Hallucinations in the psychotic represent the psychological feeding process. When the symbolism in the speech is understood, it will be found to be related to mother. Genital interpretations are not meaningful—sometimes harmful—in the early stages of treatment. The patient can only "taste" and "swallow" oral feedings and sometimes anal ones.

In the psychosis, the closest feeling of being at the breast comes from the hallucination. The psychotic cannot tolerate "your mother does not want you." This will always produce a *reaction*. Thus, a relationship is possible. For though the feeding is from the hallucinations, it is also from the good memories of infancy. But they were not enough to keep the patient from becoming psychotic. Weakness and passivity pervade the scene. With the "voices" he can remain passive, much as does a baby at the breast. "Milk, drink, bars" was the constant preoccupation of thought

---

* I have never ceased being disturbed at the confusion in outsiders as they watch me work. They do not understand, cannot comprehend. To many, I am crazy. Amusingly the more education, the more upset they become. Psychiatrists seem to react most strongly. *To fight irrationality*, seemingly irrational techniques must be used.

with one catatonic patient I have seen. He would answer a question such as "What day is it?" with such an expression. He constantly looked up at the ceiling much as a child looks up at its mother's breast.

The first important phase of treatment is to work completely through this breast fixation and the need for the incorporated mother of infancy. In various phases of treatment with this same catatonic boy, I would say, "Jimmy, your mother called and wants you to drop dead." When he was catatonic and quiet, this interpretation would be meaningless. When he was in a catatonic excitement on the way to recovery, this same sentence would drive him wild. He would foam at the mouth, scream, and shout, "Stop, don't eat him." It would take three strong men to control his thrashing around and prevent him from being hurt. Now, since he is better, he asks me please not to mention his mother. It hurts him when I do, but he says, "So what? I do not need her."

When the patient is working through the need for this infantile memory of a mother, he often cries or sobs. There may be depression or melancholia. It is as if something very basic were lost. Then there will be the gurgles, giggles, the restoration of eating, the gain of weight. It is the happy, contented baby stage.

I no longer fight with mothers. At first, I saw the patient as a helpless infant, but this is deceiving. It is humorous sometimes to take a group of women on ward rounds, where there exists a helpless psychotic . . . the women would attempt to "mother" the patient, as if "mothering" were all that is necessary for recovery. The psychosis is complicated.

I have found that it is best to work closely with a patient's mother, for she knows her daughter or son better than anyone. The patient, too, knows this. There is an intricate involvement. To understand one is to understand the other, and yet something goes wrong. Is it a maternal weakness, perhaps a defect in instinct that prevents delicate understanding early in life?

I find that my barometer of whether I'm doing the right thing for the child is the mother. Maybe the mother could not do it herself, but she knows what to do. After I have done it, she can tell me whether it has been good or bad for her child. At any rate, as I gain each new insight, I immediately share it with the mother. The mothers do want to help and the therapy engenders terrible maternal rivalry. I do know, however, that all the mothers are weak, and immature themselves, and have never been confident as mothers.

In the treatment, the therapist soon finds out that the nursing process alone is inadequate to meet the needs of the patient. The patient is an adult who has experienced growth at various levels of psycho-sexual development and the therapist must deal with the aggression and trickery that also exists. Oral giving alone is not enough. Rank stated it thus, "the strongest resistance to the severance of the libido transference at the end of analysis is expressed in the form of earliest infantile fixation of the mother."

Supporting the Budding Maturation

This is an equally important phase of treatment, although it is not as dramatic as overcoming the resistances. Patients vary in the amount of help they need toward maturation. Those who became sick early in life and always were "misfits" need much help. Those who seemed to function well until some situational trauma upset them enough to cause psychosis seem to need less help. This is probably because they have suddenly "blown a gasket" and when they recover, they are different—much stronger and more able to handle the situation that had previously upset them.

In maturation, the patient is taught to live freely in all of life's major situations. This description follows the psychoanalytic "psycho-sexual" developments of Freud, Abraham, Ferenzi, and their disciples.

The psychotic defenses are waning, and energy that was needed to maintain these defenses is transformed into free floating anxiety. With the therapist as "mother object" and the infant's new source of strength and nourishment, the feeling of being reborn begins to emerge. The food is security and knowledge. It is of great importance to "feed" the patient with delicate care, and only oral interpretations are made. Basically this means that in the unconscious a projecting object symbolizes a breast and any opening a mouth. Perhaps the oral period is the most important in schizophrenia, but the patient must pass through all the phases of psycho-sexual development, the anal, phallic and genital, before he can be considered mature. This occurs in a short space of time—perhaps a twentieth of the time it takes a normal child to mature.

I have already described the feeling of the oral sucking or breast period and shown how the concept of regression is related to Isakower's concept of falling asleep.[17] Lewin * expanded upon Isakower's work in his theories of the dream screen. Patients frequently mention feelings of choking and smothering. I believe that these feelings originate from the feelings of the mouth being enveloped by the large breast of the mother.[18]

The *schizophrenic* cannot eat gustily—bite hard, swallow or enjoy food. The oral-aggressive drive (oral period (a) sucking—passive, (b) biting—active) somehow was distorted in the mother-child relationship. In all cases there exists the ambivalence of eating the object and being eaten. One man, who screamed in horror as I came near him shouted "Don't eat me up; I feel as if my body is a bloody mess, torn apart—you've got the teeth of a whale." Another six year old autistic boy whom I would hold on my lap and feed with a bottle, would cringe in absolute terror when I opened my mouth and placed it near his. In the unconscious there

---

* Described in chapter on Epilepsy, p. 252.

is the fear of being eaten; but also the idea of being eaten by a larger object gives secret pleasure. To become like someone, one must have that person inside one's self. To be eaten means to be swallowed up, to exist no longer but also to be inside, safe and warm.

To make a person understand this is not always an easy task. Since it is deeply embedded in the unconscious of the individual—probably as deep as the early life of that person—words are not usually meaningful. Acting out the conflict can be more meaningful. For instance, it has been a clinical fact with me to see almost every patient who has emerged from a psychosis complain of pain in the teeth or mouth itself. There is a great deal of anxiety present with this. It is psychosomatic usually—unconscious—probably representing guilt for having eaten enough to overcome the hallucinations and the "bad dream" with which they were living. Few patients understand this interpretation. I always send them to a dentist. Sometimes bad teeth are found—but this does not change the interpretation. Why did they tolerate this decay for years while psychotic? While ill, they never requested a dentist.

Other patients when coming from psychosis vomit violently. It is as if they are getting rid of all the bad toxins orally.

All this occurs as the patient improves in the therapeutic environment. He is finding peace with his mouth and his digestive tract. He is now a "happy, little baby; gurgling, laughing and gaining weight." And as he takes in the environment, he cannot distinguish between what is really good for him and what tastes good. All is good—and he often gains weight. Much as with the baby—all goes in the mouth. Remember five year old Hans on his walk with Freud and his father. He saw the horse and expressed the idea that milk came from his widdler (penis). (Interpretation—when feeling good, the world gives sweet milk.)

In manic-depressive psychosis, one sees alternating patterns of high elation and deep depression. One of my patients spent several days busily loading her car with $15,000 worth of heart-shaped boxes of candy and distributing them to children on their way home from school. This was while she was manic. She would listen to no one, was extremely headstrong in manner and her words were vile and biting. Then, during treatment, she requested permission to return home. Her aged mother was there to help her. She immediately fell into a very deepening depression with rigid fixed ideation. It was delusional in depth. She said she finally realized what she had done; that she had financially ruined her family. It was all hopeless—there was no way out. She attempted suicide (ingestion of 12.5 gr. of barbiturate). In the unconscious, the inner phantasy was alternating as the feeder (one who has already eaten in full) and then the empty one who has nothing and in fact has already been eaten.

After some time in therapy the patient began to be less arrogant. She began to smile and enjoy little things. To see such softening is indeed a moment of enjoyment for me. It is a good prognostic sign, showing that normal feeling tones are seeping into the personality and that fixed psychotic defenses are beginning to loosen.

I follow with great interest the progress of a schizophrenic patient through his choosing an object in reality to gain his oral libidinal desires. Most often, as he does this, the hallucinatory symptoms of his insanity disappear. The loss of auditory and visual and olfactory hallucinations at this time reinforce my belief that these aberrations of sensation have a purpose. They probably are an oral feeding gratifying necessity. For example, one female patient has an article from LOOK about our work on her bedroom wall. A picture from it shows me hugging another patient, in this case a male.

Delusions and persecutory phenomena rather than oral feeding mechanisms or a need to fill hunger requirements represent a need to maintain status or position and are anal in type. Again, well-defined maneuvers may be more useful than simple words to deflate delusionary balloons. The therapist might be Wellington if the patient is Napoleon—refight the Battle of Waterloo—and he must always win (sometimes in full costume).

Permissiveness with anal erotic desires, where they are new feelings to the psyche, represent a step forward in development. A drooling, baby-talking, astigmatic, ataxic eight year old, recently defecated all over my lap when I fed her a bottle. This loosened her obsession of hand-washing and extra cleanliness that had been present since the age of two and a half. Her mother, a registered nurse, was early with the toilet training demands. The girl was completely bowel-trained at *age one*.

One fourteen year old boy would lean back against a door stop and let his feces glide through his anal sphincter, simply explaining that "it felt good."

The anal retentive phase is always difficult to treat. Here the patient is passively hostile, negativistic and uncooperative. One 34 year old patient was sloppy, and uncommunicative. His only expression seemed to be a sudden defecation on the bed every morning. It was certainly not a new experience but a hostile, regressive act. He was switched from a bed to an Army cot. This seemed to be the answer. He soon became toilet-trained once again.

With the therapeutic process, the ego continues to strengthen. With trial and error, patterns of behavior tend to change.

Sterba speaks of the "viscosity of the libido." [19] Each individual varies in his ability to change, even with the sharpest, quickest and shortest methods of therapy conceived by man. I wonder if in the final trial it is not the individual's own abilities that determine the rate. The therapist helps, but the patient must also be ready for help.

Phallic phases of growth are interesting. The therapist feels the challenges thrown at him. In essence, the male is testing—attempting to prove he is a better man than the therapist. He may hit with "Get off your throne, Doc!" or "Your place is falling apart; you're heading for a fall!" One young male patient decided he was going to be a professional football player and take care of a female patient's two children. He was 21, she 26. To prove his strength, he went over to the grounds of a neighboring college and when one of their football players made derogatory remarks about one of our patients, he pummeled him with his fists.

But every father is secretly proud of the son who can stand up to him. With women the therapy is different. Masculine aggressive challenges are thwarted. A woman should be feminine. She should realize her own gifts and qualities and not be forever caught in the unending struggle to prove she is as good as man.

The reward for the therapist when the patient reaches maturity is that which a parent experiences with the growth of his child. Therapists are proud to see patients leave and enter mature lives of their own. They welcome return visits from patients and are interested in their progress (as would be parents).

References

[1] Stanislavski, C. AN ACTOR PREPARES. N.Y., Theatre Arts, 1942. p. 14–15.

[2] Whyte, L. L. THE UNCONSCIOUS BEFORE FREUD. N.Y., Basic Books, 1960. p. 78–176.

[3] *idem.*

[4] *idem.* p. 146.

[5] *idem.* p. 149.

[6] Zilborg, G. "Malignant psychosis related to childbirth." AMERICAN JOURNAL OF OBSTETRICS AND GYNECOLOGY. *15*:145 (1928).

[7] Bleuler, E. DEMENTIA PRAECOX; OR THE GROUP OF SCHIZOPHRENIAS. N.Y., International Universities Press, 1950. p. 271–272.

[8] Jung, C. THE PSYCHOLOGY OF DEMENTIA PRAECOX. N.Y., Nervous & Mental Disease Pub. Co., N.Y., 1936.

[9] Federn, P. EGO PSYCHOLOGY AND PSYCHOSES. N.Y., Basic Books, 1952. p. 136.

[10] Sechahage, M. A. SYMBOLIC REALIZATION. N.Y., International Universities Press, 1951. p. 10.

[11] Reichman, F. PRINCIPLES OF INTENSIVE PSYCHOTHERAPY. Chicago, University of Chicago Press, 1950.

[12] Sullivan, H. S. INTERPERSONAL THEORY OF PSYCHIATRY. N.Y., Norton, 1953. p. 272–294.

[13] Larsen, E. F.; Vraa-Jensen, G. "Ischaemic changes in brain following electroshock therapy." ACTA PSYCHIATRICA ET NEUROLOGICA. *28*:75–80 (1953).

[14] Jacoby, J., et al. "Anorexia in electroshock therapy." JOURNAL OF CLINICAL AND EXPERIMENTAL PSYCHOPATHOLOGY. *16*:265–271 (Oct.–Dec. 1955).

[15] Bateson, G. Personal communication, October 1957.

[16] Rank, O. THE TRAUMA OF BIRTH. N.Y., Brunner, 1952. p. 74–105.

[17] Isakower, O. "Contribution to patho-psychology of falling asleep." INTERNATIONAL JOURNAL OF PSYCHOANALYSIS. *19*:331–345 (1938).

[18] Lewin, B. D. "Inferences from the dream screen." INTERNATIONAL JOURNAL OF PSYCHOANALYSIS. *29*:30–36 (1948).

[19] Sterba, R. INTRODUCTION TO THE PSYCHOANALYTIC THEORY OF THE LIBIDO. N.Y., Brunner, 1968. p. 57.

CHAPTER XI

Tobacco and Orality

The association of mental suffering and oral tension has always been observed. It is with deliberate repetitiveness that I have emphasized and re-emphasized its different associations. Throughout this book, almost in every chapter, I have approached orality in a different way, in the hopes of shedding more light. If any point is to be made at all, it is that psychosis and oral regression are interrelated.

This chapter includes my own experiences with smoking. I stopped smoking to learn more of my own oral problems because I felt they were beginning to interfere with my sensitivity as a therapist. The result (three years later) was indeed what I had hoped for. It has liberated enormous amounts of energy. All of this I now have at my command, to use at my free will—in work and pleasure.

Let us continue with a quotation from Freud, "It is clear that the behavior of a child who indulges in thumb sucking is determined by a search for some pleasure which has already been experienced and is now remembered. In the simplest case he proceeds to find this satisfaction by sucking rhythmically at some part of the skin or mucous membrane. It is also easy to guess the occasions on which the child first experienced the pleasure which he is now striving to renew. It was the child's first and most vital activity, his sucking at his mother's breast, or at substitutes for it, that must have familiarized him with the pleasure." [1]

The child's lips, in our view, behave like an erotogenic zone, and no doubt, stimulation by the warm flow of milk, with its sweet taste, results in an extremely pleasurable sensation. The satisfaction of the erotogenic is associated, in the first instance, with the satisfaction of the need for nourishment . . . extreme intensification of the eroticism persisting in the mouth will provide a powerful motive for drinking and smoking. Denial of this erotogenic fulfillment will cause oral drawing, increased salivation, pain, frustration, and other physical and mental discomforts.

Here are my own feelings, day by day, during the three week withdrawal period from tobacco.

I had smoked since the age of 18, when a friend presented me with a pipe for my birthday. Ten years later I switched to cigars. I continued smoking three to four cigars daily, and felt with false security that the increased pressure, in medical circles, on cigarette smoking was not meant for cigar smokers. It became a badge of status when I had my own locker at Dunhill's; and there a secretly pleasurable part of me remained in the moist humidor, my name enshrined with many of the city's notables.

However, late one winter, usually a time of most exhaustion for me, I did not seem to have the necessary energy to fight with one depressive paranoid, and when I reached to the depths of my storage I found I had no reserve. The patient chose electric shock treatment over a continuation of his analysis with me. I became increasingly lost and dismayed. Eight years of personal analysis for what? Searching everywhere for an answer led only to one dead end. I could give up my work with psychosis—so demanding, taxing, and at this point so unrewarding. No.

I felt that I must stop smoking. This seemed the only thing left and the right thing to do. It is now over four years and the last cigar I smoked still sits in an ashtray on my desk, discolored and partly dessicated.

Perhaps, if I, an analyst, could freely acknowledge the detrimental effects my smoking had upon my patients, I must be able to say that I, myself, was addicted.

What would satisfy the psychological needs of 70,000,000 Americans who smoked in 1963 if they were suddenly deprived of tobacco? Clearly there is no definite answer to this question but it may be illuminated by an analogy with the past.

Historically, man has always found and used substances and actual or presumed psychopharmacologic effects ranging in potency from the innocuous ginseng root to the most violent poisons. In China, traditions and custom endowed the ginseng root with remarkable health-giving properties. The strength of this belief was so strong and the supply so short that the root often became a medium of exchange. The value of the root increased in direct proportion to its similarity in appearance to the human figure. The remarkable aspect of this situation is that the ginseng root is historically the world's most renowned placebo, since science has failed to establish that it contains any active pharmacologic principle.

It would be redundant to recount here all of the potent substances at the other end of the scale. It will suffice to note that this human drive is so universal and may be so powerful that man has always been willing to risk and accept the most unpleasant symptoms and signs—hallucinations and delusions, toxicity and paralysis, violent vomiting and convulsions, poverty and nutrition, destructive organic lesions and even death.

If the thesis is accepted that the fundamental nature of many will not change significantly in the foreseeable future, it is then safe to predict that many will continue to utilize pharmacologic aids in their search for contentment. In the best interest of the public health this should be accomplished with substances which carry minimal hazard to the individual and for society as a whole. (May we not substitute heroin for tobacco here?)

Breaking the Smoking Habit

1st Day

I was working as usual in the office. I began to cough. There was a tickling in the throat. My consumption at present was 4–5 cigars daily. I felt that it wasn't the actual smoking, but the sucking. I constantly had a cigar in my mouth. I thought I was ready to stop. The cigar, only ¼ smoked, came out of my mouth and went into the ashtray.

2nd Day

There was nothing spectacular the previous night. Today the desire to smoke came upon me, I would not give in. I felt a drawing in my mouth which continued into extreme tightness and salivation. I knew this was the beginning of oral tension.

6th Day

The restlessness continued. There was no work today and I found myself walking around aimlessly. The oral tension was unbelievably strong. There was an air of apprehension. I couldn't concentrate on anything. It was like a nightmare. All day long I moved from one thing to another, never resting on anything. Everything centered around my mouth. I think it was the longest day of my life. However, that night sleep was better.

7th Day

Toward early morning I was awake to the sounds of dawn—birds chirping, the starting and stopping of the milk wagon and the clang of bottles. I was still restless but there was a looseness. I could allow myself to feel the anxiety within my body. I felt I had control. Today I knew I was less frightened and I didn't feel hopeless.

I went to the office early because I knew I had a full day. The week before I could not wait until a patient would leave so that I could be alone (for what, I do not know, because there was no relief, only the awful drawing in my mouth. But it seemed less painful than having to face people and their problems). Today was different. My anxiety made me hold on to my patients, actually hold their hands in mine. It was easiest with the weakest—the most psychotic. It was as if I really felt what they did and we shared our fear. It felt like baby play and I enjoyed what I was doing as much as the patients. All day I conducted therapy by sitting on my couch cradling a patient's head in my lap. Only once, when a domineering female therapist walked in, did the drawing in the mouth come back.

I could not look at her. (Did she represent a dominating mother to my strong conscience?) Then the drawing disappeared and in its place was a new strength—a feeling of power in my chest, neck, and shoulders.

Toward the day's end, for the very first time I noticed what I was aiming for. That cold dazed, "opium-like stupor" was gone. There was a clarity of mind that I had never before experienced.

9th Day

I spent a horrible night, tossing, turning, and moaning. My throat was quite sore. There were spurts of great alertness when my mental functioning was sharper than ever before. But there were other times when I had to be concentrating on something. It was as if I was fighting an underlying depression. I was afraid to be alone. Most of the time I could not really concentrate. A dreadful feeling pervaded my upper abdomen. At night it was all at its worst.

15th Day

Apparently my exuberance was somewhat premature. My wife suggested I should go back to smoking. For one reason, my breath smelled. (For the first time I had breath that was not tobacco tinged). Then again, there was a marked crankiness. I was snapping at everyone. That day, I fought with a storekeeper over a broken camp cot and won my argument. But my mouth was vitriolic and I know I embarrassed him in front of his associates.

16th Day

I woke up feeling better. The previous two nights I really enjoyed my bed. I found oral tension fading gradually. I understand that it will not just disappear suddenly all at once. I noticed that I could now get absorbed in television. For the first time I thought of reading. I knew that it could not be heavy reading, as the difficulty in concentration was still present.

17th Day

I was working well now, my mind relaxed and feeling confident. I thought of writing up my experiences with withdrawal from tobacco.

18th Day

The other problem was upon me: I knew that once my mind relaxed and I began "taking in" again, I would have a weight problem. I had always enjoyed eating. At times, I remembered, my appetite had been voracious. I could not seem to stop taking in food. I was gaining weight, even though I ran a mile each day that week. The pace seemed ridiculous. But I did not know how to stop. That night I went to a psychiatric meeting in town.

May 31st—Sunday

I enjoyed this Sunday around the house. I am not doing much physical work—mostly sitting and reading. The desire for a cigar is there, but it isn't an oral craving as before. It is the taste of good tobacco that I miss. I had learned the enjoyment of fine HAVANA. It is sweet, aromatic, and fulfilling. I had become somewhat of a connoisseur in recent years. Did I not have my private humidor at Dunhill's? Oh, well!

June 1st—Monday

I am once more in my stride. The pace of work is relaxing. None of the push. I know now that it was a compulsion—a driving force. My joy in smoking is now reduced to a mere recording of my experiences. But I know now that I will never go back. Not when I read what I have just written.

June 2nd—Tuesday

My hand is steady again. There is an association of pleasure at the mention of food. I must watch my weight. Something funny that evening. I had no desire to come home. During the past two weeks it was the opposite. There was a desire not to leave the house . . . it was security or protection.

June 3rd—Wednesday

Today was uneventful. There was still a feeling of indecision; but there is no return to tobacco. I know that. My desire for sleep seems great.

July 31, 1965

It is now 14 months since I have stopped. That last cigar is still in my ashtray, on my desk where I had placed it. One month ago my wife went to Dunhill's and sold my old pre-Castro Havana. $57.50 . . . I know it was worth much more . . . I could not go myself.

Will I return to tobacco? Only occasionally is the desire there. Maybe after an enjoyable meal. But then someone else lights up and I know I won't return. Perhaps it is pride—maybe stubbornness. I enjoy singing . . . my voice is much better. However I do not notice any more stamina on the athletic field as others have. There is more resourcefulness in my work and my energy seems endless, that I know, and more surprises from myself. The story is not finished. I look at those large, long, black delicacies placed side by side in cedar with envy. Oh yes, there were good moments. But today my zest for new feeling is greater than ever. I have weighed one against the other. Smoking is not for me any longer.

June 8, 1968

Four years have passed. Still no smoking, not even desire anymore. Have I "licked" it?

August 6, 1971

Still haven't smoked. All before is only a mere memory. What a relief!

Presentation of 2 hours with a patient—a professional writer wanting to give up smoking.

Withdrawal from Smoking

P. It's four weeks now—there is a foul smell—taste of death and decay—
    like I'm decaying and rotting inside. This never came out in analysis.
    I wonder if it's my sinuses.
T. How long were you in analysis?
P. With three different people—all told.
T. Most analysts smoke and most don't pay attention to orality. That's
    why it did not come out. Also you probably weren't ready for it—

you have to really reach a point where you're ready for it—it's a matter of life and death to the unconscious.

P. Realistically it's a matter of life and death, too.

T. I'm looking at it the other way. The unconscious thinks if I lose my breasts, my mother, whatever I'm sucking on—I'll rot away and I'll die. What you say is the opposite. "If I smoke I'll die." This is what we have to fight.

P. Al, can you shed some light on the business of this sucking and incorporation . . . I really don't miss the puffing—*it's the lungs that feel outraged.*

T. It's not just lips, it's the stomach, the lungs. I felt it in the lips but all down here too (pointing to my chest)—you inhale; so the whole area would be sensitive—wherever the smoke hits.

P. I have to take in this substance—breathe it in.

T. It's like a stomach; you have to take it into the lungs and it must go into your blood stream—you're a real cancer type.

P. Yes, for example, I'd switch to a lighter filter cigarette and stick to it and then I'd be puffing like hell to get my kicks out of it.

T. You are a cancer type.

P. Why I've got emphysema.

T. It's a matter of life or death for you—15 or 20 years of your life might be at stake—if it's not too late. What did your Doctor (internist) say?

P. It's not too late—it can regenerate (tissue) he said. . . . You don't believe in replacements.

T. Right now the less you can do with, the better, in form of replacements. I gave you a substitute—Milltown, 3 daily.

P. What about Lobaline Sulphate preparations.

T. I want you to incorporate me and my ideas.

P. You know—this creates a vacuum—a sensation of terrible loss; it's not only with cigarettes. How can it be that so much is tied up with tobacco? It's incredible.

T. They never know unless they go through it—you've made it into an object, a person—Freud said in melancholia—the loss of a breast (object). He was probably right. You'll have to tolerate the anxiety. After the loss the tension in the mouth is the worst thing.

P. Anger is not enough to give up smoking.

T. What do you mean?

P. You know—you get sore at yourself for being such an ass.

T. With the anger you're going to feel a sense of power. It'll come into your chest—within you—like you are your own mother.

P. You mean within yourself, you're self-perpetuating. I don't believe that.

T. Yes, you get filled up by your work, people, your wife, fucking, how's that going?

P. Not well for 1½ years.

T. With depression, there's something going on in your mouth—you can't fuck.

P. In fact, something I never found appealing is actually disgusting. I tried a few whores, that didn't work. I'm tolerating or sustaining a negative situation.

T. Suppose she had an affair.

P. It'll give me the opportunity to get out and again I'd probably kill her. I go into a rage—sometimes I hit her.

T. Right now smoking is a secret pleasure with you—you think about it—dream about it.

Second Visit: (3 days later)

P. You going to swing first! (challenging)

T. My fighting days are over.

P. It's been rough.

T. Sticking with it so far?

P. 100%—The only thing is I'm eating like a pig—it's making me uncomfortable.

T. You'll have to check that.

P. Food is unimportant to me.

T. Because you couldn't taste it—If your taste comes back you'll eat and enjoy it. Try not to give in to your mouth.

P. Suffer?

T. That's the joy of it.

P. You have the worst notion of fun. When we first talked about it—I wanted to go to the hospital.

T. Mastering your unconscious is a great pleasure—probably like climbing a mountain—driving a sports car.

P. The supreme lowering of the unconscious is suicide—what could be lower?

T. That's not what I mean. Did your mother leave a suicide note.

P. Yes, she asked for forgiveness. She was glad I married my wife. I've been thinking of linkages between smoking—2½ years before my mother died (she cracked up) we took care of her—it was rough—that's when I went into analysis—it was peculiar—often twice a year we took my mother—we dreaded it—for clothes, shopping—she was mean to sales people—she was a fuss pot—became abusive—full of anxiety—nothing looked right on her—she felt she didn't look right—her body. The grimmest thing was that in a department store you couldn't smoke—2 weeks before she died we went shopping. I was tense—and furious—we took her home. I was full of rage. I knew enough to know better—I hollered at hers—he burst into tears—a month later she jumped out a window—in many obscure ways I may have wanted her to die—she was a burden—she said it—and it was all around smoking. You make a mistake—saying 1½ years of depression—I've been about the same for 30 years. Ambiguity is involved. You know you're giving up smoking to sustain life and promote it. On the other hand, when you smoke you feel that you're killing yourself. It seems to be a paradox.

T. Maybe it's your way of killing her—pushing her out of a window—what right do you have to live?

P. Yes, it's tenuous really—take away the last of a few privileges. The hospital was a half-way house. I'm taking Bantrons, Milltown, etc. It's not cold turkey. I want to go to the hospital.

There are associations deeply associated with cigarettes. I can't write without a cigarette—when the phone rings I need a cigarette in my mouth—other instances—so, this life-death pattern bothers me. Like separating sheep from goats—those that smoke vs. those that don't—business executives I've met, high caliber—none of the top men smoke—well, fuck them—they're the worst in the world. Some nice people don't smoke—non smoking doesn't guarantee psychological happiness. My mother didn't smoke. Sneakingly there's an attempt to put myself in a framework to justify this—if no rewards I'm not going to continue this.

T. There's no guarantee—but if you do smoke you'll be in trouble—uncomfortable slow drowning.

P. Suffering from chronic asthma as I did. I should know. These are negatives though—grappling and overcoming unconscious—crap—this victory that you speak of—is what makes the world tick—

T. Let's drop this—you are talking philosophical—I'm talking something else.

P. It's more realistic—it's being a good Joe—pushing down unconscious.

T. I know. I've had it—I worked with patients—I smoked—I had eight years of analysis—I lost a case to a shock machine—I decided to quit —I went through terrible withdrawal—then there were pockets of terrible frustration—utter dream-like, opium-like states—are going to have to disappear—then problems I had began to disappear—I had more energy to work with—this is what I call mastering your unconscious.

P. Yes, in not smoking—I liberate energy to use. Smoking must suppress this. I had this thought—if I became strong, I kick out my wife—strange.

T. It might happen—you'll kick out relationships—you might kick her out.

P. You frighten the shit out of me. You're giving me only one chance. That's a bit extreme.

T. Yes.

P. I can't write; dull boring existence—there's something deeper—a block —analysis never helped.

T. That creative ability to write extends from the deep unconscious.

P. That would be exciting, interesting.

T. This creative oral urge comes from this.

P. It's just another way of using words.

T. You eat, sleep and dream, writing is a sublimation of dreaming—food for thought—the oral triad—from eating, sleeping and dreaming—comes ideas, there is a connection between writing and dreaming.

P. Does it have to be so Spartan? This is difficult—I don't think pills or booze will be a problem—smoking will. This oral thing—

T. Fear of the Talionic principle. In the unconscious—eye for eye and tooth for tooth—eat and be eaten—if you eat, will you be devoured? If you eat the food of life—will you be swallowed up. This cigarette is secret—it's a defense—you won't be eaten.

P. Why does eating at the breast appear so fearful? When is the breast threatening? He's eating him, a close friend—overcoming fear—it's pleasurable—it's related to mother—a fear—let her nurse me—more you open to me—more you'll have power over me—a fear—if this works I'll like to think it will be helpful to others.

This was the last professional visit with this patient. He said the therapy was too threatening. He was not strong enough to give up tobacco at this time. He needed more support. I was not prepared at the time to make a full commitment to this case. He was a personal friend and was really under another analyst's care. When I began to see him I stated that once he stopped smoking, if he would return, the therapy would stop. When after two visits, he resumed his cigarettes, he reminded me of our discussion on the subject. This was his way out. To treat this situation properly, his wish for hospitalization should have been honored.

Conclusion

Neither the presentation of my personal notes nor the two recorded interviews have been made to show the efficacy of any therapeutic technique in the breaking of the smoking habituation or addiction—whatever view-point one might have on the matter. Rather, the reason for the presentation is to demonstrate unconscious components of orality that might be contained in the development, continuation, and finally the separation from tobacco.

There is a similarity in psychic craving during all withdrawal, no matter what the habit or addiction. Alcohol, narcotics, barbiturates—all leave the empty, painful feeling in the upper abdomen, the cutting soreness around the umbilicus, and the dry, drawing feeling in the mouth. The same feeling is observed in psychosis—the oral yearning.

References

[1] Freud, S. THREE ESSAYS ON THE THEORY OF SEXUALITY. London, Imago, 1949. p. 60.

CHAPTER XII

Thought Process and
Subnormal Mental Functioning *

One of the areas of study most neglected by present-day psychiatry is that of subnormal mental functioning. It is growing more difficult for the psychiatrist to deny his responsibility to this great category as it becomes clear through research and treatment that his legitimate domain does indeed include this emotionally disturbed group.[1]

It has been argued by theoreticians, especially Rogers and Fenichel, that psychotherapy and mental retardation are incompatible and that the mental retardate lacks prerequisites for effective employment of psychotherapy.[2] These "lacks" include insight, verbal ability and ability to abstract and cognitively deal with acting-out impulses which are necessary components of intelligence.

I have found that many cases of mental retardation, with or without evidence of organic brain injury, respond to a confrontation type of psychoanalytic psychotherapy, if there is sufficient emotional potential.

I believe, as do Strauss, Sarvis, Rappaport, Rank, and Webster, that a person who reacts psychologically and neurologically as if brain-injured requires the same kind of understanding and treatment, whether the injury is substantiated or not.[3, 4, 5, 6, 7]

Through a basic method of communication, preverbal and verbal, it is possible to measure mature growth in patients previously diagnosed as subnormal. This growth, I believe, is similar to that found in less regressive and infantile fixated diagnostic states, such as psychosis and neurosis. I believe that psychoanalytic psychotherapy of the retardate has as its goal

* First published in Psychoanalytic Review—Vol. 53, #1 Spring 1966. Title as originally published was "Subnormal Functioning in Mental Illness."

not only "retraining" but also stimulating natural resources for personality development.

I shall attempt to present a theoretical framework for an understanding of the mechanisms of subnormal mental functioning, based on what is known about thought process, and apply this framework to therapy.

Subnormal Mental Functioning may be divided into three categories:

1. Mental Deficiency
2. Mental Retardation
3 Regressive Subnormal Functioning *
   (a) organic
   (b) functional

1. *Mental Deficiency* refers to an intellectual defect caused by a lesion of the central nervous system so initially catastrophic or actively progressive as to make the individual socially inadequate and incurable. This injury may be hereditary, constitutional or may occur at birth or shortly after.

2. *Mental Retardation* refers to that condition whereby individuals, for temporary or long-standing reasons, function intellectually below their peers. The social adequacy of this group is not questioned. If it is, there is likelihood the individual can learn to function independently in the community. Webster describes it as a clinical syndrome rather than an intellectual defect or brain disease per se. He says that there are three features in the syndrome:

1. Intellectual impairment or specific learning difficulty;
2. Slow rate of development; and
3. Disturbance in the quality of emotional development.

The development disturbance involves an impairment in the differentiation of ego functions. Slow, incomplete unfolding of the personality is associated with partial fixations, resulting in an infantile character structure. Descriptive features include autism, repetitiousness, inflexibility, passivity and simplicity in emotional life. Obvious defects in thought process together with evidences of archaic thinking include perseveration, negativism, repetitious phraseology, concreteness, neologisms, slang associations, inflexibility and fixation. There are symbolism and symbolic thinking, rationalizations, loss of concepts, loss of attention and concentration, absence of reflective awareness, and memory disturbance. Accompanying emotional activity includes deadening of affect, extreme anxiety or dread, restlessness, infantile affectivity such as searching and mouthing motions, impulsivity of actions, hyper-aggressiveness and autism. *The mental retardation syndrome* may be seen in clinical syndromes, such as

---

* Webster uses the first two categories. I have added Regressive Subnormal Functioning as a third to be able to list regressive psychosis and neurosis, both functional and organic.

infantile autism, idiot savant, childhood schizophrenia, forced mutism of childhood and in organic brain insult, acute or chronic.[8]

While environmental deficits may seem to provide causal explanations without organic pathology detected, an organic lesion does not label a person defective nor exclude him from the category of mental retardation.

3. *Regressive Subnormal Mental Functioning*—Subnormal mental functioning may occur in adult life. Evidence of its beginnings after puberty show it is regressive instead of developmental.

(a) Organic—Subnormal mental functioning is considered organic when there is definite organic injury or history of such through mental or physical examination and psychological or neurological laboratory testing. Included would be brain tumors, Korsakow's syndromes, paresis, Alzeimar's or Pick's diseases, senile dementia and other dementias, acute and chronic brain syndrome due to surgery, injury, or infection. It may occur after electric shock or other shock therapies (such as insulin or metrazol). If the injury is progressive, deterioration in all mental faculties is continuous. If the disease process is halted, there can be a gain in mental functioning but the goal remains limited.

(b) *Psychological Regressive Subnormal Functioning*—Severe thinking disorders can occur in acute and chronic schizophrenia, process or reactive schizophrenia, manic-depressive psychosis, depressive reactions in neurosis, and in normal individuals following fatigue.

Symptoms may be similar to organic regressions but more normal thought process, more lability of emotion and other qualitative responses indicate the condition is reversible.*

Theory of Thinking and Thought Process

Because of its concern with abstraction and its removal from immediate therapeutic value, the development of a theory for thought process in the field of psychology, and in the strict academic theory of thinking, is rudimentary and fragmentary. However, when the lower forms of thinking, found in all levels of subnormal mental functioning, can be understood, recognized and catalogued, they may be changed and activated into a higher grade, with more normal degree of thought and communication.

Thought can be described as:

1. primary process thought
2. secondary process thought

Freud maintained that all thinking is a detour from the direct path toward gratification.[9] Discharge of tension takes place when potential energy of an instinctual drive rises to the crucial point and the object of the drive is present. The result is GRATIFICATION. Interference with this process

---

* I and others have written on the therapy of the psychological forms of regressive subnormal functioning. It, in essence, is the therapy of psychosis.

is termed IDEATION. Here, need tension rises to the point of discharge, but discharge is delayed because the object is removed. Discharge then occurs two ways: as affect, directly into the body; as a hallucinatory image of the object or ideation.

This is the archetype of thought. It is primary process—not developed thought. This is probably why the dreamer, awakened from a dream, cannot remember it; or the psychotic, awakened from the psychosis, forgets the experience.

The primary process aims at direct discharge. If the external control (by the object, the therapist) delays gratification, beginning ideation (hallucinatory memory traces of objects) and affect result. The secondary process converts this delay (involuntary) into internally controlled delay; discharge takes place at a more suitable time, with a more suitable object, counter cathexes (prohibitions to discharge by the object, the therapist) are built into the budding ego. These isolated drives become a structured system of drives, with built-up connections of memory. They become interchanged through delay of single discharge, making particles of energy available. Conceptual, spatial, and temporal frames of reference develop in the course of experience and correspond to the relationship patterns of reality. The safeguards for reality testing are built into these new memory frames of references. As more energy is available to the growing ego, the initial process that occurred in primary process, production of ideation and affect, is energized by increased conscious control and emergence of thoughts.

There are two aspects:

1. quantitative or affective
2. qualitative or true idea

In primary thought disorders such as hallucinatory states, fugue and hypnogogic states, as well as peculiar manneristics, depressive states, and syndromes diagnosed as mental retardation, there is no clear separation of ideas and affect. This results in archaic thought process. *The energy is consumed in anxiety and defensive mechanisms (mainly repression) which serve as a displacement for feelings of world-ending catastrophe.* Great amounts of energy are consumed by the psyche to maintain the repressions of the primary process and to continue to prevent them from emerging into consciousness. Thus, an equilibrium in the organism, although unsteady, is present.

The ideal expression of consciousness is undisturbed attention, full concentration, presence of reflective awareness, sharp memory recall, pinpoint anticipation and timing—all with a proper balance of affect and thought. The result would be the formation and expression of clear concepts, judgment, creative thinking and completely understandable communication. This, an ideal state, is absent more often than present, even in the normal person. Huge gaps exist in our theory of thinking, especially in understanding states of consciousness and the forms of thought process determined by them. These gaps probably represent transitions between primary and secondary processes.[10]

Cameron has stated that thought processes are directly proportionate in growth to the development of language. Language is dependent upon social environment; as the child grows, his thinking becomes more socialized.[11]

It is my feeling that since only the medulla and spinal cord are completely developed at birth, early psychological traumas may cause psychological and neurological fixation. For instance, the pons is not completely developed until age one month, mid-brain until age four months and cortex until age thirty-six months. Slow development within normal range may be for the pons, four and one-half months; mid-brain, thirteen months; and cortex, ninety-six months.[12] It can be understood, therefore, why early psychological trauma may influence neurological development and cause fixation which simulates pontine, mid-brain and cortical lesions. This may give a youngster signs of "organicity"—clumsiness, eye symptoms, concretistic thinking—and force observers to conclude that mental retardation is of organic origin. *It is amazing to see, in a controlled environment with proper psychotherapy, these symptoms disappear.*

As far as thought process is concerned, because irreversible organic disorders show primitive or paleologic thinking, no reason exists to assume all thinking disturbance is irreversible. It would not explain why normal people regress to concretistic thinking during dream life or when fatigued. In order to escape anxiety or other devastating emotions, a person may regress to lower levels of cognition. These levels will produce thoughts and evoke emotions less traumatic than the original. There are always regressive neurological movements accompanying psychosis, for instance the rigidity and infantile-like position of catatonia.

Lower forms of Aristotelian thinking and paleological thinking are found in all forms of primitive man. Because of inherent emotional value, paleological thought, when mixed occasionally with pure logic, enriches all aspects of inner and outer life. (Kris called this "regression in the service of the ego.") [13] A completely logical man would perhaps be an extremely colorless man.

Therapy with Subnormal Mental Functioning

In therapy with subnormal mental functioning the quality of thought becomes an important index of the improvement of the patient. This fact can be measured through mental examination and psychological testing. The thinking disorder, however, is only a reflection of the underlying emotional disorder. It is to the emotional disorder that therapy is directed.

The system of therapy developed at the Delaware Valley Mental Health

Foundation, confrontation techniques directed at the primary process combined with the dedicated family living has proven extremely effective with subnormal mental functioning.

I feel that the patient's early maternal environment is perhaps the paramount influence on the retardation or subnormal mental functioning syndrome. The therapeutic family milieu is a psychological neo-nursery. In this nursery, the patient's speech and patterns of behavior are recognized for what they are—fixations or regressions to early infancy.

Many have questioned the differing qualities among childhood schizophrenia, childhood autism and mental retardation. To me, the differences are academic. If the patient has sufficient intellectual and emotional potential (if he is not mentally deficient), I will accept him and place him in this nurturing environment. The goal is the same as in the raising of a normal child or in my treatment of psychosis—realization of the greatest possible potential.

Much research has been done on the role of "early mothering" in the functional neurosis and psychosis,[14, 15, 16, 17] but little in the mental retardation syndrome. Regression is present in the mental retardation syndrome, but it has taken place so early in life it goes unnoticed. It assumes the impression of a fixation in growth. Thus, the clinical picture is both fixation and regression.

In the regressive process of schizophrenia and other psychoses, there is evidence of primitive thinking. The degree and amount of this thinking may be proportionate to the length of the illness, its inception (the earlier the origin, the more primitive the thinking), and the emotional liability.

Energy ordinarily consumed in logical thought is used by the body to thwart off harmful emotions, such as the unbearable anxiety of annihilation that prevails on all levels of mental illness. (The fear of "being eaten" or "swallowed up" is especially pronounced in this condition. For instance, if one would open one's mouth wide, growl, and approach the patient's face, the patient, most often, would cringe with fear.)

The mental retardate, the early inception of illness having crippled his personality, understands little or nothing around him. Most of these youngsters grow to adulthood without a grasp of language, no ability to read and only rudimentary speech. Many times, music is their only comfort.

In the more emotionally disturbed of this group, crude mannerisms such as sucking and mouthing motions, rhythmic rocking and violent anger are seen. Hyper-aggressive, purposeless behavior may be present, such as flinging and hurling the body, head banging, destructiveness, excessive demands and whining. There is a sadness and a loneliness, as though all human contact had been abandoned. If there is speech, it is confused, repetitive, compulsive, symbolic and thoughtless. If there are thoughts, they are magical and usually related to animal life and movement.

Whenever there is anxiety, there is the wish to escape anxiety—the wish for security. Sometimes this wish for security becomes a reality in the dream or dream-like state. In order to dream, one must sleep. Dreams are the precursors of thought. As the dreamer sleeps, a story is told. Ideation is present, sometimes actual thoughts. According to Lewin, it is necessary to eat before one can sleep and dream.[18] Lewin describes the dream screen as part of the dream:—a blank screen on which is projected a series of pictures. He describes it as being similar to a movie screen and the maternal breast. The conspicuous hunger and thirst for new experiences and impressions may be imagined as new "food for thought".

It might be said that for the production of thought, there must first occur eating, sleeping and dreaming. The hallucinatory projection of the breast occurs in the image of the dream screen. An anxious mother will engender anxiety in the infant. Anxiety hinders eating, sleeping and dreaming which are necessary for gratification and production of ideation and eventual thought process. Anxiety occurring this early in life becomes a barrier to the normal "taking in" pattern necessary for development of thought process. This, in turn, may be responsible for fixation at lower levels of mental development—the result being subnormal mental functioning.

The symptoms of mental retardation are defenses against human feeling and represent archaic compensatory mechanisms that attempt to provide homeostatic balance in an organism permeated by "root-shaking" anxiety.

The mouthing motions, the rocking and sucking motions are seen as attempts to "take in" the security of the maternal breast. The violent anger, head banging, destructiveness and hyper-activity are symptoms of bitterness and frustration in not achieving pleasure and gratification in the primary process. Inattention and poor concentration demonstrate the ever-lasting search for gratification. The repetitive, disconnected speech and recollections of only happy memories represent an attempt to repeat the early feeding experience. Perseveration is an attempt to feel oneself in relation to the world. The magical thinking and compulsive traits are attempts to control the bewildering anxiety.

Therapy with subnormal mental functioning can be divided into four stages:

1. Breaking-up of Autism
2. Focusing on Real People
3. Feeding Procedure
4. Developing Mature Thinking

1. *Breaking-up of Autism.* Through various therapeutic mechanisms,[19] energy bound by psychotic and other socially useless behavior is released.[20] It first becomes free-floating anxiety and then it becomes available for focus on real objects.

2. *Focusing on Real People.* Often the physician finds himself reacting

like a mother at her most basic level in an attempt to establish communication with the patient. He may find himself taking a secondary position to the female therapist in the therapeutic unit because of a woman's more highly developed maternal instinct and her ability to "reach" an individual through this basic bioligical attachment.

Communication is established with the patient through the skin, with baby powders and baths, through lullabies and soft voices, through gentle feeding and bedtime stories. Patients with histories of murderous assaults in mental hospitals have become docile and childlike under this continuous regime. The regression produced becomes the first step to maturation.*

3. *Feeding Procedure.* A searching, hostile, angry, cold face becomes warm and flushed, childlike and relaxed through the "feeding procedure." This is called "flush reaction". When it occurs, warmth is filling the body— the oral triad of eat, sleep and dream is being fulfilled. It is a prerequisite and stimulant to normal thinking. It usually develops after the recall of pleasant memories and their accompanying feelings of gratification. Associations to present situations occur. There is a closeness to the therapist and a feeling of "self".

At times, the physician and assistant therapists struggle for weeks with a patient's defenses, seeming to make no indentation. Then, one day, a "flushing" of the patient's face occurs and his face brightens with new understanding of his problem.

4. *Developing Mature Thinking.* By example and identification with the therapist, more mature thought process develops. The therapeutic family milieu acts as a counter-cathexis to primary process gratification—allowing gratification and regulating it in quantity. This in turn causes the patient to develop his own controls.

Emotion and feeling must be introduced by the therapist to penetrate the dead flatness of concrete thinking. This stimulates affective reaction from the patient and energy is freed for new thought process. Through continuous trial and example, mature thinking develops with the ultimate goal of verbal communication.

I could draw from the files many examples of successful therapy with subnormal mental functioning in cases of acute and chronic schizophrenia, manic-depressive psychosis and chronic depressive reactions. However, the primitiveness of the affective reaction and thinking disorder in the case I have chosen best illustrates my theory.

The Case of Henry

Henry, age 20, is a powerfully built lad and the oldest of five. His father

---

* Because of the feeling that physical and psychological origins have a somewhat similar, closely related pattern in development, several severely regressed and chronic patients were started on creeping and patterning regimes under the direction of The Institute of Human Potential, Philadelphia, Pa.

is a clergyman and his mother a teacher. She states that she was emotionally unprepared for children when she became pregnant with Henry but "my friends were having babies and I wanted one too." Birth was uneventful.

The boy's development was normal until the approximate age of two and one-half. He then suffered a high fever which was nonspecific and went undiagnosed. At about this time, rocking and biting of the hand (palmar eminences) occurred. Twirling, circular motions and general restlessness followed. At first, autism was predominant. The boyish face tightened and the eyes became intense and reddened. Hyper-aggressiveness and continuous repetitive talking followed. The parents consulted a psychiatrist and the diagnosis of childhood schizophrenia was made. The boy was placed in regular outpatient therapy.

When Henry was five years old, a sister was born. He began to steal the baby's bottle and turn over her carriage, frequently crawling inside. At six years of age, he was sent to school, first living at home, then boarding away. Because of his unmanageability, his parents were requested to remove him from one school after another. The longest he stayed at any one school was three years. He learned only rudimentary reading and writing, but read and spoke the foreign tongue of his parents, which his father had taught him before school age.

It was perhaps as a last resort that he was first seen at our clinic at the age of nineteen. During the preceding three months, he had attended four schools for the retarded. No one would keep him. At the clinic, his restlessness, hyper-aggressiveness and confused jargon confused the examiner. Through clinical examination and psychological testing, a diagnosis of childhood autism and mental retardation was made.

While the examiner was talking with his parents, Henry stripped and, although it was mid-February, ran down the highway. He was placed in therapeutic family with husband (male therapist), aged thirty-six, and a wife (female therapist), aged thirty-five, and their children, ages twelve, ten and four.

Clinical Findings

At age twelve, a neurological examination was negative and an EEG was within normal limits. Psychological examination showed (WISC IQ 77–81, PG 57–62, T.I.Q. 64–70,) that he was approximately at the upper end of the retarded category.

Henry has his own rabbit, which he cares for and feeds. When not upset, he is quite tender with it. When the bouts of psychotic anxiety return, he ignores it.

It is interesting to see beginning symptoms of projection. At a party recently, he accused one of the female therapists of stealing his potato chips. He later admitted he, himself, had had these thoughts. Since no projection mechanisms were noticed while he was hyperactive, one can speculate that paranoid symptoms develop as a projective mechanism early in life.

The most recent psychological protocol states that "although the patient is psychotic, severely disorganized and incapable of learning at a usual rate, he shows marked improvement. He is now in the process of utilizing, organizing and learning new personality resources."

Evidence further indicates that he will most likely continue to make slow improvement if the present treatment regime is continued. However, it is doubtful whether he can ever be brought to a level of independent functioning.

Selected Examples of Henry's Therapy Sessions

Example 1

(*Note: This is an example from early in the case showing the patient's rambling thoughts. He wasn't sleeping at night and a therapist stayed with him.*)

P. (talking in a babyish voice) Yeh, these people really deserted me—they don't care about me now—this fellow Mitchell, Tom, this fellow John Warner, this fellow Dave, he ran in the street. Anybody else who was as bad as you. This fellow Jimmy drooled all the time. Why? Cause he said he was in the hospital too long. This fellow, Jerry, couldn't talk —ga ha ha—make all these noises . . . this fellow Jack . . . I want to go home . . . if I keep acting up, he'll lock me up. All these people lied to me—they say I let them down—they let me down—heh . . .

Example 2

T. What did you do when you were seven or eight?

P. I bit my hands, rocked, snapped my fingers. I used to throw myself around, jump around.

T. Why did you do these things?

P. I remember I wanted to bite the doctor's kid . . . my mother didn't let me go off the property . . . she was protecting me . . . I was eight . . . (patient rocking and talking in sarcastic voice)

T. Why did you rock?

P. Maybe I was disturbed.

T. Why were you different from the other kids? How did you feel inside?

P. I felt disturbed inside; I felt cold inside.

T. Where?

P. In my tummy and my heart (baby voice).

T. How do you feel now?

P. I feel better . . . maybe I'm forgetting the past . . .

T. Why do you feel better inside?

P. Maybe I'm getting love.

T. Who do you love?

P. Joan, Phil (therapeutic unit parents)

T. Who do you think of when your tummy feels warm?

P. You.

    (*Note: This shows some understanding of normal behavior. Before treatment, the patient would have acted out and imitated any of the crazy behavior of patients around him, competing with them as to who would be the most destructive.*)

Example 3—Stimulating Emotional Response

P. Good morning, Dr. Honig.

T. Don't talk to me. What did you tell my wife last night?

P. I called you up.

T. What did you tell my wife . . .?

P. I wanted to talk to you. She said you were asleep.

T. What did you tell her?

P. I was just having a conversation with her. I wanted to talk to you. (frantic) Is that when you were asleep? There are certain things I wanted to say to you.

T. Is that how much you think of me—when I'm asleep, you want to wake me?

P. I thought maybe you would speak to me.

T. Is that what you think of me—to wake me out of a sound sleep. You didn't care about me. You did it for yourself. Where did you learn your manners? (raising voice)

P. There was an important thing I wanted to talk to you about. I wanted to talk to you about Memorial Day.

T. You act like it's one big amusement ride. Who taught you your manners? They are atrocious. Little children have better manners.

P. Yeh . . .

T. If your mother had taught you one thing, she would have taught you manners.

P. Yeh . . . she didn't teach me anything. (shifting all responsibility for behavior on mother.)

T. What are you blaming her for? You are always looking to dump your problems on someone else. Is your mother the cause of all your problems?

P. Dr. Honig, you know what I'm thinking of?

T. I'm not interested in what you're thinking of! Give me one reason why I should be interested.

P. Maybe you could explain something I thought about when I was fifteen.

T. Why should I listen to it?

P. Maybe it has some bearing on my case.

T. (soft voice) All right, tell me about it.

(*Note: Here therapist was pleased with the response of the patient.*)

P. One time when I was fifteen, I was riding my bicycle. Some boy stopped me and he asked me . . . he asked me . . . a . . . to help him put something in the trunk of his car. He asked me where I lived. Yes, he asked me. He was a very high aged boy. He offered me a cigarette and he asked me directions . . . yes, he asked me how to get to some place . . . Yes, I was fifteen . . . he offered me a cigarette (attempt at identification with older boy—showing therapist he can be like other people.)

T. Did you smoke it?

P. I tried, I think. I almost died—yeh! He once gave me a light. I wondered if I was of a high age. I think I did. I almost died, heh.

T. Why are you telling me that? Trying to show me what a big shot you are?

P. It happened the other day. A boy offered me a cigarette again—yeh, it happened again.

T. You're not telling me the whole story. Don't hold back information.

P. O.K. Yeh, I remember one time when I was fifteen, me and my parents went sleigh riding.

T. What happened?

P. We went sleigh riding, Sandra (his sister, four years younger) and me. There was a fellow in the stands.

T. Why don't you talk about something important to your case?

P. I remember when I was five. I had a story book my father gave me . . . in the story Jane said to Jim, I wonder if my cat and your dog will get along. I wonder if Nancy Adams read the story too. She and I could get along. (a former schoolmate)

T. If you had a dog and Nancy had a cat, Nancy represents your sister who was just born—you were jealous.

P. Yeh—I used to take her bottle and suck on it. Oh, I dumped her carriage.

T. Why did you do that?

P. Maybe she got more love from my mother.

T. It's a shame that a brother and sister don't get along.

P. Yeh, it is. I was jealous, that's why we didn't get along. Yeh—it's a shame, wasn't it?

Pause

P. You know what else I'm thinking of.

T. What?

P. Elaine—at one school there was Elaine, she was a counselor, Yeh—

T. You're always thinking of women—you'd think of a piece of cloth and shout "love me cloth"—anything—you're always looking for something to love you—desperate—desperate—you don't have a mind to reason.

Example 4

P. I remember when I used to fool around with Johnny Eglet. I used to fool around—we used to chase each other. Could you explain it to me—why I used to do that? I want to know—was I looking for mischief? It was crazy, annoying him that way.

(*Note: Patient sincerely wanted to understand the hyperactive destructive behavior that plagued him for fourteen years.*)

T. You were probably upset—maybe you were jealous that your sister got all the attention. Sibling rivalry—know what that is?

P. Also at Blueville School, I used to act up. Pull people's ties. Why did I do that? Was I in the way there?

T. They probably thought you were hopeless—didn't want to bother with you.

P. But it's different here, isn't it? I am trying, aren't I? What was it like—that I never tried before—what was the matter?

T. I guess you thought it was hopeless too.

P. They used to spend the time with other guys—the other guys were trying, is that right? Sometimes I think about this. I have a certain feeling about this—some boy took me in the corner—I was fooling around—I got ticklish, I had a mischievous feeling.

T. You still get that now. It's not mischievous, it's disturbed.

P. Yes, that's right—I tried to get attention. I was trying to get some of the boys to pay attention to me. May I hold your hand?

T. No . . .

(*Note: The therapist deliberately did not hold the patient's hand so as to increase the tension and heighten the emotional response.*)

P. When I was six and a half I thought of going to a fellow's house and stealing a pitcher of lemonade . . . he was having a party.

T. Why weren't you invited?

P. Probably acted crazy.

T. A guy that acts crazy is very disturbing. Come on, I want to hear something crazier.

P. I remember one time this fellow, Louis—he had a "gather up" with a lot of fellows—when I was six—got thoughts of going over and creating disturbance—I wanted to be invited, you see, so that's how come I got thoughts of creating a disturbance. There was Cyrus—I had a certain feeling—fellow I knew at six and a half—he was seven —I thought of running over there and acting up so they'd pay attention to me. I wanted to go to his house when his older brother was having a lecture. I thought of going over and talking when someone else is talking, interrupting the lecture.

T. You still do that today.

P. Yes, I realize that.

(*Note: Patient shows more understanding of his aberrant behavior and the reasons he acted that way.*)

Example 5

(*Note: An example of feeding process—producing flush reaction by slow, rhythmic "nursing-like" conversation.*)

P. I was riding my two-wheeler with my sister. I needed someone to hold me up.

T. What is the analogy between that and now? If I should say we are your helping wheels, what does that mean?

P. What do you mean?

T. That you'll feel inside and you'll grow—go on.

P. Then that day, my father put the bike in the car and we took it to be repaired. I was interested in certain things at the place, a certain tool bench, bicycle wheels. This is a fellow that repairs bikes. Then I saw something. I had no time to look so he wouldn't wait on someone else. There was a feeling inside me. My bicycle got fixed. I wanted to learn to ride. It was important that I stay. That's what my father explained to me.

T. Go ahead. How do you feel right now?

P. I feel good. I know you love me.

T. How do you know that?

P. You explained to me things about my bicycle.

(*Note: The patient's face became flushed. It showed calm, his hands became warm and a delightful boyish look was on his face. This is the flush reaction. It occurred after about an hour of this slow, rhythmic, nursing-like talk.*)

Example 6

P. I think of Mr. Jones.

T. When you are here, you talk about insanity. Now, tell me a crazy thought.

P. Oh, I think I had one thought.

T. You had more than one.

P. On Tuesday, today is Thursday, I'm supposed to tell you, I think of this, but I don't do it . . . about Julie, whenever she gets records, I think about stealing it and playing it—I don't do it, you see—I just think about it.

(*Note: This demonstrates the building of internal control in preventing gratification of this primary process wish. Before treatment, this patient would not have hesitated in acting out this wish of stealing the records or other similar behavior. He used to enjoy smashing television sets by dropping them on the floor.*)

Example 7

T. What did I ask you?

P. What thoughts I'm getting.

T. What kind of thoughts?

P. Crazy thoughts. That boy, Nicholas, wants me to help him, wants me to come to him on the double—sometime I think of it—of telling him to wait . . .

(Note: Present tense to describe a past experience.)

T. Is that crazy?

P. Yes, I did have some crazy thoughts—crazy thing—Nicholas put something on the table—I'm telling you the truth about a crazy thought—taking a wrench from the table, his wrench, and putting it on a book shelf . . .

T. Something crazier than that.

P. Can I tell you this? J.M. (counselor at previous school) once got a record for Christmas—I had a certain kind of feeling—this fella, aha, J.M. got nervous, things had to be done around the place, he was busy with something. Let me see, a . . . a . . . a, sometimes I think of taking his . . . a . . . a . . . a . . . record and saving it for myself whenever I want to hear music . . . but I don't do it, do you see? He accidentally got disgusted with me.

T. Tell me the truth, he didn't accidentally get disgusted with you . . .

P. The truth is, oh—he was putting up decorations, I didn't know.

T. How come you didn't know?

P. There were other kids there—Butch O.

T. Who am I talking about?

P. Me, Henry, I thought, now this is the truth—really the truth. I didn't know, I used to play around, tear the decorations.

T. How come you didn't know?

P. Before the holidays began . . . this is the truth!

T. Sounds like a lie to me.

P. I remember when I was home—my brothers used to take things apart when I was home.

T. Why did J.M. (school director) get mad at you?

P. I turned off the Christmas lights.

T. Come on, what did you do crazy?

P. I was getting into mischief. I said to some boy . . .

T. Tell me the truth . . .

P. If I'll tell the truth, then things will be all right? I said haloo honey, haloo . . .

T. You must have done crazier things than that . . .

P. I was pulling their legs, not really, that's just an expression.

(Note: This is an attempt to stimulate deeper unconscious thoughts with accompanying affect through constant probing and attempts to cause the patient to think.)

T. How do you know you're telling the truth?

P. Cause I remember.

T. Don't you feel better when you tell the truth?

P. Yes. Because it has to do with the way I feel now . . .

(Note: And so, each session becomes almost repetitious of the last. Gradually, through painstaking effort, the defenses are attacked and ground down. Each time, the patient gains a little more understanding of his behavioral pattern. As he becomes successful in overcoming some of the aberrant behavior, he is congratulated and accepted as more of a part of the therapeutic family. This creates more of a desire to try even harder to succeed. Soon, there can no longer be a return to former "crazy" patterns of behavior. They are forgotten and no longer give any gratification. The ability to read and write gives an added tool—language. Language development and thought process go hand-in-hand.)

Working with psychotic regression has been compared to working with childhood again. When working with a fixation, such as childhood autism, or any other clinical entity that can be included in the mental retardation syndrome, a new aspect of therapy can be described. That is, the patient is almost literally brought up all over again. He has to be taught to talk, converse, read, write and think.

It is difficult from the few interviews to describe the laborious work that goes on daily to enhance the relationship. It might be said to be a true attempt at reconstructing a human personality.

Henry has continued to improve in therapy and no longer has psychotic mannerisms: pressures of speech have become markedly reduced. His school work has become proficient in that he can read at fourth grade level; he is able to do mathematical problems using division and multiplication. At a recent conference of the staff, it was thought that he might be well enough to attend his young brother's confirmation, at which time all family relatives would be present.

He did well at the reception, but upon his arrival at the clinic, complete regression took place which lasted approximately six weeks. During this time, Henry's repetitiveness of speech changed. He began to ask continuously "Am I secure here?" "Is this my new home?" and began to cite examples from his past, always ending with "You see, my parents didn't love me. They abandoned me."

T. (angrily) Why didn't you work with Joan (female assistant therapist) on your math?

P. One time when I was walking, I was only six, I met this person. She said, "Hello, little boy. What does this design look like?" (referring to her pocketbook) I didn't know her. You are not supposed to talk to people you don't know.

(Note: This demonstrated how deeply the emotional tie with his biological mother really is. The patient is now living with his therapeutic family for almost two years and he still saw the female therapist as a stranger.)

After nearly two years of treatment, I cannot clinically assess the amount of brain damage. I can say, however, that as Henry's ability to communicate his feelings improves, obviousness of organicity diminishes.

In conclusion one might say the following: One of the areas of study of human behavior most neglected has been that of subnormal function. Subnormal Functioning has been subdivided into three categories: (a) mental deficiency, (b) mental retardation, (c) regressive subnormal functioning.

I feel that many cases of mental retardation, with or without substantiated evidence of organic brain injury, are receptive to intrusive psychotherapy. Through a very basic method of human communication, at first preverbal, then verbal, it is possible to get a measure of growth toward maturity in these patients previously diagnosed as subnormal.

A method of psychotherapy, using the therapeutic family milieu, and employing a very direct approach, has been demonstrated by clinical material.

The author has proposed a theoretical framework to demonstrate how his therapeutic approach can be used to influence a change in thought process from primitive to higher forms of thinking.

References

[1] Sarason, S.; Gladwin, T. PSYCHOLOGICAL AND CULTURAL PROBLEMS IN MENTAL SUBNORMALITY. Provincetown, Journal Press, 1958. (Review of Research and Genetic Psychology Monograph, v. 57) p. 3–290.

[2] Sternlight, M. "A theoretical model of the psychological treatment of mental retardation." AMERICAN JOURNAL OF MENTAL DEFICIENCY. *68*:618–622 (1964).

[3] Strauss, A. A.; Kephart, N. C. "Psychopathology and education of the brain injured child." In: PROGRESS IN THEORY AND CLINIC, v. 2. N.Y., Grune & Stratton, 1955.

[4] Jarvis, V. "Clinical observations on the visual problem in reading disability." In: PSYCHOANALYTIC STUDY OF THE CHILD. 1960. v. 12, p. 451–470.

[5] Rapaport, D. ON THE PSYCHOANALYTIC PSYCHIATRY AND PSYCHOLOGY, N.Y., Hallmark-Hubner, 1954. p. 423–449.

[6] Rank, B. "Adaptation of the psychoanalytic technique for treatment of young children and atypical development." AMERICAL JOURNAL OF ORTHOPSYCHIATRY. *19*:130–139 (1949).

[7] Webster, T. A. "Problems in emotional development in young retarded children." AMERICAN JOURNAL OF PSYCHIATRY. *120*:37–43 (1963).

[8] Scheerer, M.; Rothman, E.; Goldstein, K. "A case of 'Idiot Savant'." In: PSYCHOLOGICAL MONOGRAPHS, No. 4 (1945) p. 58.

[9] Freud, S. "Formulation regarding the two principles in mental functioning." In his: COLLECTED WORKS. London, Hogarth. v. 4, p. 13–21.

[10] Rapaport, D. ON THE PSYCHOANALYTIC PSYCHIATRY AND PSYCHOLOGY. N.Y., Hallmark-Hubner, 1954. (Austin Riggs, v. 1) p. 1–40.

[11] Cameron, N. EXPERIMENTAL ANALYSIS OF SCHIZOPHRENIC THINKING. Language and thought in Schizophrenia. Los Angeles, Univ. of California Press, 1954. p. 74–86.

[12] Doman-Delacata. DOMAN-MORAN PROFILE AND GRAPHIC SUMMARY. Philadelphia, Institute of Human Potential, 1963.

[13] Kris, E. ORGANIZATION AND PATHOLOGY OF THOUGHT, PRECONSCIOUS MENTAL PROCESSES. N.Y., Columbia University Press, 1951. p. 474–493.

[14] Spitz, R. "Anaclitic depression." In: PSYCHOANALYTIC STUDY OF THE CHILD. N.Y., Intnl. U. Press, 1946. v. 2, p. 313–343..

[15] Rosen, J. THE CONCEPT OF EARLY MATERNAL ENVIRONMENT IN DIRECT PSYCHOANALYSIS. Doylestown, Pa., Doylestown Fndn., 1963.

[16] Harlow, H. "Love in infant monkeys." SCIENTIFIC AMERICAN. *200*:91–100 (1959).

[17] Honig, A. M. "Analytic treatment of schizophrenia." JOURNAL OF THE AMERICAN OSTEOPATHIC ASSOCIATION. *57*:322–326 (1958).

[18] Lewin, B. D. THE PSYCHOANALYSIS OF ELATION. N.Y., Norton, 1950. p. 102–107.

[19] Honig, A. M. "Anxiety in schizophrenia." PSYCHOANALYSIS AND PSYCHOANALYTIC REVIEW. *47(3)*:77–90 (1960).

[20] Honig, A. M. "Negative transference in psychosis." PSYCHOANALYSIS AND PSYCHOANALYTIC REVIEW. *47(4)*:105–114 (1960/61).

CHAPTER XIII

Epilepsy—A Symptom of Personality Disorder

"His eyes were large, blue and dreary," writes Fyodor Dostoevsky, a known epileptic, in describing Prince Myshkin in The Idiot. "There was something gentle though heavy-looking in their expression," he goes on, "something of that strange look from which some people can recognize at the first glance a victim of epilepsy . . ."

". . . As I sat in the train," says Prince Myshkin, "I thought 'Now I am going among people. I know nothing perhaps but a new life has begun for me. I am determined to do my work resolutely and honestly. I may find it dull and difficult among people. In the first place I resolved to be courteous and open with everyone. No one will expect more than that from me. Perhaps here, too, they will look on me as a child, but no matter. Everyone looks on me as an idiot, too, for some reason'." [1]

The serious study of clinical epilepsy presents a medical enigma. No clinical entity gives a greater picture of critical organic morbidity and impending doom to the observer and the one suffering the attack than the epileptic pattern. This fact is especially true in the grand mal. Ever present in this dangerous malady is status epilepticus with resulting coma and death. Still popular is the belief of its incurability, as well as the necessity of life-long subjugation to medication.

Beginning with an aura—sometimes pleasant but more often one of impending doom—the attacks go through phases of loss of consciousness, tonic and clonic seizures and finally blissful sleep. Most often the person is awake after a half-hour, tired and vague. However, there seems to be no residuum or morbidity; perhaps a depressing of affect—but not the agonizing reaction that seems to express imminent death.

Patients themselves develop a fear of an epileptic attack. They have said that the only time they feel relatively well is after a seizure—since the impending doom of the oncoming attack is not present. This fear of an attack causes restriction of movement in all social spheres. The individual is forced into a life of helplessness, futility, loneliness, ineptness and social estrangement. Even mothers, afraid of being incapacitated by an attack, mistrust their ability to care for their children. In addition to this, an epileptic attack in any public place causes the victim great shame and embarrassment. Also the ability to earn only a meager living, most often the fate of the epileptic, produces intense despair and a sense of injustice.

Etiology

Morbid anatomy and etiology show no single cause for epilepsy.

Penfield and Erickson maintain that scar tissue from old trauma is more common than generally believed as a cause of "idiopathic epilepsy." [2] However, there is reason enough to question whether the lesions found under the microscope are not the result, rather than the cause, of epileptic seizures.[3, 4, 5]

It seems most observers agree that epilepsy is not a disease entity per se. Rather, they see it as a group of symptoms and responses that can occur in any living animal if the brain is sufficiently stimulated or irritated.[6]

Since the brain can withstand ordinary amounts of stimulation without a discharge constituting a seizure, there must then be, in the epilepsies, an abnormally lowered threshold to stimulation. Moreover, the essential feature of epilepsy is not the convulsive seizure, or even the disturbance of consciousness; it is, rather, the sudden episodic functionary disturbance in the central nervous system.

However, it seems to me various questions are still unanswered. How is it:

1. That varieties of fits occur in the same individual?
2. That the true epileptic—the one who exhibits the classical signs—can and often does recover?
3. That in the course of recovery the character of the fits may change from major to minor?
4. That in the course of recovery the first sign of improvement is the recurrence of the fits only in sleep and not during waking hours?
5. That by partially interrupting the onset of a fit, the patient can often be saved from his typical fit and display only an attack of the hysterical type of petit mal?
6. That fits are encouraged by emotional disturbance, such as fright, anger and anxiety?
7. That the epileptic fit resembles in detail the infantile convulsion, known sometimes to be the result of an emotional disturbance, such as fear or anger?

8. That typical epilepsy appears as a result of excessive emotional strain alone—especially during wartime? [7]

Even with the presence of a physical lesion, one can ask:

1. Why are the attacks periodic and why do no physical signs exist between attacks?
2. How can a localized lesion of the brain (e.g., of the uncinate convolution) produce definite mental phenomena, including the aura encountered in the various states of the attack or its equivalent?

There is another difficulty in always accepting a physical lesion as the origin of epilepsy, which is the variety of signs and symptoms in the same patient. Why do major and minor attacks occur in the same patient? Why is the tongue bitten and the urine passed on some occasions and not on others? How is it that a patient can sometimes control or prevent an attack —either voluntarily or by using some peripheral stimulus, such as tying a string around the thumb? Why do psychic phenomena vary before and after the fit?

It is true that seizures may follow severe head injury; however, a recent Walker study in the Veterans' Administration shows that only 40 percent of open head injuries result in seizures. Seizures may follow meningeal infections, cerebritis, encephalitis, disturbance in metabolic states, space occupying lesions and cerebral anoxia. Phenobarbital and tranquilizers, when withdrawn, suddenly lower the threshold to seizures. Also, alcohol "binging," with sudden withdrawal, may result in convulsive "ramfits."

However, as stated by Buzzard in 1922, there can be no doubt that the study of epilepsy has suffered much in the past from ignoring the psychological factor.[8] Fatigue, of itself, may convert potential anxieties into active anxieties because of loss of perspective and proportion by which it is always accompanied.*

Thus, it is to that large ideopathic class—those fitted into the 40–60 percent of unknown origin—that we direct inquiry. Excluding the acute processes mentioned, it can be stated that, in a large majority of epileptic illnesses, emotional disturbance was the original cause of the *first* fit.

The Epileptic Personality

There is much in the literature of epilepsy to suggest a characteristic epileptic personality-type. However, I find that most of the personality defects attributed to epileptics are the presenting symptoms of neurosis in general. There are, though, distinguishing factors present in the makeup of the epileptic—including impulsiveness, irritability and sexual naivete. The impulsiveness may be controlled by obsessive and compulsive checks

---

* Kussmaul and Turner in 1857 proved that strong stimulation of the cerebral cortex can induce a variety of convulsive reactions. In 1910 Janet, at a meeting of Society of Neurology and Psychiatry in Paris (recorded in #I, II, III of the Journal L'Encephalo) said that emotions can transform a neurosis into epilepsy.

and will not present itself except in deterioration of the personality. The irritability might mask a build-up of extreme anger and violence. Headaches, small sadistic acts and tantrums or occasional outbursts may occur. These side symptoms, however, most often accompany imperfect epilepsy —petit mal or epileptic form equivalent. With Le Grand Mal—the supreme reaction—no other neurotic symptoms are necessary. This great reaction is an entity within itself and, when active, allows the release of all psychic energy.

The personality traits of irritability and impulsiveness are elicited from childhood developmental history. These may show the central theme. Usually there is a history in childhood of violent reaction to trifling stimuli: the child threatening or even attacking another person or breaking or throwing objects near him. This reaction may alternate with a sudden mood swing of equal but opposite extreme. There may be sudden outbursts of crying, sadness, or extreme obstinacy with refusal to respond to reason.

For example, one boy at a very early age, began to "see red" whenever his little sister interfered with or thwarted him. He would assume a threatening attitude; eyes ablaze, teeth and fists clenched, sometimes a weapon ready to strike. After such an outburst he explained, "I hate her, I have always hated her. I want to kill her."

The grand mal attack probably does not solidify as a complete personality entity until puberty. It is the sexual denial at this time that makes picture complete. No other mental condition so completely denies genital sexual expression as does epilepsy. In fact, one might speculate that the complete denial of all aggressive or sexual release by the consciousness cannot exist and still allow an organism to survive. Thus, we have the safety valve that allows for everyday life—the seizure.

One boy with a history of violent rages before puberty described his feelings about masturbation. His first indulgence, at the age of 13, caused him intense remorse.

"I never indulged more than twice," he said. "Afterward I thought, well, I have done it now. I have wasted life fluid." A religious reaction followed and he said, "I will give myself to God but all the time I felt I could not make up the life fluid."

On another occasion this same boy said, "I had an overwhelming impression of the sense of unpardonable sin after the first self-abuse. I felt it could not be expiated. When I left the room in which act had taken place, I met my brothers but I didn't tell them. I was filled with remorse. At school I felt I was different from other boys after I masturbated. I stayed alone and took long walks."

After puberty the boy changed from an impulsive, upset, non-intellectual given to violent outbursts of rage to a loner, lacking in confidence and obsessed with religious mysticism. Many attacks followed, both major and minor—the major seizures followed by a depressed state lasting three or four days.

"When I was sixteen," he recalled, "I had my first attack. My brother and I were on our bicycles. At a certain spot I became confused and felt I had seen the place before. The doctor said I had an attack of petit mal. I had other attacks of petit mal; my first major attack occurred when I was 24 and in the Army . . ."

The boy's religious side had developed in an exaggerated form. Explaining his feeling, he said, "I believe that religion means a personal communication with a personal Deity. When praying sometimes I experience an overwhelming impression of something too strong for me. The depressed feeling after the fit is about religion. Perhaps I used thoughts on religion as a drug. After an attack, I seem to get into another world. St. Paul was caught up and heard unspeakable words: I do not see but I feel a sense of increased spiritual existence."

Perhaps the outstanding feature in the makeup of the epileptic is his quietness and his isolated preoccupation with the body and the illness. There is a hysteric flavor to the emotional tone. All the psychic energy is somatized. The sense of impending doom is constant. Even with epileptics who have a high degree of intellectual endowment, concreteness of thought is always present.

The Psychodynamics of Epilepsy

Perhaps the most important phenomenon of all the epilepsies is the disturbance of consciousness. This may take the form of lack of concentration, vertigo, dreary states, déja vu, hallucination, fugue, stupor or coma.

There is damage to the brain resulting secondarily from an attack. Each time an epileptic has a convulsive seizure resulting in tonic, clonic reactions and loss of consciousness, there is danger of hemorrhage,* brain edema and further scarring. The danger of hitting the skull in the fall itself is always possible. The resulting brain damage and interference with thought process from the interruptive periodic loss of consciousness interferes with the process of learning, resulting in the association of epilepsy with idiocy.

Hughlings Jackson thought that because of the disturbance of consciousness and the "Intellectual Aurae," epilepsy might be considered the prototype of all emotional illness.

It is the aura that begins the disturbance of consciousness. Jackson states "a patient describes his own mental condition as comparable to that of one who suddenly awakened from a sound sleep. He cannot get hold of the dream which seems to be quickly passing from his mind, at the same time he cannot yet appreciate the state of consciousness into which he has so suddenly awakened. Through it all, the fear of some impending catastrophe seems to be hanging over him." [9]

Most patients recall this fear of impending doom as a feeling of horror. This same feeling is described by patients as they fall into psychosis.[10] In

* The same as after electric shock therapy.

considering the dynamics of epilepsy, one compares the mother-child relationship that exists in schizophrenia. The feelings of imminent death can be compared to the dread that Sullivan describes as pre-psychotic.[11] Accompanying this feeling of impending doom in psychosis are feelings of depersonalization and estrangement. The same feelings of loss of body boundaries and separation from the immediate environment probably accompany the epileptic attack but are most often forgotten, because of the more sudden and complete loss of consciousness.

Freud wrote, "in the aura of the epileptic attack one moment of supreme bliss is experienced." [12] He related it to the triumphant sense of achievement of the primal aggressive wish—murder—the murder of the interfering father. The father is considered the disturber of the relationship in the father—mother—infant triangle. The moment of bliss—reunion with mother—is very brief. It is followed by the impending doom and subsequent loss of consciousness. However, the patients remember only the latter.

Freud also states that the moment of bliss is the triumph on hearing the news of the hated object's death (the father), but death-wish fulfillment and revenge, when fulfilled, carry the punishment of extreme guilt. There is no crime worse than patricide would be the same as if committed in actuality, an eye for an eye and a tooth for a tooth.

The total isolation of all psychic energy, however, as seen in grand mal for example, is now similar to grand hysteria. It is basically exhibited in a conversion-like somatic reaction. Large quantities of excitation that cannot be dealt with psychically are discharged through the body. To my way of thinking, this causes the only difference in types of epilepsy. In grand mal, all psychic energy is handled through somatic means; in the minor epilepsies, portions are handled psychically and portions somatically.

Since the psyche functions on a higher level of organization in epilepsy, than in schizophrenia, and the regression and disintegration of the self that accompanies psychosis are absent, perhaps the epilepsies should be considered dynamically between the psychotic reactions and the somatic hysterias.

Furthermore, it is too simple to state that the total conflict exists on a completely genital sexual level. Perhaps the obvious complete regression of all sex is really a child-like awareness but an actual non-interest in genital sex. The point of the psychic energy is at the oral level.

The epileptic attack itself, from beginning to end, can be similarly compared to the persistent nightmare occurring during the waking day. As in any dream, the epileptic reaction attempts to "act out" an infantile conflict. If one accepts this interpretation, then perhaps dynamic meaning can be given to each part of the attack. The "one moment of supreme bliss" is that nebulous joy that exhibits itself in some form of oral craving. In earlier infancy or in infantile regression and infantile states, it is always synonymous with "good mother." It is as if "mother and I" are one again —together again, symbiotic and synergistic—and everything else is a disturber of the relationship.

Lewin describes the father as the disturber of sleep.[13] I think he is more than the disturber of sleep since one who takes away the dream of "mother and I" takes away my life. If one wants to annihilate me, I have a right to destroy him before he destroys me.

A 43-year-old self-ordained Negro preacher, an epileptic for as long as he could remember, related this dream which illustrates oral deprivation: "There was a large pot of gold coins in front of me. It was to be my gift and I reached for it. Just as I was about to have it, my mother sliced off my hands. She was only carrying out the orders of a Judge who was standing there watching the whole procedure."

This dream had been recurrent. It was stimulated by the man having recently had $36.00 stolen from him while he was reaching for his wallet in a restaurant. He remembers when he was a child and his mother left him in the care of a grandmother who frequently beat him.

Freud states "the death-like seizures signify an identification with a dead person; either someone who is really dead or someone still alive and whom the subject wishes dead." [14]

The latter is more significant. The attack then had the value of punishment. One has wished another dead—now he is this other person and is dead himself. At this point psychoanalytic theory asserts that to a boy this other person is usually the father; thus the attack is self-punishment for a death-wish against hated father.

I might add that a little girl's reaction is much the same. Although she substitutes the penis for the breast (her father is substituted for the breast), it is still her mother who is the primary love object. Her father remains the hated object. It is only after genital love has superseded oral love that she is able to make the true substitution.

If one can accept the "moment of supreme bliss" as always preceding an attack, one can go on to the text component—the aura.

"The aura," states R. G. Rows, "is a disturbance of consciousness which consists of the revival of an idea, as in an intellectual aura, or of an image more or less complex in some sensory centre, or of a sensation connected with a past emotional state, or of a movement which may also have formed a part of a previous experience. The aura depends on the reactivation of paths and centres in the nervous system by a stimulation which leads to the revival in memory of a past stimulus and the results produced by it. A similar reactivation of nerve paths and centres form the basis of hallucinations which are all made up of revivals of images and ideas. Whether the image so revived by the product of the visual, auditory or of any other centre in the nervous system, it will be found to be the reawakening of some antecedent experiences of a highly emotional character."

The aura might be similar to that described as the "Isakower phenomena"—a description of falling asleep.[15] The patient loses his perceptive ego; he can no longer experience the world around him. Regressing to the archaic ego of neonatal life, he becomes concerned with body sensation. The libido, withdrawn from the external world, does not remain in the body; body distortion takes place. There is temporal and spatial distortion of all real objects.

All patients describe the aura with morbidity—the sensations involving many nervous pathways. One patient may recall the odor of burning flesh; another, the taste of blood. Still another may have heard frightening sounds or witnessed a feeling of utter blackness. Just as in the transition into hallucinatory psychosis or in suicide, there is a feeling of disintegration— as if the world were coming to an end.

Perhaps the impulsivity and raw, naked feeling of explosive violence so pronounced in the epileptic syndrome they can only be controlled by severe turning on the self. In this way, although the dynamics may be different, epilepsy can be compared to suicide.

In any case, the feeling of impending doom is justified. There next follows an actual loss of consciousness which results in a disturbance of brain function which can and has resulted in death. This is the actual attack; *loss of consciousness,* along with clonic and tonic convulsions and finally, the resulting post-epileptic sleep or coma.

Another dynamic component of the epileptic attack that appears universally, in every case and in both sexes, is related to auto-erotic genital sexuality, masturbation and orgasm. There is a complete denial of the masturbation act; Freud states the mechanism of instinctual discharge cannot stand remote from the sexual processes, which are fundamentally of toxic origin.[16] The earliest physicians described copulation as a minor epilepsy and thus recognized in the sexual act a mitigation and adoption of the epileptic method of discharging stimuli.

I cannot yet determine whether masturbation, the "secret sin," represents a pure instinctual genital desire for the parent of the opposite sex or a displaced oral need satisfied by the pleasurable feelings of the organs. If it is the latter the object might be oneself, or the parent, or oral nourishment—the unconscious phantasized mother.

It has been observed that the continuous high voltage, fast activity found in a grand mal seizure is also found at the moment of orgasm. This repressed overt infantile sexuality may only be present in the state of altered consciousness. I have treated at least one female who, after the tonic convulsion had subsided, would place her fingers in the vagina during the post-epileptic sleep. Many patients with petit mal rub their legs together, become flushed in the face and utter sounds reminiscent of sexual intercourse.

Livingston states that three patients, ages one and a half, three, and four, all females, were observed to masturbate between ages 18 months and two years. The E.E.G. (or brain wave pattern) was normal.[17] All had infantile convulsions.

One patient began to have attacks of stiffness and staring spells at the age of 18 months. A family physician diagnosed them as petit mal epilepsy and prescribed medication. When attacks continued, another physician was consulted—this time the diagnosis was grand mal epilepsy and another anti-convulsive drug was prescribed. The patient was on medication for six months with no benefit.

The patient was referred to his clinic at three and a half. The mother stated her daughter had had an average of three or four "attacks of stiffness and staring spells" daily since she was 18 months old. She described the attacks as follows: "she crosses her thighs, holds them very stiff, has a vacant and staring look in her eyes, becomes red in the face, breaks out in a cold sweat. She remains this way for 10–15 minutes and then goes into a deep sleep."

Physical and neurological exams were normal, E.E.G. revealed normal brain wave pattern. A diagnosis of masturbation was established. Following adequate psychiatric guidance, the attacks of stiffness and staring spells disappeared. When last seen at age ten, the patient was well and had had no spells since discharge from psychiatry. Another Electro-Encephalogram revealed normal brain wave pattern.

Livingston concluded "From the symptoms I have described in this case, it can be understood that the habit (masturbation) may easily be taken for some epileptic manifestation."

The Treatment of Epilepsy

Before the presentation of case material and a discussion of the psychological treatment of epilepsy, it would be prudent to mention a conclusion drawn by Ramamarthi about focal fits. The possibility of a focal attack being due to a removable organic lesion increases with the presence of objective signs. Without objective signs, the possibility is much less. Because of the possibility that, in cases of focal fits, removable organic lesions may develop, a careful follow-up is necessary.

Before I undertake the treatment of a case of epilepsy, a complete neurological and neurosurgical evaluation must be done on the patient. I must be reasonably sure no surgical organic lesion exists. This evaluation includes a clinical neurological examination, electro-encephalogram (induced sleep and awake), x-rays of the skull and arteriography and pneumo-encephalogram. When I feel sure there is no acute organic foci of irritation that might respond to surgical intervention, a psychological test evaluation is ordered.

Next is the problem of medication. Since it has no place in my armamentarium of treatment (except as temporary support), all medicine is withdrawn as soon as possible via a tapering off process. In the tapering process, I have substituted Valium orally while other medication is being withdrawn. There is evidence to support its use as a brain sedative. Only in a rare case will I re-medicate once withdrawal has been accomplished.

This withdrawal is more easily done when the patient lives at my therapeutic family unit where there is 24-hour surveillance. However, an out-patient is living at home, the medicine is still withdrawn and the family assumes the responsibility. The patient, at all times, carries my card noting his identification. Hospital calls to me have not been unusual; once I had to rescue a patient from a downtown Philadelphia store during the rush hour. The withdrawal of medicine becomes a situation of calculated risk; it is fraught with danger and frequently I have had to defend my ideas before my colleagues as well as my own conscience. One thing I have discovered, however, is that a patient soon adjusts to each lower level of medication during the tapering off process.

Recently I took on the case of a young married nurse with a history of spontaneous abortion and petit mal attacks. Neurosurgical workup was non-productive and according to the neurosurgeon's orders, the patient was placed on an anti-convulsive drug, which she took three times a day.

She had been a diligent patient and for six years took this medication faithfully. When I began to see her she was having "dizzy spells," a fogginess of mentality and a fear of taking care of her two year old daughter. She had been a cheerleader in high school and a peppy, cheerful student nurse. Now she was fearful and spent most of her time in bed while a maid (whose services she could not afford since her husband was an auto mechanic) tended her home and child.

Once I was on the case I tapered off the medicine to one pill a day, one every other day and finally one per week. There were no symptoms (of which I have described) until that last week when she took the last 1½ gr. of the drug. She immediately became somnolent, dizzy and foggy. It was obvious that the drug itself was causing these symptoms. It was then withdrawn completely, with immediate beneficial effects.

CASE I—Irene L., age 19

Following is the letter sent to the referring psychiatrist Dr. M., re. Irene L., first examined January 17, 1961.

Dear Dr. M.:

I saw your patient, Irene L., at G.F. on Wednesday, January 17th. She is a 19 year old single female showing the position of a chronically ill patient. She has the stooped shoulders, short hair and fixed faces often seen in the state hospital. Upon questioning I find that, since the age of 10 or 11, boys as well as others have been making sounds with their mouth that indicate she smells. She has had this thought for at least eight or nine years and is convinced that indeed, she does smell. She feels that the gas escapes through her rectum but she is not aware when it happens. This fixed idea is with her all the time. Apparently there are no compulsive acts. The patient is a middle child; she has an older sister and a younger sister. She has had no suicidal thoughts; many times, however, she feels everyone would be better off if she weren't around.

She feels that her mother loves her although, in a subsequent interview at my office, she told me that nobody loves her. She has a strong desire to go home; she feels there is more to do there.

As far as I can elicit, she had had electric shock treatment between one and three times a week for over a year. I feel I would like to see more records on this treatment.

While interviewing her in the office one day, she went into a Jacksonian-type episode in which she began to shake both arms and talk gibberish, almost in a motor-type of aphasia. She later said she remembered while it was happening but could not get her speech out. This has been going on for a month, her mother says.

Impression: Obsessive compulsive personality. It is possible to discover on deep questioning, that this patient may have somatic delusions; the diagnosis would then be changed to chronic schizophrenia and olfactory delusions. (In fact, diagnosis was changed to chronic schizophrenia and olfactory delusions.)

Recommendation: There is no doubt in my mind that this is a chronic case and will be of several years' duration if it is possible to cure this patient. I feel an E.E.G. examination should be done because of the seizure in my office. I will attempt to treat this patient with direct psychotherapy and elicit the older sister's and brother-in-law's support at home; if this does not work, I will hospitalize the patient.

Thank you for allowing me to examine your patient. I remain

Sincerely yours,
Albert M. Honig

Following is Dr. M.'s letter to the family physician who first referred Irene L.

Dear Dr. S.:

The following is a note for your records to supplement our several phone conversations in reference to your patient. As you know, she was hospitalized at G.F. and was finally discharged after a consultation with Dr. Honig. At the present time plans are being made for her admission to the sanitorium under Dr. Honig's service.

I feel that I. could be diagnosed as schizophrenia—simple type. Unfortunately, we are not dealing with a regressive phenomenon in this case but a fixation from about the age of eleven, which makes the case much more difficult or refractory as far as prognosis is concerned. In addition to quite a few hours of psycho-therapeutic investigation, we did a battery of psychologic tests and there is evidence that this is a simple type of schizophrenia, which is particularly refractory to known treatments of any type. My only suggestion—and we must remember that this patient has had psycho-pharmaceuticals and electroshock therapy by a previous psychiatrist—would be the Rosen technique, and thus the consultation with Dr. Honig.

I discussed the entire case, prognosis, possibilities of cure, etc., with her mother and brother-in-law, the latter something of a spokesman for the family, and offered a poor prognosis even with Dr. Honig. However, I told them if they wanted to try there is always hope. I also felt that Dr. Honig should most certainly be allowed to form an opinion and prognosis of his own after examining the patient.

I will, of course, be "looking in" on Irene from time to time with interest and, if this treatment is sterile, I would be very happy to assist you and the family in further recommendations if they are needed at the time.

Thank you very much for your kind reference of this patient.

Sincerely yours,

As this letter states, I began to treat Irene out of the hospital. She lived with her mother and nine year old sister. Nearby lived her recently married older sister, a school teacher and her husband, who was a graduate engineer. Since the mother understood little of the treatment procedure, the young couple was deputized as family assistants.

The family lived in a big brick house built by the father before his death two years before from coronary thrombosis. During the summer they worked at a seashore grocery store originally owned by the father.

The patient came to my office twice a week, accompanied by her mother. Her main symptoms were:

1. The delusion that air came out of her; therefore she smelled.

2. Her grand mal seizures—sometimes two daily. All medication was withdrawn. The seizures had a history of one to two years. This girl was receiving sub-convulsive shock twice a week during this time. I felt that, though the shock treatment might be contributing to the frequency of seizures, they were not the initial cause since she had apparently suffered seizures before.

3. The cessation of menses was of approximately two years' duration. This is about how long the condition had been chronic.

The following are descriptions of the somatic delusion pertaining to the rectum that I. felt:

I started to get sick when I was about 12 years old. I remember coming home to my mother and telling her that I smelled of perspiration under my arms. I truly believed in this. Many times after this I still came home after school and was telling my mother that I still smelled under my arms. I kept changing my school blouse every single day when before this I used to change my school blouse about every other day. About three months later I started to believe in the fact that air was coming from my body and making me smell. I truly believed in this for many years. I was conscious of it every single day for every single second all through the years and still am. I feel now that it is a part of my life.

I have worked in the store for today. I have enjoyed and liked it very much. It has seemed very different.

I have always loved my mother and father. I have always loved my sisters very much. I have never been jealous of them. E. (9 years) my sister I always thought that she never made fun of me or said anything about air coming out of me because she just accepted me as being that way. I always thought that it wasn't necessary to say anything about air coming from me to my mother or father because they understood what was wrong with me and were just waiting for the day like I was when I could tell again when air was coming from me. I am sorry for all the trouble I have caused my family. I know they must have spent much money on doctor's bills and still are. It seems very confusing and I only wish I could really believe and know what I am and if air does really come from me and when it does and even if it is only maybe a couple times a day that still means that air comes from me and if I am near a person they would smell me.

It will be two years in July that my father has passed away. It doesn't seem possible. I am just beginning to realize that my father has passed away. I know there must be much worry for my mother.

Lately it happened a couple of times that I felt about the dreams that I had told you about. There are many feelings and different things I feel in myself that I can't explain or understand. I know how you say that like there are two parts of a person's mind—a conscious and a subconscious, and like how Sissy's husband Frank was explaining to me that when a person goes to sleep their mind relaxes and there are many thoughts that come to them in their dreams that they don't think during the day. I know like how I was telling you that a couple times I can recall how I seemed half asleep and half awake how great the fear was in me of whether air came out of my rectum or not. And how deeply I believed this for many years. I was always conscious of this for many years and still am all through the day. I know that many times when you ask me if I had any crazy thoughts, this seems very strange to me because of being always conscious of it and I don't know how to tell you because then you would probably wonder if my appointments with you are doing any good. I know that during the day it doesn't really bother me or hurt me as much as it does at other times but I am still conscious of it and it seems more of a *friend* or *part* of me and seems part of my life and seems hard to understand how the other people cannot be conscious of one thing all through the day and how they can be so free of any thought like this.

I know how my mother was telling me of the many spells I had after and before I was put in the hospital and the many spells I had during the night in my sleep. I do not remember any of these spells coming over me and do not remember when at any particular moment these had happened. My mother had told me I remember a few times and I could remember how surprised I was that it had happened then. Although when I started to get these spells before I was put in the hospital I could understand the reason why a spell would come over me. Because of how I felt.

I am beginning to feel during the day just a couple times it happens maybe lately a couple times every other day a feeling of swish like air coming from my rectum. Although I have no control over this no more than you would have of perspiration coming from your pores. Maybe you can feel it and see it but you have no control to stop it or know when or what exact moment it will come out.

Tonight when I was walking on the boardwalk a couple times I felt like if I had to go to the bathroom. After when we walked off the boardwalk I felt this same feeling of which I described.

I do not know whether this means that maybe I am that kind of person that is this way and has air coming from them and because I am so afraid of it is not conscious of it and that because I am getting better at least being able to feel it. Or if it really could be true that air does not come from me. And that maybe these are blood vessels of which you were telling me ones.

It was about this time that I learned from Irene's previous therapist that, early in her illness, she had been more paranoid; she had written letters to different politicians, the President and Premier Castro, concerning her feelings of persecution.

I now began to attack her delusion, determined to destroy it at all cost. I felt I had nothing to lose; the patient was a backward type case, burned out, and the only way we could go was uphill.

I began making headway after approximately one month of treatment. The delusion was still intact but the patient was not so convinced of its truth. Her mother was lending a great deal of support at home, providing the nourishment necessary after my attack on the psychosis.

But then, about February 20th, the seizures became more frequent and occurred in public places. I placed the patient in a hospital for evaluation under the care of a neurosurgeon. Following is his report:

This very interesting patient was admitted to the hospital on March 28, 1961. As you well know the reason for admission was the occurrence of several seizures. These were supposed to have been present on two or three occasions over a period of about a month. Prior to this the patient had been receiving frequent electroshock treatments for about a year until she came under your treatment. Apparently she had been diagnosed as a paranoid schizophrenic.

At the time of her admission the patient was very withdrawn, quiet and appeared lethargic. She also appeared only fairly-well oriented as to space and time. (Examination revealed a suspicion of bilateral ankle clonus and delayed Babinski on the left side. Hoffman sign was negative. All deep tendon reflexes were hyperactive. The Rhomberg test was normal. No headache or visual difficulty was noted. No nystagmus was evident.

An electro-encephalogram (EEG) was performed and found to be essentially the same as her previous (six weeks ago) examination. A pneumoencephalogram was attempted but was incomplete due to a spinal fluid reading taken. This revealed a suspicious area in the right hemisphere. A bilateral cerebral arteriogram was performed and this was reported as showing an area of arterial collection in the right hemisphere 1 cm. in diameter at the junction of the body and the posterior horn of the right ventricle.)

. . . (there was a questionable tumor but) . . . questionable tumor was causing her symptoms. The seizures and positive Babinsky were more likely as a result of her shock therapy. It was felt that additional consultation was advisable and the services of Dr. S. were sought. He felt that no tumor was present and the patient should not be exposed to surgery.

Therefore, we have discharged the patient to your continued care and suggest that she be kept under observation. (If the seizures continue (she exhibited none while in the hospital), then in about three (3) months, she should have another arteriogram. I would continue her on Dilantin sodium 1½ gr. t.i.d.)

Thank you for referring this case to me for attention.

Respectfully

Following are abstracts of sessions from May 18, 1961 to May 2, 1965 —at which time this patient decided to pay for her own sessions and see me only on occasion (taken from my notes).

May 18

The patient had a convulsion in bed at six A.M. Her mother had guests for the first time two days ago and Irene talked with them spontaneously. She asked: "Where was I when my father died three years ago?" She remembers no feeling for the event. The delusion of air coming from her persists. She had amnesia concerning an event that happened one month ago, when a boy walked her home. She remarked, "Mom, did I really do that? Do I really have spells? If I do, I don't know about it." She rationalized, "If I do this (epilepsy) without control then I can lay air and not know about it."

Her family physician gave her progesterone to induce menstrual flow. Her first period lasted three days and was very weak.

Her convulsions have somewhat lessened. Yesterday's seizure was the first in three weeks.

Today I told her how to test for air coming out of her: (a) smell (b) feel (c) sound.

She says she has no love for anyone.

May 24

Patient said, "I know I don't smell."

"How do you know?" I asked.

"When my younger sister said 'Why don't you go out and get a job' I knew she wouldn't say this if she didn't think I was all right."

Yesterday, the patient went to her relatives and told them things that were on her mind—not caring what they thought. She started Saturday in a bad way. She began to hit her mother. After this she had a seizure. Since then she has felt well and there have been no spells for the last two days. She expressed a desire to be as well as her older sister. She wanted to operate a cash register at the family food store at the shore. At present, there are many doubts in her mind concerning her delusion and its truth.

July 11

Today Irene related her first dream: "I was walking with my younger sister. I see a three or four year old child in a baby carriage, with one foot off. It was my older sister, M.'s carriage." At the same time, she began to ask me questions about sex. Irene thought that when her mother and father fought, they made babies. She can understand how normal people feel, she says. Her hair under her arms doesn't bother her anymore.

July 14

Irene related the following dream: "I got fat and the doctor said this is the way to get well." I made the interpretation that food is knowledge and that in her re-learning process she would have to even re-learn what food is and means to her.

July 20

Another dream: "There was a man holding me on the bed (an older man)." She said it was the butcher down the street. Then her mother came in to them. Today, Irene brought in a doll that she had made.

July 28

Today Irene missed an appointment. I got extremely angry. She told her brother-in-law that I must really care for her.

July 29

Another dream: Her father and mother were fighting. She said that it was because of this that she stayed away from boys. She said to me in tears, "If my father had intercourse with my mother he must have loved her."

August 4

There were two seizures of importance this week. The first occurred in Grant's 5 and 10 cent store three days ago. The patient was taken to a nearby hospital. By the time I was called (she had my card in her possession), she had recovered.

The second occurred today in my office. We were talking superficially about sex for the first time. I had asked her to buy me a travel alarm clock since I was about to begin a vacation trip. She thought this was wrong and that my wife should have bought it. Her reasoning was "that it gets you up in the morning, out of bed."

Before the spell took place she said she thought "this isn't life; it's death and I am in purgatory as punishment for my sins."

Description of the Seizure

The patient looked depressed when she entered the office. She started to talk about her dreams. She mentioned having a dream similar to the one she had had the previous week. Soon after, she went into seizure.

During the seizure she spread her legs. There followed both tonic and clonic contractions. Then there was tongue biting, pallor, eye rolling. She kicked off her shoes then she screamed "father". An orgasm-like attack followed and the seizure ended, the patient uttering passionate sounds, her hands in her vagina.

September 20

There have been no spells since the last one. Today Irene related the following dream: There was a knife. She tried to put it into her mother, then into her older sister. With this came a feeling of wanting to be free. She talked fervently of school and a job.

November 1

The patient has been learning shorthand and typing at a local secretarial school. She said she hasn't made a good adjustment to her fellow students, although she is applying herself diligently and seriously to her work.

She related an incident that happened in her car. She got angry at her mother and her mother slipped extra candy bars into Irene's pocket—to appease her. Where before, this action might have quieted her, now it only increased her anger.

She related this dream: "I was driving with my father. We found a certain stone which solved all the family problems. . . . Then I met some boys in their car."

Her interpretation was "all my life I waited for the family to be a family. It never happened and now we are all grown up."

November 20

Irene was upset this week. She locked her mother out after taking a shower. She had the irritating feeling that she had wasted all these years.

There was also the feeling of having kissed a female schoolmate with whom she had been fighting.

December 21

This was a turbid week. After having seen her cousin and her new baby girl, Irene had two seizures. During the seizures she masturbated as she had done previously.

Another dream: She went to the bathroom; there she saw her second cousin, a handsome boy of 18.

She associated the dream with the fact that this boy's family had been asking her to visit. She then said, "I don't know where I am—I must be growing up—I am now having feelings of being a woman."

January 10

This dream was unusual: A little girl says "I'm sweating; throw water on me. The mother complies each time. However, what the girl really needs is a sweater because it is cold."

She interpreted this as her mother never having really told her the truth. The patient has expressed a desire to work for me as an assistant.

Following is a letter I received from Irene during the summer of 1961, while she was working at the family store. It was her first summer working; she was still convulsing and, as can be seen, still somewhat delusional:
(letter)
Summer 1961:

"I am beginning to recognize things now and remember. I know I have promised to you that I would write a couple more pages but I don't know what to write. I have been getting no more dreams. I don't mean in the night but those feelings of dreams during the day. I have gotten another spell during the night, Sunday. When I have spent those few days at my Aunt C.'s house last week, when it was for my last appointment with you. I felt sort of more worse. Then when I got back to the beach it was sort of harder for me to get used to getting back in the store. Although when I have come back up for my appointment I was just waiting to get back to the shore. This morning we have gotten up early to come to the city. I have not slept all night. I have eaten some chicken noodle soup that my mother had made at night. Maybe this was what kept me awake.

Last night my sister had said that the cash register was twenty dollars short. I use to think that psychiatrists use to listen to people talk of their problems and then try to talk to them. But now I can see that a psychiatrist gets paid to use psychology and lately I can see that my family has been using much of this on me. I am still very much confused. If I can understand what my family is using on me, then I can understand the fact that a feeling has gone away from my body and when it comes back then I will know that I am cured."

May 2, 1962

Treatment continued uneventfully until this time. The patient ceased to have seizures and her menstrual periods became regulated. She continued at school. Her mother related one of her own dreams to me: a bearded man was trying to get into her window to take her daughter away from her.

The patient states that she wants to quit school and get a job and see life.

About June 14, 1962, the patient became arrogant and refused to keep her appointments. Her brother-in-law called me. He said she was saying she was well and didn't want more treatment. I urged him to get her to my office. He complied with force. She came in fuming. She had scratched him; he had treated her roughly during the trip. She screamed angrily and hysterically for an hour in my office. Mainly, she did not want to listen to anyone anymore—she wanted to be independent now. She decided to continue her visits, but to pay for them herself.

She made one more visit after this—June 27th. This visit she paid for herself. I have had no further sessions with I. She applied for work and in 1963 (May 6), the following review from the Bureau of Vocational Rehabilitation was sent to me:

May 6, 1963—Re. I.L.

The following is the pre-vocational evaluation report on the above named client.

General Observations

I. dressed appropriately for this work setting and makes a neat appearance. She also speaks in a low, but clear voice, and seems to be able to communicate with her fellow co-workers. It is felt that both her physical and emotional problems do not significantly limit her work performance. Her energy level is adequate and she makes good use of her psychic energy by engaging in constructive work situations. Medically, she is reported to have a brain tumor and be susceptible to epileptic seizures. Psychiatrically, she was admitted to the M hospital on March 28, 1961 and discharged on April 7, 1961. The final diagnosis was schizophrenic episode, brain tumor suspect. At the present time she is reported to have made a remarkable recovery from this episode under intensive private psychiatric care. She is a cooperative friendly person, who exhibits an appropriate effect.

In her interpersonal relationships with co-workers she is rather reserved. Being a passive individual, she makes a good follower and readily conforms to the demands of the group. In her male-female relationships she seems equally at ease with both sexes. In her interpersonal relationships with supervisors she demonstrates an adequate degree of sociability and is highly cooperative. She required only occasional supervision. During pre-vocational evaluation she attended work regularly and was always punctual.

Worker Characteristics

Irene manifests an adequate self-image and good work approach. She is highly motivated to do a good job, and needs only occasional support when difficulties are encountered. She can persist at her work and her frustration tolerance seems to be adequate. Initiative is rarely demonstrated, yet she is a very dependable person. The quality of her work is good. Since she paces herself smoothly and rapidly, she produces at a good rate. Her learning speed is adequate and she can retain what she has learned. Instructions are always followed and a good attention span is manifested. Her conceptualization ability is adequate on both an abstract and concrete level, indicating her ability to plan and organize work materials. She can also adequately transfer old skills to new learning situations. A highly sensitive color and tactual discrimination ability is exhibited. However, her perceptual, clerical, weight, and measurement discriminations are only adequate. In addition, her visual-motor coordination, gross, fine muscle, and finger-hand dexterities are also adequate. She achieved up to level V complexity on certain clerical tasks. She did her best work on clerical, mailroom and bindery tasks, and poorest on electrical activities.

Summary and Recommendations

Although Irene does not seem to be ready for competitive employment, she demonstrates many good worker characteristics. Her major vocational problem at the present time is her lack of work experience. Continuation in this work adjustment program for eight (8) additional weeks is recommended for the following reasons:

1. To give her the opportunity to have a successful work experience so that she is better prepared to engage in competitive employment.

2. To see how she handles the increased tensions and pressures of a more demanding work setting.

Reauthorization should be dated as of May 15, 1963.

Termination report Re: I.L.—September 6, 1963.

The following is the termination report for the above named client.

General Observations

Irene's primary vocational problem will continue to be her psychiatric involvement. Although there are still residual symptoms of psychopathology, she appears to be in relatively good remission at this time. She is an attractive young lady who, throughout the work adjustment program, made an excellent appearance. She was well groomed and appropriately attired for this vocational setting.

Early in the process, she impressed one as being moderately depressed but as she became more familiar with her environment, she exhibited more appropriate affect. Related to this was a lowering of internal anxiety, resulting in greater ability to deal effectively with daily tensions and pressures.

Although she was fearful of close emotional involvement, she appeared to become less aloof and considerably more responsive. Her level of confidence has also increased but basic insecurity still exists. However, she can, at this time, utilize her defensive system in a psychologically more positive manner. She was highly motivated for the vocational rehabilitation and by the date of her termination was able to perceive herself as a potential employee. Throughout, her attitude was good, she accepted the program and exerted energy in her own behalf. Her regular and punctual attendance were indicators of a good sense of worker responsibility.

Interpersonal Relationships

Irene was more reserved than withdrawn but she was never a particularly active member of the group. She still preferred to remain on the periphery of social interactions. She had the potential to enter into meaningful relationships but was fearful of rejection. She did not exhibit leadership potential and this, in addition to her retiring personality pattern, negated the possibility of placing her in a cadre position. She was basically a conformist, adhering to group wishes.

She complied with all work demands and graciously accepted supervision. She had no difficulty with authority figures, was always co-operative and was never a disciplinary problem. She rejected her dependency needs and attempted to function autonomously. As a result, she required only minimal support.

Worker Characteristics

Irene developed a more positive vocational self-image. By experiencing work successes, she became less fearful of exposing what she perceived as personal inadequacies. A reduction of internal anxiety resulted in a longer attention span. She became less distractible and began to follow all instructions to their completion. Although there was never a question of mental deficiency, she began to more effectively utilize her intellectual resources. During the course of the program, she learned new operations more quickly by both the insight and trial and error methods. Her memory for detail was good and she had no difficulty transferring skills to new situations. Although she conceptualizes considerably better on the concrete level, she was able to handle abstract material.

She persisted at all job duties and even began to initiate her own work activities. This indicated greater willingness to assert herself in an appropriate manner. After initial structuring, she was capable of independent organization and planning.

She became less erratic and developed a relatively smooth work rhythm. This improved pacing resulted in increased productivity. At termination her average weekly rate reached a competitive level (90¢). Because of her compulsivity, she was an excellent quality worker. However, she was able to channel this psychological characteristic positively and never permitted it to interfere with the speed factor. Her visual motor coordination, gross dexterity and final manipulative skills were always potentially good but were further developed as a result of the program.

Summary

Irene's principal vocational liability will be the residual effects of a primary thought pathology. The possibility of an organic involvement (brain tumor) is also suspect. If this is found to be true, it will seriously complicate already existing problems.

In general, she has made a rather good vocational adjustment and there have been many noticeable improvements, such as increased productivity, smoother work pace, excellent quality, higher frustration tolerance and greater self confidence. She was still fearful of genuine emotional involvement, although the potential exists. For this reason, she would function best in a permissive setting where she could enter into casual interpersonal relationships.

At termination, she was producing at a competitive rate of employment (90¢ an hour). She was capable of performing both complex and simple factory jobs as well as routine clerical duties. She preferred to become employed in the latter vocational area but did not reject the former.

Recommendations

1. Terminated 8/24/63
2. Placed in Competitive Employment (contact Mr. S. for details of placement)
3. Supportive psychotherapy
4. Neurological examination to confirm or refute the possibility of an existing brain tumor.

Sincerely,

The patient has been working and living at home; I see her at our Clinic Christmas parties. She remains non-psychotic and non-epileptic. Unmarried, she is shy with boys, but at this time is beginning to date.

June 1967

In June 1967 I attended I.'s wedding to a local fireman. She seemed happy, alert and in love. My family and I were treated as something special. It was indeed flattering.

Since then, the young couple have started housekeeping in their own home. Irene works as a secretary 40 hours per week. In every respect she is living the life of a young newly married woman. She has told her husband everything of her past. This has only enhanced his love for I.

July 1968

In July 1968, I received an announcement of the birth of a daughter, wt. 6 lbs. 5 oz.—normal birth, mother and baby doing fine.

CASE II—Jimmy, age 17

Another case concerns Jimmy, a 17 year old male, younger of two siblings, who has been living at home with his father, mother and sister. Both parents work in factories; the father is an electrical laborer, the mother works in the clothing industry. The sister is separated from her husband, works out of the house, and employs a babysitter to care for her four small children.

My report to the referring general practitioner stated the following:
Dear Dr. J.:
I saw your patient, Jimmy on April 11, 1964. He came accompanied by his mother.

History

The history was taken from the patient and his mother. The patient had had uncontrollable rages since a child. The mother says this began at approximately age of three. At the age of seven or eight, he developed what looked like grand mal epilepsy. He was taken to the hospital and a diagnosis of grand mal epilepsy was made. The patient was placed on dilantin sodium and phenobarbital. The records from the hospital have been requested. It is only recently that the mother has come to feel that there may be a psychological problem. The rage attacks seem to build up and the patient can feel when an attack will come. They are preceded by an increase in tension and frequently sibling rivalry with the sister will tee it off. At times the patient has made attempts to strike his sister and the sister feels he may harm her at night. He is doing poorly in school and he has always been labeled an "oddball". He has few friends and even the teachers have been making fun of him recently. The patient has remained in bed many days at a time rather than face the world. His father is in the throes of a mental breakdown, and the mother has been hospitalized with the same condition. His sister, who is separated from her husband and has several children, is now seeing a psychiatrist.

Impression

Grand mal epilepsy, possibly on a psychogenic basis. I want to examine all the records in the case. I have sent to the places where the patient has been hospitalized.
It is possible that this boy is suffering from an underlying psychosis.

Recommendation

Because of this boy's murderous rages and the inability of his parents to tolerate him if he was treated at home, the following recommendation is made. The patient should be hospitalized in one of our family units, and taken off all medication and treated, well knowing of his murderous rages and possible underlying psychosis.
Psychological evaluation should be made before treatment is started.
Thank you for letting me examine your patient, I remain

Sincerely yours,
H.

Records of his previous admissions to a hospital for neurologic workup were obtained. It is noted that the boy was an RH negative baby transfused. He was first diagnosed as grand mal epileptic at the age of eight and placed on medication.

Hospital Record Re: Jimmy—April 17, 1964

The following is the summary as requested on the above named case:

On the evening of March 3, 1953, the patient complained of pain in his left eye. He went to bed and spent an uneventful night, arising the next morning with no complaints or objective symptoms as observed by the parents. He went to school that morning and came home for lunch. At that time he again complained of pain over the left eye. While eating, he apparently lost motor control and smeared pie over his face while attempting to eat it. He then vomited. The child was noted to walk with a stumbling gait with the direction of fall toward the left side. The patient was placed at bed-rest and the doctor was called. Paralysis of the left side developed immediately. The child was hospitalized.

Past History

Child represented a known RH problem at birth and was paralyzed on one side (unknown). He suffered a convulsion at feeding time, was transfused and apparently recovered.

The patient was discharged on the tenth hospital day in good condition and ambulatory. The next admission was on May 24, 1953. Discharged 6/16/53.

The patient was admitted in what appeared to be a grand mal attack. Examination at this time was essentially the same as on the first admission.

The final diagnosis was non-specific infectious enteritis. The following was recommended.

1. Continue the depressive therapy as previously established . . .
2. Further observation and search for focus of infection.

Very truly yours,

The patient was admitted to one of our units approximately two weeks after the first interview. Medication was discontinued and a complete psychological evaluation was obtained. Withdrawal continued over two weeks with no reaction.

Psychological Evaluation

Jimmy, aged 17 years, was seen for psychological testing on May 3, 1964, at the Delaware Valley Mental Health Foundation with the purpose of making a differential diagnosis. The testing was conducted with a view toward establishing the role of organic and/or pathological emotional factors in his behavior, previously diagnosed epileptic. At the time of testing he had been without medication for five days after 11 years of continuous treatment.

The psychological results were interesting. The psychologist felt that, in general, then, this boy seems to be suffering from an inability to cope rather than from neurotic or psychotic problems. This inability is organically based, typically epileptic, and suggests a program of retraining more than of psychotherapeutic intervention. However, the psychological structure is going to be difficult to ameliorate by now because of the death-like rigid grip on thinking and emotion which Jim erects as his only defense. It is not correctly described as passivity, but rather as immobilization and depression. Better discharge of anger in smaller amounts and better organization of his environment so that he isn't so often made angry, seem the clues to therapy.

Specific Recommendations

Jim appears to need a protective environment for a while; one which will not take advantage of his tremendous drive to fuse and identify and cling, but will use it to provide him a good model. In this environment he should not be provoked but should be encouraged to express, without retaliation, his view of things as they happen. He should not be allowed to argue. Jim needs to know the boundaries between himself and others and his statements of opinions, unqualified by another's intrusions, should help him establish some identity of his own.

More fundamental help is also necessary. He needs to be taught concepts from scratch and in a concrete manner at first. He needs to review every new situation with someone who can teach him how to think about it. He needs to be given many rules, concrete ones for concrete situations and to practice them and report on the outcome. He needs to learn new skills that are within his literal-minded capacity and to be praised and encouraged to master them. In short, Jim needs to have his environment organized for him so that he can control it. If this is accomplished this testing suggests that there will be no further behavior problem.

It is suggested that Jim receive some "perceptual training" by a specialist before he takes his next academic or work step. And he should be given a full battery of vocational tests with his particular handicaps in mind.

Basically we had a 17 year old boy with a history of grand mal epilepsy who had been free from seizures several years. It was thought that the medication had kept the attacks under control.

There was some eye muscle difficulty. (There was a residual strabismus and a hyperactive horizontal nystagmus. All other abnormal neurological signs were absent.) There were many symptoms that might have been residuum of previous epileptic aurae. These included "bouts of peculiar smells and odors" that usually preceded moods of deep depression and stubbornness.

At these times, Jimmy would lie on his bed and not eat or talk. There were moments of great irascibility and anger. He was a powerfully-built lad; on all but one occasion, when he broke the furniture in his room, he was able to control his rage by taking long walks (against advice). This action was apparently a safety valve. He once walked over 30 miles and returned with his feet blistered and swollen.

Another of Jimmy's symptoms was preoccupation with what was called "the dribbles". This term was used between him and his mother when he soiled his bed with small drops of urine. Perhaps this was a carry-over from spontaneous urination at the time of an earlier grand mal attack.

There were various defects in Jimmy's character structure. For example, he was a fabricator of stories. One Monday morning, for instance, he told his classmates he had gotten married over the week-end. This was an apparent way of drawing attention to himself.

There was marked ambivalence in Jimmy's attitude toward certain value systems. He would change from one extreme to the other in an attempt to manipulate others.

While we battled with his defenses at the Foundation and he found the situation difficult, he would frequently disappear to find his mother, either at her place of employment or at home. He would then distort, with obvious intent, what was happening at the Foundation. Most often I could help the parents understand his behavior by long telephone conversations. (Discontinuance of treatment was frequently threatened.) Finally, after 15 months, one of these maneuvers did end the therapy. The boy convinced his parents we were paying more attention to another patient in the unit and were keeping Jimmy because of our need for his money. (Actually the case was being financed by a major medical policy of an insurance company.) In reality, the boy was faced with returning to high school and to earn the necessary credits for entrance to college. Apparently, he chose to work in a factory beside his father rather than continue his education.

Jimmy felt a great guilt about masturbation and a great latent rage toward his father—a weak, passive man who had spent time under an electric shock machine for overwhelming depression. Jimmy was afraid of "bettering" his father; in the long run this anxiety about success was too much for Jimmy to handle. However, the boy is young and the whole story has yet to unfold. He still calls me when he becomes distressed. The Foundation is still a source of refuge to him.

The following are Jimmy's actual hand-written notes:

"My first memory is of my mother coming into the bedroom where my crib was one morning. I believe it was an Easter Monday, before she went to work and giving me a kiss. I think that I was about two or three years old. The next thing that comes to mind is when I started kindergarten (4½ or 5). I walked into the class and was fairly surprised to see our doctor's daughter, Janice. She was crazy about me and pestered me all the time. Every time she got a chance to, she would try to kiss me.

But for the most part even then, I felt strange and stayed pretty much to myself at all times. The bigger kids always used to bully me around even when I tried to be friends. After that, school seemed to be one mess of trouble for me. It was a mess.

When I started first grade (I started early) it seemed as though not even the teacher liked me. She would punish me for no reason whatsoever and used to pull my hair, make me stand in the corner. While I did this the kids in the class would laugh at me and try to get my goat when they got the chance.

In 1953, I lost so much time when I was in the hospital that I felt hopeless because of all the time and work I missed and also because certain kids like this Bobby and his pals would all try beating me up and seeing if they could get me into trouble. They always worked in crowds against me. Finally, by the time I got in about third or fourth grade I was pretty fast to get going and I would fight back, and usually only got hurt worse in the deal.

While all of this was going on, I seemed to become more irritable and I'd wind up arguing with everyone and fighting with them.

My sister and I have never gotten along and I don't feel as if I was ever very close to my family, especially my father.

After my bout in the hospital when I was young it seems as if Mom is always with me when I do anything and even so now, but I don't like it. After a while, in school, they would have the teachers watching me closely, and at recess, my dad would always be there watching or else I'd have to stay near the teacher.

That didn't help much because the kids still found ways to torture me without the teacher's knowledge—like tripping me when I walked past, or waiting outside to get me when I started home.

I think a lot of my trouble might have been my own fault. I was never very much for fooling around in class—I took my work too seriously.

Also, I think I may have been too far searching. This especially whenever I would go to ask a girl to go out with me. It would take me about a month to get up enough nerve to ask her out. Maybe I could have felt this way because a lot of times before when I would ask a girl out she would say no or maybe even just laugh.

One time I asked a girl why she said no and she said she didn't want to go out with me because she didn't want to get mixed up with me because the fellows who used to bother me would maybe start on her and she didn't want to get involved.

When I went into seventh grade, I started to sing. Also, I started having more trouble with the kids and with school. It seemed to start on the bus. I didn't know anyone and the bus was so crowded that when I got a chance to sit down, I sat quietly and looked out the window. The kids thought I was odd and they used to tease me and hit me a lot. And when I would get into the bus after a while, if there was an empty seat or one with only one person sitting in it, I would have to practically fight to sit down.

Then, the first day that we had gym, the instructor called us in to mark all of our equipment. When he came to me, I handed him my gym suit, socks and sneaks. He asked me where my "jock strap" was. When he heard that I wore it under my street clothes he made a big thing of it in front of the rest of the class and after that the fellows started calling me Jocko.

Soon it spread all around the school and everyone was calling me Jocko and making fun of me. Then too, they started making fun of me because I sang in the school choir. After a while, the thing got so far out of hand that kids I didn't even know would come up to me and start threatening me and beating me up.

One time it got so bad that when I went to a school dance, a group of boys and even some of the girls wanted to beat me up right there. Finally, I called Mom and she called one of the committeemen around our area and told him about it. He came over and got me and at the same time brought the police with him and they questioned some of them and picked up some of them.

Then the school board got into it and tried to find out who was at fault. After having me watched, they found I was not at fault and that my cousin was behind most of it.

Eighth grade, what I remember of it, was almost the same but not as bad. When I went out to H High for ninth grade, the same thing started all over again and it got so bad that I took to walking to and from school.

After the first time my homeroom teacher found out that I sang he started calling me canary. This picked up and became so bad that again I would wind up fighting.

That was the first year I ever had a girl friend and the kids made it as bad for the both of us that I finally wound up breaking up with her. In tenth grade, I was in the High School honors choir out there and the kids started in again with the picking fights again.

Then I transferred to B. Here I got along fairly well until a big shot up there started in fighting with me again. Even though I was not at fault, I still got suspended when this fellow started after me in science class and I went after him. It took four teachers to break us up.

This sort of thing went on throughout the rest of the year periodically. Also I remember that no one in the choir liked Miss Kennedy the choir director and they showed it specifically before the Spring Concert. The other kids refused to work and learn their music. Then, they had enough guts to ask Miss Kennedy to step out and let one of the other instructors take over the choir. Here was where I got into it again. I stood up for Miss Kennedy and told the kids, trying to be nice about it, that they should not let their dislike for the instructor stop the concert and that they could at least go through the last concert of the year with her. They walked out. After quite a session with administration, they finally came back and we put on the concert.

But while all this was going on, some of the kids started a tale around that I was having an affair with the instructor because we got along so well.

About three weeks before the concert I started taking voice lessons from her and I was given the Valentin aria (Even Bravest Heart May Swell) from Faust to learn.

Then I was told that I was to sing the aria in the concert. The kids started again.

When the student concert came up, and it came time for my solo and I got up, the kids all started laughing, stamping and booing. I waited until the noise stopped and I saw them taking a lot of kids to the office. When I saw that I figured that here it goes again. But after the concert the kids who I thought would start, surprisingly only some did. The rest of the ones who usually start jumped to my defense saying how good I was. Sometimes it seems as if I lose feeling in my hands.

I can be smoking a cigarette while I'm working and accidentally burn my hand or the like, and I never feel pain or anything until I notice that I did hurt it.

It really used to bother me when I went to school because I wanted to get good grades just like my sister (all A's and B's) so I'd spend hours on each assignment writing it and rewriting it trying to improve my work, but I never could quite make the grade.

It really shook me that Mom and Dad kept trying to decide for me what I was going to do when I would get out of high school. At first, and even still, I wanted to go to college and became a music teacher, but Mom said no because there was too much eye work. I tried explaining that I had checked into the physical therapy work, and there is just as much eye work in that as in studying music."

One sees the struggle to get close to the warm source (girls) and harassment and conflict with the group of boys. This became a part of Jimmy's problem while he was at the Foundation and attending school and it became obvious that there was some need in him to provoke these incidents.

Jimmy writes about his past treatment at home and how it has affected him:

"It's hard because all of my life I have been allowed to hide behind Mom and Dad, and phony sickness that probably never existed to begin with, and I have always been allowed to "put off until tomorrow things that are better done today." I've got a responsibility to society, to my parents, to my future family, and to myself to throw off this deadweight and the cord that binds, and at least try, although it is kind of late in the game, to score that touchdown. I think I did a little bit of growing up yesterday, and I was sore partially at you, but mainly, for one of the rare times, at myself.

I've been working overtime trying to figure myself out, I think, that the reason why I never did well in school and why, after a fair report during the first report, I turned around and gave up the ship. The answer, God knows, galls me because I've already got, and always have had, what I've been looking for—attention. I know that this kind of attention is the wrong kind (the kind that comes with being a goof-off) and if I can just unlock this warped brain of mine, I'm going to try and make good."

Jimmy's stubbornness is illustrated in a letter he wrote home on December 1, 1964. His attempts at manipulation and lying are illustrated in his note of December 31, 1964.

"Hi Everybody:

I am very fine tonight. Today some of the boys and I took a trip to Jersey. It was rather stupid in a way, but in a way not so, because at last I took off without running to 'Mommie'. I'm looking forward to seeing you all this weekend if you can make it.

Now I'm sure that I am not going to get out of here in June. I say this because as I was telling Eddy that some of the boys and I were planning to take a trip cross country—working our way this summer if I get out, he said you know how you can do it—finish school this year.

I dislike school anyway, but if it is going to be hung over my head like the Damocles Sword, well, then I'm going to louse up because I don't like to be brow-beaten or badgered into doing one thing in order to get something else. I'm very dissatisfied and depressed over this deal and about myself. I put my foot right in it this time, I fear, because I feel as if, and all indications point to the fact, that if I hadn't decided to be bull-headed about going back to school in September, no one would have even tried to make me go. I've been thinking of some things that you could get me for Christmas and I thought I would give you the list so that you could maybe get some ideas.

December 31st

I may be wrong in my reasoning, but it seems pretty logical to me. It seems that Mom is just wishing out loud about your possible motive for the long visit. It leads me to believe that they miss me. Also, I think they are beginning to feel that maybe they were a little wrong in thinking they would be better off with me gone, and that they are starting to want me back. What do you think is wrong with my reasoning? The night before last, even though I had been up since early in the morning, I could not sleep. I wound up watching television until all the channels closed down for the night. That was after five o'clock. I still didn't get to sleep until eight o'clock yesterday and then back up again at ten.

I'm sorry but I couldn't stay away from Jane. I guess I must, in your eyes, have an awfully strong desire to kill myself, but I cannot help it. Regardless of what anyone says, I love her and that is the only reason that I keep going back for more.

I also have a feeling that I will have to leave the Clinic soon anyway. I'm going to have to get a job. You see, during the show last night, we were laying it on pretty heavily, and after the show I had intercourse with her. I was carried away, and I didn't have a contraceptive on, so I suspect she will get pregnant. When Mom finds out I do not think she will allow me to stay up there any longer because she will figure it is my responsibility to get a job and marry Jane and support our kid."

Jimmy's stubbornness is illustrated below:

"You probably think that if you did let me go back now, I'd never come for treatment, and I'd stop going to school. But I wouldn't because Mom and Dad wouldn't allow me to stop seeing you and I have become used to school and am determined to get out in June. Not only that, but I realize that now, of all times, that diploma is more important to me than ever, and I'm not about to let it slip through my grasp now. In regard to school, also, if you didn't want me to finish at P.H.S. or Clement, I would go to one of the other high schools.

I know it may sound as if I am practically begging to get out of here and maybe I am, but at least I have something and someone to go to now, and I do have a responsibility to Jane now also. I've also been thinking that even though I have Jane now, I have shot all hopes of ever working for you in the head. If we do get remarried up here in a church, I guess that it would still work out with her down there and me up here, wouldn't it? Well, I guess that's it for tonight."

His fabrication about his running away to get married is illustrated:

"You see, I lied last Monday night. I did not marry Jane over the holidays. It was just a story to try to get someone to realize that I am not a nutty kid. But, as it turned out, I think I did the exact opposite. Especially because I ran my mouth off at both ends at school, and now I'm sorry because I've probably cut off almost all possibilities of my getting any more dates."

Jimmy's fear of his own strength can be illustrated by the following school incident:

"When I was back in the last two years of elementary school, I was on the Safety Patrol off and on. When I was on the patrol, the others used to ride me about the way I used to do my job. One time, after we went on a trip with the class, two kids were riding me pretty hard, as usual. Well, anyway, when we got back it was time for the safeties to leave, so this boy and I left the room and started to go on patrol. (He was one of the guys who was riding me.)

When he left the school building he started to fight with me, and the other safeties who were his friends, went to help him. The captain started with me and I took off my safety belt and threw it in his face. When I went to leave the other safeties jumped me and in the scuffle I tore my books. Well, anyway, I managed to get to the bridge about four or five blocks away from the school before the safety lieutenant tried to take me on. I grabbed him and held him in a choke hold and walked with him until he passed out. Then I dropped him, kicked him into the street and started on my way. In the scuffle my lunch box was parted from its handle and when another safety went to tackle me, I slugged him, without dropping the handle and

I cut him pretty bad. Then I beat it home and a while later his mother came over and raised hell. I don't remember too much more about that, but on Monday morning when I went to go to school, I was sent to the office before I could go through the class anymore.

At the outset my Dad was on the other side, even though I was not at fault. This depressed me very much but my having fought like I did really depressed me and shook me so much so that I showed visible shakyness when relating this story. I was thinking about what I had related and I am positive that this has the answer to a lot of my problems. I think that the reason, one of the main reasons, that I had so much trouble with everyone and everything, was that I take things—anything—too seriously. I would just like to be able to sit and talk about everything, that comes to the top of my head for a day or two straight, no matter what the outcome would be because I feel that if I could do this I could get out more information that is pertinent to this and get it over faster."

Perfection and its effect on Jimmy:

"I felt as if one mistake, and I couldn't take it. But I am going to try and lick that. Who the hell cares if I mess up a job, the important thing is to try. If I mess it up, I mess it up. At least I will have done my best. I think I know where I started picking this perfection bit up. It started when I realized that my sister was good in almost everything she did, and that she seemed to be the favorite to my childish mind. It seemed to me that if I could learn to do things perfectly, and outshine her I would be the favorite for a change.

So in everything I did, school, studies, shop work, singing and in later years, even dating, I would try and shoot as high as possible in order to get the attention that I was lacking."

Jimmy's explanation of his epilepsy:

"I invented the epilepsy to get the attention that I needed. And when these two still didn't do the trick I caused myself to have a loud voice, the itches and aches and pains in order to attempt to get what I needed. And when all of this still didn't work, I invented the whistling, foot tapping, drumming with my hands to add to everything else. When these still didn't work, I started holing myself up in my room with my books and not really studying, but demanding absolute quiet still with the pretense that I couldn't concentrate.

When these didn't work, I took up smoking, hoping that it would stir up a little bit of attention for me. When this didn't work, I started having attacks, two and three times a week, ending up in the hospital in February. When that didn't seem to satisfy my needs, I dropped out of school in March with the excuse that I couldn't work like that with breaking of the new medicine into my system. And a month later, I was here.

My rages were also an attention seeker that I invented. I think that this is all true because since I came up here, where people pay more attention to me, I have noticed a drop in a lot of this:

1. First, I saw that I could do without the medicine.
2. Next, I saw that the rages weren't really necessary.
3. The epilepsy went.
4. Loud voice modulated.
5. Itches not so bad; no more aches and pains.
6. Studying without too much ado."

In this case, as in all epileptics I have seen, erection and orgasm played an active part in the personality picture.

When Jimmy first became my patient, he had never had an orgasm with ejaculation. I felt, now, that his great rages were his orgasmic equivalents whereas before it had been the epileptic seizures. The boy, therefore, was ordered to masturbate. There was a great deal of guilt included in his act. Violence entered the sexual act along with obvious feelings of castrations.

Following are some of Jimmy's thoughts and dreams about sex:

"I remember back when I was 12, I somehow got interested in seeing a girl with no clothes on. Well, I suddenly found myself mixed up with a couple of real young girls goofing around. Once, when my mother and dad found out, my mother really gave it to me, up one side and down the other, and even threatened to cut my testicles off and tie them around my neck.

Once in a while I get this dream that my penis was real stiff and it was big and sickeningly white.

I never used to like to be around girls. Because I felt as though every time I was around girls, I felt that I would start having sexual thoughts about them, and that I would say or do something that I shouldn't. In fact, when I was living in Elmer, two things happened that really shook me. I had met this girl through a few friends of mine. I took her out a few times. She had an older sister but I think she was in a lower grade. I had heard from these friends of mine that this girl's sister was a real tramp, and so I got interested. Then they invited me to a party that they were throwing for a friend of theirs. The party was held in the basement of this house, and there was dancing, games and a little necking here and there. Then they had this game where there were four people up front with a flashlight and if the person with the flashlight flashed the light on a couple that were necking, the girl with the flashlight would change with the girl in the necking group. We, the girl and her sister, and me worked out a system by which she would always pick up. That way I was sure to get the girl that I was told was a tramp. When I did, besides necking with her, I felt her breasts and tried to put my hand up her dress. I was scared stiff and after that very guilty.

For about three-quarters of an hour after I masturbate and come, semen still seeps out. Also I've rubbed a little raw spot on my penis.

I wish I could stop smoking. I think the reason I associated Jane with my wet dream when asked this morning was because I am crazy about her and her about me also.

On our second or third date I casually asked her what she thought she would be doing two years from then if we were still going together. She said she wouldn't be sitting in the movies, but probably be in her own home, etc. And besides it would seem that you would want that sort of relationship with someone you really like and want.

I tried masturbating tonight. I didn't come but I get an erection. Woke up at 6:30 A.M. with a circular wet spot on my pants. Sticky. I didn't know if it was a wet dream or not because I didn't note an erection but I think it was a wet dream. I don't think I bounced around so much last night. About 9:40 I started to have an erection! Nine forty-eight I urinated and afterward had the dribbles. Four o'clock I did above again. I've been forcing myself to lay down and relax today.

I dreamt that a girl resembling someone I know and I were, I believe, down at Dad's house and she was lying on a bed or couch of some kind and I came in and half-sat, half-laid on the edge of the bed facing her and we were talking. Then Dad came into the room and was shocked. He seemed to think that we were about to have intercourse. An argument ensued. I don't remember what was said but I surmised that he was degrading us for being indecent. I tried to explain what was really going on but no one would listen to this. I think this dream was spurred by a play I saw on television.

4/16/67

I was talking to Mom tonight and between us I think I found out what was really bugging me. It almost broke my heart on Saturday night to tell Jane what I did. It is true that I am not sure if I really love her and I probably never will be sure, but I must feel something for her because it hurt me terribly to do what I did that night. I want her even if I may not really love her. Maybe that's because she is the only one I have ever known that makes me feel as if they would really care for me and is willing to accept me for what I am.

But I probably would never find out for sure now, because I have literally burned my bridges behind me. I tried to make it seem that I didn't mind if she went out and had a good time with that guy at the dance. But deep inside I was beside myself and burning up. A few times before I checked myself, I almost walked up to him and busted him in the mouth and told him to stay away from my girl. But I didn't want to cause a scene and I did not want to give her the satisfaction of knowing that I really cared. I am not really concerned with the consequences that could come from it. All I really know is that I want her back at any cost.

When I am with her and we're just talking I get so charged up that I almost have an orgasm right on the spot, so she must please me sexually because I have never even had an erection when I was out with any other girl, that I can remember. And she seems to want me even more than I want her, so I'm game if she is, no matter what the outcome.

I feel as if I am not really getting as much out of this as I probably could if I would just break down and trust people, but it is just not in my nature to really trust anyone. I don't seem to get anywhere by trying to trust anyone because I start trusting and then I get scared off. I don't think that I can really benefit from this because until I can start to trust I can't really do anything to help myself."

Jimmy continued as a patient for 15 months and became emotionally stronger. When he left I was disappointed he didn't stay another year and complete his college credits. But he was well enough to live a normal life and he could grow further in his own way.

Here is Jimmy's final letter and his reasons for leaving the unit:

"Just what is my position here now? Will I be getting paid for covering when therapists go out, or am I to get paid an allowance for doing nothing? The reason that I am asking so stupid a question is that from what I understand that everybody has someone to cover for them. And the therapist with whom I'm living is not getting another patient while I'm here.

Also I was told that I was to be paid and yet the office knows nothing about it. I'd like to know just what is going on. Also I am a bit burned up about my file. I had been given permission to read it so I did and I have caught you in two apparent bald-face lies.

1. The score on the tests that were applied by the woman from New York. You told both my parents and myself that I had scored 135 and possibly more on the IQ. I checked out the IQ and it comes to 127.

2. You said I would be getting to do work around here, but apparently that is not so since everyone seems to have coverage—besides, I was told that I'd be doing little if anything and getting paid for it.

On top of this, I thought we had made a deal several months ago about checking the mail. You agreed that you would not have my mail checked unless you asked my permission first. Yet while checking the folder, I not only found a letter I had never even seen to my knowledge, dated after you and I made the agreement. And to add insult to injury, the therapist even went into the trash can and pulled a letter that I had written and decided not to send.

Now, I ask you, is this fair? You pounded at me for months to trust you and confide in you and finally I did. But you evidently didn't trust me. I've talked this over with Mom and Dad and they are leaving this up to me. I'm telling you the same thing. I catch you in any more lying through your eye teeth and I leave.

Both Mom and Dad were so mad at this mess that they were both in favor of coming up here and ripping you and this place wide wide open. I'm beginning to wonder if some of the other things that you have said are false also. Take, for instance, that bit about the scholarship for college, getting me into medical school if I wanted to go and also my "being your right hand man around here".

I like you—I want to trust you, but in the last two weeks I've been finding so many apparently false statements on your part that I don't know what to think. I've had trouble sleeping for awhile. A few times I had visions (dreams) of obtaining my license and either have it torn up by you or one of your therapists."

It can be seen that Jimmy had a desire to be free and on his own. He found reasons to leave.

Conclusions

A. Emotional disturbance, in a large majority of epileptic illnesses, is the original cause of the first fit.

B. There is a definite pattern to the epileptic personality, although the personality traits of epileptics can, in essence, be considered traits seen in neurosis, borderline psychosis and psychosis. The greater the form of epilepsy, the less other neurotic symptomatology exhibited. The grand mal attack is a complete psycho-physiologic reaction that allows discharge of all mental energies. When it is present regularly there is no need for other neurotic discharge. This lack of neurotic traits and complete discharge allows the personality a denial affect and presenting calm. The result has given the epileptic pattern an organic and "non-neurotic" look and, therefore, fostered the belief that epilepsy is first and always an organic disease.

C. The grand mal attack (or the minor epilepsies) solidify as personality entities with the arrival of puberty. It is the sexual denial that makes the picture complete at this time.

D. The frequent and complete loss of consciousness interferes with the pattern of thought process and learning. The result is the "idiot" label to epileptics. In considering the psychodynamics of epilepsy, one might say that the disorder shows personality traits and dynamic origins of both schizophrenic and grand mal hysteria. The aura is similar to the twilight period of beginning psychosis. The total attack can be considered a complete psychic equivalent or "way of life". This is a similarity to psychosis.

E. Epilepsy must be considered foremost as a symptom of brain irritability. It is a duty of the physician to seek out all causes of this symptom picture. In doing this, it is first necessary to rule out all surgical causes of the epileptic pattern. Where no history of surgically-treated lesion can be demonstrated, the physician must recognize that the epileptic pattern can be a symptom of behavior disorder. If this is demonstrated, psychological help is in order. It is possible to effect a discontinuance of the epileptic syndrome and produce further personality development.

References

[1] Dostoevsky, F. THE IDIOT. N.Y., Bantam, n.d. Ch. 1.

[2] Penfield, W.; Erickson, T. EPILEPSY. Springfield, C. C. Thomas, 1941. p. 466.

[3] Fay, T.; Winkelman, N. W. "Widespread pressure atrophy of brain and its probable relation to function of Pacchionian Bodies and cerebrospinal fluid circulation." AMERICAN JOURNAL OF PSYCHIATRY. 9:667–685 (1930).

[4] Tanzi, E. MENTAL DISEASES. N.Y., Rebman, 1909. p. 620–625.

[5] Bianchi, L. and Torino, F. B. LA MECCANICA DEL CERVELLO. E. la funzione dei labi frontali, 1920.

[6] Schwab, R. S. "Epilepsy." WORLDWIDE ABSTRACTS OF GENERAL MEDICINE. *8(8)*:12 (1965).

[7] Rows, R. D.; Bond, W. E. EPILEPSY, A FUNCTIONAL MENTAL DISEASE. N.Y., Hoeber, 1926. p. 7.

[8] Buzzard, W. F. SOME ASPECTS OF MENTAL HYGIENE. Presidential address, Section on Psychiatry, Royal College of Medicine, 1922.

[9] Jackson, H. PAPERS. Philadelphia, Lewis Library of Physicians & Surgeons, 1885. p. 105–113.

[10] *loc. cit.*

[11] Sullivan, H. S. INTERPERSONAL THEORY OF PSYCHIATRY. N.Y., Norton, 1953. p. 315.

[12] Freud, S. "Dostoevsky and parricide." In his: COLLECTED PAPERS. London, Hogarth. v. 5, p. 222–242.

[13] Lewin, B. "Inferences from the dream screen." INTERNATIONAL JOURNAL OF PSYCHOANALYSIS. *29*:12–14 (1948).

[14] Freud, S. *loc. cit.*

[15] Isakower, O. "Contributions to the psychopathology of falling asleep." INTERNATIONAL JOURNAL OF PSYCHOANALYSIS. *13*:331–345 (1938).

[16] Freud, S. *loc. cit.*

[17] Livingston, S. THE DIAGNOSIS AND TREATMENT OF CONVULSIVE DISORDERS IN CHILDREN. Springfield, Thomas, 1954. p. 97–98.

CHAPTER XIV

Conclusion

The next generation is already pushing at our established institutions. Soon it will be here. Changes are inevitable. What might we expect it to be like?

What will happen to Delaware Valley Mental Health Foundation? Will it survive? Will it survive in principle or will it change?

History has shown that any dedicated, unique, small co-operative enthusiastic group united in purpose, successive in achievement must face a problem of expansion. Expansion by necessity, involves more personnel, more central control and less individualism. Such expansion at Delaware Valley Mental Health Foundation could be self destructive. There might be several reasons for this.

A. Compromise of ideology. An ideology that is good and effective cannot be compromised. For instance, it is important that money from the lay community be given with no contingent attachments. Already county mental health boards will administer state and federal funds. Expansion might necessarily mean dependency on these funds. To receive this money our institution must adhere to county, state, and federal regulations. These regulations could force a compromise in ideologies.

B. Stotland and Kobler state that the "viability and excitement of any institution are enhanced by active support—financial, moral and in other ways—from people who adhere to its basic philosophy or ideology." [1] Whenever a new idea in mental health, especially one that involves an open door policy that needs community acceptance is to be tried, it will be faced with a force of negativism. This probably will be voiced by a minority that is negative to any change. It is the community leaders on the Board who can prevent this force from coming into the open. The community and neighbors are afraid of *large institutions*. They might actively object to expansion. Such objection could result in court fight, zoning disagreements and general unfavorable publicity.

C. Problems of professional status, power and hierarchy arise in any organization. It is state law in Pennsylvania, that any licensed mental health center must be under the directorship of a physician, licensed to practice medicine and trained in psychiatry. Many clinical psychologists are disgrunted with this law, feeling that it is unnecessary to have medical leadership in a community clinic. I do not want to get embroiled in such discussions and feel that it is more important to work as a therapeutic team, each lending one's own background discipline tinged with personal imagination, to the battle.

D. It is essential that the director be identified with the philosophy of the organization for its continual survival. Any administrator must wed himself to the philosophy of the Foundation and to the services of its staff.

E. Robert Felix sees the future of American Psychiatry synonymous with increased insurance coverage.[2] This, he feels, will enable the poor to get acceptable help. In my experience, it has been the middle class too that has suffered. Many private insurance companies have clauses, sometimes inconspicuously placed, especially in major medical policies, that cleverly exclude mental health coverage.

At D.V.M.H.F., almost 75% of patient applicants cannot be accepted because of inadequate insurance coverage or insufficient personal resources. This is heart breaking because it makes adequate mental health care a privilege instead of a *RIGHT*.

Rather than expansion let us envision growth. Becker has stated "there is something in the close family living, the homelike atmosphere and in intensive personal supervision that motivates the patient to grow. If these results continue, a new modality of social rehabilitation will have proved itself." [3]

Perhaps eight family units with a maximum of 30 patients would not be too much.

Training facilities for several resident physicians per year are planned. A training program for family therapists is in operation. At present, negotiations with the community college to provide a two year Associate in Arts degree in family therapy, with practical training at the Foundation, is in the talking stage.

Instead of expansion, why not a model for mental health—available to all communities, based on family care.

It is the hope of the Delaware Valley Mental Health Foundation that eventually it will serve as this model for mental health projects. Thus it will never become a factory for turning out "well" human beings, but rather a place where other people interested in mental health can come to study, to research, and to work and establish similar mental health clinics in other parts of the world. I do not believe in copying, but rather in absorbing ideas. We at the Delaware Valley Mental Health Foundation invited everyone to visit us; to understand our concepts and share ideas. From this will come increasing growth.

Research could be conducted in different areas as yet untouched. For instance, the area of crime has eluded the behavioral scientists as yet. Recently the Commission of Mental Health in Pennsylvania and the Attorney General's office have asked me to serve as consultant to the state hospital for the criminally insane. They have been concerned with rehabilitation of long termers. Twenty-five percent of the inmates are convicted murderers; few repeat this crime when rehabilitated. There would be a problem here in legal commitment. At present many have questioned its legality and its injustices are magnified when there isn't enough public concern.[4, 5, 6] A person under the influence of his unconscious isn't a reasoning human being and needs protection and help, even though he may have committed a crime. There are few psychotics who can recognize the destructive nature of their illness and also will accept help voluntarily. Commitment allows others to take action to give the patient more protection. Therefore, I do not think it should be abolished. At present commitment papers in Pennsylvania are nothing more than the family's commitment to the treatment—little more than agreement of fact. . . .

All in all, all work should be fun. It has been fun putting this book together. My work in psychiatry has been fun. When the fun ceases, I will look for something else to do.

References

[1] Stotland, E. and Kobler, A. LIFE AND DEATH OF A MENTAL HOSPITAL. Seattle, University of Washington, 1965. p. 214.

[2] Felix, R. H. "Mental health 10 years from now." THE PHYSICIANS PANORAMA. (Sandoz Drug) *4(2)*:29 (1966).

[3] Becker, A.; Murphy, N. M.; Greenblatt, M. "Mental health, recent advances in community psychiatry." N. E. JOURNAL OF MEDICINE. *272*:621–626 (1965).

[4] Szasz, T. S. "Some observations on the relationship between psychiatry and the law." AMA ARCHIVES OF NEUROLOGY & PSYCHIATRY. #75, p. 297 (1956).

[5] Gutmacher, M. S. "Critique of views of Thomas Szasz on legal psychiatry." ARCHIVES OF GENERAL PSYCHIATRY. *10*:238 (1964).

[6] Szasz, T. S. LAW, LIBERTY AND PSYCHIATRY. N.Y., Macmillan, 1963. p. 142–144.

Bibliography

Abraham, K. "Oral eroticism and character." In his: SELECTED PAPERS. N.Y., Basic Books, 1954.

Abraham, K. A SHORT STUDY OF THE DEVELOPMENT OF THE LIBIDO. London, Hogarth, 1947.

Alexander, F. DYNAMIC PSYCHIATRY. Chicago, Univ. of Chicago, 1952.

Arendt, H. "Understanding and politics." PARTISAN REVIEW. 20:392 (1953).

Arlow, J. A. and Brenner, C. PSYCHOANALYTIC CONCEPTS AND THE STRUCTURAL THEORY. N.Y., Intnl. Univ. Press, 1964.

Aubanel, H. ESSAI SUR LES HALLUCINATIONS. Paris, 1839. 95 p. Thesis.

Bacon, C. L. "The Rosen treatment of the psychoses from the viewpoint of identity." In: English, O. S. DIRECT ANALYSIS AND SCHIZOPHRENIA. N.Y., Grune & Stratton, 1961.

Becker, A.; Murphy, N. M.; Greenblatt, M. "Mental health, recent advances in community psychiatry." N.E. JOURNAL OF MEDICINE. 272:621–626 (1965).

Beers, C. W. A MIND THAT FOUND ITSELF. N.Y., Longmans, Green, 1917.

Bianchi, L. and Torino, F. B. LA MECCANICA DEL CERVELLO. E la funzione dei labi frontali.

Birdwhistle, R. INTRODUCTION TO KINESICS. Louisville, Univ. of Louisville, 1952.

Bleuler, E. DEMENTIA PRAECOX OR THE GROUP OF SCHIZOPHREN-ICS. N.Y., Intnl. University Press, 1950.

Bleuler, M. "Conception of schizophrenia within the last fifty years and today." INTERNATIONAL JOURNAL OF PSYCHIATRY. 1(4):501–523, 2(1): 135–137 (1966).

Bouisson, M. MAGIC: ITS HISTORY AND PRINCIPAL RITES, N.Y., Dutton, 1961.

Bowen, M. SCHIZOPHRENIA AND THE FAMILY. Philadelphia, Conference held at Temple University Medical Center on Oct. 10, 1958.

Brierre de Boismont, A. J. F. ON HALLUCINATIONS. Trans. by R. L. Hulme. Columbus, Riley, 1860.

Brossard, C. and Herron, M. "Breakthrough in psychiatry—Revolutionary treatment of the mentally ill."●LOOK MAGAZINE. p. 30–39, April 5, 1966.

Bush, C. K. "The growth of general hospital care of psychiatric patients." THE AMERICAN JOURNAL OF PSYCHIATRY. *113*:1059 (1957).

Buzzard, W. F. SOME ASPECTS OF MENTAL HYGIENE. Presidential address Section on Psychiatry, Royal College of Medicine, 1922.

Cameron, D. E. & Ewen, M. D. "Treating the mentally ill in general hospitals." CONNECTICUT MEDICINE. *22*:290–299 (April 1958).

Cameron, N. EXPERIMENTAL ANALYSIS OF SCHIZOPHRENIC THINKING. Los Angeles, University of Calif. Press, 1954.

Carus, P. THE SOUL OF MAN. Chicago, Open Court Pub. Co., 1831.

Cooper, W. M. A HISTORY OF THE ROD. London, Reeves, 1900.

Curran, W. J. "Legislative progress and planning for community mental health." In: FRONTIERS OF HOSPITAL PSYCHIATRY. Nutley, Roche, Jan. 1966.

Delsarte, F. A SYSTEM OF EXPRESSION. N.Y., Stebbins, Werner, 1902.

Desmonde, W. H. and Mead, G. H. and Freud, S. PSYCHOANALYSIS AND THE FUTURE. N.Y., N.P.A.P., 1957.

Dewey, J. PHILOSOPHY, PSYCHOLOGY AND SOCIAL PRACTICE. N.Y., Putnam, 1899.

Doman-Delacata. DOMAN-MORAN PROFILE AND GRAPHIC SUMMARY. Phila., Institute of Human Potential, 1963.

Dostoevsky, F. THE IDIOT. N.Y., Bantam, n.d.

Eisenberg, L. "Hallucinations in children." In: West, L. J. HALLUCINATIONS. N.Y., Grune & Stratton, 1962. p. 204.

English, O. S. "Clinical observations on direct analysis." In his: DIRECT ANALYSIS AND SCHIZOPHRENIA, N.Y., Grune & Stratton, 1961.

Erikson, E. CHILDHOOD AND SOCIETY, 2nd ed. N.Y., Norton, 1965.

Esquirol, M. ILLUSIONS OF THE INSANE. London, Liddell, 1833.

Fay, T.; Winkelman, N. W. "Widespread pressure atrophy of brain and its probable relation to function of Pacchionian Bodies and cerebrospinal fluid circulation." AMERICAN JOURNAL OF PSYCHIATRY. *9*:667–685 (1930).

Federn, P. EGO PSYCHOLOGY AND PSYCHOSES. N.Y., Basic Books, 1952.

Feinberg, Irwin. "A comparison of the visual hallucinations in schizophrenia with those induced by mescaline and LSD-25. In: West, L. J. HALLUCINATIONS. N.Y., Grune & Stratton, 1962. 64–76.

Felix, R. H. "Mental health 10 years from now." THE PHYSICIANS PANORAMA. (Sandoz Drug) *4(2)*:29 (1966).

Fine, H. J.; Zimet, C. M. "Process-reactive schizophrenia and genetic levels of perception." JOURNAL OF ABNORMAL AND SOCIAL PSYCHOLOGY. *59*:83–85 (1959).

Fisher, S. "Body image boundaries and hallucinations." In: West, L. J. HAL-LUCINATIONS. N.Y., Grune & Stratton, 1962. p. 255.

Frank, L. K. "Tactile communication." GENETIC PSYCHOLOGY. #56, p. 209–255 (Nov. 1957).

Freud, A. "Aggression in relation to emotional development: Normal and pathological." THE PSYCHOANALYTIC STUDY OF THE CHILD. Vol. III/IV, p. 37–42 (1949).

Freud, A. PSYCHOANALYTIC TREATMENT OF CHILDREN. London, Imago, 1947.

Freud, S. "Analysis of phobia in a five-year old boy." In his: COLLECTED PAPERS. London, Hogarth, 1925. Vol. 3.

Freud, S. CIVILIZATION AND ITS DISCONTENT. London, Hogarth, 1953.

Freud, S. COLLECTED WORKS. London, Hogarth, various editions.

Freud, S. COMPLETE PSYCHOLOGICAL WORKS, N.Y., Macmillan, 1953.

Freud, S. THE EGO AND THE ID. London, Hogarth, 1950.

Freud, S. GROUP PSYCHOLOGY AND THE ANALYSIS OF THE EGO. N.Y., Liveright, 1951.

Freud, S. INTERPRETATION OF DREAMS. VI. N.Y., Basic Books, 1955.

Freud, S. INTRODUCTORY LECTURES OF PSYCHOANALYSIS. N.Y., Liveright, 1950.

Freud, S. THE PROBLEM OF ANXIETY. N.Y., Norton, 1936.

Freud, S.; Breuer, J. STUDIES IN HYSTERIA. London, Hogarth, 1957.

Freud, S. THREE ESSAYS ON THE THEORY OF SEXUALITY. London, Imago, 1949.

Friedman, P. ON SUICIDE. N.Y., Intnl. Univ. Press, 1967.

Fromm, E. INDIVIDUAL AND SOCIAL ORIGINS OF NEUROSIS. N.Y., Knopf, 1948.

Fromm, E. PSYCHOANALYSIS AND RELIGION. New Haven, Yale, 1958.

Geleerd, E. R. "Some aspects of psychoanalytic technique in adolescence." In: PSYCHOANALYTIC STUDY OF THE CHILD. v. 12 p. 263–283 (1957).

Gheel, GHEEL ET LE PLACEMENT FAMILIAL. Gheel, Belgium, Gheel Colony, 1953.

Gheel, THE PRESENT POSITION OF FAMILY CARE AT GHEEL. Brussels, S. C. T., 1951.

Goethe, J. W. von, THE WISDOM OF GOETHE. N.Y., Carlton, n.d.

Gorman, M. "Psychiatry and public policy." THE AMERICAN JOURNAL OF PSYCHIATRY. *122*:55–60 (1965).

Green, L. J. "Functional neurological performance in primitive cultures." HUMAN POTENTIAL. *1(1)*:17–18 (1967).

Green, R. S. "A comparison of sanitoriums and psychiatric units in a general hospital." JOURNAL OF THE MICHIGAN MEDICAL SOCIETY. *58*:1474 (1959).

Gutmacher, M. S. "Critique of views of Thomas Szasz on legal psychiatry. ARCHIVES OF GENERAL PSYCHIATRY. *10*:238 (1964).

Handelsman, I. "The effects of early object relationships on sexual development —autistic and symbiotic modes of adaptation." In: PSYCHOANALYTIC STUDY OF THE CHILD. v. 20. N.Y., Intnl. Univ. Press, 1965.

Harlow, H. and M. "The effect of rearing conditions on behavior." BULLETIN OF THE MENNINGER CLINIC. 26(5):6–12 (1962).

Harlow, H. "Love in infant monkeys." SCIENTIFIC AMERICAN. 200:91–100 (1959).

Harlow, H.; Harlow, M.; Hansen, E. W. THE MATERNAL AFFECTIONAL SYSTEM OF RHESUS MONKEYS. Madison, University of Wisconsin, 1958.

Harlow, H.; Rheingold, H. MATERNAL BEHAVIOR IN MAMMALS, N.Y.; Ley, 1963.

Harlow, H.; Cross, H. A. OBSERVATION OF INFANT MONKEYS PERCEPTUAL AND MOTOR SKILLS. Baton Rouge, Southern University Press, 1963.

Harlow, M. "The nature of love." AMERICAN PSYCHOLOGIST. 13:673–685 (1958).

Hartmann, H. "Comments on the scientific aspects of psychoanalysis." In: PSYCHOANALYTIC STUDY OF THE CHILD. v. 13, 1958.

A HISTORY OF FLAGELLATION. N.Y., Medical Pub., 1924.

Hlasko, M. "The savage protest dies; from Icarus to James Bond." REFLECTIONS (Merck, Sharpe & Dohme) 1(1):12–17 (March–April 1966).

Hollander, B. IN SEARCH OF THE SOUL. N.Y., Dutton, 1920.

Honig, A. M. "Analytic treatment of schizophrenia." JOURNAL OF THE AMERICAN OSTEOPATHIC ASSOCIATION. 57:322–326 (1958).

Honig, A. M. "Analytic treatment of schizophrenia." PSYCHOANALYTIC REVIEW. 45(3):51–62 (1958).

Honig, A. M. "Anxiety in schizophrenia." PSYCHOANALYSIS AND PSYCHOANALYTIC REVIEW. 47(3):77–90 (1960).

Honig, A. M. "Negative transference in psychosis." PSYCHOANALYSIS AND PSYCHOANALYTICAL REVIEW. 47(4): 105–114 (1960/61).

Hunt, M. "A neurosis is just a bad habit." REFLECTIONS. Merck, Sharp and Dohme. 2(4):2 (1967).

Hunt, M. A REPORT ON THE STATE MENTAL HOSPITAL. West Point, Merck, Sharpe and Dohme, 1965. 1(2):4 (1965).

Isakower, O. "Contributions to the psychopathology of falling asleep." INTERNATIONAL JOURNAL OF PSYCHOANALYSIS. 13:331–345 (1938).

Jackson, D. "Community psychiatry." TRENDS IN PSYCHIATRY. 2(3):5.

Jackson, H. PAPERS. Phila., Lewis Library of Physicians & Surgeons, 1885.

Jackson, H. SELECTED WRITINGS. London, Hadder and Staughton, 1931.

Jacoby, J. et al. "Anoxia in electroshock therapy." JOURNAL OF CLINICAL AND EXPERIMENTAL PSYCHOPATHOLOGY. 16:265–271 (1955).

Jarvis, V. "Clinical observations on the visual problem in reading disability." In: PSYCHOANALYTIC STUDY OF THE CHILD. p. 451–470 13 (1958).

Joint Commission on Mental Health and Illness. ACTION FOR MENTAL HEALTH. Final report of the Commission. N.Y., Basic Books, 1961.

Jung, C. THE PSYCHOLOGY OF DEMENTIA PRAECOX. N.Y., Nervous & Mental Disease Pub. Co., 1936.

Kato, M. "Rehabilitation and community care of psychiatric patients in Japan." THE AMERICAN JOURNAL OF PSYCHIATRY. 121:844 (1965).

Kennedy, J. F. "Message from the President of the United States." THE AMERICAN JOURNAL OF PSYCHIATRY. *120*:729 (1964).

Kierkegaard, S. FEAR AND TREMBLING AND THE SICKNESS UNTO DEATH. Garden City, Doubleday, 1954.

Kierkegaard, S. "The sickness unto death." In: Bretall, R., ed. KIERKE-GAARD ANTHOLOGY. Princeton, Princeton University Press, 1951.

Klein, M. "Origins of transference." INTERNATIONAL JOURNAL OF PSYCHOANALYSIS. *33*:433–438 (1952).

Klein, M. THE PSYCHOANALYSIS OF CHILDREN. London, Hogarth, 1954.

Kolb, L. "Phantom sensations, hallucinations and body image." In: West, L. J. HALLUCINATIONS. N.Y., Grune & Stratton, 1962. p. 239.

Kris, E. ORGANIZATION AND PATHOLOGY OF THOUGHT. N.Y., Columbia University Press, 1951.

Kris, E. PSYCHOANALYTIC EXPLORATION IN ART. N.Y., New York University, 1952.

Laing, R. D. THE DIVIDED SELF. London, Pelican, 1960.

Larsen, E. F.; Vraa-Jensen, G. "Ischaemic changes in brain following electro-shock therapy." ACTA PSYCHIATRICA ET NEUROLOGICA. *28*:75–80 (1953).

Leary, T. THE PSYCHEDELIC EXPERIENCE. New Hyde Park, University Books, 1964.

Lewin, B. D. "Inferences from the dream screen." INTERNATIONAL JOUR-NAL OF PSYCHOANALYSIS. *29*:12–14 (1948).

Lewin, B. D. THE PSYCHOANALYSIS OF ELATION. N.Y., Norton, 1950.

Liebman, J. L. PEACE OF MIND. N.Y., Simon & Schuster, 1956.

Link, H. C. THE RETURN TO RELIGION, N.Y., Macmillan, 1936.

Livingston, S. THE DIAGNOSIS AND TREATMENT OF CONVULSIVE DISORDERS IN CHILDREN. Springfield, C. C. Thomas, 1954.

"LSD" LIFE MAGAZINE. *60(12)*:40–46 (March 25, 1966).

MacLean, P. E. FRONTIERS OF PSYCHIATRY. (1967).

McNeill, J. T. A HISTORY OF THE CURE OF SOULS. N.Y., Harper, 1951.

Merton, T. "A devout meditation in memory of Adolf Eichman." REFLEC-TIONS. Merck, Sharpe & Dohme, *2(3)*:21–23 (1967).

Modell, A. "Hallucinations and psychic structures." In: West, L. J. HALLU-CINATIONS. N.Y., Grune & Stratton, 1962. p. 172.

Morris, D. THE NAKED APE. N.Y., McGraw-Hill, 1967.

"Mother begs mercy for her son—says he fears whipping post." PHILADEL-PHIA BULLETIN. Nov. 18, 1962. p. 15.

Nevious, J. L. DEMON POSSESSION AND ALLIED THEMES. London, Redway, 1897.

Nietzsche, F. THE PHILOSOPHY OF NIETZSCHE. N.Y., Random House, 1954.

Odoroff, M. E. and Brooks, B. W. "General Hospitals Lighten Load of St Long-Term Care." THE MODERN HOSPITAL. *93(5)*:84–86.

Page, C. MECHANICAL RESTRAINT AND SECLUSION OF INSANE PERSONS. N.Y., Longmans, 1964.

Parish, R. HALLUCINATIONS AND ILLUSIONS. London, Scott, 1897.

Parsons, T. THE STRUCTURE OF SOCIAL ACTION. N.Y., McGraw-Hill, 1937.

Penfield, W.; Erickson, T. EPILEPSY. Springfield, C. C. Thomas, 1941.

Piaget, J. THE CONSTRUCTION OF REALITY IN THE CHILD. N.Y., Basic Books, 1954.

Piaget, J. PLAY, DREAMS AND IMITATION IN CHILDHOOD. N.Y., Norton, 1962.

Plato. THE LAW. Book XI. London, Dent, 1960.

"Provocation and manifestations of anxiety in schizophrenia. Panel discussion." BULLETIN OF THE AMERICAN PSYCHOANALYTIC ASSOCIATION. 6(4):37–42, 144–148 (1950).

Ramsey, I. "Toward a hidden God." TIME MAGAZINE. 87(14):85 (April 8, 1966).

Rank, B. "Adaptation of the psychoanalytic technique for the treatment of young children with atypical development." AMERICAN JOURNAL OF ORTHOPSYCHIATRY. 19:130–139 (1949).

Rank, O. BEYOND PSYCHOLOGY. N.Y., Dover, 1941.

Rank, O. THE TRAUMA OF BIRTH. N.Y., Brunner, 1952.

Rapaport, D. ON THE PSYCHOANALYTIC PSYCHIATRY AND PSYCHOLOGY. N.Y., Hallmark-Hubner, 1954.

Reich, W. CHARACTER ANALYSIS. N.Y., Orgone Inst. Press, 1949.

Reichman, F. PRINCIPLES OF INTENSIVE PSYCHOTHERAPY. Chicago, Univ. of Chicago Press, 1950.

Reidy, J. P. ZONE MENTAL HEALTH CENTERS. Springfield, Thomas, 1964. p. vii–x.

Reisman, D. THE LONELY CROWD. Garden City, Doubleday, 1953.

Rosen, J. THE CONCEPT OF EARLY MATERNAL ENVIRONMENT IN DIRECT PSYCHOANALYSIS. Doylestown, Pa., Doylestown Fndn., 1963.

Rosen, J. DIRECT ANALYSIS. N.Y., Grune & Stratton, 1953.

Rosen, J. "Transference, a concept of its origin, its purpose and its fate." ACTA PSYCHOTHERAPEUTICA. 2:301–314 (1954).

Rows, R. G.; Bond, W. E. EPILEPSY. N.Y., Hoeber, 1926.

Sarason, S.; Gladwin, T. PSYCHOLOGICAL AND CULTURAL PROBLEMS IN MENTAL SUBNORMALITY. Provincetown, Journal Press, 1958. (Review of Research and Genetic Psychology Monograph, vol. 57). p. 3–290.

Scheerer, M.; Rothman, E.; Goldstein, K. "A case of 'Idiot Savant'." In: PSYCHOLOGICAL MONOGRAPHS, No. 4. (1945).

Scheflen, A. "One to one relationship." PSYCHIATRIC QUARTERLY. 34:692–710 (1960).

Schimel, J. "Physicians panorama." MENTAL HEALTH ACHIEVEMENT AWARDS. 2(5):17–19 (May 1965).

Schulberg, H. "Psychiatric units in general hospitals." THE AMERICAN JOURNAL OF PSYCHIATRY. 120:30 (1963).

Schwab, R. S. "Epilepsy." WORLDWIDE ABSTRACTS OF GENERAL MEDICINE. 8(8):12 (1965).

Sechahage, M. A. SYMBOLIC REALIZATION. N.Y., Intnl. Univ. Press, 1951.

Senn, J., ed. CONFERENCE ON PROBLEMS OF INFANCY AND CHILD-HOOD, SYMPOSIUM ON THE HEALTHY PERSONALITY. N.Y., Josiah Macy Fndn., 1950. p. 213.

Simpkinson, C.; Fine, H.; Pollio, H. THE POETIC FUNCTION OF META-PHOR IN PSYCHOTHERAPY. Memphis, University of Tennessee.

Solomon H. S. "The Presidential Address: The American Psychiatric Association in Relation to American Psychiatry." *115*:1–9 (1958).

Spitz, R. "Anaclitic depression." In: PSYCHOANALYTIC STUDY OF THE CHILD. v. 2, p. 313–342. N.Y., International Universities Press (1947).

Spitz, R. "Anxiety in infancy: A study of its manifestations in the first year of life." INTERNATIONAL JOURNAL OF PSYCHOANALYSIS. *31*:138–145 (1950).

Stanislaviski, C. AN ACTOR PREPARES. N.Y., Theatre Arts, 1942.

Sterba, R. INTRODUCTION TO THE PSYCHOANALYTIC THEORY OF THE LIBIDO, N.Y., Brunner, 1942.

Sternlight, M. "A theoretical model of the psychological treatment of mental retardation." AMERICAN JOURNAL OF MENTAL DEFICIENCY. *68*:618–622 (1964).

Stierlin, H. and Searles, H. PSYCHOTHERAPY OF SCHIZOPHRENICS AND ITS REPERCUSSIONS IN THE HOSPITAL STRUCTURE. N.Y., Basic Books, n.d. p. 269.

Still, A. T. FOUNDER OF OSTEOPATHY. Waukegan, Hunting, 1925.

Stotland, E. and Kobler, A. LIFE AND DEATH OF A MENTAL HOSPITAL. Seattle, Univ. of Wash. Press, 1965.

Strauss, A. A.; Kephart, N. C. "Psychopathology and education of the brain injured child." In: PROGRESS IN THEORY AND CLINIC., v. 2. N.Y., Grune & Stratton, 1955.

Sullivan, H. S. INTERPERSONAL THEORY OF PSYCHIATRY. N.Y., Norton, 1953.

Sullivan, H. S. THE COLLECTED WORKS, N.Y., Norton, 1956.

Szasz, T. S. LAW, LIBERTY AND PSYCHIATRY. N.Y., Macmillan, 1963.

Szasz, T. S. THE MYTH OF MENTAL ILLNESS. N.Y., Hoeber-Harper, 1964.

Szasz, T. S. "Some observations on the relationship between psychiatry and the law." AMA ARCHIVES OF NEUROLOGY AND PSYCHIATRY. #75, p. 297 (1956).

Tanzi, E. MENTAL DISEASES. N.Y., Rebman, 1909.

Thomas, E. W. "The validity of brain injury as a diagnosis."

Tinbergen, L. THE STUDY OF INSTINCT. London, Oxford, 1951.

Trotsky, L. THE RUSSIAN REVOLUTION. Garden City, Doubleday, 1959.

Webster, T. A. "Problems in emotional development in young retarded children." AMERICAN JOURNAL OF PSYCHIATRY. *120*:37–43 (1963).

Whyte, L. L. THE UNCONSCIOUS BEFORE FREUD. N.Y., Basic Books, 1960.

Will, O., Jr. HALLUCINATIONS IN THE SCHIZOPHRENIC REACTION. N.Y., Grune & Stratton, 1962.

Wittkower, E. and Bijou, L. "Psychiatry in developing countries." THE AMER-
ICAN JOURNAL OF PSYCHIATRY. *120*:218 (1965).

World Health Organization. Expert Committee on Mental Health. THIRD
REPORT. Tech. rpt. v. 73 (1953).

Wrong, D. H. THE OVERSOCIALIZED CONCEPT OF MAN IN MODERN
SOCIOLOGY. N.Y., Random House, 1956.

Zilborg, G. "Malignant psychosis related to childbirth." AMERICAN JOUR-
NAL OF OBSTETRICS AND GYNECOLOGY. *15*:145 (1928).

Appendix

January, 1971

Dear Friends:

In 1971, the Delaware Valley Mental Health Foundation will have been in existence for ten years. These have been exciting and fruitful times in which we have been able to develop a new concept in mental health communities. Now we have to look forward to the future, something which we haven't had time to do until this point. Success in our work has created such a tremendous demand for both inpatient and outpatient services that our present facilities are currently being taxed to the utmost. Buildings that were suitable for a struggling new community have become time-worn and inadequate for their purpose. Right now it is impossible for us to totally fund capital improvements from our everyday operating expenses. So we have to turn to friends and other contributors for help. The following pages are intended to familiarize you with the Delaware Valley Mental Health Foundation. Your subsequent interest will be greatly appreciated.

Sincerely yours,

Albert M. Honig, D.O.
Medical Director

DELAWARE VALLEY
MENTAL HEALTH FOUNDATION

Who We Are:

The Delaware Valley Mental Health Foundation is a service, training and research center located in semi-rural Bucks County, Pennsylvania, about 25 miles outside of Philadelphia. Founded in 1961 as the Honig-Fine Clinic, the Foundation incorporated as a private non-profit entity under its present name in 1964, in order to increase the scope of its services to the general community. We are a licensed mental hospital, License #235, in the Commonwealth of Pennsylvania, maintaining unique inpatient facilities at our Doylestown address, and two outpatient offices at Doylestown and Levittown, which provide the full range of psychiatric and psychological services.

The Foundation is administrated by an Executive Staff Committee, headed by the Medical Director, who in turn is a member of and responsible to the Board of Directors.

What We Do:

In an era when large bureaucratic institutions have reduced instead of increased clinical efficiency and services rendered to patients, the Delaware Valley Mental Health Foundation has maintained a highly humanistic approach to the treatment of mental disorders. Our philosophy has evolved from two basic premises. First, that it is important to treat the "whole" person by participating continuously in his physical and emotional world; and second, that the road back from mental illness is a long and arduous one, requiring a great amount of time and human effort. To accomplish our goals, we have attempted to build a therapeutic community that will respond to the needs of our patients for all their waking hours. Family units, comprised of a trained husband and wife team, and four or five patients all living together in an informal family atmosphere have replaced the traditional ward setting of state and other private mental hospitals. The expectations of the new family help each patient to give up previously learned maladaptive patterns of behavior and substitute in their place new functional modes of behavior. This is a continuous re-educative process emerging from the experience of everyday living. In individual and group sessions, the dynamic material produced by the patients is handled by an experienced psychiatrist or psychologist, and the "family" is encouraged to become a testing ground for the working out of psychoanalytic insights and practical, everyday living experiences. This arrangement insures an intense experience for all participants, and an unusual opportunity for training and research.

Our outpatient department gives psychiatric and psychological services to all residents of the Bucks County area, and beyond, regardless of color, creed, or the ability to pay. These services include psychiatric evaluation, psychological testing, individual psychotherapy, group therapy, family therapy, and the maintenance of a 24 hour/day telephone emergency service. In addition we provide consultative services to the Bucks County Prison and to the Delaware Valley Hospital in Bristol, Pennsylvania.

What We Have:

Inpatient facilities are located on 14 acres of Bucks County farmland at 833 E. Butler Avenue, Doylestown, Pennsylvania. There are five patient units, holding from two to six patients. Current buildings include an old, renovated, white frame house, a reconverted, renovated barn with two units, and two mobile trailer homes. Another small frame building houses both administrative offices and doctors' offices for outpatient practice. In Levittown we rent a small, three bedroom home that has been reconverted into office space for our Lower Bucks outpatient department. We also rent a small home in Plumsteadville for the convenience of coverage family therapists when they are not on duty.

What We Propose:

The Delaware Valley Mental Health Foundation must grow to keep pace with the present demands of inpatient and outpatient services. Already completed are plans for the construction of a "therapeutic community" designed by Louis I. Kahn, F.A.C.P., noted Philadelphia architect. These buildings were specifically designed with recommendations of the Medical Director and the staff of the Delaware Valley Mental Health Foundation to meet therapeutic needs of our patients. It is estimated that five such units will be required over the next five years. Each unit is comprised of three bedrooms, which comfortably house two patients each and a two bedroom family suite for the family therapists. Also included is a treatment room for group and individual therapy and family meetings as well as a large living room and dining area and a kitchen. Of course, all the specifications of the Pennsylvania Department of Labor and Industry with regard to the construction of buildings used for mental health facilities will be followed. Cost of construction of each unit is currently estimated at $76,900. A copy of the lowest bid received on construction costs is attached.

In addition, in order to accommodate the rapidly expanding needs of our outpatient department, several renovations are required on the existing administrative and office building. These renovations are estimated at $25,000. No formal bid has yet been submitted, but this will be solicited as soon as specifications are made available.

GROWTH PROPOSAL

Immediate Needs:

1. The Foundation requires one inpatient unit as described in the preceding section, with another ready by 1973. (See illustration page 6.)

COST: $76,900. (present cost)

2. To implement our method of treatment, the Foundation requires a special unit to serve as a half-way house for patients who no longer need intensive care. This would be a one or two story apartment-type dwelling located in the rear portion of the grounds. It will be self-governed by expatients, under staff supervision, who are actively participating in life by working or going to school. These people will pay rent and provide their own food.

COST: $153,800.

3. Immediate additions of three or four rooms to present office and administrative building in Doylestown.

COST: $25,000.

Long Term Needs:

1. Completion of the therapeutic community to include indoor recreational facilities, classrooms, library, workshops for vocational training, and a patient-operated commercial enterprise, as well as two further inpatient live-in units.

2. Conversion of present barn structure into day school and residential setting for autistic and emotionally disturbed children.

Index